Fayette County, Tennessee

Marriages

1838 – 1871

Byron and Barbara Sistler

JANAWAY PUBLISHING, INC.
Santa Maria, California

Originally Published:
Nashville, Tennessee
1989

Reprinted by

Janaway Publishing, Inc.
732 Kelsey Ct.
Santa Maria, California 93454
(805) 925-1038
www.JanawayGenealogy.com

2006, 2013

ISBN: 978-1-59641-055-8

Made in the United States of America

FAYETTE COUNTY, TN MARRIAGES

1838-1871

Where two dates appear on an entry, the first one is the date license was issued, the second (in parentheses) the date marriage was solemnized. If only one date, it usually means that the date of execution was the same as the date of license issuance.

Sometimes the execution of the marriage was not reported to the courthouse, and occasionally the clerk failed to note in the marriage book that the license was returned. We would usually make a notation in the entry to indicate the non-execution of a marriage if the book so stated.

The marriages are arranged alphabetically, the first half of the book by groom--the second by bride.

The records included in this book were transcribed by us directly from microfilm of the original marriage books. Error, where it occurs, may be attributed to us, or to the clerks of the period, many of whom did an appallingly sloppy job of entering the information.

If the bride and groom were black, a B is placed at the end of the entry.

It should be remembered that this and other marriage books we have prepared are indexes, and do not include all the information to be found in the original marriage book. Such data as names of bondsmen, ministers, justices of the peace, churches, etc., are omitted. Often such information is helpful to the researcher. Consequently the serious researcher, to obtain this additional information as well as to check on the accuracy of the transcriber, should examine the original marriage record if at all possible.

Byron Sistler
Barbara Sistler

Nashville, TN
January 1989

Abbernathy, M. C. M. to Mary Donaldson 9-9-1846 (9-10-1846)
Abbington, W. T. to Mary J. Plant 12-3-1866 (12-4-1866)
Abel, J. M. to Mary F. Cowan 12-24-1867 (12-26-1867)
Abel, William to Mary S. Coulter 8-9-1853 (no return)
Abels, Joseph to Delilah Lindsey 10-1-1846 (10-4-1846)
Abernathy, Abraham to Ann Crawford 9-3-1869 (11-25-1869) B
Abington, Hardamon to Margaretta Blair 9-19-1839 (9-26-1839)
Abington, Jas. to Billy Waller 12-12-1851 (no return)
Able, H. C. to M. H. Bull 9-2-1867 (9-5-1867)
Able, John F. to R. J. Tiller 10-19-1867 (10-23-1867)
Ables, B. S. to Mary E. Gilbreth 7-8-1844 (no return)
Ables, John W. to Lucinda Beavers 2-26-1839
Adair, James B. to Mary R. Cocke 1-20-1849
Adams, A. H. to Ann E. Upshaw 12-3-1847
Adams, David to Pricilla S. Walker 9-19-1855 (no return)
Adams, J. C. to M. J. Sanders 4-15-1859 (4-20-1859)
Adams, J. M. to Cornelia A. Stafford 2-7-1866
Adams, James B. to M. E. Bradly 1-23-1860 (1-24-1860)
Adams, Martin H. to Susan McConnell 1-24-1854 (no return)
Adams, Warren to Martha Moore 1-11-1849 (no return)
Adkins, Isaac to Matilda Okelly 8-17-1867 B
Adkins, Larkin to Mary Harvey 5-29-1851 (no return)
Adkins, Sam to Bettie Taylor 4-6-1867 (4-7-1867) B
Adkins, W. C. to Cinthia A. Birdsong 6-27-1851 (6-30-1851)
Aiken, Richd. to Sarah E. Sevier 12-13-1851 (no return)
Akin, George to Martha Durham 2-8-1844
Alexander, Abner to Mary E. Davis 5-26-1853 (no return)
Alexander, Charley to Lou Miller 11-12-1870 (11-17-1870) B
Alexander, Daniel to Fanny Heaslet 12-24-1869 (no return) B
Alexander, E. R. to Maryann Provine 12-15-1841 (no return)
Alexander, Emanuel to Noah Shephard 7-21-1869 (7-29-1869) B
Alexander, Henry to Betsy Tate 7-19-1867 (no return) B
Alexander, J. E. to Mollie Cisco 1-27-1869 (1-28-1869)
Alexander, James to Martha Alexander 1-18-1841 (1-21-1841)
Alexander, John A. to Elizabeth A. Boswell 5-1-1865
Alexander, John to Sophia Ann Jones 6-16-1866 (no return) B
Alexander, R. B. to Sarah M. Taylor 3-29-1838
Alexander, Russel to Charlotte Mask 12-30-1868 (12-31-1868) B
Alexander, Uriah M. to Ann Abernathy 1-30-1871 (2-1-1871)
Alexander, Wm M. to J. M. Hart 3-28-1854 (no return)
Alexander, Wm. J. to Mattie Kyle 11-27-1865 (no return)
Alexander?, Rob. S. to Mary C. Alexander 11-15-1846
Alford, J. H. to Anna Sloan 12-14-1870 (12-15-1870)
Allen, Andrew A. to Ann B. Allen 12-22-1845 (12-23-1845)
Allen, Benj. J. to Fannie R. Sims 11-6-1855 (no return)
Allen, Charley to Permella Stephens 2-7-1871 (2-9-1871) B
Allen, Edmond to Rebecca M. Smith 12-30-1838
Allen, G. W. to Jennie Dowdy 11-29-1870 (11-31?-1870)
Allen, George N. to Mary Sisco 11-24-1845 (no return)
Allen, Henry to Love Carter 1-13-1867 (1-19-1867) B
Allen, Henry to Milly Watkins 9-25-1869 (no return) B
Allen, Isaac to Louisa Williamson 1-16-1871 (1-19-1871) B
Allen, James M. to Laura E. Hawley 9-14-1852 (no return)
Allen, John C. to Jane Price 3-21-1844 (3-23-1844)
Allen, John to Puss Wright 3-19-1870 (4-16-1870) B
Allen, Joseph to Elizabeth D. F. Grissom 12-27-1852 (no return)
Allen, Marion to Roberta Gloster 4-25-1866 (6-17-1866) B
Allen, Milton S. to Margaret J. Knott 11-9-1868 (no return)
Allen, Robert S. to Mariah S. Griffin 1-13-1844 (1-25-1844)
Allen, Robert to Rachel A. Morrow 8-26-1870 (8-28-1870) B
Allen, Robt. to Emily Webb 12-20-1848
Allen, Sam to Allice Bentley 6-14-1867 (no return) B
Allen, Sam to Lou Murrell 2-22-1868 (2-26-1868) B
Allen, Thomas to Mary Thompson 1-7-1869 B
Allen, William C. to Margaret M. Wall 12-23-1847
Allen, William C. to Sarah C. Dunbar 6-20-1846 (6-21-1846)
Allen, William M. to Mary W. Watts 12-2-1847 (12-14-1848?)
Allen, William M. to Sarah E. Menees 10-21-1847 (10-23-1847)
Allen, Wilson to Lottie Sneed 2-1-1871 (no return) B
Allen, Wilson to Mary Rives 2-3-1841 (2-4-1841)
Allen, Wm. H. to Lizzie J. Yancey 5-14-1866 (5-15-1866)
Allison, Robert F. to Mary M. Taylor 1-3-1871 (1-5-1871)
Amis, E. H. to A. H. Peviard? 6-26-1869 (6-27-1869)
Amis, J. S. to S. J. Reames 11-14-1865 (11-16-1865)
Amis, J. W. to A. L. Anderson 8-12-1867 (8-13-1867)

Amis, Lewis to Catharine Lee 11-11-1839
Amis, Samuel S. to Clara Amis 12-10-1866
Ammen, Peter to Mary Cooker 10-17-1843 (no return)
Ammons, Dorriss to Jane Belote 7-10-1843 (no return)
Ammons, E. to L. F. Sullivan 12-9-1854 (no return)
Ammons, G. W. to Ann P. Rodgers 8-22-1851 (no return)
Amones, James to Sarah J. Harris 9-12-1865 (9-13-1865)
Ancromb, Charles to Agnes Hobson 12-11-1869 (no return) B
Anderson, A. J. to Nancy P. Williamson 7-4-1853 (no return)
Anderson, Adolphus to Matilda Jones 11-2-1866 (11-3-1866) B
Anderson, Andrew to Perlina Rivers 11-18-1869 (11-21-1869) B
Anderson, Andrew to Virginia G. Crews 1-27-1869 (2-4-1869)
Anderson, Andy to Victoria Mitchell 9-4-1865 (9-6-1865)
Anderson, Bill to Lucy Taylor 4-5-1871 (4-6-1871) B
Anderson, Carter to Frances Lindsey 1-2-1869 (1-5-1869) B
Anderson, D. W. to M. E. M. Eastham 3-7-1853 (no return)
Anderson, Edward A. to Mary Jane Whitten 11-9-1846 (11-12-1846)
Anderson, Edward H. to Mattie O. Evans 1-2-1871 (1-8-1871)
Anderson, George to Nancy Moody 12-22-1866 (no return) B
Anderson, Hal to Margaret Poke 12-28-1869 (1-1-1870) B
Anderson, Jabize S. to Mary J. Elder 12-4-1847 (12-7-1847)
Anderson, Jacob to Levina Ann May 4-28-1838
Anderson, James A. to Louisa C. Trent 5-24-1852 (no return)
Anderson, James W. to Margarett C. Alexander 1-17-1842 (1-23-1842)
Anderson, James to Amy Miller 8-13-1870 (8-14-1870) B
Anderson, John A. to Julia A. Thompson 12-13-1870 (12-17-1870) B
Anderson, Joseph B. to Permelia Harper 1-20-1845 (no return)
Anderson, M. Logan to Cordelia Smith 3-25-1870 (3-30-1870)
Anderson, Thomas G. to Susan Cage 4-8-1838 (no return)
Anderson, Tobias to Mary E. Morgan 11-6-1869 (11-9-1869) B
Anderson, W. G. to Florence I. Johnson 7-27-1869 (7-29-1869)
Anderson, W. T. to Mollid A. Green 7-6-1869 (7-8-1869)
Anderson, William to Adeline Edmunston 12-27-1843 (no return)
Anderson, Wm. W. to Mary Settle 3-16-1866 (no return)
Anker, Solomon to Ginnett Greenwall 6-21-1856 (no return)
Anthony, G. W. to Bamley Hollowell 11-8-1862 (not endorsed)
Anthony, Peter to Sally Gammons 1-9-1869 (1-10-1869) B
Anthony, T. L. to M. A. Pleasant 10-29-1849 (11-4-1849)
Appleberry, J. D. to E. A. Privett 12-23-1863 (12-29-1863)
Appleberry, R. G. to Matilda J. Privette 1-13-1865 (1-18-1865)
Appleberry, Richd. to Mary L. Newton 9-21-1846 (no return)
Archbell, Dave to Mary Shelton 12-26-1868 (12-28-1868) B
Archer, David to Cressy Taylor 12-26-1866 (12-28-1866) B
Archibald, T. K. to Sue T. Neblett 7-6-1870 (no return)
Archie, Rufus to Mary A. Motley 1-29-1861 (1-30-1861)
Armour, David to Sallie Jordan 3-29-1869 (4-1-1869) B
Armour, Wm. C. to Susan E. Gardner 9-2-1850 (9-4-1850)
Armstrong, Alfred to Jollie? Mitchell 8-29-1870 (no return) B
Armstrong, J. B. to M. E. Holland 1-13-1870 (1-18-1870)
Armstrong, W. C. to Sallie A. Phillips 10-21-1868 (10-22-1868)
Arnold, Reddick to Lucy J. Floyd 10-14-1839 (10-24-1839)
Arragon, R. T. D. to Dennie Felts 6-26-1866 (7-4-1866)
Arter, Wm. to Elizabeth Oliver 11-18-1838
Asbury, Willis to Charity Moorman 1-28-1870 (2-5-1870) B
Ashford, Jackson to Rebecca J. Okelly 12-6-1870 (12-7-1870)
Ashley, Henry to Sally Tucker 2-18-1869 (2-21-1869) B
Askew, Sandy to Edy Reddick 1-15-1869 (no return) B
Aston, C. S. to Martha M. Bell 12-6-1847
Aston, William to Frances R. Flippin 11-18-1845
Atherton, A. C. to C. M. Beavers 1-8-1866 (1-10-1866)
Atkin, E. F. to Sarah Jane Gowen 1-28-1848 (1-30-1848)
Atkins, Abea to Mary Lanier 4-10-1848 (4-11-1848)
Atkinson, R. D. to Agnes Griggs 1-30-1869 (2-4-1869)
Austin, Edwin K. to Marion W. Hanley 7-15-1845 (7-18-1845)
Avery, A. H. to Henrieta E. Polk 4-10-1848 (4-12-1848)
Ayers, J. L. to D. F. Redus 4-16-1850
Babb, Peyton to Polly Gooden 7-13-1870 (7-14-1870) B
Babbett, Thos. F. to Barbary A. Ward 5-16-1860
Babbs, Silas to Hester Montague 9-25-1869 (6-15-1870) B
Baggett, Thos. D. to Martha M. Pyron 2-21-1853 (no return)
Bailey, Arter to Catharine Peebles 11-4-1869 (11-9-1869) B
Bailey, Benj. A. to E. A. Clark 11-27-1855 (no return)
Bailey, Charles to Mattie Shelton 12-23-1869 (no return) B
Bailey, H. H. to Ann J. Fuller 2-4-1867 (2-5-1867)
Bailey, Harris to Mary (Mrs.) Cotner 5-5-1852 (no return)

Bailey, Harris to R. E. Baily 12-28-1859
Bailey, John J. to Emma R. Parr 1-6-1851
Bailey, Robert B. to S. E. Philips 3-15-1843 (3-18-1843)
Bailey, Silas to Sarah Ann Logan 11-13-1869 (11-14-1869)
Bailey, Tom to Mary Black 8-26-1868 (no return) B
Bailey, Wash to Nancy Richardson 1-25-1871 (1-26-1871) B
Bailey, Wm. C. to Fanny P. Farrill 10-8-1849 (10-11-1849)
Bailey, Wyatt to Sallie Boyd 1-11-1871
Bain, David L. to Ella Benton 7-27-1866 (10-15-1866)
Baird, J. S. to Penelope Newsom 9-24-1866 (9-25-1866)
Baker, A. to Martha E. Farley 2-9-1846 (2-11-1846)
Baker, Calib to Katherine Moore 12-31-1868 (1-1-1869) B
Baker, Daniel to Agnes Watson 12-17-1868 (12-25-1868) B
Baker, Dick to Candis Strickland 4-4-1868 B
Baker, James B. to Sarah J. Bram 6-19-1854 (no return)
Baker, Jesse to Levena Golen 10-18-1840
Baker, John W. to Mary Tatum 1-31-1842 (2-2-1842)
Baker, John to Hester Walker 10-19-1868 (10-30-1868) B
Baker, Jones to Lizzie Parish 4-24-1867 (4-28-1867) B
Baker, Sam to Lucinda Dowdy 12-27-1865 (no return) B
Baker, Stephen to Laura Ann Wilson 7-5-1866 (7-6-1866) B
Baker, W. R. to Lucy J. Maury 3-26-1855 (no return)
Baker, William to Margarett Beard 1-25-1844
Balam, Tom to Caroline Lewis 12-25-1869 (12-20?-1869) B
Baldwin, Joseph T. to Clarecy A. Shaw 11-14-1851 (no return)
Baldwin, W. C. to M. C. Pickens 1-31-1842 (2-6-1842)
Ball, Stephen C. to Nancy C. Raper 11-28-1859 (11-29-1859)
Ballard, Ed to Evey Hunter 12-12-1868 (12-21-1868) B
Ballard, H. G. to Hardenia A. Taylor 5-3-1847 (5-4-1847)
Ballard, Henry to Mary Beaver 2-1-1867 (8-15-1867) B
Ballard, Samuel O. to Mary F. Williams 3-25-1841
Ballard, W. E. to Mary A Shinault 2-22-1866
Ballard, William to Nancy E. Shepherd 10-26-1846 (10-27-1846)
Balthrop, John L. to Eliza T. Hinson 12-20-1869 (12-22-1869)
Bankhead, James to Martha Webster 2-5-1845 (2-6-1845)
Bankhead, Robert to Nancy Oliphant 3-4-1846 (3-5-1846)
Bankhead, Thos. R. to Dora McAnulty 10-10-1868 (10-11-1868)
Barberry, Mathew to Rebecca Ann Beaver 9-15-1842
Barham, Thos. to Eliza J. Holloway 1-5-1848
Barker, W. G. to Elizabeth Brame 1-8-1848
Barmon, Henry to Eliza Bazzel 10-3-1849 (no return)
Barnard, C. L. to A. J. Scarbrough 9-28-1852 (no return)
Barnes, George to Mary F. Hernes 12-5-1867
Barnes, James to Elizabeth Hargrove 9-22-1845 (9-25-1845)
Barnett, Lawson T. to Dionitia A. Preston 1-5-1847 (no return)
Barringer, Calvin L. to Tommie Patton 12-24-1862 (no return)
Barrington, Dennis to Missouri Roberson 12-28-1867 (1-1-1868) B
Barrom, Thomas to Mary A. E. Mathews 2-28-1867 (3-5-1867)
Barron, Sanders to Mary Barron 9-18-1869 (no return) B
Barron, W. J. to Mollie E. Culp 12-11-1866 (12-13-1866)
Barrow, S. L. to E. A. Culp 12-20-1864 (12-24-1864)
Bartlet, Gabriel M. to Elizabeth G. Glasgow 12-3-1846
Bartlett, Emanuel to Celia Hare 12-13-1869 (12-14-1869) B
Bartlett, G. M. to Rebecca Cross 1-4-1854 (no return)
Barton, William to Mary L. Mitchell 4-30-1847
Barwell, D. M. to Ann E. Thompson 10-8-1860 (10-24-1860)
Base?, John W. to Mary A. Cossett 8-21?-1843 (9-5-1843)
Baskerville, Richard to Frances Booker 12-22-1870 (12-28-1870) B
Bason, Isaac to Mary Elizabeth Standley 12-26-1840 (12-29-1840)
Bass, David S. to Agnes C. Ruffin 8-9-1866 (8-12-1866)
Bass, Gilbert to Ann Joy 2-15-1869 (3-8-1869) B
Bass, Rufus to Laura N. Clark 2-5-1868 (2-6-1868)
Baswell, John to Susanah Davis 8-2-1848 (no return)
Baswell, W. W. to M. A. D. Newton 3-17-1860 (3-22-1860)
Bateman, John to Emily J. Roberts 11-15-1848
Bates, Esau to Lucinda Honey 12-11-1843 (12-14-1843)
Bates, John to Julia Baird 2-1-1867 (2-2-1867) B
Batt, John M. to Elizabeth F. Woodfin 9-19-1840 (9-24-1840)
Battle, W. B. to Elizabeth A. Bonner 12-8-1846
Batts, Pleasant to Emily Wilkes 1-26-1871 (1-28-1871) B
Baty, H. B. to Elizabeth G. Wash 12-18-1838 (12-20-1838)
Baucum, Danl. to Isabella Graves 1-7-1841 (1-10-1841)
Baugh, Josiah R. to Sarahjennett Holloway 11-2-1847
Baum, John D. to Martha F. Margrove 6-26-1865 (6-27-1865)
Baum, Thos. D. to Mary J. Hargrove 11-26-1849

Baw, Edward B. to Martha Jane Shaw 1-15-1844 (1-18-1844)
Baw, William A. to Julina Stone 1-13-1852 (no return)
Baxter, J. F. to Eliza E. Morton 1-7-1870 (1-13-1870)
Baxter, S. W. to A. V. Branch 12-19-1850
Baxter, Wesley to Emily Trent 7-6-1867 (7-7-1867) B
Bayless, Samuel H. to Martha A. Hatley 7-22-1844
Beacham, Calvin to Mary An Armour 8-?-1842 (no return)
Beal, W. H. to E. E. Baxter 12-12-1865
Beale, Enoch to Eliza Brown 2-22-1868 B
Beard, John H. to Susan Jane Laughter 4-29-1846 (4-6?-1846)
Beard, T. C. to Nancy Boon 6-7-1852 (no return)
Beasley, Charles to Mariah Walker 12-12-1868 (12-13-1868) B
Beasley, Isam to Sarah Black 3-3-1845 (no return)
Beasley, James W. to Martha Broom 10-1-1847 (10-2-1847)
Beasley, James to Amelia Tripp 2-23-1867 (3-4-1867) B
Beasley, Reuben to Leathy White 12-3-1870 (12-29-1870) B
Beasley, Thos. J. to Agness Griffin 1-21-1867 (1-24-1867)
Beasly, Henry to L. A. O. Kelly 4-29-1865 (5-2-1865)
Beaver, Wilson T. to Martha W. Jackson 7-19-1841 (7-22-1842?)
Beavers, Michael to Mary Jackson 11-30-1839 (12-5-1839)
Beavers, W. B. to Mary J. Harris 2-19-1866 (2-20-1866)
Beck, Thomas to Caroline Hall 4-16-1849 (4-18-1849)
Bedford, John to Eliza Parker 9-12-1862 (9-18-1862)
Belan, Stephen to Lucy Brooks 10-5-1870 B
Bell, Jacob to Ellen Brown 12-28-1867 (12-13?-1868) B
Bell, John W. to Flora Jones 5-6-1869
Bell, Martin to Mattie Wilson 8-19-1867 (8-24-1867) B
Bell, Moses to Paralee Coleman 4-25-1867 (no return) B
Bell, Spencer to Jane Mitchell 8-5-1869 (8-7-1869) B
Bell, Tho. J. to Lucy A. Hudspeth 12-16-1845 (12-17-1845)
Bell, Wm. A. to Joe Winsett 10-19-1865 (10-22-1865)
Beloate, John M. to Mary F. Godbey 1-10-1871 (1-11-1871)
Belote, Brown to Tennessee Ann Williams 8-28-1846 (no return)
Belote, Smith C. to Lydia M. Rogers 7-15-1844
Belote, Smith C. to Maryann Williams 7-10-1848 (no return)
Benchbark, T. G. to Catharine E. Tomlinson 7-8-1852 (no return)
Beninger, William H. to Caroline C. Gate 12-25-1843 (12-28-1843)
Bennett, Archibald to Nancy Taylor 7-25-1839
Bennett, E. H. to Martha J. Allen 11-29-1870 (11-30-1870)
Bennett, Franklin to Malinda Lee 10-31-1843
Bennett, Green to Mary Ammons 8-20-1845 (8-21-1845)
Bennett, Joshua E. to Adelia N. Garvin 3-18-1864 (3-22-1864)
Bennett, T. W. to Ragile G. Hood 10-5-1848 (no return)
Bennett, William A. to Lusinda Stations 7-22-1848 (no return)
Benson, Earby to Susan Stacy 9-25-1852 (no return)
Benson, Henry to Ellin Carter 9-2-1839 (no return)
Benson, Jesse to Mary J. Eason 10-17-1846 (no return)
Benson, P. D. to A. J. Humphreys 8-18-1843 (9-8-1843)
Bentley, James A. to Elizabeth Coffee 12-15-1845 (12-18-1845)
Bently, D. H. to Elizabeth C. Phillips 12-27-1852 (no return)
Benton, Robert F. to Frances E. Barnes 8-31-1852 (no return)
Berdon, Gustavus to Martha T. Baugh 6-11-1867 (6-18-1867)
Berry, Abraham W. to Martha E. Thornton? 5-20-1849
Bert?, Henry C. to Mary Wade 10-26-1844 (10-31-1844)
Best, R. H. to M. J. Dearren 11-6-1865 (11-14-1865)
Beuford, Gideon J. to Mary S. May 3-29-1852 (no return)
Bevins, A. to Elizabeth Iley 12-18-1847 (12-17?-1847)
Bevlin, Isaac to Lelia Alkire 2-13-1868
Bickers, Benjamin to Martha Woodard 8-15-1840 (8-17-1840)
Biggers, A. J. to Martha E. Morrison 2-11-1850 (2-12-1850)
Biggs, Henry to Cassanda H. Neville 4-3-1854 (no return)
Biles, John S. to Frances M. Shaw 6-23-1845 (6-24-1845)
Bill, Geo. W. to Sarah Wallace 7-10-1850 (no return)
Billeps, Hamp to Rachel Tatum 12-14-1869 (no return) B
Bird, Governor to Pink Kirkpatrick 4-9-1866 (no return) B
Bird, King to Lizzie Skipper 12-24-1869 (12-29-1869) B
Birdsong, Thomas to J. D. Groves 10-22-1859 (8-12-1860)
Birdsong, Thomas to Penny Balcum 9-29-1866 (9-30-1866)
Birdwell, James M. to Margarett M. Brown 4-6-1853 (no return)
Bishop, J. H. to Amanda Johnson 8-12-1869
Bishop, John D. to Charity A. Daugherty 12-30-1868 (1-6-1869)
Bishop, Wm. J. to Mary P. Black 3-8-1849 (3-13-1849)
Bistwick, Henry to Martha A. Faldwell 9-20-1847 (9-26-1847)
Bivren, John to Sarah W. Bryan 1-22-1839
Black, A. A. to Rebecca J. Hunter 7-30-1853 (no return)

Black, Charles R. to Elenor B. Benson 9-8-1864 (9-11-1864)
Black, J. M. to O. J. Slaughter 1-29-1866 (2-1-1866)
Black, James W. to Nancy C. Alston 5-8-1848
Black, L. to Louisa Walker 8-14-1854 (no return)
Black, Leander to Mary A. S. (Mrs.) Harwell 5-20-1844 (5-29-1844)
Black, Mebane to Sarah McGinnis 2-2-1871 (2-11-1871) B
Black, R. W. to Aminta J. Cross 10-22-1867 (10-23-1867)
Black, Robert C. to Lydia A. Clendenen 8-15-1840 (8-21-1840)
Black, Robert H. to Martha A. Cross 2-19-1867 (2-20-1867)
Black, Sterling M. to Eugenia E. Burroughs 10-23-1869 (10-27-1869)
Black, Thomas S. to Analiza Yancy 3-6-1852 (no return)
Black, Thomas to Elizabeth Guyn 10-21-1840 (12-6-1840)
Black, Wm. to Arabella Ross 4-19-1851
Blackwell, John to Mary A. (Mrs.) Philpott 1-18-1843 (no return)
Blackwell, Warren to Margaret Dow 4-15-1871 (4-17-1871) B
Blain, Nathanl. to Sarah J. Pleasants 4-9-1842 (4-14-1842)
Blair, Abnur to Eliza J. Craft 10-21-1853 (no return)
Blair, James T. to Lizzie H. McDowell 2-26-1867 (2-28-1867)
Blake, William to Eliza J. Shaw 1-8-1852 (no return)
Blake, Wm. R. to Aley A. Biddy 11-20-1867 (no return)
Blakeley?, D. L. to Mary E. Morgan 5-14-1851 (5-15-1851)
Blalock, F. S. to Mary A. Linebarger 12-7-1868 (12-9-1868)
Blalock, Horace to Caroline Kirkland 3-22-1870 (3-26-1870) B
Bland, Andrew to Sucky Macklin 2-4-1869 (no return) B
Bland, Jack to Cornelia O'Kelly 8-10-1866 (8-11-1866) B
Bland, Thos. Nash to Marietta Mason 5-10-1867 (5-11-1867) B
Blane, A. J. to Mary Ann Butler 2-15-1864
Blankenship, Calvin M. to Emelia Hays 9-22-1838 (9-23-1838)
Blankenship, E. H. to Emily A. Baxter 12-12-1865
Blankenship, Wm. F. to Rebecca S. Holloway 11-7-1854 (no return)
Blare, James to Mary C. McLeod 2-22-1851 (no return)
Blaydes, J. D. to Rebeccca Garrison 2-26-1866 (3-1-1866)
Blaydes, James to Eveline Chaffin 7-3-1867 B
Blaydes, William to Celia Ross 1-19-1871 B
Bledsoe, William to Julia Flowers 12-29-1870 (12-31-1870) B
Boals, John W. to Martha R. Nesbit 5-22-1869 (5-23-1869)
Boals, Nelson to Harriet Hilliard 9-13-1867 (9-14-1867) B
Boals, Nelson to Margaret Norman 5-12-1866 (no return) B
Bobbitt, Charles to Margaret Atkins 11-23-1846 (12-1-1846)
Bobbitt, Green W. to Sarah Plant 12-15-1845 (12-16-1845)
Bobbitt, T. F. to S. D. Ward 1-6-1871 (1-10-1871)
Bobins, John W. to Susan O'Kelly 5-3-1847 (5-13-1847)
Bobo, Allen H. to Sarah Ann Hargus 6-3-1844 (no return)
Boggs, Kitchen to Maggie Ray 12-7-1869 (12-8-1869)
Boggs, Saml. to Mary Brown 1-5-1867 (1-6-1867)
Bogsen?, William to Elizabeth Jane Foust 2-20-1846 (2-22-1846)
Boile, Washington to Hannah Buford 12-27-1869 (12-31-1869) B
Bolder, Gust to Dora Basin 12-17-1870 (12-24-1870) B
Boles, Nathan 3-31-1845 to Louisa Norman (4-1-1845)
Boling, G. W. to Ann E. Stafford 1-14-1854 (no return)
Bolling, Burgess to Mary A. Stamper 5-5-1851 (no return)
Bolling, Thornton to Dinah Houston 3-29-1866 (4-1-1866) B
Bomar, Booker to Mary O. Daniel 12-17-1854 (no return)
Bond, Calvin to Eliza Sherrod 12-24-1866 (no return) B
Bond, Eaton to Sarah S. Hare 7-27-1840 (no return)
Bond, Edward to Julia Lacey 3-19-1867 (3-21-1867) B
Bond, Henry R. to M. H. Mathews 7-12-1847 (7-15-1847)
Bond, J. P. to Sarah A. Clary 1-21-1867 (1-24-1867)
Bond?, S. D. to Caroline E. Bourne 4-24-1854 (no return)
Bondurant, P. M. to L. B. Hilliard 4-3-1854 (no return)
Bondurant, Robert M. to Margarett Watkins 7-2-1847 (no return)
Bondurant, W. W. to Sallie P. Woodson 11-8-1869 (11-9-1869)
Bone, Henry to Frances Ivie 11-12-1866 (12-1-1866) B
Boner, Booker to Susanah Notgrass 8-7-1851 (no return)
Bonner, William T. to Judy Mosley 7-25-1843
Booker, A. T. to Lucinda Webb 1-21-1845 (no return)
Booker, J. B. to Isabella Jones 6-3-1851 (6-4-1851)
Boon, Jesse to M. E. C. Pool 12-12-1865 (12-15-1865)
Booth, David C. to Amelia J. Jernigan 3-9-1839 (no return)
Booth, William to Rebecca Dickson 10-23-1839 (10-31-1839)
Booth, Wm. A. to Martha A. Moore 4-2-1845
Booth, Wm. to Mary F. Slaughter 2-12-1868
Bordeaux, Anthony to Fannie Price 8-4-1869 (no return) B
Boroughs, Henry C. to Martha O. Bivins 12-23-1846 (12-24-1846)
Borun, Thomas T. to Ann Notgrass 11-11-1847 (no return)

Bostick, Thos. A. to Rebecca J. Luckado 1-1-1850 (1-2-1850)
Boswell, W. H. to Harriett Burnett 12-5-1853 (no return)
Bouchette, R. M. to Emma O. Polk 12-31-1842 (1-3?-1843)
Boult, John H. to Caroline Trotter 12-9-1839 (12-19-1839)
Bounds, George to Ida A. Nobles 2-28-1870 (3-2-1870)
Bounds, J. J. to Nisha A. Winfield 7-18-1865
Bounds, Joseph B. to Margarett A. Boales 9-21-1847 (10-10-1847)
Bounds, Sterling to Marry A. East 8-29-1843 (9-5-1843)
Bounds, Thomas to Margarett Floyed 12-7-1841 (12-9-1841)
Bowden, Jesse to Elizabeth Smith 2-19-1847 (no return)
Bowen, George to Mary Jane Jordan 3-11-1840 (no return)
Bowen, James W. to Lucinda Adkins 9-13-1843 (9-14-1843)
Bowen, P. H. to V. G. Polk 3-9-1864 (3-15-1864)
Bowers, Andy to Mary Baird 7-6-1867 (no return) B
Bowers, B. to Susan H. Cunliffe 10-31-1859 (11-1-1859)
Bowers, Ed to Arena Hudson 3-28-1870 (3-29-1870) B
Bowers, Finis to Ida Watson 12-26-1870 (no return) B
Bowers, Henry to Anna Flippin 12-17-1868 (no return) B
Bowers, Isaac to Veniann Taylor 5-19-1868 B
Bowers, Jacob to Rebecca H. Doudy 4-2-1845 (4-9-1845)
Bowers, Joe to Julia Miller 9-7-1867 B
Bowers, Lewis to Becky Pettus 12-27-1869 (12-23?-1869) B
Bowers, Lewis to Emma Brown 12-27-1869 (12-23?-1869) B
Bowers, Luke to Christianer Athens 4-22-1871 (4-23-1871) B
Bowers, Mack to Susan Boyd 3-27-1869 (3-28-1869) B
Bowers, Robbin to Florrence Bowers 1-5-1867 B
Bowland, Alexander to Elizabeth Blessing 7-29-1841
Bowman, Thos. T. to Fanny B. Bass 4-24-1867
Boyd, Aleck to Jane Morrow 3-28-1866 (3-31-1866) B
Boyd, B. K. to S. A. McFadden 4-11-1864 (4-12-1864)
Boyd, Felix to Mary Crosby 1-6-1871 (no return) B
Boyd, Henry to Amy Cobbs 2-6-1869 B
Boyd, J. Y. to Virginia A. Wray 1-1-1851
Boyd, James S. to Iva McMullen 5-7-1860 (5-10-1860)
Boyd, Jessee to Emily Morrow 1-19-1867 B
Boyd, John to Elvira Poindexter 12-26-1867 (12-27-1867) B
Boyd, L. L. to Musadora Reeves 1-27-1866 (1-30-1866)
Boyd, M. M. to Eliza Green 7-19-1865
Boyed, D. T. to Eliza A. Cloyed 12-6-1854 (no return)
Boyed, John J. to Mary E. Dalton 5-25-1848
Boyed, Presley D. to Manervy Ann Trotter 10-28-1852 (no return)
Boyed, Thomas G. to Julia A. Macon 9-17-1840 (9-24-1840)
Boyed, Whitfield to Locky Mariah Henderson 2-25-1841
Boyers, Rodwier? J. to Missouri S. Turner 5-19-1843 (5-21-1843)
Boykin, Edmund to Claricy Nevills 10-30-1869 B
Boylan, Balam to Katie Stewart 2-18-1871 (no return) B
Boylan, Isiah to Lina Tucker 4-8-1871 (no return) B
Boyle, Anderson to Mat Rivers 1-12-1869 (1-17-1869) B
Bracken, Jerry to Lizzie A. Whitmore 1-1-1868 (2-3-1868) B
Bracken, Tom to Eliza Boyd 5-19-1868 (5-22-1868) B
Brackin, A. F. to Eliza Looney 4-15-1838
Bradberry, Charles to Elizabeth Sanders 2-9-1843
Braden, B. P. to Sarah Harris 2-3-1849
Braden, Frank to Jemima Johnson 2-28-1866 (no return) B
Braden, George to Annie Williams 8-9-1867 (8-10-1867) B
Braden, Gus to Mary Martin 8-27-1869 B
Braden, James P. to Laura Paine 11-10-1869 (11-11-1869)
Braden, John D. to Elisabeth Stewart 11-23-1848 (11-30?-1848)
Braden, Joseph P. to Elizabeth Melton 11-1-1843 (11-3-1843)
Bradshaw, Moses J. to Frances Montague 3-12-1844 (3-28-1844)
Bradsher, Stephen G. to M. E. Boyd 12-7-1869 (12-16-1869)
Bragg, Wm. to Frances Wollerford 9-30-1850 (no return)
Brakefield, Wm. H. to Elizabeth A. Craigg 1-22-1846
Brame, C. B. to R. H. (Mrs.) Mitchel 8-20-1855 (no return)
Branan, August to Martha J. Gallery 8-6-1855 (no return)
Branch, Burrell to R. S. Appleton 12-18-1847 (no return)
Branch, Davy to Louisa Dowdy 12-28-1865 (no return) B
Branch, L. H. C. to M. B. Allen 12-18-1865 (12-20-1865)
Branch, R. to Eugene P. Dyer 5-11-1853 (no return)
Branch, Thomas to Margaret J. Davis 12-19-1846 (no return)
Branch, William to Polly Gordon 7-13-1866 (no return) B
Brannon, G. W. to Mollie A. Cowan 12-11-1862 (12-16-1862)
Braswell, Wm. to Ella Seymour 7-19-1866 (7-21-1866) B
Brewer, B. to Lucretia Tipton 10-30-1849 (11-2-1849)
Brewer, J. W. to Rosina B. Skeggs 11-21-1866 (11-22-1866)

Brewer, Kit to Cathrine Littlejohn 3-1-1869 (3-5-1869) B
Brewer, Matthew to Mariah Tappan 3-1-1871 (3-2-1871) B
Bridges, York to Abbie Crawford 11-11-1870 (11-20-1870) B
Bridgewater, William to Rocky (Rody) Hardin 2-2-1871 (2-8-1871) B
Bright, A. D. to A. R. Rives 10-18-1867 (10-24-1867)
Brightwell, Thomas H. to Annie L. Shaw 1-14-1869
Brim, John A. R. to Elizabeth I. Brame 6-14-1838 (no return)
Brinkley, James to Sarah McCulley 3-1-1847 (3-3-1847)
Brinkley, Jeremiah to Sarah Brinkley 1-27-1849 (2-1-1849)
Brinkley, Richard to A. E. Sawyers 2-16-1842 (2-17-1842)
Brinkley, Richd. to Mary Ann Weller 12-26-1848 (no return)
Brinkley, Thos. W. to Jennie Covington 10-18-1870 (10-20-1870)
Brinkley, Wm. R. to Nancy Emily Floyed 2-1-1841 (no return)
Britt, Benj. W. to Mary S. Ewell 8-3-1846 (no return)
Britton, William to Patsy Cogbill 12-22-1870 (12-27-1870) B
Broadnax, Martin to Martha Broadnax 10-16-1869 B
Brobbeck, J. R. to Jyncy Ballaw 9-20-1851 (no return)
Brockman, Ben to Susan Bivens 4-9-1845 (4-10-1845)
Bronte, Matthew to Jane Whitney 8-2-1842
Brook, J. D. to J. P. Hargess 1-16-1852 (no return)
Brookes, James to Maria L. Davis 6-21-1842 (6-22-1842)
Brooks, Archie to Caroline Marr 12-28-1867 (no return) B
Brooks, Braddock to Susan Mcguire 1-1-1867 (1-3-1867) B
Brooks, Henry R. to Laura E. Gill 12-21-1866 (12-30-1866)
Brooks, Jas. W. to Nannie B. Bell 6-22-1865 (6-23-1865)
Brooks, John C. to Emaly Y. Montague 8-8-1848
Brooks, Samuel C. to Elizabeth J. Tatum 3-23-1843 (3-24-1843)
Brooks, W. G. to E. S. Smithson 12-31-1866 (no return)
Brooks, William to Dora Cummins 3-30-1870 (4-2-1870) B
Broom, Absolem to Rebecah Crawley 6-15-1847 (no return)
Broom, John H. to Eliza Farris 4-1-1844 (no return)
Broom, Julius to Lizy Flippin 11-26-1869 B
Broom, Peterson P. to Mary C. Bowers 11-5-1838 (11-17-1838)
Broom, Taylor to Mozella Blaw 12-21-1868 (12-25-1868) B
Broom, Tho. M. to Susan T. King 1-19-1865 (1-24-1865)
Broom, Thomas M. to Louisa E. V. Yancy 3-20-1860 (3-22-1860)
Brown, Abraham to Jennie Harper 5-26-1869 (5-29-1869) B
Brown, Adam to Nerva Tucker 7-13-1867 (8-3-1867) B
Brown, Belton to Jennie Williams 9-17-1868 (9?-19-1868)
Brown, Granison to Isadore Coe 2-26-1869 (no return) B
Brown, H. W. to J. B. McFaddin 12-31-1849 (1-1-1850)
Brown, Harrison to Rose Stewart 6-9-1868 (6-10-1868) B
Brown, Harvey W. to Mary Posey 1-28-1854 (no return)
Brown, Harvey to Sarah Elmore 7-29-1847
Brown, Isiah to Myra Johnson 12-28-1870 B
Brown, J. F. to Elizabeth Pearson 7-24-1854 (no return)
Brown, J. J. to Belsia Abernathy 1-2-1871 (no return)
Brown, James to Emily Allen 12-28-1866 (12-30-1866) B
Brown, James to Milla Reed 9-25-1868 B
Brown, Jesse B. to A. M. Buford 6-19-1840 (6-24-1840)
Brown, John C. to Mary C. Neiley 1-8-1849 (1-10-1849)
Brown, John to Elizabeth P. Alston 5-25-1840 (5-26-1840)
Brown, Joseph to Amanda Warren 12-24-1870 (12-25-1870) B
Brown, Lenard to Nancy J. Johnson 11-8-1849
Brown, Neill S. to Elizabeth J. Gwynn 2-14-1871
Brown, Ransom to Anna Lucas 9-28-1870 (no return) B
Brown, Reddick to Eliza Jenkins 2-18-1867 B
Brown, Robert to Rebecca Elmore 4-5-1847
Brown, Royal F. to Mary J. Palmore 1-15-1847 (1-17-1847)
Brown, Tho. J. to Frances Branch 1-14-1846 (1-15-1846)
Brown, Thomas W. to Mary Hamlett 12-15-1838 (12-20-1838)
Brown, Thos. to Rhoda Humphreys 1-4-1851 (1-5-1851)
Brown, Tom to Sarah Young 8-31-1867 (9-7-1867) B
Brown, William J. to Susan Jane Palmer 2-3-1847 (2-4-1847)
Brown, William S. to Mary A. Wilson 8-27-1846 (no return)
Brown, William to Elizabeth Moanings 1-5-1870 (no return)
Brown, William to Violet Lee 1-20-1870 (1-22-1870) B
Brown, Wm. F. to Priscilla P. (Mrs.) Boylan 3-14-1839
Browne, Wm. A. to Mallissa C. Sherfield 11-29-1844 (11-30-1844)
Brownlow, James J. to Edney J. Williams 7-13-1840 (no return)
Broyles?, M. B. to Adeline W. Blain 11-30-1855 (no return)
Bruce, George to Emeline Adams 10-3-1840 (10-4-1840)
Bruce, J. R. to H. E. Jackson 7-24-1848 (no return)
Brumley, A. J. to Sarah A. Campbell 8-20-1846
Brumley, C. H. to Analiza High 5-6-1841

Bryan, John A. to Margarett E. Teller 9-12-1854 (no return)
Bryan, Jonathan T. to Elnory E. Watkins 3-23-1844 (3-28-1844)
Bryan, W. A. to E. J. Simmons 4-26-1853 (no return)
Bryant, Clark to Mary Webb 6-15-1867 (6-20-1867) B
Bryant, Columbus to Virginia Bell Frasier 10-21-1865 (10-22-1865)
Bryant, Geo. W. to Martha A. Pollock 7-24-1865 (7-25-1865)
Bryant, James D. to Lavinia F. Tiller 1-27-1852 (no return)
Bryant, Jesse to Sarah Biddy 11-21-1866 (11-22-1866)
Bryant, Jim to Martha Lacy 8-31-1867 (9-7-1867) B
Bryant, John to Sarah Sumner 3-5-1849 (3-11-1849)
Bryant, Wm. A. to Rebecca A. Love 1-1-1866 (1-4-1866)
Buchanon, L. A. to Rutha An Sulivant 2-3-1848 (2-7-1848)
Buck, Edward to Sarah Davis 7-28-1848 (7-30-1848)
Buckelew, R. F. to Elizabeth Johnson 8-30-1851 (no return)
Buckley, W. D. to Mary E. Phillips 3-20-1869 (3-23-1869)
Buckley, William to Nancy A. Kelley 4-30-1850 (no return)
Buckner, Jonathan to Jane L. Wood 1-21-1846 (1-28-1846)
Buffum, Rufus E. to Eliza M. Laughorn 7-15-1846
Buford, Austin to Clara Jackson 1-8-1867 B
Buford, Henry to Fanny Beasley 2-6-1867 (2-7-1867) B
Buford, John O. H. to Caroline A. Black 11-2-1846 (11-5-1846)
Buford, Mingo to Priscilla Maclin 4-1-1870 (12-28-1870) B
Buford, Robt. C. to Martha D. Suttle 11-27-1848 (no return)
Bull, D. R. to M. F. Able 9-2-1867 (9-5-1867)
Bull, Jeremiah to Edna F. Robertson 7-12-1851 (no return)
Bullock, C. L. to Mary Carter 9-25-1854 (no return)
Bullock, John to Rhodie Mitchell 1-11-1868 (1-21-1868) B
Bullock, Robert to Ann S. Mathews 9-24-1839
Bumpass, George W. to S. A. Mayo 12-22-1868 (12-23-1868)
Bunton, Johnson to Susan Brown 10-23-1845
Burford, Philemon T. to Caroline J. Ingram 5-22-1839 (5-24-1839)
Burford, Philemon T. to Frances A. Smith 3-4-1842 (no return)
Burford, William to Loomy McLeod? 7-6-1844 (7-7-1844)
Burge, Saml. B. to Marthaan Wootten 10-20-1839 (10-24-1839)
Burkhart, A. to Nancy J. Chambers 1-24-1855 (no return)
Burkhart, Alexder. to Mary A. Harris 12-4-1856 (no return)
Burleyson, Archey to Sarah Ann Hunsucker 12-21-1866 (12-22-1866)
Burnes, William H. to Mary E. Magett 4-19-1847 (4-29-1847)
Burnett, Edmond to C. A. Boykin 7-20-1866 (8-11-1866) B
Burnett, G. W. to N. A. Alexander 5-29-1860 (not endorsed)
Burnett, Leonard to Caroline Black 1-26-1869 (no return) B
Burnett, W. L. to Ellen J. Tomblinson 12-20-1852 (no return)
Burns, E. A. to Mary Ann E. Dayley 12-25-1848 (12-26-1848)
Burns, Jno. P. to Edna M. Johnson 7-23-1868 (7-24-1868)
Burrell, Michael to Emma Taylor 12-30-1868 (12-31-1868) B
Burris, Henry to Ellen Picket 8-2-1851 (no return)
Burris, Solomon to Rose Abington 12-22-1868 (12-23-1868) B
Burrow, Green to Martha Henley 5-19-1840
Burrow, Reuben to Permelia Murrell 3-7-1842 (4-5-1842)
Burrows, B. F. to Matilda Young 3-2-1866 (no return)
Burruss, Benj. F. to Mary Elder 6-3-1851 (no return)
Burt, Ben to Missouri Boylan 8-31-1867 (no return) B
Burton, Albert C. G. to Eliza J. Hutchinson 2-15-1871 (no return) B
Burton, Frederick to Melvina Reed 12-28-1868 (12-29-1868) B
Burton, H. L. to A. A. Manier 2-4-1862 (2-10-1862)
Burton, James W. to Lucy W. Cocke 7-12-1865
Burton, John M. to Mary Halloway 11-4-1847 (11-5-1847)
Burton, John to Martha P. Wells 6-28-1839 (6-29-1839)
Burton, William to Nancy Morgan 2-13-1851 (no return)
Burton, William to Sarah C. Watson 8-23-1848
Burton, Wm. C. to Mallissa Higgason 10-23-1860 (10-24-1860)
Burtus, John S. to Sarah Word 7-27-1853 (no return)
Butcher, Manuel to Netty Harvy 1-14-1870 (1-16-1870) B
Butterworth, Jesse T. to Maryann Branch 9-13-1847 (9-16-1847)
Butterworth, William P. to Martha A. Branch 2-17-1843 (2-23-1843)
Butts, L. C. to Martha A. Martin 2-15-1844 (2-25-1844)
Byles, Marcus to Mary Montgomery 8-26-1841
Cabness, John to Rose Tucker 3-17-1869 (no return) B
Caffey, J. N. to Pernalia S. Cloyeds 7-6-1841
Cain, William to Ann Martin 1-30-1843 (2-1-1843)
Cain, William to Sarah Ann Boatman? 6-4-1852 (no return)
Cal, Bently to Chany Peebles 4-22-1867 B
Caldwell, A. W. to Mary Ann Walker 11-2-1868 (no return)
Caldwell, Robt. to Mary E. Bumpass 11-3-1846
Caldwell, Simon W. to Josephine J. Dickason 1-23-1867 (1-30-1867)

Caldwell, Theophilus to Elizabeth C. Hodges 1-19-1846 (no return)
Calewell, Robert to Nancy S. Hargis 1-29-1844 (2-5-1844)
Calhoun, A. F. to Ann R. Morphis 4-10-1865 (4-13-1865)
Calway, John to Rose Green 4-30-1868 (no return) B
Campbell, A. B. to E. V. Leech 6-13-1842
Campbell, Alfred W. to Sarah F. Giles 10-13-1851 (no return)
Campbell, J. W. to Mary A. Eubanks 6-21?-1855 (no return)
Campbell, Jas. B. to Caroline V. Black 1-30-1866
Campbell, John to Parisade Rogers 12-24-1869 (no return) B
Campbell, Lawrence A. to Mary Thompson 4-26-1869 (4-27-1869)
Campton, Richard to Sarah E. Hill 5-20-1854 (no return)
Canada, Thos. S. to Mary Lay 4-8-1868 (no return)
Cannon, Gabriel to Clara J. Davis 2-24-1853 (no return)
Cannon, Haywood to Elling Adams 1-1-1854 (no return)
Cannon, John to Martha Davis 3-24-1865 (3-28-1865)
Cannon, Stephen to Nancy Stafford 3-16-1866 (3-21-1866)
Cannon, Steven to Annis Harris 3-11-1863 (3-17-1863)
Cannon, Wm. J. to Catharine Wirt 11-9-1854 (no return)
Caperton, James B. to Nancy C. Brooks 10-15-1844 (no return)
Caple, Littleton to Polly Sanders 1-8-1840 (1-9-1840)
Caple, Phillip to Julia Ann Ingram 9-6-1839 (no return)
Carelton, Calvin to Nancy M. Pierce 1-9-1861 (1-10-1861)
Cargal, Thomas H. to Sarah Jane Read 11-8-1851 (no return)
Cargil, Wiley T. to Josephine Hooks 12-13-1866 (12-24-1866)
Cargil, Wily to Mary Folwell 7-7-1851 (no return)
Cargil, Wm. W. to Penelope A. Brown 4-6-1849 (5-2-1849)
Cargill, Tom to Lucinda Cargill 8-8-1867 (12-28-1867) B
Carl, Jacob E. to Mary E. Norman 12-26-1853 (no return)
Carlton, Sterling to Julia Ann Scott 1-3-1867 (1-6-1867) B
Carmack, Baccus to Mitta A. McCree 11-8-1867 (11-10-1867) B
Carnes, George to Lucy Walker 4-28-1866 (5-13-1866)
Carnes, James A. to Elizabeth M. Jones 10-28-1840 (10-29-1840)
Carnes, Stephen G. to Bettie B. Cooper 3-30-1869
Carney, D. P. to Virginia Scott 11-4-1867 (11-5-1867)
Caroway, Jno. B. to Martha J. Smith 1-14-1868 (1-16-1868)
Carpenter, Fondell to Mary Jane (Mrs.) Bowes 5-28-1853 (no return)
Carpenter, George to Jane Dodson 3-24-1866 B
Carpenter, Mat to Alice Higgason 4-12-1871 B
Carpenter, Wm. to Eliza Fort 6-19-1869 (6-20-1869) B
Carroll, Elias to Amelia L. Durham 1-29-1840 (1-30-1840)
Carroll, Frank to Sarah Webb 7-17-1866 (7-26-1866)
Carroll, George W. to Margarett Wallace 12-21-1870 (12-22-1870)
Carroll, Johnun? to Adaline Price 12-30-1839 (no return)
Claunch, Joseph to Sarah McFadden 8-30-1842 (no return)
Carroll, William to Martha Lucas 8-25-1855 (no return)
Carson, Thos. S. to Mary A. Glover 4-20-1853 (no return)
Carter, Alfred to Mary Newsom 8-26-1868 B
Carter, B. to Lititia Clancey 2-7-1865
Carter, Charles to Mattie Smith 4-11-1871 (4-15-1871) B
Carter, Isaac J. to Mary C. Morris 5-25-1844
Carter, James D. to Sarah A. O. Shore 5-28-1846 (6-10-1846)
Carter, James T. to Ada Cisco 12-30-1867 (1-14-1868)
Carter, Jefferson to Harriet Holmes 10-30-1866 (no return) B
Carter, John E. R. to E. Lumsley 12-13-1844 (12-14-1844)
Carter, John to Ibby Wilson 4-10-1840 (4-12-1840)
Carter, Sam to Lucy Carter 1-7-1867 (1-12-1867) B
Carter, Simon to Ann Palmer 10-22-1870 (10-23-1870) B
Carter, Stephen L. to Nancy Howell 5-25-1851
Carter, W. F. to Martha J. Hood 3-11-1849 (no return)
Carter, Washington to Lucy Jackson 12-28-1867 (12-29-1867) B
Cartwright, A. to Angeline Walker 1-19-1869 (2-5-1869) B
Cartwright, Timothy M. to Sallie W. McFerrin 11-7-1870 (11-10-1870)
Caruthers, Dee to Daffne Walker 1-17-1868 B
Cary, H. to Ella Rhea 5-1-1866
Cash, Elkins to Ellen Evans 5-3-1845 (5-8-1845)
Cash, Paul to Malinda Brown 4-26-1870 (4-30-1870) B
Cassell, William to Elizabeth Montcreath 10-18-1852 (no return)
Castleberry, Stephen to Cathrine Moore 1-8-1867 (1-16-1867) B
Castles, John D. to L. A. Neel 10-19-1866 (10-23-1866)
Cather, Josiah to Cynthia Jones 12-25-1866 (12-26-1866) B
Catnar, Phillip to Mary M. Whitaker 11-14-1848 (11-16-1848)
Catron, John to Feddie Fraser 12-9-1868
Catron, William to Rebecca Catron 7-23-1870 (no return) B
Cavenness, James to Maryann Gaines 2-8-1840 (2-11-1840)
Cavnes, Eli to A. Bridgewater 12-9-1869 (12-25-1869) B

Cawbourn?, Hansell to Mariam Barrett 7-9-1839 (no return)
Chaffin, D. L. to Sarah E. Stephens 1-30-1851 (1-31-1851)
Chaffin, E. H. to L. A. White 2-9-1854 (no return)
Chaffin, Harris to Charlotte Yancey 12-28-1868 B
Chaffin, Harris to Keziah Battle 2-1-1871 (no return) B
Chaffin, Haywood to Tillah Pettis 1-2-1869 B
Chaffin, J. B. to Mary Jane Vaughn 11-30-1838 (no return)
Chaffin, James to Bettie Bracken 2-13-1869 (2-16-1869) B
Chaffin, Leonidas C. to Sallie J. Rives 12-20-1869 (12-21-1869)
Chambers, Benji. to Juatt? Edwards 9-22-1847 (9-16?-1847)
Chambers, Elias to Sarah Atkinson 12-22-1866 (12-23-1866)
Chambers, Gloster to Palina Chambers 11-6-1869 (12-4-1869) B
Chambers, J. G. to Mary F. Taylor 8-3-1859
Chambers, M. L. to E. F. Wade 10-24-1859 (10-26-1859)
Chambers, Madison H. to Martha Ann Laughn 12-8-1843 (no return)
Chambers, Wm. M. to Catharine Burrows 1-29-1855 (no return)
Chambliss, W. F. to P. T. Yancey 11-27-1866
Champion, E. W. to Emeline Marshall 7-9-1868
Champion, Saml. E. to Allice E. Simms 3-4-1868 (3-5-1868)
Champion, Saml. E. to Drucilla B. Witt 1-12-1871
Champion, W. C. to O. J. Alexander 10-22-1868
Chaney, Ephraim to Caroline Cleaves 2-20-1869 (2-27-1869) B
Chaney, Joseph J. to Martha E. Arnold 10-16-1866 (10-17-1866)
Charles, T. J. to Mary A. J. Mooberry 12-24-1855 (no return)
Cheairs, Joseph to Nancy Wilkerson? 11-7-1842 (no return)
Cherry, C. W. to Anna M. Williamson 7-17-1849 (7-18-1849)
Cherry, John R. to Martha D. Stone 4-10-1849
Chersey, John to Martha McNeill 11-9-1867 (no return) B
Chester, Fil to Minerva Williamson 5-11-1868 (no return) B
Chiles, Henry B. to Arabella E. Mitchell 1-4-1851 (1-6-1851)
Chiles, Silas M. to Permelia Hutchins 2-28-1838
Choat, Jno. W. to Permelia Moncreiff 9-19-1844 (9-20-1844)
Christian, James to Nancy Porter 7-16-1870 (5?-11?-1870) B
Christian, Robt. N. to Valeria Shaw 7-28-1866 (8-?-1866)
Clampet, Victor to Martha J. Smith 10-17-1854 (no return)
Clampet, William to Nancy Levesque 1-30-1839 (1-31-1839)
Clapp, Gilbert to Olia Campbell 1-4-1871 (2-14-1871) B
Clark, Moses C. to Mary A. Johnson 8-13-1846 (8-14-1846)
Clark, Thos. G. to Margier B. Rolyere? (Rogers?) 10-8-1838 (10-9-1838)
Clark, William to Elizabeth Jane Whitehead 1-29-1839
Clark, William to Jane Thompson 6-30-1866 (no return) B
Clark, Wm. A. to Martha Wylie 9-28-1868
Claunch, William M. to Jane C. Gilmore 7-22-1844 (7-25-1844)
Claxton, James A. to Elsworth Nelson 10-4-1865 (10-5-1865)
Claxton, T.J. to A. M. Lemons 1-8-1866
Clay, Henry to Eliza Cartwright 12-20-1867 (no return) B
Clay, Henry to Matilda Foster 10-8-1870 B
Clay, J. A. to Anna J. Cartwright 11-18-1867 (11-20-1867)
Clay, Squire to Arenar Dun 1-5-1870 (2-1-1870) B
Clayton, Henry to Louisa Williams 1-14-1869 (1-16-1869) B
Clayton, James H. to H. T. Reeves 10-24-1855 (no return)
Clayton, William to Ellen Yarbrough 2-3-1871 B
Clayton, Wm. L. to Mary E. Martin 3-1-1853 (no return)
Clear, Robert to Clarissa Jones 1-13-1871 (no return) B
Cleare, John to Julia Crockett 12-28-1870 (no return) B
Cleaves, Henry to Juda McDowell 1-6-1871 (1-16-1871) B
Cleaves, James D. to Julia Sanderman? Bucy 5-11-1852 (no return)
Cleaves, John D. to Sidney T.D.H.E. Mason 6-11-1852 (no return)
Cleere, J. L. to Minerva Word 10-3-1854 (no return)
Cleere, John to Liddie Dupree 12-26-1867 (no return) B
Cleere, Mack to Malissa Jackson 2-12-1867 (2-14-1867) B
Clements, Asa to Nancy Elder 10-4-1841 (10-6-1841)
Clements, J. C. to Mary A. Brown 2-8-1842 (no return)
Cleveland, Handy to Laura Moore 6-21-1867 (6-22-1867) B
Clifton, Ridley to Elizabeth Harris 4-11-1846 (no return)
Cline, Dennis to Allice Goode 1-5-1869 (1-6-1869) B
Cloyd, John to Eliza A. (Mrs.) Murry 11-26-1855 (no return)
Cloyed, David P. to Eliza Hope 4-21-1841
Coapland, N. W. to Isabella D. Kerr no dates (with Jun 1838)
Coates, Edward to Eliza H. Hart 9-13-1852 (no return)
Coates, John to Salina Boswell 4-21-1845
Cobb, Alfred to Sallie Ross 3-2-1867 (not endorsed) B
Cobb, R. T. to M. B. Worrell 11-9-1870 (11-10-1870)
Cobbs, Edwin H. to Lucy H. Young 12-15-1845 (no return)

Cobbs, Jas. H. to Mary T. Tanner 4-11-1850
Cobbs, Wm. to Callie Nelson 2-16-1867 B
Cobern, Abraham to Maria Cross 12-21-1868 (no return) B
Cocke, B. J. W. to L. V. Carpenter 9-17-1860
Cocke, H. C. to Bettie A. Marlar 5-11-1867 (no return)
Cocke, Hal to Patience Jones 11-16-1869 (11-18-1869) B
Cocke, Henry M. to Fannie A. Herron 1-16-1861
Cocke, Henry to Cornelia Williamson 1-23-1869 B
Cocke, J. D. to A. E. Ricketts 12-27-1864 (12-29-1864)
Cocke, James H. to Mary P. Cocke 5-4-1870 (5-5-1870)
Cocke, Lindsey to Anikee McNeill 2-7-1868 (no return) B
Cocke, N. J. to Lucy W. Pleasants 10-14-1845 (10-15-1845)
Cocke, N. J. to Mary S. Higgarson 9-1-1847
Cocke, Ned to Martha McClain 1-5-1871 B
Cocke, Robert to Watsie? Ann Link 9-15-1869 B
Cocke, Solomon to Lucy Martin 2-18-1869 (2-20-1869) B
Cocke, Stephen W. to Ann Mariah Mann 4-2-1838
Cocke, Thomas R. to Mary Jane Jones 3-5-1840
Cockrahane, Daniel K. to Catharine A. Smith 5-17-1843 (5-18-1843)
Cockran, Tecumseh to Josephine Allen 1-19-1870
Cody, F. M. to Mary A. Wilson 1-14-1860 (1-17-1860)
Cody, James to Lucy E. Exum 2-1-1870 (no return)
Cody, Jos. L. to Harriet A. Cody 1-2-1868 (no return)
Coe, Harcus to Mary Frances Coe 5-31-1869 (6-13-1869) B
Coe, Levin H. to Lucy E. Stainback 12-20-1866
Cofield, Thomas to Margaret Tharp 3-9-1870 (no return) B
Cogbell, Burrell to Verda Newby 2-11-1871 (no return) B
Cogbill, C. H. to Frances L. McCauley 10-30-1854 (no return)
Cogbill, C. H. to H. A. Ballard 7-21-1859
Cogbill, Henry to Adaline Heaslett 2-2-1867 (no return) B
Cogbill, Jas. C. to Mollie C. Holman 1-2-1866 (1-11-1866)
Cogbill, Thos. C. to Lucy A. Owen 10-18-1867 (10-30-1867)
Coghill, George W. to Sarah E. Massey 6-25-1847 (6-29-1847)
Cohn, David to P. D. A. L. Eskridge 1-17-1853 (no return)
Coker, James to Mary Shaine 3-22-1844 (3-23-1844)
Coker, Leonard to Sarah Nutt 7-11-1846 (7-12-1846)
Cole, Clem S. to Lydia A. Ross 12-17-1867 (12-19-1867) B
Cole, Henry Clay to Lucinda Shackelford 5-14-1866 (no return) B
Cole, J. E. to P. Benson 12-6-1859 (12-13-1859)
Cole, James W. to Eliza A. Hudson 11-28-1866 (11-29-1866)
Cole, John A. to Martha A. Swift 3-13-1843 (3-22-1843)
Cole, Mumphred H. to Elizabeth Young 4-24-1840 (5-5-1840)
Cole, Samel E. to Martha O. Manees 4-3-1850 (no return)
Cole, Shed to Manerva Dickinson 12-9-1870 B
Cole, William L. to Sarah Burtus 12-22-1847 (12-23-1847)
Coleman, E. G. to Margaret C. Patton 10-12-1847
Coleman, Henry to Frances Cody 3-15-1871 (1-?-1872) B
Collier, D. W. to M. E. Maury 4-27-1865
Collier, Wm. to Malinda Jordan 9-21-1869 (no return) B
Collins, E. R. to Parlee Clayton 4-28-1863 (4-30-1863)
Colter, Geor. C. to Mary Malone 1-4-1845
Colter, Geor. C. to Mary Malone 12-20-1844 (no return)
Combes, Charles A. to Caraline Traylor 1-26-1848 (1-27-1848)
Comer, James to Liza Jane Thomas 8-5-1867 (8-9-1867) B
Compton, Eli R. to Mildred Ann Clark 8-13-1840
Conish, John to Polly Simmons 7-2-1870 B
Conn, J. L. to Nancy B. Malone 2-24-1849 (2-25-1849)
Conn, Robert W. to Caroline Duke 2-17-1842 (2-24-1842)
Connell, A. J. to M. F. Warren 10-5-1868 (no return)
Conner, J. W. to Lutisha Brister 2-1-1847 (2-2-1847)
Conner, Wash to Amanda Young 12-26-1866 (12-27-1866) B
Conway, John W. to Elizabaeth Winn 11-4-1841
Conway, John W. to Martha J. Elder no date (with Dec 1847)
Coody, W. F. to C. A. Ray 11-14-1853 (no return)
Cook, R. H. to N. B. Carraway 8-16-1851 (no return)
Cook, T. J. to N. J. Watkins 11-5-1867 (no return)
Cook, Willis to Allice Coffman 3-19-1870 (no return) B
Cook?, A. to Sarah Johnson 7-4-1842
Cooper, Hugh J. to Lucinda A. Fisher? 10-5?-1853 (no return)
Cooper, Richard F. to Mary E. Burdaux 2-9-1839 (2-10-1839)
Cooper, Willingham to Nancy Brinkey 6-18-1839 (6-20-1839)
Copeland, Charles E. to Eliza Reese 11-23-1841 (no return)
Coppidge, James A. to Susan Kerr 3-12-1866
Cossett, F. D. to Martha L. Moore 6-7-1855 (no return)
Cothran, John S. to Mary J. McCombs 12-19-1853 (no return)

Cotter, Thos. N. to Tobitha J. Cotter 1-11-1848 (1-12-1848)
Couch, Levi to Sarah C. Shafter 12-1-1849 (no return)
Coulter, Allen to Louisa Bounds 9-18-1854 (no return)
Coulter, James A. to Martha A. ____ 9-19-1855 (no return)
Covey, James J. to S. C. Morrison 11-21-1865 (11-26-1865)
Covey, John E. G. to Jane Hamrick 11-13-1865 (no return)
Covington, John A. to Virginia A. Harris 2-26-1866 (2-27-1866)
Cowan, A. F. to Rebecca Bull 10-22-1845
Cowan, D. P. to Luzenia Bull 3-11-1851
Cowan, John S. R. to E. A. C. Thompson 2-8-1869 (2-10-1869)
Cowan, John to Willie A. Fitsgerald 8-17-1867 (8-18-1867)
Cowan, Moses to Levina Pool 6-13-1844
Cox, Bernard to Sallie Mosley 12-27-1866 (1-12-1867) B
Cox, Isaac to Frances Finney 6-23-1866 B
Cox, J. F. to Emma C. Chambers 4-19-1870 (4-21-1870)
Cox, Jas. A. to Rebecca Caldwell 12-15-1868 (12-16-1868)
Cox, Levon H. to Tela Mebane 6-30-1866 (7-15-1866) B
Cox, T. W. to Mollie Johnson 11-4-1867 (11-5-1867)
Crabb, Isaiah to Mary Hammons 2-23-1839 (2-26-1839)
Crabtree, Samuel to Barthema Thacker 7-6-1844 (no return)
Craig, B. F. to R. E. Dunlap 1-31-1849 (2-1-1849)
Craig, Daniel M. to Nancy E. Nokes 12-23-1848 (12-24-1848)
Cranford, J. F. to Susan E. Braden 11-26-1867 (12-1-1867)
Crawford, Franklin to Ann L. Eathan 3-2-1840 (3-5-1840)
Crawford, George to Ann Irvin 9-14-1867 (9-15-1867) B
Crawford, J. B. to Sarah A. Wall 4-21-1859 (4-20?-1859)
Crawford, J. J. to Margarette P. McKnight 9-19-1844 (no return)
Crawford, James L. to Eliza J. Pickins 2-6-1867 (2-7-1867)
Crawford, Jerry to Abby Forest 2-2-1867 B
Crawford, Matthews to Cornelia Wainwright 12-29-1868 B
Crawford, P. D. to M. A. Newby 10-10-1866 (10-11-1866)
Crawford, Simon to Ada Walker 7-16-1870 (no return) B
Crawford, Stephen to Margaret Moore 12-29-1868 B
Crawford, W. T. to Sarah Cursey 11-22-1862 (12-4-1862)
Crenshaw, Azariah L. to Mary E. Magness 8-31-1846 (9-2-1846)
Crenshaw, F. B. to M. L. Webber 7-11-1859 (7-13-1859)
Crenshaw, J. M. to Mary A. McNees 2-9-1850 (2-10-1850)
Crenshaw, John H. to Ida Frances Eddings 11-6-1866 (11-7-1866)
Crenshaw, L. C. to L. C. Tomlin 5-16-1867
Crenshaw, L. C. to Sallie Jane Boswell 8-18-1866 (no return)
Crenshaw, M. L. to Martha C. Martin 12-13-1849 (no return)
Criddle, Jerry to Laura Henry 12-25-1869 (6-25-1871) B
Crisp, Daniel J. to Sallie E. Frazier 12-13-1869 (12-15-1869)
Cromwell, O. B. to M. C. Kennon 4-20-1867 (4-21-1867)
Crook, G. M. to Mary J. Averett 5-2-1854 (no return)
Crook, James B. to Martha J. Southern 7-?-1844
Crook, Peter A. to Emely M. Simmons 9-17-1853 (no return)
Crook, Wm. F. to Amanda Pattilo 6-25-1849 (no return)
Crooms, George to Mariah Moore 1-24-1867 (1-25-1867) B
Cross, Elijah to Dicy Miller 5-31-1838
Cross, Isam to Arena Fletcher 1-31-1867 (1-8?-1867) B
Cross, Jacob to Julia Braswell 1-28-1870 (no return) B
Cross, Jessee to Margaret Lipscomb 6-6-1842 (no return)
Cross, Joe to Elizabeth Shore 12-20-1867 (12-22-1867) B
Cross, Sam to Mariah Shaw 8-9-1866 (no return) B
Crossett, J. G. to Frances J. Watkins 1-18-1854 (no return)
Crossett, John D. to Harriet F. McClaren 11-25-1868 (11-26-1868)
Crossett, Joseph J. to Elizabeth A. Goodwin 12-26-1846 (1-14-1847)
Crouch, John J. to Mary Neel 10-1-1847
Crowder, Jas. M. to Harriet Johnson 9-4-1849 (9-5-1849)
Crowder, John to Harriet Crowder 10-31-1868 (11-14-1868) B
Crowder, R. A. to L. A. Bridgwater 1-11-1859 (not endorsed)
Crowder, T. W. to Mary F. Reeves 12-16-1865
Crunch, G. W. F. to F. A. Smith 4-27-1852 (no return)
Culberson, King to Ellen Lightle 1-7-1868 (2-9-1868) B
Culbreath, Huel D. to Sarah M. Moore 1-3-1868 (no return)
Culbreath, Jas. M. to G. A. Simms 3-25-1868 (3-26-1868)
Culbreth, C. F. to Marry Ann Bever? 6-26-1840
Culbreth, John to Elizabeth Hughes no date (12-28?-1838)
Cullom, A. J. to Sarah Durham 5-8-1850 (no return)
Cullum, B. H. to Martha A. Portis 11-?-1853 (no return)
Cullum, Hugh A. to Nancy J. Alexander 11-17-1854 (no return)
Cullum, Mathew M. to Cinetia M. Childes 1-26-1848 (no return)
Cullum, William E. to Mary A. Porter 7-20-1848 (no return)
Culp, Cleiborn to Susan Bobbitt 9-27-1869 (10-2-1869) B

Culp, Eli to Juli Ann Hendley 12-27-1842 (no return)
Culp, Judson A. to Elizabeth L. Norman 12-13-1850 (12-15-1850)
Culp, L. T. to Cassie Jones 12-19-1870 (12-22-1870)
Culp, Leroy to Alzora Gofourth 2-29-1844
Culp, Robert to Martha Phillips 1-12-1866 (1-15-1866) B
Culpeper, J. B. to Louisa Ivey 10-8-1849 (10-10-1849)
Culpepper, Calvin to Lizzie Ann Warr 7-2-1870 (no return)
Culpepper, Henry to Gracey Mebane 12-28-1870 (12-29-1870) B
Culwell, C. H. to Martha A. Bradshaw 5-3-1869
Cummings, Jacob to Sidney Alexander 5-19-1866 (8-11-1866) B
Cunliff, H. C. to Priscilla Reed 11-28-1860 (11-29-1860)
Cunningham, John to Mary Ward 12-27-1869 (12-28-1869) B
Cunningham, Tho. to Elizabeth Scalion 1-8-1846
Curl, Jesse B. to Mandy Wade 2-20-1847 (3-10-1847)
Curl, Jesse B. to Margaret Ann Mathews 11-20-1843 (11-28-1843)
Curray, Mack to Caroline Finney 12-17-1870 B
Currie, W. T. to Araminta H. Ivie 12-18-1860 (12-20-1860)
Currin, Alfred to Ellen Young 10-31-1866 B
Curtis, N. G. to Sarah A. Nelson 12-5-1855 (no return)
Dacus, D. D. to S. A. M. Johnson 10-30-1860 (11-2-1860)
Daley, Wm. J. to Tennie B. Matthews 2-28-1868 (no return)
Damron, Thomas S. to Clara Jane Fisher 3-8-1851 (3-12-1851)
Danaher, Mike to Adelia P. Kennedy 7-20-1866 (7-25-1866)
Dandridge, Baker to Manerva Wilks 8-26-1865
Dane, Noah to Mary Blair 11-1-1841 (11-10-1841)
Daniel, Alexander to Caroline Emerson 12-29-1855 (no return)
Daniel, Jno. M. to Nancy J. Muray 11-21-1860
Daniel, John to Martha Jefferson 1-2-1869 (no return) B
Daniel, R. H. to Rutelia Miller 1-22-1867
Daniel, Spencer P. to Celia Ann Rice 12-31-1845 (1-8-1846)
Daniels, C. C. to Ellen Webb 1-23-1867 (1-24-1867)
Darbey, James D. to Janie F. Roberts 1-28-1839 (1-29-1839)
Darby, Joseph to Ann Moncreiff 9-21-1844 (9-22-1844)
Darby, Joseph to Druciller Moncreef 11-7-1838 (11-15-1838)
Darby, William R. to Clancy D. Roberts 1-12-1841
Darden, A. H. to Eliza Goodwin 7-30-1869 (8-1-1869)
Darden, J. W. to Sarah J. Preston 1-7-1855 (no return)
Darden, Joshua to Nancy Witt Reeves 11-23-1865 (11-28-1865)
Daugherty, Nathan to Mollie Jane Price 8-3-1867 (no return)
David, And. F. to Margarette W. Boon? 5-20-1844 (5-22-1844)
David, Geo. W. to Sarah Paschal 12-9-1845 (12-10-1845)
David, T. R. to Mary Land 7-14-1870 (7-17-1870)
David, Timothy K. to Mary H. Humphreys 10-14-1840 (10-22-1841?)
Davis, A. J. to Susan J. Richey 1-6-1869 (1-7-1869)
Davis, Benjamin to Sarah E. Dodd 12-19-1845 (12-23-1845)
Davis, Benjn. to Mary Rachels 8-27-1850 (8-29-1850)
Davis, David to Mary Lackey 6-14-1838
Davis, E. B. to Sallie P. Loving 2-6-1860 (2-7-1860)
Davis, Fed to Julia Ann Pewett 5-2-1867 (no return) B
Davis, Francis E. to Jane E. Steel 5-10-1842 (no return)
Davis, Fredk. to Isabella M. Alexander 8-26-1842 (8-31-1842)
Davis, G. H. to Elizabeth A. Brooks 1-4-1854 (no return)
Davis, G. W. to Anna Childress 7-16-1870 (7-17-1870)
Davis, Geo. to Mary A. Polk 11-19-1842 (11-17?-1842)
Davis, J. D. to F. E. Stevens 1-15-1866 (1-16-1866)
Davis, J. M. to Josephine Bowen 1-1-1866 (1-4-1866)
Davis, James C. to Jane Allen 1-16-1855 (no return)
Davis, James to L. A. Teams 12-10-1865 (12-10-1865)
Davis, James to Lavina Moore 11-18-1840 (11-19-1840)
Davis, Jerome to Catharine Bobbitt 9-16-1870 (9-18-1870) B
Davis, John Calhoon to Nannie Wilborn 1-5-1854 (no return)
Davis, John L. to Lucy Ann Thomas 12-2-1844 (12-20-1844)
Davis, John Wesley to Martha E. Davis 3-9-1870 (3-10-1870)
Davis, John to Emeline Gay 4-9-1870 (4-12-1870)
Davis, John to Levinia Westbrook 12-29-1846 (12-31-1846)
Davis, M. L. to Sarah Walton 1-19-1854 (no return)
Davis, Pink to Caroline Gage 11-26-1870 (11-21?-1870)
Davis, S. M. to Mary McClaren 1-28-1853 (no return)
Davis, W. T. to Permilia Snow 9-27-1865 (9-28-1865)
Davis, Wesley to Esther Harris 8-21-1869 (8-13?-1869) B
Davis, Wm. H. to Elmira Jones 4-25-1866 (4-28-1866) B
Davis, Wm. to Sarah Ann Rachel 10-7-1850 (no return)
Davis, jr., John to Eliza Jane Davis 12-18-1856 (no return)
Davison, J. C. to J. A. R. Whitehead 9-25-1848 (9-28-1848)
Daviss, John to Araminta Eveline Harp 3-4-1845

Davy, John C. to Angirary? Eddins 4-18-1843
Dawson, David to Lila Brooks 12-3-1870 B
Dawson, John L. to Mary Hunter 2-2-1866 (2-4-1866)
Dawson, Robert to Margaret Jones 1-12-1871 (no return) B
Day, A. S. to Eliza D. Lewis 11-9-1854 (no return)
Day, Billy to Ellen Finney 12-31-1866 (1-5-1867) B
Day, W. G. to Frances Patton 12-7-1853 (no return)
Dazey, J. N. to Emma Evans 12-3-1869 (12-8-1869)
DeAragan, R. T. to E. V. Dyer 6-21-1854 (no return)
DeBow, R. G. to M. V. Grissom 12-14-1868 (12-15-1868)
DeGraffenreid, Ben to Margaret Cole 10-2-1868 B
DeGraffenried, London to Charity Ashe 1-8-1866 (1-13-1866) B
Dean, Henry H. to Frances E. Abbington 5-18-1846 (5-22-1846)
Deardolph, S. R. to Mary E. Kent 10-6-1854 (no return)
Deener, J. J. to S. A. Gober 11-12-1851 (no return)
Deener, John to Lucinda Wade 1-7-1869 (no return) B
Deener, R. H. to Virginia W. Porter 2-27-1869 (2-28-1869)
Deener, Thos. W. to Susanah M. Galeor 11-20-1848 (11-23-1848)
Degraffenreid, Jesse to Lucy Douglass 12-22-1866 (12-27-1866) B
Degraffenreid, Nathan to Judy Springfield 12-25-1866 (12-27-1866) B
Delap, Jim to Alsey Patterson 8-11-1866 (8-12-1866) B
Denney, William to Eliza M. Rogers 7-12-1847 (7-18-1847)
Dennis, Giles to Ruth Tatom 6-1-1868 (no return) B
Denniston, James S. to Mary Ann Bounds 10-23-1844
Denton, Joseph to Lucinda Stallings 4-2-1849
Devenport, John R. to Anna E. Dairden 10-24-1867
Devenport, W. J. to Susan J. Sutherland 3-28-1870 (3-29-1870)
Devenport, Wm. J. to M. L. Surpit 2-13-1849 (2-14-1849)
Devereux, William H. to Ann E. Williams 11-18-1852 (no return)
Dewitt, Jack to Ellen Taylor 12-26-1870 (12-27-1870) B
Dick, James to Mary Finch 1-22-1841 (1-27-1841)
Dickason, John to Mary Harris 10-25-1851 (no return)
Dickerson, Jordan to Charlotte Herrod 5-26-1866 B
Dickinson, Benj. to Winny Goodwin 12-19-1866 (1-16-1867) B
Dickinson, Bernard P. to Carrie F. Rogers 1-28-1869 (no return)
Dickinson, C. R. to P. A. Lowery 12-12-1867 (12-15-1867) B
Dickinson, Edwin D. to Cornelia A. Neal 4-21-1841
Dickinson, Kirk to Frances Moore 7-16-1870 B
Dickinson, Sam to Dinah Dickinson 12-25-1866 (no return) B
Dickinson, Sam to Violet Carpenter 5-1-1869 (5-3-1869) B
Dickinson, Shadrack to Mary E. Old 1-24-1843 (1-25-1843)
Dickinson, Wesley to Nancy Williamson 3-16-1867 B
Dickinson, Willis to Mary Tatum 12-26-1868
Dickinson, Wm. to Virginia Williams 12-27-1865 (12-28-1865) B
Dickinson, jr., Ed to Bettie J. Shaw 12-17-1868
Dickinson, sr., Edwin to Mary Lucette Rivers 12-27-1870 B
Dickson, Pinkny to A. E. Harris 10-22-1851 (no return)
Dickson, W. P. to Arbella White 10-13-1870 B
Dildia, Jesse to Mariah Mathews 12-29-1847 (1-4-1848)
Dillard, Miles A. to Lucinda O. Burrow 7-28-1854 (no return)
Dilliard, H. B. to Matilda Goodwin 7-4-1851 (7-6-1851)
Dilliard, Henry M. to Lizzie W. Lucas 1-20-1859
Dilliard, Henry to Jennie Mosley 12-27-1866 (1-2-1867) B
Dilliard, Thomas J. W. to Susan J. Bromly 12-19-1866
Dishourgh, Sam to Rebecca Ann Whitton 8-10-1844 (8-13-1844)
Dixon, John H. to R. E. Devenport 2-5-1870 (2-10-1870)
Dodds, Isaac C. to Margaret L. Fisher 3-1-1848 (3-2-1848)
Dodds, Isaac to Mary J. Allen 4-29-1845 (no return)
Dodson, Jack to Rose Lemons 5-10-1871 (no return) B
Dodson, Thomas to Martha Ann Patton 10-21-1844 (10-23-1844)
Dolton, John C. to Demarious Bryant 10-3-1853 (no return)
Doolin, James to Sallie Spiller 12-23-1869 (12-29-1869) B
Dorman, Allen to Harriet Woolly 12-5-1846
Dortch, Edmond to Martha Gloster 4-9-1866 (4-30-1866) B
Dortch, George to Minerva Patterson 8-16-1867 (8-18-1867) B
Doty, George to Frances Brinkley 7-3-1841 (no return)
Dougan, E. W. to C. A. Hampton 11-16-1869 (11-18-1869)
Dougan, E. W. to Virginia Hampton 10-16-1866 (11-10-1866)
Dougan, George to Maryan Worthen 11-27-1843
Dougan, John to Ritteran Harris 1-15-1845
Dougan, S. T. to Laura W. Leverett 3-3-1871 (no return)
Douglas, Sandy to Patience Finney 8-27-1869 B
Douglas, Silas to Martha Reed 1-6-1870
Douglass, Carroll to Hannah Levy 8-23-1867 (9-7-1867) B
Douglass, E. C. to Marietta C. Neel 12-1-1868 (12-3-1868)

Douglass, Fred to Julia Hunter 1-6-1871 (no return) B
Douglass, Hugh J. to Mary B. Perkins 9-7-1843 (9-8-1843)
Douglass, James A. to Elizabeth J. Salmon 10-26-1841 (10-27-1841)
Douglass, John to Caroline Martin 12-29-1866 (12-30-1866) B
Douglass, John to Martha Messenger 4-9-1867 (4-13-1867) B
Douglass, Jordan to Lucy Prewitt 12-27-1867 (1-5-1868) B
Douglass, Joseph E. to Frances I. Stegar 2-15-1838
Douglass, Robert to Ann Jane Taylor 12-22-1866 (12-26-1866) B
Douglass, Robert to Emeline Franklin 4-1-1867 (no return) B
Douglass, Wm. B. to Ann E. Fleming 8-25-1866 (8-29-1866)
Dover, Mansell to Maggie Kincaid 7-6-1870 (7-14-1870)
Dowdy, Archy to Lizzie Rawlings 2-14-1868 (2-21-1868) B
Dowdy, Armsted to Susan Henley 3-1-1852 (no return)
Dowdy, Benj. F. to Susan Akin 2-2-1839 (no return)
Dowdy, Linsey to Fanny Culp 12-15-1870 (12-28-1870) B
Dowdy, P. L. to Nancy Williams 4-7-1842 (4-13-1842)
Dowdy, William P. to Lucy E. May? 12-15-1846 (12-16-1846)
Dowdy, Willis to Adeline Phillips 3-13-1869 (3-27-1869) B
Downey, John W. to Eliza Riggs 2-20-1860
Downing, T. M. to Virginia M. Scott 9-10-1850 (9-11-1850)
Downs, Baltimore to Martha Johnson 12-4-1867 (12-5-1867) B
Doyerl?, Wylie to Martha F. Hudson 2-11-1840 (2-13-1840)
Dozier, V. to Mary Williams 3-1-1854 (no return)
Drake, Sam to Lucy Spike 8-19-1868 (no return) B
Draper, Robert H. to Julia E. Jackson 3-3-1855 (no return)
Driggers, Thomas A. to Adah Honey 8-30-1843 (8-31-1843)
Drysdale, Robt. to Eliza W. Paine 7-30-1849 (8-2-1849)
Duberry, Wistley to Mary Lewis 10-15-1847 (10-17-1847)
Dudney, J. T. to Elenora Bailey 11-4-1867 (11-6-1867)
Duggins, P. H. to Harriett O. Manley 1-24-1854 (no return)
Duke, James M. to Tempy R. Williams 1-28-1854 (no return)
Dulin, J. H. to L. A. Anderson 3-14-1866 (3-15-1866)
Dunaho, Richard A. to Louisa Granbery 4-3-1848 (4-5-1848)
Duncan, C. A. to Sallie Andrews 12-14-1870
Dunkin, Frank to Martha Haselette 12-23-1867 (12-28-1867) B
Dunkum, R. A. to D. Ellen Bowers 2-25-1854 (no return)
Dunlap, Samuel to Ama Mitchell 3-27-1867 (no return) B
Dunlap, Wm. to Sarah Gohlson 8-9-1867 (8-11-1867) B
Dunn, E. M. to Ann E. Aaron 2-7-1849 (no return)
Dupree, George F. to Sallie E. Astin 12-12-1868 (12-17-1868)
Dupree, Peter M. to Rebeca M. Washington 11-21-1840 (11-25-1840)
Duprey, Starke to Rosa B. Abington 2-15-1838
Durden, Wiley to Mary E. Tucker 11-14-1870 (11-15-1870)
Durham, H. C. to Mary F. Manley 12-12-1865 (12-13-1865)
Durham, Jim to Eliza Hood 12-26-1866 (12-27-1866) B
Durham, John M. to Trilucia Robertson 1-23-1845
Durham, Samuel M. to Mary J. Brady 1-27-1852 (no return)
Durham, Stephen C. to Martha Ingram 1-29-1842 (2-3-1842)
Durrett, Robert D. to Martha H. Polk 11-8-1841
Durrum, T. L. to M. J. McFadden 10-21-1862
Duvall, T. J. to Harriett J. Irwin 3-17-1851 (no return)
Dye, Benjamin B. to Nancy Lane 1-31-1843 (2-2-1843)
Dyer, Beverly L. to Sarah R. Branch 10-27-1852 (no return)
Dyer, John W. to Virginia Wellar 1-29-1849 (1-30-1849)
Dyer, M. B. to D. E. Smith 4-26-1859 (4-28-1859)
Ealey, William A. to Lucy Jane Carpenter 7-20-1852 (no return)
Ealy, Sam to Sarah Dickenson 12-29-1868 (12-30-1868) B
Earl, John K. to Martha B. Stafford 10-7-1863 (10-8-1863)
Earl, Turner to Caroline Stewart 9-9-1870 (no return) B
Earnhart, Daniel to Sarah M. Holland 10-17-1855 (no return)
Earnhart, G. W. to Mary E. Scott 11-13-1867 (11-14-1867)
East, Joseph to Rebecca Miligan 2-6-1838
Eastham, James S. to Antoinette A. Graves 10-11-1852 (no return)
Eaton, Abraham to Susan Williams 1-18-1847 (no return)
Eaton, D. W. to R. P. Pollock 11-5-1869
Eaton, Willis to Leonah Jones 2-4-1869 B
Eddins, Jas. A. to Caroline C. Hooker 12-10-1850 (12-11-1850)
Eddins, John M. to Martha A. D. Standley 12-22-1841 (12-23-1841)
Eddins, John to Mary Munn 12-13-1846
Eddins, Monroe to Mahala Reddick 9-8-1866 (no return) B
Eddins, Washington to Elizabeth Bynum 5-12-1846 (5-22-1846)
Edenton, Jas. C. to H. C. Moore 11-21-1868 (11-24-1868)
Edmonds, Charles to Samanthy Pollock 12-13-1869 (12-16-1869)
Edwards, Caswell to Emily Trousdale 1-7-1867 B
Edwards, Harry to Celia Wright 8-4-1870 (8-11-1870) B

Edwards, Henry to Louisa Granberry 6-1-1866 (6-3-1866) B
Edwards, Joseph B. to Sarah T. Hodges 11-6-1865 (11-15-1865)
Edwards, Joseph L. to Martha Finney 10-23-1844
Edwards, Lewis to Sarah Ragland 3-9-1868 (3-21-1868) B
Edwards, O. T. to Anna E. Dickinson 1-30-1867
Edwards, S. M. to C. C. Crawford 10-23-1865 (10-24-1865)
Edwards, William A. to Cornelia B. Durham 12-28-1868 (12-31-1868)
Edwin, W. M. to Mary V. Lewis 10-26-1849 (10-30-1849)
Egan, John to Elizabeth Suckett 1-6-1855 (no return)
Eitle, W. M. to Mary Ozier 1-13-1869
Elam, Mark to Elizabeth Maberry? 1-10-1855 (no return)
Elbertson, Tobert to S. Cothran 2-8-1838
Elcan, Cyrus to Martha Bledsoe 10-10-1870 (10-29-1870) B
Elder, Benj. to Fannie Dickason 3-17-1862
Elder, J. M. to Eliza E. Hughes 1-6-1871 (1-12-1871)
Elder, J. M. to S. A. Dickason 1-15-1861
Elder, Patrick H. to Sarahann Driver 7-17-1844 (7-18-1844)
Elgin, John to Mary Mitchell 10-18-1844
Elington, E. to Jane Thomas Ellington 5-8-1848 (5-9-1848)
Eliott, John J. to Sarah C. Petty 9-1-1840 (9-2-1840)
Ellington, Phil to Mariah Neil 2-16-1867 B
Elliot, Wm. C. to Emma J. Williams 12-17-1870 (12-22-1870)
Elliott, A. S. Pasco to Lucinda Snow 12-19-1844
Elliott, Flanders to Martha Goodloe 3-6-1871 (3-11-1871) B
Ellis, Joseph F. to Emma E. Davis 3-16-1852 (no return)
Ellis, S. to Martha J. Shoemaker 1-25-1871 (1-26-1871)
Ellis, W. A. to Mollie Crowder 9-13-1869 (9-15-1869)
Elms, Amos to Rebecca Johnson 7-9-1840 (no return)
Emberson, W. H. to Caroline Davis 9-6-1847 (9-9-1847)
England, B. A. to F. C. Saunders 12-2-1859 (12-6-1859)
Epps, H. L. to Helen Eagan 11-1-1869 (11-2-1869)
Erickson, Francis to Tempe. S. Bryant 1-28-1851
Error, Turner to Margaret Mason 8-30-1867 (8-31-1867) B
Ervin, George to Mary E. Hogan 9-28-1848 (9-29-1848)
Eskridge, Thos. to Penelolpe Smith 4-7-1849
Estridge, Jerry to Junetta Hamer 4-30-1868 (5-10-1868) B
Evans, Benjamin W. to M. D. C. Whyte 3-19-1839 (3-21-1839)
Evans, David to Malinda Nelson 12-14-1839 (12-24-1839)
Evans, E. L. to Evaline H. Degraffenreid 10-6-1841 (no return)
Evans, Ephraim to Lucy Westmoreland 2-1-1871 (2-6-1871) B
Evans, Isaac D. to Martha R. Cargit 10-20-1849 (no return)
Evans, J. S. to Ellen Stansberry 9-18-1855 (no return)
Evans, James S. to Cornelia F. Trotter 1-28-1851 (1-29-1851)
Evans, John L. to L. J. Cargil 12-28-1849 (no return)
Evans, John to Tabitha Ritchie 6-26-1847
Evans, Joseph S. to Nancy Baldridge 5-15-1847 (no return)
Evans, Plummer to Frances Reeves 1-21-1869 B
Evans, R. L. to Elizabeth P. Allen? 10-13-1847 (11-12-1847)
Evans, Sam to Puss Mitchell 12-25-1868 (12-26-1868) B
Evans, Thomas S. to Marthaann Neal 1-30-1841 (2-18-1841)
Evans, William to Maria Mary Lewis 2-3-1846 (2-5-1846)
Evans, Wm. H. to Carolin M. Forbbs 4-28-1846
Ewell, Harry to Julia Ewell 5-12-1870 (5-15-1870) B
Ewell, P. D. to Bella C. Falls 11-12-1863 (11-17-1863)
Ewell, P. D. to Mollie A. Chaffin 8-5-1867
Ewell, Silas to Lou Branscomb 2-24-1868 (2-29-1868) B
Ewell, Thos. A. to Estell Turner 2-9-1870 (2-10-1870) B
Ewing, Tom to Lizzie Wills 12-23-1866 (12-29-1865?) B
Ewing, William to Judy Gwynn 12-23-1866 (12-29-1865?) B
Exum, John to Jane Young 4-15-1840 (4-16-1840)
Exum, Wm. C. to M. J. Exum 9-17-1859 (9-20-1859)
Fain, Hiram to Sarah R. Pety 4-5-1842
Falkner, John to Pamelia Gwin 11-30-1850
Fall, Gilberth to Frances D. Menice? 11-26-1839
Falls, Frank G. to Bettie A. Evans 2-24-1871 (3-1-1871)
Falls, John to Lucy F. Finch 5-13-1862 (5-14-1862)
Faris, Washington to Hariett McCarley 12-16-1850 (12-18-1850)
Farley, J. M. to Virginia Thorpe 12-29-1870 (no return)
Farley, Joseph J. to Rebeca Tatum 11-20-1840 (11-26-1840)
Farley, Sterling to Lucinda F. Stone 7-7-1847
Farley, Thomas to Martha Tatum 10-6-1843 (10-10-1843)
Farley, William to Julia Baw 12-15-1854 (no return)
Farley, William to Manerva Ann Stone 10-4-1848 (no return)
Farmer, H. M. to Ann J. Hesler 7-13-1849 (7-17-1849)
Farmer, Harry (Henry) M. to Mary Ann Price 4-27-1871

Farmer, Huy M. to Rebeca C. Lorrence 11-2-1840 (no return)
Farmer, Uel H. to Ann Butterworth 10-10-1839
Farmer, Wm. F. to C. F. Hurley 1-30-1871 (2-14-1871)
Farrar, Geo. W. to Virginia E. Flippin 11-5-1866 (11-7-1866)
Farrar, J. S. to R. Harris 1-21-1861 (1-23-1861)
Farrell, Daniel S. to Malisa Hall 11-17-1851 (no return)
Farrell, James to Sarah Warren 8-4-1866 (no return)
Farrer, J. T. to Martha S. Farrer 7-21-1851 (7-24-1851)
Farrer, Thos. J. to Zany Ann Benson 12-14-1844 (12-19-1844)
Farrington, Andrew H. to Areadna Ray 7-15-1845
Farris, Dandrage to Tabby Trent 12-1-1868 (12-27-1868) B
Farris, W. H. to E. A. Smith 2-3-1868 (2-5-1868)
Faulk, John to Samantha Hendrix? 6-22-1850
Fausett, David to Margaret Stockinger 4-27-1862 (4-30-1862)
Fawlk, Jonathan to Louisa Cothran 1-17-1848 (1-20-1848)
Fellow, William to Martha Birdwell 10-16-1841 (10-17-1841)
Ferrel, John to Elizabeth Hughes 5-2-1846 (no return)
Ferrell, C. W. to Tempy Ann Hudson 2-9-1846
Ferrell, N. P. to M. N. Waller 10-2-1854 (no return)
Fewell, William to F. M. Barron 1-17-1848 (1-18-1848)
Field, Alex. to Eliza J. Brown 10-15-1842 (no return)
Field, J. G. to Ann Eliza Caples 10-23-1865 (10-26-1865)
Field, Robert to Fanny Jordan 9-17-1870 (no return) B
Fields, Isham to Henrietta Boyssian 11-28-1843 (11-29-1843)
Fields, Jack to Rose Fields 12-24-1866 (12-29-1866) B
Fields, John B. to Lucy L. Williamson 1-3-1868 (1-9-1868)
Fields, Rawley to Lucinda Holland 11-10-1869 (not executed) B*
Fields, Richard to Jane Parker 8-28-1869 (no return) B
Figgins, Joseph M. to Harriet V. Cassel 2-16-1867 (2-22-1867)
Finch, A. C. to S. A. Gardner 11-17-1859 (11-18-1859)
Finch, B. to S. A. Pickens no date (1864 or 65?)
Finch, John W. to Lucy? J. Botts 9-16-1849
Finley, William to Jane Brown 4-23-1870 (no return) B
Finney, B. D. to Elizabeth J. Jernigan 5-18-1846 (5-26-1846)
Finney, Moses to Rose Cloyd 3-14-1870 (no return) B
Finney, Richd. F. to Martha Ann Finney 1-5-1839 (1-6-1839)
Finney, W. P. to Martha J. Finney 9-28-1849 (9-10?-1849)
Finny, A. B. to H. W. Burt 10-29-1854 (no return)
Firth, Richard M. to Martha F. Adams 2-18-1841
Firth, T. J. to S. J. Branch 8-28-1868 (9-9-1868)
Firth, W. S. to Maggie G. Leach 3-1-1870 (3-2-1870)
Firth, Wm. T. to Martha E. Smith 11-15-1859 (12-13-1859)
Fisher, Henry to Josaphine Fisher 3-10-1868 (no return) B
Fisher, J. H. to Bettie A. Matthews 5-7-1866 (5-9-1866)
Fisher, Lacey to Margaret Nutson 1-22-1870 (no return) B
Fisk, Samuel W. to Penniah Dodds 3-6-1854 (no return)
Fitch, Young to Margaret Brown 11-25-1865 B
Fitchugh, Wash to Lucynda Rawlings 1-8-1867 (1-12-1867) B
Fitts, William H. to Mary Edwards 1-8-1852 (no return)
Fitzgerald, _____ to _____ Adams 9-5-1838 (no return)
Fitzpatrick, Granville to Ellen Bridly 1-26-1842 (1-27-1842)
Fitzpatrick, Samuel to Susanah Bradly 11-2-1840 (11-5-1840)
Flemming, John to Winny Johnston 4-11-1849 (4-12-1849)
Flemming, Robert to Nancy Torrence 2-21-1859 (2-23-1859)
Flemming, W. A. to Mary J. Elliott 5-31-1859 (6-8-1859)
Flemmings, G. S. to M. N. Phillips 12-7-1864 (not endorsed)
Fletcher, Asberry to Martha Sanders 4-6-1866 (4-10-1866) B
Fletcher, Felix to Eliza Smith 11-19-1869 (no return) B
Fletcher, G. W. to Sarah F. Dowdy 3-4-1841 (no return)
Fletcher, Simon to Mary E. Dortch 1-25-1870 (1-26-1870) B
Flippin, Booker to Jantha Brewer 1-7-1870 (no return) B
Flippin, J. A. to Bettie E. Ddupree 4-11-1864 (4-16-1864)
Flippin, T. J. to Betty N. Word 2-24-1864 (2-25-1864)
Floyd, Calvin S. to Elizabeth F. Sisco 10-16-1850 (10-17-1850)
Floyd, James to Caroline R. Rawlings 12-21-1865 (12-24-1865)
Floyd, William J. to Edna J. Brownlow 8-8-1846 (no return)
Floyed, R. W. to Mary Catharine Walker 4-13-1852 (no return)
Folkner, Francis C. to Nancy T. Willingham 11-10-1855 (no return)
Foote, T. H. to Mary A. Pickens 11-23-1869 (11-25-1869)
Forbes, Francis M. to Lucinda Aulsup 7-2-1870 (7-4-1870)
Forbes, Henry T. to Fannie G. Webb 9-12-1855 (no return)
Forbess, A. B. to Sarah And. Airs 9-4-1848 (9-27-1848)
Ford, Edward C. to Elizabeth Bagley 8-30-1845 (9-25-1845)
Ford, Johnson G. to Sarah T. Soap 12-19-1842 (no return)
Forrest, Dock to Tempe Simmons 2-22-1866 (no return) B

Fort, David W. to Adeline D. Goode 12-6?-1841 (no return)
Fortner, Lewis D. to Martha A. Taylor 12-16-1854 (no return)
Fortson, George to Winney Granberry 4-27-1869 (no return) B
Foster, A. G. to Elizabeth Campbell 4-27-1853 (no return)
Foster, C. A. to F. D. Weston 12-4-1838 (1-22-1839)
Foster, James C. to Maryann Roe 1-25-1843 (2-2-1843)
Foster, James to Laura Mebane 10-28-1868 (no return) B
Foster, Robert L. to Lucy M. Crank 5-6-1852 (no return)
Fowler, Joseph to Eliza Shaw 2-25-1869 (2-26-1869) B
Fowler, William H. to Nancy C. Payne 12-26-1846 (12-27-1847?)
Fox, Henry C. to Emily F. Gates 3-17-1862 (3-20-1862)
Francis, Oliver to Rebecca Mangrum 2-14-1842 (2-16-1842)
Frank, W. H. to F. J. Robertson 5-30-1859
Franklin, Alexander to Charlotte Doss 12-30-1866 (1-1-1866?) B
Franklin, Cornelius to Becky Shaw 12-25-1867 B
Franklin, Henry to R. Jane Allen 1-22-1870 (1-27-1870) B
Franklin, Meshack to J. P. Wilborne 4-26-1866 (5-2-1866)
Franklin, Thomas D. to Mary L. C. Moodey 5-3-1845 (5-7-1845)
Franklin, Wm. E. to Willie Wilkinson 2-7-1871 (2-8-1871)
Franklin, Wm. to Lucy Baldwin 1-1-1869 (1-2-1869) B
Fraser, Henry to Jennie Pattillo 1-2-1867 B
Fraser, John to Frances Swift 2-21-1867 (no return) B
Fraser, M. G. to Harriet Wortham 2-20-1867
Fraser, R. C. to Mollie Graham 9-5-1866 (9-6-1866)
Fraser, Silo to Berlin Dickinson 1-3-1868 (no return) B
Fraser, Wm. L. to Hattie E. Fraser 6-8-1865
Frazer, Mark M. to Louisa Blessing 9-11-1845 (12-6-1845)
Frazer, Milton G. to Mary H. Harvey 2-11-1854 (no return)
Frazier, Daniel G. to Betsey J. Hill 2-23-1846 (2-25-1846)
Frazier, Daniel W. to Perlina C. Morriss 12-1-1843 (11?-16-1843)
Frazier, G. B. to Lanith White 11-13-1855 (no return)
Frazure, Jeremiah to Louiza E. Wall 11-13-1851 (no return)
Freear, E.H. to Lucey A. Towls 4-29-1853 (no return)
Freeland, Joseph J. to Margaret J. Johnston 11-15-1870 (11-22-1870)
Freeman, Binkley to Eady Harriss 4-17-1839 (4-18-1839)
Freeman, Daniel to Mary A. Cocke 4-23-1870 (4-28-1870) B
Freeman, G. W. to Martha Allen 10-15-1854 (no return)
Freeman, H. F. to S. A. Darden 12-15-1862 (12-17-1862)
Freeman, King to Clara Mebane 12-24-1868 (12-25-1868) B
Freeman, W. H. to Harriet J. Braden 11-4-1865 (11-5-1865)
Freeth, George to Ann Eliza Malone 1-9-1863 (1-10-1863)
French, James to Mary Ann Lanthrop 7-23-1845
Frierson, Benjamin to Margarett Thompson 12-24-1870
    (no return) B
Frothschild, Joseph to Ellen Van Campen 9-18-1866 (9-20-1866)
Fulks, Andrew to Peggie Reid 3-8-1869 (no return)
Fuller, David to Matilda J. Clark 4-21-1866 (no return)
Fuller, James T. to Lucyann Trezvant 7-25-1848 (no return)
Fuller, John to Candis Haily 12-22-1853 (no return)
Furgason, Benjamin F. to Elisabeth L. Daniel 12-6-1848 (no return)
Furr, James A. to Fanny Ballard 11-5-1870 (11-10-1870)
Gabbie (Gallbie?), Robt. M. to Margarett J. Allen 1-27-1845
    (1-28-1845)
Gabley, John to Eveline Booth 4-17-1852 (no return)
Gaither, E. to Emily T. Guy 3-14-1864 (3-15-1864)
Gaither, Ham to Bettie Cobbs 2-1-1870 B
Gaither, Henry to Caroline Hudson 12-28-1869 B
Gaither, Saml. E. to Martha A. Roberts 3-31-1871 (4-4-1871)
Gallagher, James to Mary Macklin 4-23-1867 (not executed)
Gallagher, James to Tennessee Sullivan 1-4-1870 (1-6-1869?)
Galloway, Enoch to Lucretia J. Edwards 2-2-1855 (no return)
Galloway, N. W. to Susan H. Harris 5-1-1871 (5-2-1871)
Galloway, Richd. E. to Martha H. Exum 5-14-1849 (no return)
Gant, Ed to Mira Warren 3-1-1871 (3-3-1871) B
Gant, Edward to Martha Jordan 8-22-1868 (no return) B
Gant, Wm. J. to Catharine Parish 3-16-1870
Gantling, Briggs to Frances Wills 1-12-1839 (1-15-1839)
Gardner, Fielding C. to Caroline Williamson 5-21-1839 (5-25-1839)
Gardner, James M. to Martha J. Webster 5-13-1869 (5-17-1869)
Gardner, John E. to Jane McGee 9-27-1838
Gardner, Moses to Milla Stidham 9-13-1867 (no return) B
Gardner, T. C. to Ann Benton 10-9-1862 (not endorsed)
Garnett, Jno. H. to Mary F. Rutledge 12-15-1868
Garrett, J. T. to Sally Hamrick 12-31-1866 (no return)
Garrett, R. C. to Sarah A. Rhodes 5-1-1848 (5-3-1848)

Garrett, Rufus K. to Sarah E. Luckey 1-21-1851 (1-22-1851)
Garrison, B. P. to Isabella Seymour 4-4-1864
Garrison, James L. to Lucy Ann Ivey 8-31-1847 (no return)
Garrison, James V. to Susannah Baker 12-14-1846 (no return)
Garrison, John T. to Mary H. Cleaves 5-7-1863
Garrison, M. to Marinda Howell 6-24-1869 (6-30-1869)
Garvin, H. to Mary Eddins 7-27-1863 (8-11-1863)
Garvin, J. G. to M. T. Burnett 9-6-1862 (9-9-1862)
Garvin, John A. to Albenia T. Culp 12-11-1866 (12-13-1866)
Gaston, Chas. A. to Jennie Campbell 6-18-1867 (6-20-1867)
Gately, Robert to Biney Parks 2-1-1859
Gates, Jno. H. to Mattie V. Yancy 12-2-1867 (12-6-1867)
Gates, John to Mary A. Benge 8-29-1840 (9-3-1840)
Gatling, Richard B. to Sarah E. Granberry 7-8-1844 (7-9-1844)
George, John H. to Margaret Henderson 1-24-1845 (no return)
Geyer, J. to M. J. Hawkins 7-23-1853 (no return)
Gibson, J. N. to Victoria J. March 6-3-1868
Gibson, Matthew T. to Mima Brown 5-27-1870 (5-28-1870) B
Gibson, William to Isabella Sanders 7-21-1841 (7-22-1841)
Gilbert, William to Ellen Carpenter 4-16-1867 (not executed) B
Giles, Ned to Emeline Hunter 12-12-1868 (12-19-1868) B
Giles, T. L. to Lenora C. Lock 3-7-1853 (no return)
Gilford, Elias to Caroline Lane 11-25-1870 (no return) B
Gill, J. C. to Candace Lile 10-13-1847 (no return)
Gillespie, Andrew J. to Julia ann Wright 2-12-1844 (2-13-1844)
Gillespie, Davis to Martha Ann Morris 6-17-1848 (no return)
Gilliam, James B. to Lucy K. Ritchey 1-18-1870 (1-20-1870)
Gilliam, James M. to Elizabeth F. Hall 6-3-1852 (no return)
Gilliam, James M. to Margarett A. Wall 1-16-1843 (1-17-1843)
Gilliam, John A. to Mary Curtis 1-22-1853 (no return)
Gilliam, Thomas P. to Sarah High 12-23-1847
Gilliam, Wm. A. to Emma D. Holloway 2-17-1869
Glasgow, Isaac to Martha Moore 1-11-1867 (1-19-1867) B
Glenn, John to Eliza Jane Griffin 10-25-1845 (10-28-1845)
Glover, C. C. to Eliza N. Shaw 4-29-1854 (no return)
Glover, J. W. to Rebecca Perry 7-8-1868 (7-9-1868)
Glover, Wilie A. to Lee G. Southall 12-5-1863 (12-13-1863)
Gober, James A. to Eliza H. Watters 8-6-1845 (8-7-1845)
Gober, M. A. to M. A. Penn 11-24-1865 (11-29-1865)
Godby, James M. to Susanah E. Williams 9-14-1852 (no return)
Godby, Wilson J. to _____ 7-19-1849 (no return)
Goins, C. A. to Sarah F. B. Elder 3-17-1843 (no return)
Golden, John to Eliza Moorman 1-28-1869 (1-30-1869) B
Golin, George to Rebecca Tatum 8-27-1869 (no return) B
Goode, Daniel to Nola Johnson 6-11-1869 (no return) B
Goode, J. A. V. to Elizabeth F. Murphey 11-30-1853 (no return)
Goode, James to Maria Hare 12-24-1866 (no return) B
Goode, Wm. P. to Lucinda Baker 12-27-1870 B
Gooden, Gus to Lucy Ann Morris 11-5-1869 (11-6-1869) B
Gooden, Ned to Susan Hart 12-30-1869 (12-31-1869) B
Goodloe, G. W. to Emily W. Jones 12-29-1852 (no return)
Goodman, John F. to Elizabeth J. Crump 8-9-1854 (no return)
Goodman, Monroe to Ann Baskerville 12-29-1866 B
Goodwin, Washington to Harriet Bobbitt 12-9-1869 (12-16-1869) B
Gordan, George to Hannah Moore 10-16-1867 (10-19-1867) B
Gordon, Jesse to Susan Gambrell 2-14-1844 (no return)
Gordon, Nathaniel to Ann H. Aston 4-22-1838
Gore, James M. to M. H. Morris 10-30-1866 (11-2-1865?)
Gormon, Parish A. to A. E. Mallory 9-6-1848 (9-12-1848)
Goss, John to Lillie F. Darlin 12-30-1868 (no return)
Gossett, A. T. to Cornelia W. Pope 1-14-1871 (1-17-1871)
Gourdlock, Milton to Ann Scott 9-4-1869 B
Grable, Samuel A. to Sarah T. Watkins 3-28-1862 (4-4-1862)
Grace, Abel to R. C. Harvey 10-20-1849 (10-28-1849)
Graham, A. K. to Eva Marshall 1-15-1866 (no return)
Graham, Harrison to Frances Washington 1-2-1871 (1-4-1871)
Graham, James C. to Jane Ballard 1-16-1841 (1-20-1841)
Graham, Jehu to Mary A. D. Smalman 6-26-1851
Grammar, P. H. W. to Mary A. Harper 12-24-1853 (no return)
Granberry, Dudley to Mary J. Ketchum 10-24-1868 (no return) B
Granberry, Everett to Margaret Granberry 10-23-1869
    (10-24-1869) B
Granberry, J. H. to L. J. Brown 4-9-1866 (4-11-1866)
Granberry, J. L. to Sallie T. Williamson 10-9-1865 (10-12-1865)
Granberry, Jackson to Lucy A. Taylor 1-18-1868 (1-26-1868) B

Granberry, John to Lydia Williams 12-25-1866 (12-27-1866) B
Granberry, Milton to Luvenia Granberry 1-18-1868 (1-26-1868) B
Grant, Elijah to Charlotte Biggs 2-10-1871 (2-15-1871) B
Grant, R. D. to Polly Branch 6-23-1849
Graves, A. P. to Amelia A. W. Eastham 12-4-1852 (no return)
Graves, G. to Malinda Torrence 9-22-1849 (11-27-1849)
Graves, Joseph to Sarah ANn Edwards 11-7-1844 (11-14-1844)
Graves, Lewis to C. C. Arbuckle 12-6-1849 (no return)
Graves, Solm. O. to Elizabeth Perkins 9-9-1853 (no return)
Graves, Thomas J. to Artelia J. Wills 1-28-1840 (1-30-1840)
Graves, W. W. to Julia A. Phillips 12-25-1850
Graves, William to Shemima McInteref 1-30-1849
Gray, Claiborne to Mary Jane Bowls 9-22-1866 (no return) B
Gray, Geor. C. to Harriet Parham 1-22-1845
Gray, H. to Hariett Roberson 1-30-1851
Gray, James M. to Louisa F. Beasley 4-17-1839 (4-18-1839)
Gray, Joseph Y. to Mary Wortham 8-19-1840 (9-22-1840)
Gray, Robt. to Rebecca Brown 7-21-1870 (7-22-1870) B
Gray, W. C. (Rev.) to Maggie Trent 5-11-1863 (5-20-1863)
Grear, Tom to Easter Johnson 8-2-1867 (no return) B
Green, Ambrose E. to Ann Henry Ford 10-3-1868 (10-8-1868)
Green, Carter to Charlotte Green 6-16-1866 (no return) B
Green, David to Maria Stainback 11-27-1866 (12-2-1866) B
Green, G.? J. to M. A. Slaughter 10-22-1866 (10-25-1866)
Green, Geo. R. to Martha J. Monroe 5-27-1846 (no return)
Green, George to Ann Deener 11-14-1868 (11-15-1868) B
Green, Hamilton J. to Lucy A. Davis 11-19-1850 (11-21-1850)
Green, Harry to Catherine Fraser 3-20-1866 (3-28-1866) B
Green, Henry D. to India M. Swift 12-21-1859 (12-22-1859)
Green, Ira N. to Rebecca Jackson 10-7-1840 (10-13-1840)
Green, J. D. to J. J. Robertson 12-23-1862 (12-30-1862)
Green, James F. to Virginia A. Hare 10-14-1848 (10-18-1848)
Green, Lee to Amanda Walker 2-12-1870 (2-25-1870) B
Green, R. Moses to Mary F. Owen 11-25-1854 (no return)
Green, Richard W. to Harriet H. Scott 5-8-1839 (5-15-1839)
Green, Simon W. to Melvinie Clements 6-23-1862
Green, Solomon to Sarah B. Degraffenreid 10-30-1848 (no return)
Green, Washington to Elizabeth Fraser 2-13-1869 (2-17-1869) B
Green, William E. to Emily S. Jordan 11-4-1845 (11-5-1845)
Green, William E. to Mary E. Jordan 10-9-1843 (10-11-1843)
Green, William S. to Viola L. Chaffin 12-20-1870 (no return)
Green, Willis M. to Catharine Wirt 3-15-1838
Greenberry, John to Hester Wright 10-7-1867 (no return) B
Greenbery, John F. to Mary c. Mitchell 1-4-1851 (1-6-1851)
Greenlaw, Anguss to Ellenorah E. Bayless 7-13-1844 (7-14-1844)
Greenlee, Abram to Julia Hilliard 7-25-1870 B
Greenway, William W. to Elisabeth M. Young 5-2-1848
Greenway, Wm. W. to Mary A. E. Rhodes 9-5-1850
Greer, Charles to Ellen Currie 7-5-1869 (7-17-1869) B
Greer, Robt. E. R. to Mary J. Johnson 11-5-1867 (11-7-1867)
Gregory, Robt. C. to Sarah Jane Martin 12-9-1851 (no return)
Gressom, Jerome B. to Sarahann Teague 7-16-1844 (no return)
Grider, B. H. to Rebecca C. Worrell 1-28-1845
Grider, Tobias to Mary B. Worrell 1-5?-1839
Griffin, B. P. to H. A. C. Lile 10-5-1860 (10-18-1860)
Griffin, Benjamin to Winney Birdson 2-8-1847
Griffin, Durell to Maria Rosser 11-3-1870 (11-8-1870)
Griffin, Francis M. to Margaret E. Pickins 12-24-1847 (12-28-1847)
Griffin, G. W. to Eliza J. Spurlock 12-21-1852 (no return)
Griffin, Gus to Margaret Boals 2-24-1869 (2-25-1869) B
Griffin, James C. to Clotilda Lay 6-25-1851 (no return)
Griffin, James H. to Z. A. Thomas 1-6-1851 (no return)
Griffin, John W. to Amelia J. Morison 12-30-1848 (12-31-1848)
Griffin, John to Isabella Coffey 5-2-1840 (5-3-1840)
Griffin, Robert to Caty Loving 2-4-1867 (no return) B
Griffin, William E. to Mary Ann Crenshaw 9-11-1846 (9-18-1846)
Griffin, Wm. L. to Mary L. Jones 10-14-1868 (10-15-1868)
Griffith, David to Ann Morrow 11-9-1868 (11-13-1868) B
Grifford, Robert to Frances E. Fausett 12-3-1851 (no return)
Grisham, William to Stacy Bounds 10-31-1845 (no return)
Grissom, John W. to Mary Outlaw 11-15-1869 (11-16-1869)
Grizzle, R. R. to Susan A. Hood 10-3-1868 (10-7-1868)
Grundy, Henderson to Patience Hammon 2-20-1869 (2-12?-1869) B
Guardner, Pleasant to Jane Read 8-31-1838 (no return)
Guarrant, Robert D. to L. A. Exum 8-26-1847 (no return)

Guthra, William J. to Elizabeth James 1-24-1842 (5-16-1842)
Guy, H. P. to C. A. Tomlinson 8-9-1854 (no return)
Guy, H. P. to Martha L. J. Rogers 1-4-1865
Guy, Henry to Mary Williams 7-5-1870 (7-17-1870)
Guy, John to E. J. Tomlinson 7-3-1849 (7-11-1849)
Gwin, James to Isabella S. Bobbitt 1-10-1853 (no return)
Gwyn, Albert to Lavenia Brewster 12-23-1866 (12-27-1866) B
Gwyn, Elijah to Mary Wilkerson 12-28-1868 (12-5?-1868) B
Gwyn, H. L. to America J. Poor 2-4-1865 (2-6-1865)
Gwyn, R. R. to Elizabeth A. Smith 12-19-1842
Gwyn, Richd. R. to S. E. Butterworth 11-10-1859 (11-15-1859)
Gwynn, Henry C. to Julia L. Rich 6-25-1866 (6-28-1866)
Gwynn, Henry C. to Susan Roberts 12-18-1865 (12-20-1865)
Gwynn, James to Georgia Ann Jones 7-13-1866 (7-28-1866) B
Gwynn, James to Viney Crawford 3-21-1870 (3-31-1870) B
Gwynn, N. to Susan Wilkerson 8-10-1866 (8-12-1866) B
Gwynn, S. J. to S. M. Gwynn 1-28-1866 (1-30-1866)
Hacket, George W. to Susan E. Rogers 11-8-1845 (11-18-1845)
Hacklin, Neverson to Susan Broadnax 12-26-1867 B
Haden, J. S. to Isabella Armour 1-4-1844 (no return)
Haden, R. M. to Laura J. Paulson 6-23-1869 (6-24-1869)
Hadley, Ike to Jenney Monroe 12-4-1865 (12-9-1865) B
Hafford, W. D. F. to Mary Belle Palmer 3-8-1859
Hailey, James H. to Margaret Irwin 3-11-1869
Hailey, L. S. to Elizabeth Sanders 12-22-1847 (no return)
Hale, Bernard to Emma Brewer 12-20-1867 (12-28-1867) B
Haley, D. S. to Mary J. Hilliard 2-15-1853 (no return)
Haley, H. S. to Nancy E. Cocke 12-16-1867 (no return)
Haley, James to Martha J. Kelly 10-2-1849 (no return)
Hall, Dennis to Margaret Dickinson 9-7-1867 (9-8-1867) B
Hall, Henry W. to Martha B. Lavier 5-15-1867 (5-16-1867)
Hall, James H. M. to A. K. Rhodes 4-22-1838
Hall, John to Annette Williamson 6-23-1866 B
Hall, W. L. to Susan R. Hansel? 2-14-1852 (no return)
Hall, William L. to Armelia Patton 12-11-1847 (12-23-1847)
Halley, Creed P. to Mary W. (Mrs.) Spencer 7-18-1839
Halloway, Saml. F. to Harriett Ford 11-9-1847
Ham (Haines?), Thomas I. to Martha Fisher 2-1-1838
Ham, G. W. to Martha P. Fisher 1-4-1841 (1-7-1841)
Ham, James M. to R. C. Farley 3-9-1850 (no return)
Hamerick, Saml. to Juliana Wright 3-13-1847 (3-16-1847)
Hamilton, George F. to Martha McLoad 11-17-1853 (no return)
Hamlet, James W. to Mary Jane Broom 5-8-1840 (5-14-1840)
Hammond, James H. to Eliza J. Rideout 1-17-1861 (1-20-1861)
Hammond, James M. to Rebecca Marcum 10-27-1848 (10-29-1848)
Hammons, Edward D. to Elizabeth C. Roberts 10-7-1870 (10-9-1870)
Hammons, L. B. to Caroline Simmons 3-2-1854 (no return)
Hammons, Wm. to Lucy Able 7-3-1838
Hamon, Nuton A. to Martha J. Leonard 9-7-1852 (no return)
Hampton, J. T. to Paulina Oberley 2-5-1842 (no return)
Hampton, J. W. to H. McAvoy 9-30-1847
Hampton, John P. to Catharine Stewart 8-23-1869 (8-26-1869)
Hamrick, William to Marey E. F. Coby 12-14-1859
Hancock, A. S. to Sarah J. Ball 1-11-1841 (1-12-1841)
Hancock, J. C. to A. P. Galloway 3-14-1859 (3-28-1859)
Haney, David to Lydia Vanpelt 10-1-1869 (10-2-1869) B
Harbson, Jas. H. to Eliza J. Stegall 7-1-1850 (7-9-1850)
Hardin, George W. to Sarah A. E. Harris 6-11-1838 (no return)
Hardin, John H. to Martha A. Bridgewater 7-26-1849 (7-31-1849)
Harding, Augustus to Dollie Irwin 11-8-1869 (no return) B
Hardy, Davy to Rosanna Crewer 12-21-1867 B
Hardy, George to Dilly Grundy 12-28-1867 (no return) B
Hardy, George to Jane Jones 3-16-1867 (3-19-1867) B
Hardy, George to Mary Ann Fletcher 5-18-1868 (no return) B
Hare, Frank to Amanda Mebane 10-1-1870 (10-4-1870) B
Hare, Jacob to Margarett E. Neal 10-31-1853 (no return)
Hare, Paten to Charity Carroll 11-16-1869 (no return) B
Hare, Starkey S. to Ann T. J. Ware 8-15-1846 (8-18-1846)
Hare, Starky S. to Eda A. Brown 2-14-1859 (2-22-1859)
Hare, Thomas P. to Oliver B. Turbeville 1-10-1848 (1-13-1848)
Harendon, Hankins E. to Virginia A. Miller 9-3-1839
Hargis, J. W. L. to Augustine L. Hargis 12-22-1841 (12-23-1841)
Hargiss, James A. to Amanda L. Barnes 6-11-1852 (no return)
Hargiss, Marion S. to Tranquilla E. Lester 5-30-1846 (6-10-1846)
Hargrove, R. W. to Caroline C. Loving 10-15-1860 (10-16-1860)

Hargus, Washington B. to Elizabeth J. Bradberry 5-16-1844 (5-17-1844)
Haring, J. W. D. to Nancy Moss 3-26-1850 (3-28-1850)
Harper, E. to Mary Ann Kyle 1-14-1851 (no return)
Harper, J. A. to Frances Rich 9-3-1850 (no return)
Harper, Lewis W. to Mary Gresham 9-2-1850 (9-4-1850)
Harper, Nat to Gertrude R. Maxwell 12-28-1867 (1-8-1868)
Harper, Robert B. to Mary M. Hart 9-12-1864 (9-13-1864)
Harper, W. A. to Lucy H. Rich 11-11-1853 (no return)
Harrel, W. J. to Callie V. Griffin 9-14-1869 (no return)
Harrell, Asburry to Sarah Blain 12-13-1866 (no return)
Harrell, David to B. Carter 3-2-1838
Harrell, J. C. to Fanney Mitchell 3-16-1859
Harrell, Levi to Jenny Crawford 10-6-1866 (10-8-1866) B
Harris, A. G. B. to M. A. E. Blair 9-14-1866 (9-16-1866)
Harris, Alford W. to Mary Lucinda Sale 2-24-1846 (no return)
Harris, Austin to Nellie Shaw 10-25-1870 (10-30-1870) B
Harris, C. H. to Minerva Jones 12-2-1865 (12-3-1865) B
Harris, Caleb T. to Mary E. Rodgers 2-3-1869 (2-24-1869)
Harris, Curtis to Sarah J. Cothran 5-27-1854 (no return)
Harris, Elisha W. to Sarah B. Payton 11-19-1846 (11-24-1846)
Harris, F. P. to Sarah A. E. Leverett 8-7-1867
Harris, H. to Martha Jane Williams 7-30-1851 (no return)
Harris, Henry to Julia Braden 3-8-1867 (3-9-1867)
Harris, Henry to Lou Rieves 8-15-1867 (8-17-1867) B
Harris, Henry to Rose Boyd 3-23-1867 (3-30-1867) B
Harris, J. R. to Mary F. Winbourne 12-15-1869
Harris, Joe to Caroline Garvin 5-9-1866 B
Harris, John W. to E. C. Young 4-3-1871 (5-2-1871)
Harris, Joseph to Jane Askew 5-15-1869 (no return) B
Harris, Nathanl. to Elizabeth Starling 7-23-1850 (no return)
Harris, Nelson to Priscilla Jones 12-29-1870 B
Harris, Newel W. to Sally P. Whitmore 10-4-1852 (no return)
Harris, Newit to Malsey Harris 2-14-1853 (no return)
Harris, Newitt to Sallie M. Newsom 10-24-1867
Harris, Orange to Amanda Marshall 12-9-1868 (1-3-1869) B
Harris, Overton to Eliza Cumings 2-23-1867 (3-2-1867) B
Harris, Reuben to S. E. C. Gardner 5-5-1851 (no return)
Harris, Sterling to Mary Isabella Forbs 3-25-1851 (no return)
Harris, T. B. to H. M. Jones 12-13-1859 (12-14-1859)
Harris, T. P. to Lucy Martin 5-13-1863 (5-14-1863)
Harris, Thomas W. to Caroline Burford 8-21-1843 (no return)
Harris, Thomas to Mary Stovall 12-6-1842 (12-7-1842)
Harris, Turner to Ary Ann Mitchel 6-11-1847 (6-17-1847)
Harris, Wesley to Amanda Farris 3-18-1854 (no return)
Harris, Wesley to Rebecca Reeves 3-11-1869
Harris, Whitson A. to Mary E. Winston 1-24-1848 (1-28-1848)
Harris, Wilkerson to Emeline Jones 12-24-1866 (12-27-1866) B
Harris, Wm. C. to Lucinda J. Demming 1-21-1850 (1-22-1850)
Harris, Wm. F. to Martha E. McSpadden 7-16-1844
Harris, jr., J. W. to Mary Goode 9-12-1865 (9-13-1865)
Harris?, Nathl. to Elizabeth Starling 7-25-1850 (no return)
Harrison, E. W. to Sarah E. McCully 9-18-1854 (no return)
Harrison, Jno. E. to O. E. Murphey 8-13-1838 (no return)
Harrison, Joe to Rosa Warren 12-27-1865 (12-30-1865) B
Harrison, John to Martha Moore 7-6-1867 B
Harrison, Landon to Clara Brown 12-12-1868
Harrison, Wm. J. to Sarah A. T. Ellington 10-4-1849
Harriss, J. C. to Rhody Frasier? 1-6-1845 (1-8-1845)
Hart, S. A. to Susan Smith 7-31-1855 (no return)
Hart, W. L. to Sallie Holt 10-16-1865 (10-17-1865)
Hartis, Andrew S. to Josaphin Marshall 10-31-1851 (no return)
Harvey, Blunt to Sarah E. Sullivan 3-4-1868 (3-10-1868)
Harvey, Jesse to Nancy Rodgers 11-10-1866 (11-20-1866)
Harvey, Lot to Nancy Boyd 3-23-1866 (4-1-1866) B
Harvey, Marcus D. to Rebeca C. Burford 4-8-1839 (4-9-1839)
Harvey, R. H. (Dr.) to Mary J. Rogers 6-16-1869
Harvey, Richd. H. to Della Ann Harrison? 12-19-1848
Harvey, W. B. to J. C. Rhodes 3-31-1869 (no return)
Harvy, James L. to Elizabeth A. Walker 11-14-1842 (11-15-1842)
Harwell, Buckner to Mary J. Ross 10-2-1867 (10-3-1867)
Harwell, Buckner to Rose Ann Hamlett 7-8-1840 (7-9-1840)
Harwell, Thomas to Elizabeth W. Eddins 1-17-1848 (1-20-1848)
Harwell, W. F. to Rosina Wells 11-15-1865 (11-21-1865)
Hasbey, Burwell S. to Rebecca M. Eddins 1-13-1840 (1-14-1840)

Haselet, James A. to Darcus Branch 9-21-1867 (no return) B
Hashler, D. M. B. to Jane Locke 10-11-1854 (no return)
Haskins, Calvin to Mary Young 12-22-1866 (12-24-1866) B
Hatcher, Augustus to Elizabeth Thomas 1-11-1868 (1-12-1868) B
Hauf, Joseph to Roselia Beer 1-24-1854 (no return)
Havercamp, Harmon to Isabella A. M. Montgomery 2-5-1867
Hawkins, G. B. to Sallie A. Worrell 1-17-1866
Hawley, W. S. to Margaret F. Shoemaker 2-9-1871 (2-24-1871)
Hays, Booker to Sarah Cole 5-11-1871 (5-27-1871) B
Hazlewood, J. D. to Julia S. Irby 12-8-1866
Hazlewood, W. T. to B. J. Hazlewood 12-19-1865 (12-20-1865)
Heaggins, James to Isabella Owens 2-11-1871 (no return) B
Heaslet, Abraham to Anna Deener 12-3-1869 (no return) B
Heaslet, Fielding to Blanch Ann Dobbs 12-2-1869 (no return) B
Heaslet, Robert to Mary Deener 11-29-1869 (no return) B
Heaslett, Adam to Emily Shackleford 11-15-1867 (no return) B
Heaslett, Jesse to Easter Blaine 9-27-1871? (SB 1870?) B
Heaslett, Mitchell to Mary Grider 1-11-1870 (no return) B
Heath, Z. W. to Bettie Yancy 1-26-1869 (1-27-1869)
Heflin, H. L. to Mary J. Maxwell 12-28-1867 (1-8-1868)
Hemly, Thos. to F. A. Thomas 12-23-1851 (no return)
Hemson, W. J. to F. M. Edwards 11-27-1865 (11-28-1865)
Henderson, George to Julia Williamson 12-27-1869 B
Henderson, Jackson R. to Ann Eliza McPherson 4-30-1846 (no return)
Henderson, James to Ann Harvell 12-25-1866 (12-26-1866) B
Henderson, Pleasant to Emily V. Mays 1-30-1841 (2-3-1841)
Henderson, Robt. to Fillis DeGraffenreid 10-3-1868 (10-4-1868) B
Henderson, Tho. B. to Sarah J. Honnell 9-1-1846 (9-3-1846)
Henderson, Wm. H. to Sarah W. Mays 5-8-1843 (no return)
Henderson, Wyatt to Kitty Rogers 11-1-1867 (11-2-1867) B
Hendon, Dock to Cloe Haskins 7-30-1870 B
Hendrick, B. G. to Martha A. Old 5-30-1842 (no return)
Hendrick, Bernard G. to Sarah P. Higenbothem 2-19-1851 (no return)
Hendrick, Wm. J. to Lucina T. Anderson 12-31-1849 (1-1-1850)
Hendron, O. T. to Agnes Gregory 11-28-1842
Henley, Elijah D. to Lucinda Hubbard 11-11-1846
Henley, Isaac A. to Christina Bryant 1-28-1848 (no return)
Henley, Isaac P. to Manda C. Ellison 12-8-1842
Henley, William H. to Mariah Cowan 9-9-1840
Henley, Wm. H. to Sarah E. Henley 11-9-1868 (11-11-1868)
Henley, Wmson. to Nancey Green 3-10-1845
Henley, jr., Elijah to Pantha Grissum 9-28-1843
Henry, James W. D. to Lizzie Heit (Hart) 2-8-1867 (2-12-1867)
Henry, John G. to Estelia Worthan 2-18-1840 (2-20-1840)
Henry, Richard to Rilda Carpenter 5-29-1869 (no return) B
Herly, Thomas N. to Mary E. Jones 3-12-1848
Hern, Stephen to Emley Stafford 8-5-1844 (8-8-1844)
Herndon, John S. to Elizabeth A. Wall 11-5-1862 (11-6-1862)
Herndon, John S. to Mary E. Dodson 1-18-1854 (no return)
Herndon, R. H. to F. H. Peak 12-24-1854 (no return)
Herndon, Thomas H. to Sarah J. Kent 5-17-1865
Herndon, Wm. M. to Martha A. Howard 12-5-1856 (no return)
Herrick, Alonzo to Sarah Reeder 12-23-1868 (12-24-1868)
Herrington, D. J. to Sarah E. Harris 1-27-1842 (2-2-1842)
Herron, A. H. to Mary Featherston 2-6-1838
Herron, Harrison to Sallie A. V. Shore 10-7-1867 (10-17-1867)
Herron, Jno. to Sallie Baird 8-5-1868 (8-6-1868) B
Herron, John S. to Lucy Burford 10-14-1854 (no return)
Herron, John T. to Eliza Broom 3-22-1838
Herron, Ned to Virtue Heaslet 3-5-1870 (3-6-1870)
Herron, W. G. to Callie Webb 1-15-1868 (1-16-1868)
Hess, N. J. to R. E. Dayton 12-10-1870 (12-13-1870)
Hester, James to Mahala Lewis 12-25-1865 B
Hester, John W. to E. S. Brame 1-7-1841
Hester, John W. to Mary J. Harris 12-12-1854 (no return)
Hester, William H. to Sinia E. Wall 4-3-1841 (4-5-1841)
Hesther, James D. to S. A. Breene? 6-28-1842 (7-14-1842)
Hewin, Asa to Catharine J. Huddleston 5-2-1853 (no return)
Hewlet, John C. to Sallie A. Mitchell 2-2-1866 (2-8-1866)
Hicks, J. N. to Mary A. Nelson 2-7-1866 (2-8-1866)
Hicks, John W. to Martha E. Andrews 2-26-1868 (2-27-1868)
Hicks, R. B. to Rosa L. Andrews 12-19-1866 (no return)
Hicks, Wm. to Martha A. Lightie 3-12-1859 (3-18-1859)

Hiflin, George H. to Mary F. Robertson 11-28-1854 (no return)
Higbee, Adam to Ella Woods 12-25-1868 (12-26-1868) B
Higgs, Isham to Barbary Foust 1-9-1840 (no return)
High, Jno. W. to Sarah Eliz. Simmons 9-11-1850
High, M. to Matilda P. Vaughn 1-11-1851 (1-16-1851)
Hill, Alfred to Martha Parrish 9-7-1870 (9-18-1870) B
Hill, Ben to Patience Harris 8-29-1868 (8-30-1868) B
Hill, Charles to Emily Sanders 12-17-1869 (no return) B
Hill, Francis to Sarah J. Culp 12-2-1850 (12-3-1850)
Hill, Jessee to Millie Moody 12-5-1870 (12-8-1870) B
Hill, John H. to Nancy C. Brown 9-23-1853 (no return)
Hill, Joseph A. to Rachel C. Pulliam 6-6-1859 (6-7-1859)
Hill, Nathan to Mary Mason 12-24-1869 B
Hill, R. S. to Frances C. Craig 9-13-1862 (9-14-1862)
Hill, W. H. to Elizabeth Williams 12-27-1845 (12-28-1845)
Hill, W. H. to Mary F. Evans 2-1-1868 (no return)
Hill, William to Polly Taylor 5-18-1866 (5-19-1866) B
Hill, Wm. B. (Rev.) to Virginia J. Laughy 10-30-1851 (no return)
Hilliard, A. T. to Jennie R. Tuckniss 12-1-1866 (12-2-1866)
Hilliard, Albert to Phillis Jefferson 3-20-1869 (3-24-1869) B
Hilliard, Charney to Blanch Pollerd 2-4-1871 (2-12-1871) B
Hilliard, David B. to Martha Ann Blair 2-2-1846 (2-5-1846)
Hilliard, Henry E. to Sallie Anna Old 7-18-1860
Hilliard, J. P. to C. S. Tripp 3-24-1866 (3-29-1866)
Hilliard, J. T. Z. to Mary V. Trotter 9-24-1860 (9-25-1860)
Hilliard, J. W. T. to Mary A. Chambers 12-6-1854 (no return)
Hilliard, J. W. T. to Nancy A. Willis 9-16-1854 (no return)
Hilliard, Michell G. to Elizabeth Craig 6-7-1838
Hilliard, N. S. to Elizabeth Evans 12-29-1865 (1-3-1866)
Hilliard, W. A.? to Elizabeth D. Chambers 2-1-1847 (2-4-1847)
Hilliard, W. H. to E. C. Haley 10-5-1866 (10-7-1866)
Hineman, D. G. to M. A. Stockinger 2-9-1859
Hines, Ellet to Emeline Mebane 12-27-1870 (12-30-1870) B
Hinshaw, Addison to Calidona B. Martin 1-9-1844
Hinshaw, Pleasant to Margarett A. Martin 11-6-1841 (11-7-1841)
Hinson, John G. to Narcessus Compton 8-15-1838
Hinson, William to Malvina Compton 11-10-1838 (11-11-1838)
Hite, Francis to Mary Ingram 4-26-1853 (no return)
Hix, Merrit D. to Elizabeth Holloway 9-14-1853 (no return)
Hobbs, Francis M. to Susan Hickey 8-23-1865
Hobson, W. H. to Temperance J. Sullivan 4-27-1840 (5-2-1850)
Hodge, James R. to Virginia A. Beasley 6-13-1854 (no return)
Hodge, Samuel to Sally D. Brown 8-12-1843 (no return)
Hodge, Thomas to Anna Maclin 3-20-1869 (no return) B
Hodges, Jno. W. to Virginia Hamblet 12-2-1867 (12-11-1867)
Hodges, W. K. to D. E. C. Krouth 6-10-1860 (6-14-1860)
Hodman, Daniel to Elmira J. Hoskins 1-20-1850 (no return)
Hogan, Granville H. to Mary Jane Taylor 7-23-1845 (7-24-1845)
Hogan, S. E. to Nancy Ramsey 9-21-1843
Hogan, William C. to Levina Massy 1-26-1842 (1-27-1842)
Holcomb, P. to Martilla _____ 8-28-1851 (no return)
Holden, George to Lucinda Atkinson 12-20-1869 (12-23-1869) B
Holden, John to Ann Eliza Wilkins 12-11-1841
Holiday, T. M. to Martha Rogers 1-24-1871 (1-25-1871)
Holland, Thomas to Mary Ann Wilson 11-23-1852 (no return)
Holleman, Joe to Cornelia Poor 12-26-1866 (12-27-1866) B
Hollice, James to Frances Hammons 12-15-1863 (12-17-1863)
Holliday, George W. to Julia A. Williams 8-6-1847 (8-15-1847)
Holliday, John to Eveline Armstrong 3-12-1848 (no return)
Hollin, John S. to Harriet Winder 5-11-1866 (5-12-1866) B
Hollis, Jno. W. to Mary Jane Woolley 8-15-1868 (8-16-1868)
Hollis, Thos. J. to Patsy Garrett 11-16-1867 (11-17-1867)
Holloway, D. T. to Jane Cothran 7-16-1866 (7-18-1866)
Holloway, J. J. to Mary Brumley 10-27-1849 (10-28-1849)
Holloway, John to Rebeca Bryles 1-8-1841
Holloway, M. C. to Elizabeth Jane Henley 11-20-1845
Holloway, Q. T. to Mary J. England 10-12-1852 (no return)
Hollowell, M. D. to Dixie E. Graves 12-21-1868 (no return)
Hollowell, S. S. to Laura Culpepper 2-16-1869 (2-18-1869)
Holman, Mark to Charlotte E. Burnset 9-10-1846 (9-17-1846)
Holmes, Levy to Sarah Davis 12-27-1869 (1-1-1870) B
Holmes, Meredith to Sarah H. Stokes 5-25-1838
Holt, A. G. to Martha J. Wall 10-28-1847 (no return)
Holt, Carter to Margaret Dors 1-6-1868 (no return) B
Holt, Freeman to Hannah Chambers 11-6-1869 (12-4-1869) B

Holt, Labon to Elizabeth Ann Batt 5-25-1842
Holtzclaw, Ezra to Manerva S. Grisham 12-8-1852 (no return)
Honey, John to Mary Ann Lynch 2-15-1847 (2-21-1847)
Honley, Geo. to A.a C. Dilliard 3-15-1866
Hood, A. M. to M. J. Reams 2-3-1864 (not endorsed)
Hood, Adrian to Beckey Wade 7-10-1868 (no return) B
Hood, George W. to Mary Bennett 2-23-1841
Hood, James to E. J. Clampit 1-3-1842 (1-13-1842)
Hood, Jno. A. to Angeline Ray 3-10-1860 (3-13-1860)
Hood, L. D. to Ciney Carter 10-6-1840 (10-27-1840)
Hood, Mathew to Mary Duberry 10-3-1853 (no return)
Hood, Matt to Martha Wray 12-27-1867 (12-31-1867) B
Hood, Richard to Martha Ann Lewis 3-17-1851 (no return)
Hood, Robertson to Catharine Teage? 10-10-1848
Hooey, Daniel T. to Ellen Smith 7-9-1869 (7-11-1869)
Hooker, S. J. to Mary G. Gwyn 12-8-1866 (no return)
Hooker, Wm. to Jane Brown 1-3-1849 (no return)
Hooks, Jno. Henry to Mildred N. Compton 12-12-1867 (no return)
Hooks, Robt. B. to Laura J. McIntosh 12-12-1867 (12-15-1867)
Hooper, Benj. F. to Lauryan Hooper 1-18-1843 (no return)
Hooper, Franklin to L. A. Bounds 2-8-1838
Hooper, Jack to Elvira Cogbell 6-15-1870 (no return) B
Hope, Wm. M. to E. J. David 4-19-1854 (no return)
Horner, B. B. to Susan Newby 2-16-1850 (2-20-1850)
Horton, Needham to Mary Folwell 5-1-1840 (5-6-1840)
Houk, B. F. to Isabella Beaver 4-20-1867 (4-21-1867)
House, J. A. to Julian Seward 11-15-1838
House, James to Mary House 11-5-1869 (11-11-1869) B
House, William R. to Emily Jane Dodson no dates (with Dec 1845)
House, William to Mary Rhine 11-5-1869 (11-11-1869) B
House?, David C. to Letitia F. Hazlewood no date (with Dec 1852)
Houston, Benjamin to Henrietta O. Wilkins 10-27-1845 (10-29-1845)
Houston, Charlie to Lettie Cross 12-27-1870 (12-29-1870) B
Houston, Willis to Roan Bailey 1-17-1859 (1-19-1859)
Howard, Nat to Lyddia Reeves 12-25-1869 (12-31-1869) B
Howard, Samuel to Sarah A. Wright 12-29-1868 (12-30-1868) B
Howell, Charles C. to Frances E. Carpenter 12-21-1847 (12-23-1847)
Howell, George S. to Agnis M. Bankhead 4-24-1841 (4-30-1841)
Howell, Joel C. to Ann J. Carpenter 9-13-1851 (no return)
Howse, Lewis C. to Mollie E. Hazlewood 11-9-1866 (11-14-1866)
Hubbard, Champ to Helen Walker 10-4-1869 (no return) B
Hubbard, E. J. to Elizabeth M. Durham 7-15-1844 (no return)
Hubbard, Frank to Indiana Cleave 8-27-1870 (no return) B
Hubbard, Freman to Nancy Jane High 9-11-1850 (9-12-1850)
Huchins, Merite to Elizabeth Crossett 11-4-1850 (11-7-1850)
Hudson, A. F. to S. E. Clark 12-24-1853 (no return)
Hudson, G. G. to Martha Gillaspie 12-26-1860 (12-3?-1860)
Hudson, Isaac to Susan Williams 12-30-1868 (12-31-1868) B
Hudson, Mack to Matilda Mabin 4-18-1867 (no return) B
Hudson, P. T. to Mary E. Perkins 5-9-1866
Hudson, William T. to Tappan Marsh 1-28-1840 (2-12-1840)
Hudspeth, Samuel M. to Marthaann M. Long 4-19-1840 (6-19-1840)
Hudspeth, Seaton to Agnis Winn 10-17-1848 (10-19-1848)
Hudspeth, Seten to Agnis Winn 10-17-1848
Huffman, John R. L. to Fanny C. Hackney 12-20-1869 (12-23-1869)
Huffman, William to Frances Johnson 9-4-1865
Hugg, E. B. to Lavicia Lane 4-13-1869 (4-15-1869)
Hughes, F. M. C. to Catherine Collins 4-9-1867 (4-11-1867)
Hughes, George to Gray Boswell 6-18-1867 (no return) B
Hughes, J. H. W. to Ellen Baucum 6-12-1854 (no return)
Hughes, J. W. to S. J. Clayton 11-29-1866 (11-30-1865?)
Hughes, Jesse to Mary Bradley 7-7-1840 (7-9-1840)
Hughes, Jessee M. to Fidelia A. Fausett 9-10-1852 (no return)
Hughes, John A. to Nancy Haney 2-9-1869 (2-11-1869) B
Hughes, Joseph to Milly David 12-18-1849 (no return)
Hughes, R. E. to Sallie Ann Wade 12-18-1868 (12-20-1868) B
Hughes, Silas to Matilda Rushen 11-17-1852 (no return)
Hughes, Silas to Minta E. Davis 7-11-1863 (7-22-1863)
Hughes, T. N. to Mary P. Gilliam 2-18-1868 (2-27-1868)
Hughes, Wm. to Catharin Allen 8-26-1850 (9-1-1850)
Hull (Hall?), Sip to Jane Berry 12-30-1869 B
Hull, Sip to Jane Green 12-29-1865 (1-30-1865) B
Hull, Spencer to Catharine Murphy 5-19-1866 (8-11-1866) B
Humphrey, Elsey to Harriet M. Kelly 12-12-1844
Humphrey, J. A. to R. M. Moore 9-4-1860 (9-5-1860)

Humphrey, Jesse to Nancy Brown 11-24-1848
Humphrey, Thomas to Mary Taylor 12-25-1869 (12-26-1869) B
Humphreys, Collin to Emma Isbell 4-18-1867 B
Humphreys, J. F. to Sallie E. Baxter 12-18-1860
Humphreys, Wm. T. to Margaret R. Wall 11-2-1850 (no return)
Hundly, Wm. H. to Fannie W. May 5-23-1859 (5-24-1859)
Hunsucker, A. to Louisa Ross 3-11-1869 (3-23-1869)
Hunt, Douglass R. to Mary E. Polk 4-3-1846 (4-8-1846)
Hunt, Hukbald? D. to Sallie M. Wilson 12-21-1848
Hunt, Isaac to Ann Parks 12-24-1867 (12-26-1867) B
Hunt, John W. to Virginia E. Marton 1-13-1842 (1-20-1842)
Hunt, Tennessee to Nellie Springfield 12-31-1868 (1-2-1869) B
Hunt, William T. to Carolin Petty 7-1-1844 (no return)
Hunter, A. J. to Ann M. House 1-16-1851 (1-22-1851)
Hunter, Andy to Vina Bluford 1-10-1871 (no return) B
Hunter, Geo. T. to Ann Eliza Broom 11-2-1846 (11-5-1846)
Hunter, James to Orelia Ann Allen 5-20-1870 (5-21-1870) B
Hunter, John D. to J. L. Brown 5-30-1870 (no return)
Hunter, Marshall to Margaret Jones 6-21-1867 (7-13-1867) B
Hunter, Marvin to Nancy Ann Hunter 4-3-1869 (4-18-1869) B
Hunter, Nelson to Nancy J. Williams 2-13-1868 (no return) B
Hunter, Wm. C. to Nancy C. Bull 5-19-1847 (5-20-1847)
Hurley, Andrew B. to Eliza E. Womac 6-6-1848 (6-8-1848)
Hurly, John to Gerusha Adams 11-26-1839 (11-28-1839)
Hutchins, Lewis to Lucinda Bell 9-30-1865 (10-1-1865)
Hutchins, Nathaniel M. to Martha A. Apleton 12-16-1847
    (12-18-1847)
Hutchins, Wm. P. to Tonser Wheeler 11-3-1866 (11-4-1866)
Hutchison, J. K. to Isabella Garrison 8-20-1867
Hyde, W. B. to Margaret A. Kinnon 12-29-1866 (12-30-1866)
Iby, Richard to Hepsabeth Caple 2-22-1841 (2-24-1841)
Ing, John to Susan Knox 9-15-1855 (no return)
Ing, R. W. to Ellen Galloway 12-3-1856 (no return)
Ingram, Washington to Mary Parker 12-13-1869 (12-26-18689) B
Ingram, Wm. M. to Allice M. Stainback 10-21-1867 (10-24-1867)
Ingram, Wm. P. to Martha Harris 6-4-1849 (6-5-1849)
Irbey, Silas C. to Jane C. House 12-15-1846 (12-22-1846)
Irby, J. P. to Nancy J. York 1-16-1871 (no return)
Irby, Silas R. to Nancy M. Irby 3-12-1847 (no return)
Irvin, Samuel to Agnes King 1-13-1844 (1-14-1844)
Irvy?, James H. to Martha E. Garrison 4-12-1844 (no return)
Irwin, Grandison to Octavia McNeill 11-10-1868 (11-11-1868) B
Irwin, Jesse R. to Margarett R. Miller 9-14-1844 (no return)
Irwin, Samuel L. to Sarah L. Roach 4-29-1847
Irwin, Thomas J. to Mary C. Pucket 4-23-1841
Irwin, William to Nancy Alexander 3-30-1841 (4-1-1841)
Isbell, Beverly to Sue Chaffin 9-26-1867 B
Isbell, Daniel to Roanna Holloway 7-9-1870 B
Isham, Elijah to Charlotte Able 4-8-1847 (4-9-1847)
Isham, G. A. to Sarah Simmons 1-8-1870 (1-13-1870)
Isom, W. C. to P. E. Appleberry 7-20-1864 (7-24-1864)
Iverson, Captain to Dicey McNeal 7-14-1866 (7-15-1866) B
Ivey, A. V. to Philadelphia F. Cooper 5-1-1847 (5-2-1847)
Ivey, R. L. to Mary L. Barren 7-11-1865
Ivie, Washington to Elizabeth Mitchell 12-7-1846 (no return)
Ivy, A. J. to Nannie J. Thompson 1-21-1867 (1-24-1867)
Ivy, Wyott to Nora Holloway 2-9-1870 (2-10-1870) B
Izard, F. J. to Sarah E. Whittaker 5-2-1854 (no return)
Jack, Daniel B. to Martha R. Ward 1-21-1871 (1-24-1871)
Jack, Wm. to Elizabeth W. Beckham 6-26-1868 (7-5-1868)
Jackson, Andrew to Amy Shephard 3-13-1869 (3-15-1869)
Jackson, Andy to Bettie Mayo 7-3-1868 (7-4-1868) B
Jackson, Bob E. to Sophia S. Marshall 3-17-1845 (no return)
Jackson, David R.? to Louisa E. McClinsley 4-10-1848 (4-13-1848)
Jackson, Dennis to Julia Ann Porter 7-2-1869 (no return) B
Jackson, Edmond S. to Rebecca B. Cothran 11-30-1866 (12-4-1866)
Jackson, Frederick S. to Susa C. Malone 5-17-1841 (5-20-1841)
Jackson, Gabriel to Susan Willis 11-20-1841 (11-23-1841)
Jackson, Geo. W. to Clara A. Vaughan 1-7-1847 (1-14-1847)
Jackson, Henry to Patience Bolling 3-17-1866 (3-21-1866) B
Jackson, John A. to Mary A. Dodson 9?-17-1853 (no return)
Jackson, John to Susan Ann Porter 4-6-1867 (4-14-1867) B
Jackson, Joseph to Mary Morrow 1-13-1845
Jackson, M. L. to Priscilla J. Hammon 3-11-1850
Jackson, Robt. T. to Mary J. Bruce 7-28-1845 (7-30-1845)

Jackson, Sam to Cary Holmes 3-18-1869 B
Jackson, Thos. S. to Mary Harris 5-26-1845 (no return)
Jackson, William to Mary Smith 2-6-1867 B
James, C. P. to Dilly Polk 9-17-1849 (no return)
James, Elias to Amelia Crowder 1-14-1869 (1-16-1869) B
James, John to Martha Bailey 12-14-1868 (12-17-1868)
James, Thompson to Amanda Gill 10-16-1840 (no return)
Jarrett, David P. to Jane Newsom 4-10-1839 (no return)
Jarrett, J. W. to Susan E. G. Lundal 12-10-1838 (12-12-1838)
Jefferson, Adam to Susan Farrar 12-19-1866 (no return) B
Jefferson, Andy to Ruthy Hilliard 8-17-1869 (8-18-1869) B
Jefferson, John to Leana Marshall 1-28-1871 (no return) B
Jeffries, John E. to Martha Capps 12-9-1840 (no return)
Jelks, John A. to Elizth. Guarrant 11-25-1844 (no return)
Jemerson, James M. S. to Mary Jane Ayres 10-4-1838
Jenkins, Abraham to Luncinda Price 11-9-1840 (11-12-1840)
Jenkins, Ed D. to Mary Pickett 9-23-1844 (9-26-1844)
Jenkins, James L. to M. E. Blain 11-6-1865 (no return)
Jenkins, W. C. to E. L. Blain 3-3-1868 (3-5-1868)
Jenkins, Wm. C. to Penelope Sumner 12-21-1840
Jernigan, David J. to Martha J. Caraway 9-30-1844 (no return)
Jeter, Albert G. to Sintha Gilmore 6-9-1847 (no return)
Jeter, Benj. W. to Sarah M. Busey 4-13-1868 (4-16-1868)
Johnson, A. J. to V. J. Nicholson 12-23-1865 (12-26-1865)
Johnson, Aden to Matilda Ann Smith 10-1-1842 (10-6-1842)
Johnson, Albert to Cynthia Cloyd 7-23-1870 (7-29-1870) B
Johnson, Alfred to Lettie McClane 6-15-1867 (no return) B
Johnson, Andrew to Lavenia Worsham 12-28-1869 (12-9?-1869) B
Johnson, Andrew to Rosanna McNeel 7-3-1868 (7-4-1868) B
Johnson, Bodley to Eliza B. Hampton 11-23-1846 (11-24-1846)
Johnson, Daniel to Sarah A. Watkins 2-11-1871 (2-16-1871) B
Johnson, David H. to Elizabeth P. Allen 8-?-1842 (not endorsed)
Johnson, David H. to Sarah A. Carraway 11-26-1845 (11-27-1845)
Johnson, Dick to Mariah Rivers 2-9-1867 (2-10-1867) B
Johnson, Elisha T. to Catharine Downey 12-24-1844
Johnson, Frank to Ann Phillips 2-22-1867 (2-24-1867) B
Johnson, G. T. to N. E. Crawford 11-27-1865 (11-30-1865)
Johnson, G. W. S. to Mary Stidham 1-8-1845 (1-9-1845)
Johnson, Gaines to Sarah Dortch 1-2-1869 B
Johnson, George F. to Jane Johnson 7-6-1844 (no return)
Johnson, Grant to Lina Ann Mask 10-30-1868 (no return) B
Johnson, Harvy to Ellen Carpenter 3-17-1869 (3-19-1869) B
Johnson, Henry to Bettie Warren 12-24-1869 (no return) B
Johnson, J. I. to Fannie F. Harris 2-7-1866 (2-8-1866)
Johnson, J. M. to Margaret J. Williamson 1-10-1849 (1-11-1849)
Johnson, J. R. to Mary V. Crowder 12-1-1869 (12-8-1869)
Johnson, Jake to Artemecia Haselett 1-18-1868 (no return) B
Johnson, James H. to F. M. Cogbill 12-15-1852 (no return)
Johnson, James to Mandy Rightsdale 12-16-1867 B
Johnson, James to Mary Messenger 4-13-1871 (4-16-1871) B
Johnson, Jas. K. to Rosa West 1-8-1867 (no return)
Johnson, Jeff to Sallie Ivy 2-15-1868 (2-16-1868) B
Johnson, John S. to Manerva A. Hope 10-1-1851 (no return)
Johnson, John to Lucinda Flowers 10-29-1870 B
Johnson, Joseph to Agnes A. Elliott 1-31-1870 (2-4-1870)
Johnson, Joseph to Cintha Browne 2-3-1845 (2-4-1845)
Johnson, Joshua to Altha Birdsong 9-9-1847
Johnson, Julias to Sarah A. Dilliard 9-25-1865 (9-26-1865)
Johnson, Mack to Mareno Wilson 2-12-1868 (2-15-1868) B
Johnson, Newton to P. A. Tarry? 9-8-1849 (no return)
Johnson, R. J. to M. D. Doyle 1-6-1868 (1-7-1868)
Johnson, Robt. to Allice Baw 12-3-1867 (no return)
Johnson, Rolling H. to Mariah Davis 12-15-1851 (no return)
Johnson, Samuel to Harriet W. Erwin 6-12-1839
Johnson, Spencer to Kittie Alley 4-12-1868 (no return) B
Johnson, Thos. J. to Sallie Rivers 6-12-1867
Johnson, Tom to Alice Sumner 1-12-1871 (no return) B
Johnson, Vincent to Pataline McMurry 2-20-1867 (no return)
Johnson, W. C. to Martha G. Thompson 6-1-1867 (6-2-1867) B
Johnson, W. R. to Annie E. Plummer 1-21-1869
Johnson, Washington to Laura Mayo 12-30-1869 B
Johnson, William A. to Amanda J. Heathcock 11-9-1870 (11-10-1870)
Johnson, William H. to Susan A. Hudson 7-28-1842
Johnson, William to Emily J. Poindexter 3-20-1871 B
Johnson, William to Fanny Allen 8-17-1869 B

Johnson, William to Margaret Stafford 8-1-1870 (8-2-1870)
Johnson, William to Margarett V. Tate 5-25-1848 (5-31-1848)
Johnson, William to Martha Morgan 4-28-1871 (no return) B
Johnson, Wm. H. C. to Ripsey Steadham 12-17-1838 (12-20-1838)
Johnson, Wm. to Penny Ann Nellums 3-14-1839
Johnson, Wm. to Susan A. Alexander 2-15-1847 (2-16-1847)
Johnston, Ben W. to Harriett H. Hood 10-11-1855 (no return)
Johnston, Haden to Charlotte Riddle 4-24-1850 (no return)
Johnston, J. H. to E. W. G. Bowers 10-14-1868 (10-25-1868)
Johnston, J. H. to S. A. Edwards 12-1-1866 (12-5-1866)
Johnston, James to Henrietta Bridgewater 11-15-1865 (11-16-1865)
Johnston, John R. to Eleanor A. Nolly 11-15-1865 (11-22-1865)
Jones, A. B. to Mary E. Neesbit 11-23-1839 (11-27-1839)
Jones, Aaron to Flora Lockhart 4-25-1866 (no return) B
Jones, Alfred to Lee Harvey 2-26-1870 (12-28-1870) B
Jones, Andrew to Frances Wray 7-9-1870 B
Jones, Arther B. to Eliza C. Swift 12-14-1852 (no return)
Jones, Ben to Darcus Flippin 11-3-1866 (11-4-1866)
Jones, Ben to Hannah Baird 2-22-1867 (2-23-1867) B
Jones, Charles G. to Camilla Porter 10-9-1865 (10-11-1865)
Jones, Charles to Casandra Reddick 10-13-1866 (no return) B
Jones, Charley to Malinda Buford 12-27-1869 (12-30-1869) B
Jones, D. T. to L. A. Stewart 8-11-1869 (8-13-1869)
Jones, Daniel to Eveline Teague 1-1-1867 B
Jones, Edmund to Harriet Campbell 5-21-1868 (5-23-1868) B
Jones, Fayette to Tempy Williamson 12-25-1866 (12-29-1866) B
Jones, Frank to Chaney Black 2-3-1871 (5-20-1871) B
Jones, Gilliam to Eliza Armstrong 12-30-1867 (12-31-1867) B
Jones, Green to Lou Ely 12-30-1868 B
Jones, Henry to Adaline Harrell 6-2-1866 (no return) B
Jones, Henry to Aregon Parham 8-22-1867 (no return) B
Jones, Henry to Eveline Mitchell 12-28-1870 B
Jones, Hiram B. to Ann King 1-31-1867 (2-1-1867)
Jones, Hiram M. to Mary Jane Morris 2-3-1845 (no return)
Jones, Isaac to Nancy Baskerville 12-28-1866 (12-29-1866) B
Jones, J. V. to Emma V. Word 12-11-1867 (no return)
Jones, Jack to Louisa Pulliam 4-14-1866 (4-22-1866) B
Jones, James I. to Iola Clay 11-15-1869 (11-17-1869)
Jones, James to Mary B. Gardon 1-24-1840
Jones, Jasper to Frances Rainer 8-29-1867 (9-23-1867) B
Jones, Jerry to Minda McKinley 10-29-1870 B
Jones, John T. to Narcissa Cathey 11-9-1848 (no return)
Jones, John to Amy Meriweather 3-2-1867? (3-3-1867) B
Jones, John to Betty Murrell 1-11-1870 (2-9-1870) B
Jones, John to Mary Brown 3-16-1867 (3-17-1867) B
Jones, John to Mary Jones 12-28-1866 (12-29-1866) B
Jones, John to Rachel A. Crippin 5-12-1860 (5-13-1860)
Jones, Joseph to Lilly Kee 12-8-1868 (12-12-1868) B
Jones, Joshua J. to Sarah W. Freeman 10-23-1843
Jones, L. P. to Sallie Owen 1-17-1861
Jones, Larkin P. to Mary E. Hodges 8-9-1838
Jones, Lewis to Mag Williamson 4-24-1867 (no return) B
Jones, Logan to Ann Higgason 3-19-1866 (no return) B
Jones, Lou to Alice Simmons 12-26-1870 B
Jones, Louis to Margaret Pippin 3-15-1871 (3-20-1871)
Jones, M. A. to Sarah Morris 1-8-1850
Jones, Manuel to Jane Bullock 1-27-1866 (no return) B
Jones, Marshall B. to Eliza J. Griffin 12-15-1870
Jones, Morgan to Jane Eley 7-13-1867 (7-14-1867) B
Jones, Ned to Emeline Turnley 1-11-1868 B
Jones, Oswell F. to Julia A. Gwyn 10-31-1838 (11-1-1838)
Jones, Richard to Sallie Davis 3-6-1871 B
Jones, Robert to Priscilla Bishop 10-17-1868 (10-18-1868) B
Jones, Russel to Harriet Ealy 8-7-1869 (8-9-1869) B
Jones, Saml. to Gracey Flurnoy 12-28-1870 B
Jones, Saml. to Susan A. Stewart 9-9-1867 (not endorsed)
Jones, Sylvester to Betty Ann E. Martin 12-19-1850
Jones, Thomas to Sally P. Sparkes 7-7-1853 (no return)
Jones, Thos. W. to Cordelia Williamson 5-29-1866
Jones, W. F. to Julia A. Anderson 3-2-1864
Jones, Wash to Peggy Brown 5-2-1867 (5-5-1867) B
Jones, Wes to Harriett Matthews 1-2-1868 (1-3-1868) B
Jones, Wiley to Laura Dickinson 5-4-1870 (5-7-1870) B
Jones, William H. to Mary B. Oliver 6-6-1855 (no return)
Jones, Wm. A. to Mary Jane Granbery 3-2-1848

Jones, Wm. F. to Mary E. Cleere 9-2-1845 (9-4-1845)
Jones, Wm. S. to Aillvice? Slaughter 12-31-1839
Jones, Wm. to Frankey Taylor 9-20-1867 (9-21-1867) B
Jones, Wm. to Martha Randal 1-8-1869 (1-16-1869) B
Jones, Wm. to Susan Springfield 1-23-1869 (no return) B
Jordan, Burrell to Bettie A. Holmes 1-11-1871 (1-12-1871)
Jordan, Charles W. to Callie B. Boswell 12-10-1866 (12-12-1866)
Jordan, Dandridge M. to Susanah R. Johnson 9-25-1852 (no return)
Jordan, Edward T. to Ann S. Green 10-27-1846 (10-28-1846)
Jordan, George to Sarah J. McFadden 7-29-1867 (8-7-1867)
Jordan, John W. to Margery E. Neely 10-7-1842 (12-12-1842)
Jordan, John to M. Whitehead 12-11-1847 (12-16-1847)
Jordan, John to Maggie Jones 10-18-1870 (no return) B
Jordan, Mack to Lucy Williams 4-24-1869 (4-29-1869) B
Jordan, Peter to Frances Wirt 2-20-1869 (3-21-1869) B
Jordan, Tom to Betsy Poindexter 1-4-1869 B
Jordan, Wm. C. to Juliand Lester 12-23-1839 (12-24-1839)
Jordon, Saml. B. to Eliza W. Hilliard 1-31-1849
Justice, Louis to Martha Dickinson 8-28-1869 (10-17-1869) B
Karr, J. W. to Lizzie C. Wray 1-3-1853 (no return)
Kee, Isaac to Lydia Sullivan 3-30-1844
Kee, James L. to Adaline Adams 9-4-1865 (9-6-1865)
Kee, Robert to Florida Dunn 8-7-1867 B
Keeble, J. W. to Binga H. Powell 9-10-1855 (no return)
Keer, John to Puss Taylor 3-4-1868 (3-7-1868) B
Kelley, Edmond to Ela Ann Williams 7-5-1838
Kelley, M. H. to S. E. Hood 12-26-1867
Kelly, Alfred to Martha Boswell 3-9-1847 (no return)
Kelly, Augustus to Martha P. Williams 7-20-1846 (7-23-1846)
Kelly, George to Mary E. Fisher 10-25-1849
Kelly, James C. to Louisa W. Nowlin 11-15-1846 (11-19-1846)
Kendall, Isaac to Mary J. Wilson ?-24-1844 (2-29-1844)
Kendrick, Lewis to Gracy Neel 10-19-1867 (11-6-1867) B
Kendrick, Robt. to Ann Notgrass 5-7-1846 (no return)
Kenedy, Vinson to Sarah (Mrs.) Bell 4-21-1841 (no return)
Kennedy, John to Sallie E. Crutcher 12-5-1866 (12-10-1866)
Kennedy, Riley S. to Sarah Ann Hargas 9-17-1842 (9-21-1842)
Kennon, Nelson to Tempy Frazier 4-15-1871 (4-17-1871)
Kennon, Thos. W. to Tennessee C. Carpenter 9-26-18686 (9-27-1866)
Kerniham, Lawrence to Nancy A. Rodgers 7-29-1868 (no return) B
Kerr, J. R. to Mary J. Alexander 11-10-1847
Kerr, Samel M. to Rebecca O. Williams 12-21-1850 (12-25-1850)
Kersey, Hall to Rebecca Buckley 12-1-1863 (12-3-1863)
Ketcham, James to Jane Garrison 10-4-1848
Ketchum, Frank to Rosella Rainer 10-28-1868 (no return) B
Keyor?, Francis C. to Hetty Shinel 9-21-1841 (no return)
Keywood, L. D. to Jane R. Brinkley 3-7-1855 (no return)
Kidd, William A. to Sarah E. Barnes 6-19-1851 (no return)
Kindrick, James to Mary Crabtree 4-13-1838
Kindrick, Saml. to Amelia Davis 10-17-1846 (no return)
King, D. C. to Mary Harris 2-6-1869 (2-8-1869)
King, George to Mary Elizabeth Irwin 4-8-1869
King, J. G. to Maggie A. Scott 10-22-1866 (10-4?-1866)
King, James A. to Martha An Robertson 3-6-1848 (3-16-1848)
King, W. A. to Mary J. Stidham 1-13-1868 (1-14-1868)
King, William J. to Harriet A. Fisher 9-12-1846 (9-17-1846)
Kirk, Allen to Cornelia Mebane 9-6-1866 (no return) B
Kirkland, David to Margaret A. Henshaw 7-6-1846 (7-12-1846)
Kirkland, Henry to Mahala Jeffries 1-24-1870 (1-25-1870)
Kirkpatrick, R. Y. to Carni Litton 7-31-1854 (no return)
Kirkpatrick, W. J. to Sarah J. Stackerd 5-10-1854 (no return)
Kirksey, John to Slalie Green 12-27-1868 (no return) B
Kirtland, Richd. Mc. to Martha Firth 8-24-1863
Kitchem, Levi to Georgeann Walker 1-19-1844
Kizer, Francis C. to Martha Abels 2-1-1842
Knight, John H. A. to Jane C. Fillmore 7-26-1844 (no return)
Knight, W. M. to Emily S. Roberts 11-16-1847 (11-17-1847)
Knott, Jas. W. (Rev.) to Sally W. Miller 5-27-1849
Knox, Milton H. to Emily Teague 12-30-1843 (no return)
Knox, R. L. to Fannie C. Steger 1-29-1866 (1-31-1866)
Knox, Samuel to Louisa Marshall 3-27-1869 B
Knox, W. S. to Mahala Parks 3-17-1866 (3-18-1866)
Knox, William S. to Frances A. E. Hale 8-24-1847 (no return)
Koen, Benjamin F. to Margaret M. Ragan 10-7-1839
Koonce, R. M. to S. E. Cotner 1-12-1871

Krider, John to Elizabeth McConnell 10-3-1851 (no return)
Kyle, Dallis to Ann Murrell 12-26-1870 (no return) B
Kyle, Samuel B. to Josie M. Astin 12-12-1868 (12-17-1868)
Lacey, Jos. B. to Sally Benson 10-13-1866 (10-17-1866)
Lackie, Thos. to Elizabth. Lackie 12-9-1849 (12-11-1849)
Lacy, Beverly to Clara Broom 12-28-1868 B
Lacy, Isaac to Lucinda H. Christman 2-7-1843 (2-9-1843)
Lacy, James to Judah Edwards 4-26-1848
Lacy, Stephen to Catharine Dowing 2-?-1838
Laine, J. M. to Jane Karr 2-16-1846 (2-17-1846)
Lake, Levin to Maggie E. Williams 10-28-1864 (10-29-1864)
Lakey, James H. to Sarah Lakey 1-15-1851
Lalusan?, J. S. to Martha A. Cross 7-7-1849 (not endorsed)
Lamb, L. B. to Martha V. Douglas 12-16-1865 (12-19-1865)
Lamb, W. T. to M. A. F. Cook 11-22-1851 (no return)
Lambeth, N. W. to Mary A. Sanford 7-10-1865 (7-12-1865)
Land, James T. to Mary A. Crawford 8-8-1852 (no return)
Landreth, W. F. to M. P. Clay 4-8-1863 (4-30-1863)
Lane, Daniel to Harriet Morris 6-8-1867 (no return) B
Lane, Felix D. to Leah Phillips 8-11-1847
Lane, Sampson to Sarah E. Wilburn 9-7-1854 (no return)
Langdon, J. J. to Margaret Davenport 10-19-1866 (10-28-1866)
Langdon, Wm. R. to S. Downy 12-29-1869
Langham, A. J. to Jane Brown 2-7-1842 (no return)
Langham, Lemuel to Susan Jane Laughter 1-1-1846 (no return)
Langley, William to Priscilla Winfrey 12-30-1868 (12-31-1868) B
Langly, Wm. B. to Cornelia A. Smith 3-12?-1842 (no return)
Langum, A. J. to Vernelia Scott 12-21-1844 (no return)
Lappet, John Jesse to Mary Bass 4-13-1871 (no return) B
Largent, W. H. to Lucy A. Averett 11-26-1860 (12-5-1860)
Largent, Wm. H. to Sarah J. Dinkins 2-12-1855 (no return)
Lashley, James to Mary Ann Ward 8-17-1840
Lassiter, Jesse to Emla Hammons 11-11-1840
Laudaman, James B. to Frances Marial 11-5-1850 (11-7-1850)
Lavender, Joseph to Elizabeth Outlaw 4-28-1852 (no return)
Lawrence, John W. to Annis Wilson 12-14-1841 (12-21-1841)
Lay, Elisha to Elizabeth Ingram 9-16-1839 (no return)
Lazenby, Wm. to Nora Baxter 11-20-1869 (11-25-1869)
Lea, R. C. to Mary P. Mitchell 12-6-1847 (12-23-1847)
Lea, Wm. A. to Martha E. Brown 6-14-1852 (no return)
Leach, A. G. to Fannie A. Lockhart 1-14-1868 (1-15-1868)
Leach, John L. to Amanda F. Lockhart 2-19-1866 (2-21-1866)
Leake, E. M. to Catharine T. Watkins 3-20-1844 (no return)
Leavy, Robt. to Hannah Dickinson 10-17-1868 (10-18-1868) B
Ledger, Geo. H. to Mary F. Dowdy 2-26-1851
Lee, Berry to Mary Rogers 10-7-1845 (10-9-1845)
Lee, Felix W. to Elizabeth Howard 2-12-1839
Lee, Henry to Marth M. Williams 10-11-1854 (no return)
Lee, James to Mary Simmons 2-8-1842
Lee, Robt. to Mary Morris 1-5-1866 (1-6-1866) B
Legon, Benj. H.? to Ann C. (Mrs.) White 5-11-1855 (no return)
Lemons, C. P. to Susan J. Buford 5-5-1840 (5-7-1840)
Lemons, Ed to Eliza Fields 1-6-1871 (no return) B
Lenard, Wm. to Charlott Chaffin 7-20-1867 (7-27-1867) B
Lenow, J. to Frances Broom 1-7-1845 (1-9-1845)
Lester, Stephen J. to Ann J. Woods 2-7-1838
Leverett, Joseph T. to Marthena Harris 11-26-1870 (11-27-1870)
Levett, Frank to Mattie Mebane 2-4-1870 (no return) B
Levisay, D. T. to Salina Crawford 1-11-1842 (no return)
Levy, Green to Julia Carter 10-19-1867 (10-20-1867) B
Levy, King to Isabell Rhea 12-29-1868 (1-16-1869) B
Lewis, Edmond to Laura Donelson 9-2-1868 (no return) B
Lewis, H. Walter to Lucy Winfield 8-9-1870 (8-10-1870)
Lewis, Henry to Lucrecia Loney 1-20-1840 (12?-27-1840)
Lewis, Isaac to Malinda Baxter 12-21-1867 (12-24-1867) B
Lewis, James to Fanny H. Sample 5-10-1842 (5-12-1842)
Lewis, John N. to Kerron R. Rice 3-16-1846 (no return)
Lewis, Leonard to Adeline Brown 7-23-1869 (7-24-1869) B
Lewis, Mark to Harriet Hunter 1-1-1869 (1-2-1869) B
Lewis, Nathan to Emily C. Capps 8-16-1845 (no return)
Lewis, Owen to Laura Hill 1-12-1867 (1-13-1867) B
Lewis, Ransom to Jenny Taylor 4-4-1868 (4-5-1868) B
Lewis, Tom to Kitty Witt 2-1-1868 (2-2-1868) B
Lewis, William to Ella Brown 8-28-1869 (8-29-1869) B
Lewis, Zack to Charlotte Newsom 12-10-1868 (12-11-1868) B

Lightfoot, Moses to Serena Miller 10-25-1870 (no return) B
Lightle, John C. to Jane C. Steadham 12-20-1864 (12-22-1864)
Ligon, George to Margaret Finney 9-3-1869 B
Ligon, Owen to Ellen Whitt 12-27-1866
Ligon, William to Ann White 3-15-1867 (3-17-1867) B
Limbarger, John to Caroline M. Aynesworth 8-25-1841 (8-29-1841)
Lindley, James to Susan Pippin 7-30-1866 (7-31-1866)
Lindsey, Jesse T. to Delila Lindsey 8-29-1843 (9-5-1843)
Lindsy, W. H. to Delila Harris 10-22-1839
Linebarger, Wm. C. to Mary E. Tatum 11-21-1865 (11-22-1865)
Lipscomb, Geo. R. to Mary R. Branch 2-21-1870 (2-22-1870)
Lipscomb, George A. to Catharine G. Yancey 9-4-1847 (no return)
Lipscomb, George A. to Priscilla S. Simmons 12-25-1854 (no return)
Lipscomb, J. A. to Anna Shirley 12-29-1868 (12-31-1868)
Lipscomb, W. P. to Mary Pullen 2-4-1868 (2-26-1868)
Lipscomb, W. P. to N. E. (Mrs.) McNamee 2-15-1870 (3-2-1870)
Little, Wm. to Amanda C. Hase? 10-6-1840
Littlejohn, Joseph B. to Ann M. (Mrs.) Sneed 1-9-1843 (1-10-1843)
Littlejohn, Willie J. to Margaret H. Chesolm 1-18-1843
Littleton, William to Edie Thompson 12-29-1870 (no return) B
Lloyd, A. B. to Martha J. Johnson 12-19-1868 (12-22-1868)
Lloyd, T. B. to Anna E. McMullin 12-25-1865 (1-1-1866)
Lock, F. A. to Lucy M. Wesson 3-12-1853 (no return)
Lockett, F. H. to Susan Smith 6-2-1847 (no return)
Lockhart, S. H. to Mollie E. Adams 6-30-1862 (not endorsed)
Lockheart, L. H. to Mattie G. Leach 10-27-1870 (no return)
Logan, W. P. to Ada F. Griffin 2-13-1860 (2-14-1860)
Londa, York to Liza Wade 7-13-1867 B
Londrith, Pliney B. to Helen M. Zellner 6-21-1859 (6-23-1859)
Long, J. W. S. to Elizah Smith 8-29-1838 (8-30-1838)
Long, Nicholas to Margarett J. Rhea 7-12-1848
Long, Nicholas to Sarah Humphrey 9-10-1844
Long, Saml. D. to Margaret Ann Dodson 2-9-1846 (2-12-1846)
Long, Wm. H. to Bettie M. Hunt 11-30-1868 (12-8-1868)
Looney, G. G. to Rose Ann Deloach 6-26-1838 (no return)
Louch, Henry to Nancy Honey 12-23-1843 (12-24-1843)
Love, J. P. to Elizabeth J. Wiley 3-22-1855 (no return)
Love, Jas. P. to Sallie P. Brock 12-19-1868 (1-13-1869)
Love, Wm. R. to R. J. Bell 9-17-1859 (9-18-1859)
Lovelace, Thos. to Genett Gaither 11-9-1865
Lovelady, John to Elizabeth Campbell 7-15-1839
Lovelady, T. H. to S. L. Moore 9-28-1854 (no return)
Loveless, William E. to Josephine Cogbell 9-20-1848 (9-27-1848)
Loving, Francis to Susan T. Rayn 11-28-1839 (no return)
Loving, Jim to Fannie Hare 1-15-1868 B
Loving, Josephus to Edwanna? Alston 1-21-1840 (1-22-1840)
Low, Saml. to Bettie Wright 1-1-1868 (no return) B
Lowery, Thomas to Sarah Richie 12-14-1853 (no return)
Lowrey, George to Caroline Harvey 8-18-1866 (not endorsed) B
Lowry, Wm. to Elinora Abington 3-25-1839 (4-3-1839)
Loyd, Jackson to Sarah Coker 3-26-1846
Lucas, Anderson to Susan Sterling 4-17-1850 (4-18-1850)
Lucas, B. H. to Mattie O. Simms 10-2-1865 (10-3-1865)
Lucas, Granville to Martha Blackwood 12-24-1870 (12-25-1870) B
Lucas, James Y. to Mary E. Lanier 12-25-1847 (no return)
Lucas, Mike to Sophia Ann Wells 4-5-1869 (4-6-1869)
Luck, Alen P. to Sarah C. Tilman 11-24-1849 (12-5-1849)
Luck, J. S. to Lucy Clear 11-5-1869 (11-9-1869)
Luckado, Edward P. to Jane W. Irby 6-23-1845
Luckado, Wilson to Grissey Slauson 6-20-1853 (no return)
Lundy, Joshua? C. to Sophia W. Simmons 8-4-1845 (8-5-1845)
Lusby, James L. to Elizabeth Baker 12-16-1841 (12-23-1841)
Luster, Henry to Marcindy Brook 3-12-1867 (3-15-1867) B
Lyles, W. W. to Martha E. Hunsucker 1-30-1867
Lynch, David to Emily Montcrief 10-30-1853 (no return)
Lynch, Moses to Selena C. (Mrs.) Sutherland 12-31-1839
Lynch, R. W. to Mary Webb 6-3-1854 (no return)
Lynn, Benson F. to Maryann Garrett 12-20-1840
Lynn, Charles to Esther V.? Kerr 7-18-1841 (6?-22-1841)
Lynn, Charles to Henry Orr 1-4-1869 (1-5-1869)
Lynn, Sidney to Amanda McDowell 12-24-1866 (12-25-1866) B
Lyons, Patrick J. to Mary Jones 11-26-1868
Maberry, James to Fanny Walker 2-9-1867 (2-16-1867) B
Mabin, Dempsie to Harriet Porter 4-28-1868 (no return) B
Mabin, Wiley to Malissa Mabin 5-3-1867 (6-3-1867) B

Mackey, Aleck to Fanny Rains 11-30-1870 (12-1-1870)
Mackey, Cyrus to Molly Moseley 12-26-1868 (12-29-1868) B
Macklin, Joshua to Polly A. Tucker 12-24-1870 (no return) B
Maclin, Bevly to Henrietta Broadnax 2-20-1869 (2-23-1869) B
Maclin, J. N. to Florence Brodnax 5-24-1869 (5-30-1869)
Maclin, J. W. to Mary J. Brodnax 6-17-1861 (6-19-1861)
Maclin, Jerry to Bettie Maclin 12-23-1866 (no return) B
Maclin, Rasmus to Lemon Buford 12-23-1869 (no return) B
Maddin, Calvin D. to Martha Hollemon 6-10-1847
Madding, David to Lucretia Taylor 12-20-1869 (12-28-1869) B
Maddox, Frank to Julia Carpenter 1-13-1869 (1-14-1869)
Madison, James to Patsey Thompson 2-1-1867 (2-16-1867) B
Magee, B. F. to Susan E. Price 9-1-1852 (no return)
Mallard, Jefferson V.? to Didama Jackson 2-10-1841
Malone, B. to Emily Ellison 9-16-1847 (no return)
Malone, Calvin to Nancy A. Lewis 1-8-1839
Malone, L. H. to Mary Jones 7-29-1851
Malone, Louis to Maria Middlebrooks 12-27-1867 (12-28-1867) B
Malone, R. H. to Mary C. Cassett? 10-2-1849 (10-3-1849)
Malone, Taylor to Mary Thompson 2-28-1870 (3-2-1870)
Malone, Tho. to Piny E. Ozier 12-16-1846 (12-17-1846)
Malone, W. C. to E. M. Gardner 7-20-1850 (8-8-1850)
Malone, William to Mary C. Riggs 12-8-1862
Mamier?, Tom to Felicia Day 5-19-1866 (8-11-1866) B
Mangum, Owen to Hannah Conner 2-27-1871 (2-28-1871) B
Manifee, Mansfield to Ann Ross 9-1-1869 (no return) B
Manley, F. C. to E. A. Buford 12-22-1869
Manley, R. to Catharine Downey 12-27-1839 (3-9-1840)
Manley, Richard to Margaret G. Durham 9-6-1854 (no return)
Manley, Richd. M. to Ann E. Davis 8-5-1846
Manley, Theof J. to Mary Manley 5-4-1847
Manly, T. J. to Mary E. (Mrs.) Jackson 2-23-1867
Mann, James A. to Fannie W. Hall 1-2-1869 (1-6-1869)
Manning, A. to Sarah Jane Williams 2-14-1852 (no return)
Manning, James W. to Martha W. Smith no date (with Oct 1852)
Manning, John R. to Mary S. Hansil 12-23-1851 (no return)
Manuel, Rob. T. to Frances Duberry 12-6-1845 (12-7-1845)
Maples, Josiah to Mary A. Marshall 10-1-1853 (no return)
Marlar, Jesse to Cynthia Smith 8-15-1846 (no return)
Marler, John C. to Eliza S.? Thrift 1-1-1841 (1-5-1841)
Marler, Simpson L. to Caroline Yeates 3-4-1841
Marler, Thomas J. to Sarah Devenport 8-12-1838
Marsden, James to Mary V. Williams 5-23-1842 (5-24-1842)
Marsh, Bird to Harriet Dunn 12-28-1852 (no return)
Marshall, Clarence to Lucinda Knox 12-20-1870 (12-22-1870) B
Marshall, Liz to Tempy Knox 4-6-1871 (4-7-1871) B
Marshall, Newt to Emma Morgan 3-13-1871 (4-5-1871) B
Martin, Alfred to Fannie Rhodes 9-5-1868 (9-6-1868) B
Martin, Geo. W. to Eleanor C. Brown 12-11-1849
Martin, George to Caroline Hunter 12-29-1869 (no return) B
Martin, J. M. to Eliza J. Worrell 12-26-1863 (1-17-1864)
Martin, James C. to Susan Strickland 2-27-1869 (2-28-1869) B
Martin, James to Mary Jones 9-25-1869 (no return) B
Martin, Jas. M. to Sarah J. Sasser 2-16-1853 (no return)
Martin, John G. to H. R. E. Taylor 5-23-1859 (5-25-1859)
Martin, Michael B. to Susan Godbey 9-14-1846 (no return)
Martin, Moses to Lucy Ann Palmor 11-22-1848
Martin, Saml. B. to Ardis Meredith 2-17-1846 (no return)
Martin, William H. to Rosa A. Edwards 1-10-1848 (1-11-1848)
Mason, Chas. G. to Emma Young 1-22-1866 (1-24-1866)
Mason, Frank to Eveline May 12-24-1868 (12-27-1868) B
Mason, Nickolas to Martha Williams 12-24-1868 (12-26-1868) B
Mason, Robert E. to Josephine M. Neal 5-16-1854 (no return)
Mason, Robt. to Frances Brewer 2-7-1868 (2-9-1868)
Mason, Stephen to Easter Miller 2-21-1871 (2-26-1871) B
Mason, Wm. to Rose Ann Harris 12-26-1867 (12-29-1867) B
Massey, D. B. to Mary Darden 12-16-1850 (no return)
Massey, F. A. to Lucy A. McCauley 3?-13-1850 (no return)
Massey, Thomas J. to Sarah A. M. Gwyn 9-5-1866 (7?-11-1866)
Massey, Wm. to Missouri Jones 11-11-1868 (11-14-1868) B
Mathews, Aretny to Jane Stedham 4-2-1849 (5-3-1849)
Mathews, Barney to Mary A. E. Gablin 3-5-1841 (3-9-1841)
Mathews, John H. to Sarah A. B. Allen 3-21-1839
Mathews, John to Celia Shackleford 3-23-1867 (no return) B
Matkins, L. D. to Mary Mason 1-21-1848 (no return)

Matmass, Madison to Victoria Green 12-14-1870 (12-18-1870) B
Matthews, Aaron to Catherine McDowell 12-26-1870 (no return) B
Matthews, George to Harriet Ealy 4-8-1871 (4-3?-1871) B
Matthews, George to Lucy McCully 9-4-1868 (no return) B
Matthews, Henry to Mary Humphreys 3-22-1870 (3-18?-1870) B
Matthews, James S. to Effie P. McDowell 11-17-1866 (11-20-1866)
Matthews, Joe to Louisa Williamson 9-5-1868 (9-6-1868) B
Matthews, Richmond to Laura Taylor 12-24-1868 (12-28-1868) B
Matthews, Thomas to Catherine Jones 1-19-1866 (1-27-1866) B
Matthews, Wash to Gracy Maxwell 1-2-1868 (1-3-1868) B
Matthews, William to Lelia Winfrey 10-27-1865 (10-28-1865) B
Matty, J. J. to J. M. Cullom 12-17-1859 (12-20-1859)
Maurach?, Samuel to Margarett Pinket 11-2-1840
Mavis, Wm. to Sarah (Mrs.) Wainwright 7-17-1855 (no return)
Maxwell, Charles J. to Armedia A. Sharp 9-21-1852 (no return)
Maxwell, H. P. to Charlotte M. Morrison? 3-19-1841
May, M. A. to Susan W. Clark 1-20-1847
May, P. A.? to Amy Branch 12-7-1852 (no return)
May, Phil to Mary Beavers 1-6-1868 (no return) B
May, Thomas to Eliza Bounds 1-13-1870 (1-31-1870) B
Mayfield, Virgil H. to Mary D. Lane 7-3-1846
Mayfield, William S. to Kitty A. Jarrett 10-13-1843 (no return)
Mayo, C. B. to Martha A. Trotter 4-1-1850 (4-9-1850)
Mayo, F. A. to Laura Cocke 2-23-1869 (2-25-1869)
Mayo, James to Mary A. Gramer 12-12-1854 (no return)
Mayo, John W. to Emily A. Winston 2-2-1842
Mayo, L. S. to Mary E. Terrill 12-27-1850 (12-28-1850)
Mayo, Wm. C. to J. E. Anderson 12-23-1844 (12-24-1844)
Mays, F. M. to Rebecca Shinn 9-24-1851 (no return)
Mays, William L. to Margaret E. McClellan 2-5-1851
McAdams, B. W. to Mary E. Smith 4-6-1869
McCall, James to M. Andrews 7-27-1866 (no return)
McCall, John M. to Emaline E. Spivey 8-30-1843 (8-31-1843)
McCall, Robert to Eliza Gravault 9-2-1848 (9-3-1848)
McCally, Robt. to Charity McCully 2-24-1850 (3-5-1850)
McCarley, Dean to Mary Barrett 8-9-1838
McCarley, Peter to Ann Pulliam 6-11-1868 (6-13-1868) B
McCarson, C. C. to Laura Norris 8-14-1867 (8-15-1867)
McCarty, J. R. to M. A. Slaughter 1-29-18686 (2-1-1866)
McCaskill, James A. to F. E. Smith 12-19-1856 (no return)
McCaskill, Wm. C. to Mary M. Ozier 10-5-1854 (no return)
McCaughan, John to Margarett G. Allen 10-21-1854 (no return)
McCharen, J. A. to A. J. Green 11-9-1868 (11-11-1868)
McCheven, R. E. to M. F. Slaughter 12-3-1866 (12-5-1866)
McClanahan, Henry to Nancy J. Patterson 2-2-1869 (2-7-1869) B
McClarren, Alexander J. to Margarett J. Fisher 2-4-1840 (2-19-1840)
McClarty, W. W. to Laura L. Slaughter 4-7-1868 (4-12-1868)
McClellan, John to Paralee Mosby 11-16-1867 (1-4-1868) B
McClellan, T. D. G. to Frances E. Porter 8-29-1848
McClerrin, Robert to Millie Batt 12-6-1870 (no return) B
McClerry, Thomas to Isabella Moon 12-4-1869 B
McClurere?, James B. to Susan D. Alexander 3-24-1848 (4-16-1848)
McCoard, Isaac M. to Nancy Long 11-23-1846 (11-5?-1846)
McComack, R. S. to Malina Shaw 11-29-1841 (12-9-1841)
McConnell, C. W. to L. M. Baw 4-23-1860 (4-26-1860)
McConnell, Marton to Patsey Brownlow 9-30-1841 (10-15-1841)
McCoy, A. J. to M. M. Morton 1-4-1869 (1-5-1869)
McCraw, Henry to Margarett Fields 1-3-1871 (no return) B
McCraw, John to Margaret Johnson 9-21-1866
McCraw, Jonathan H. to Mary B. Jackson 10-16-1843
McCraw, Jonathan to Elizabeth P. Harris 1-4-1851 (no return)
McCray, M. to M. Thomas 10-26-1869 (10-28-1869)
McCrillis, Lafayette to Augusta Montgomery 12-27-1865 (12-28-1865)
McCulley, Tom to Louisa Word 12-25-1866 (no return) B
McCullough, James to Martha Ballard 7-11-1855 (no return)
McCully, Gabe to Lucy Woodfolk 12-24-1870 (no return) B
McCully, J. M. to M. C. McCully 4-3-1860 (4-5-1860)
McCully, John H. to Margaret Earl 12-6-1853 (no return)
McCully, W. H. to Berlin Amis 11-10-1866 (11-11-1866)
McDade, John to Josephine Womble 10-22-1844
McDonald, Cash to Martha Haskins 1-5-1871 B
McDonald, David to Nancy E. Sullivan 12-24-1866 (12-26-1866)
McDonald, Richard to Katty Sullivan 10-17-1868 B
McDonald, Taylor to Bell Isbell 1-3-1868 (1-7-1868) B
McDowel, Henry to Mariah Lucas 2-23-1867 (2-26-1867) B

McDowell, Allen to Anna Sanders 10-6-1869 B
McDowell, George to Malissa Brooks 9-26-1868 (9-27-1868) B
McDowell, Henry to Clara Johnson 10-10-1868 (no return) B
McDowell, Jos. to Anna McDowell 8-13-1866 (8-15-1866) B
McDowell, Solomon to Victoria Morton 1-6-1871 (no return) B
McEllroy, Virginius A. to Fanny Capers 10-14-1869 (10-18-1869)
McElwain, Ned to Maranda Rives 2-19-1870 (2-20-1870) B
McFadden, J. M. to Fannie Sharp 11-4-1863 (11-5-1863)
McFadden, Jno. M. to Sarah E. Watson 1-8-1846
McFadden, John M. to Mary M. Morrison 11-27-1844 (no return)
McFadden, Thomas to Ruth Watson 11-10-1838
McFarland, Felix to Martha A. Douglass 6-28-1842
McFarland, George to Sara Ragland 11-27-1865 (12-30-1865) B
McFarland, Henry to Angeline Poindexter 5-11-1868 (5-16-1868) B
McFerren, William M. to Nancy M. Walker 11-20-1852 (no return)
McFerrin, Addison to Mary Hamilton 7-23-1869 (no return) B
McFerrin, John H. to Tommie Matthews 1-24-1866 (1-31-1866)
McFerrin, Ned to Sidney Jones 1-4-1868 (1-7-1868) B
McGee, R. G. to Mary Jane McGee 12-12-1839 (no return)
McGee, Thos. to Sarah Moore 8-?-1842 (no return)
McGehee, Fountain to Cyntha Thompson 1-13-1839 (1-24-1839)
McGehee, Fountain to Cynthia Thompson 1-13-1839 (no return)
McGinnis, Dennis to Rosah Black 4-30-1868 (no return) B
McGinnis, J. R. to Mary E. Boyd 12-21-1862 (1-1-1863)
McGowan, James E. to Willy Ann Lucado 9-23-1850 (no return)
McGregor, Rob Roy to Ada B. Martin 6-10-1867 (7-6-1867)
McGuirk, John to Louisa A. Mahaffy 5-24-1853 (no return)
McKendree, W. C. to Mattie Loving 1-8-1866 (1-9-1866)
McKindry, Frank to Ella Parks 12-20-1870 (no return) B
McKinley, Andy to Kitty Williams 1-17-1871 B
McKinley, H. B. to Salina A. Alender? 11-26-1850 (12-3-1850)
McKinney, N. M. to Susan E. Lacy 2-6-1865
McKinney, Perry to Mary McNeill 8-5-1867 (8-10-1867) B
McKinney, Samuel to Lucy A. Sanders 8-15-1854 (no return)
McKinny, Candour to Margaret C. Morton 11-20-1844 (no return)
McKinstry, J. W. to P. E. Parrott 11-16-1869 (11-17-1869)
McKisick, Wm. H. to Matilda Lee 12-24-1867 B
McKnight, Franklin to Eliza M. Buckley 11-7-1843 (11-14-1843)
McKnight, James to Susan M. Jones 5-5-1841 (5-6-1841)
McKnight, Joseph to Jane McCarley 12-7-1839 (12-10-1839)
McKnight, Thos. R. to Margart A. Howell 12-12-1850 (no return)
McLean, William J. to Elizabeth A. (Mrs.) Bartis 7-3-1848 (7-4-1848)
McMillon, J. M. to Mary Hart 12-15-1849 (12-18-1849)
McMullen, Stuart to Martha W. Jones 10-4-1869 (10-6-1869)
McMullen, Wm. P. to Georgia Lloyd 4-20-1868 (4-22-1868)
McMullin, Silas W. to Sarah Adaline McKeasy 12-31-1845
McMullin, Wm. R. to Frances Agee 3-19-1840
McNama, John to Isabella D. Adams 2-17-1841 (2-18-1841)
McNamee, Charles to Emily Finch 1-11-1849 (no return)
McNamee, Charles to Mary Kedd 1-27-1840 (no return)
McNamee, Chas. to Eliz. Bryant 6-21-1845 (no return)
McNamee, W. F. to Fannie M. Freeman 11-2-1866 (11-7-1866)
McNary, Isaac to Sallie Ford 5-21-1868 (5-27-1868) B
McNary, Wm. to Caroline Montgomery 2-3-1870 (2-5-1870) B
McNeely, Wm. C. to Rhoda C. Morton 1-1-1869 (no return)
McNees, Robert L. to Lucy F. Arbuckle 11-6-1854 (no return)
McNeil, Buck to Martha Jones 1-6-1866 (1-14-1866) B
McNeil, Henry to Martha Jones 12-28-1865 (1-14-1866) B
McNeil, Horace to Caroline McNeil 3-17-1866 (8-26-1866) B
McNeill, Green to Milly Derden 12-31-1866 (1-6-1867) B
McNeill, J. A. to Kate E. Austin 1-9-1865 (1-10-1865)
McNeill, J. R. to M. P. Perry 12-16-1862 (12-24-1862)
McNeill, Jordan to Rose Reeves 11-9-1867 (no return) B
McNeill, Simon to Mary E. Perry 12-9-1867 (12-16-1867)
McNelis, Michael to Sarah Frances Dodson 3-9-1869 (3-21-1869)
McPherson, William to Jane Buford 2-27-1871 (3-4-1871) B
McQuirter, George M. to Margaret Douglas 10-20-1869
     (no return) B
McQuistin, Wm. to Jane W. Allen 2-24-1845 (2-25-1845)
McRee, C. W. to Emma H. Johnson 10-11-1869 (10-12-1869)
McShaw, John to Nancy Brown 12-5-1870 (no return)
McSwine, John to Ann W. Bailey 2-19-1852 (no return)
McVay, Basel to Cladus Laughter 9-25-1847
McVay, John to Margaret Johnson 11-18-1848 (no return)
McVey, William to Adaline Smith 6-12-1867 (6-25-1867)

Meacham, Abram to Caroline Kelly 1-4-1869 (1-10-1869) B
Meak, John M. to Jane Burrow 10-24-1848 (no return)
Means, Thomas M. to Ann E. Boley 10-4?-1853 (no return)
Mebane, Baker to Edmonia Wigglesworth 12-29-1870 (no return) B
Mebane, Dave to Nannie Pittman 2-20-1871 (2-21-1871)
Mebane, Freeman to Chaney Jordan 6-4-1869 (6-5-1869) B
Medford, Jonathan to Isabella Wilson 4-20-1871
Medley, James A. to Matilda P. Lochridge 6-2-1851 (6-5-1851)
Meigs, A. L. to Catharine E. Kirkpatrick 6-11-1855 (no return)
Meliam, Benjamin F. to Nancy O. Pickins 10-13-1851 (no return)
Melton, Braxton to Catharine McCraw 12-29-1869 (no return) B
Melton, Henry to Mary M. Montgomery 7-17-1850 (7-18-1850)
Melton, James H. to Sarah A. Willson 3-16-1853 (no return)
Melugin, T. M. to C. V. Stewart 12-11-1862
Mench?, _____ to Amanda Anderson 2-12-1849 (no return)
Mendeth?, David to Artis Y. Capp 12-28-1840 (no return)
Mercer, Isaac B. to Sarah D. Alexander 8-13-1849 (no return)
Mercer, James P. to Marieller Burton 5-12-1855 (no return)
Mercer, Joseph S. to Mary Notby 8-13-1849 (no return)
Meriwether, D. J. to H. L. Williamson 4-2-1860 (4-4-1860)
Merrick, James C. to Nancy Thompson 4-17-1839 (4-21-1839)
Merriwether, James to Martha Hunter 11-4-1843 (no return)
Merriwether, Jesse to Eliza Coe 12-28-1865 (12-29-1865) B
Merweather, Francis A. to Eliza J. Hardy 3-2-1853 (no return)
Mewborn, James C. to Mary L. McFerrin 11-2-1867 (11-7-1867)
Mewborn, Joseph L. to Mary Mathews 11-16-1866 (11-20-1866)
Mewborn, Joshua W. to Mattie Lou McFerrin 11-2-1867 (11-7-1867)
Mewborn, William to Caroline Dupree 1-3-1871 (no return) B
Michie, John to Almira Pulliam 4-9-1866 (no return) B
Mickleberry, J. S. to Mary Cothram 11-30-1841 (12-2-1841)
Middlehook, James to Lucy Arnold 3-5-1867
Middleton, Vincent to Martha E. Dodson 7-14-1855 (no return)
Milam, T. M. to Kitty L. Perkins 12-20-1865 (12-27-1865)
Miller, Anderson to Mary Ann Simmons 12-28-1868 B
Miller, H. G. to Lizzie S. Hart 12-7-1859
Miller, Haden to Emma Bledsoe 2-11-1871 (no return) B
Miller, Haywood to Eliza Ann Cartwright 6-3-1869 (no return) B
Miller, Henry to Emma Cross 1-4-1870 (no return) B
Miller, Isom to Adeline Barken 12-22-1869 B
Miller, James M. to Evelina Reese 12-24-1844 (no return)
Miller, Jan L. to Mariah Buck 7-15-1851 (no return)
Miller, Lewis to Mary Jane Trip 12-25-1867 (12-28-1867) B
Miller, Richd. to Mildred Exum 8-30-1867 (8-31-1867) B
Miller, Robert to Sallie Patrick 12-22-1869 B
Miller, S. A. to Lucinda Rhea 8-28-1849
Miller, William J. to Mary Jane Turner 3-9-1852 (no return)
Miller, William to Susan Taylor 2-25-1871 (no return) B
Miller, Wilson to Mary E. Gardner 12-21-1847 (12-30-1847)
Milliken, L. H. to Livinia Moody 7-5-1841
Milliken, W. A. to Mary Humphreys 2-3-1870
Millirons, George to Frances E. Doddridge 4-23-1838
Mills, Curtis to Marta Jane Holloway 1-27-1848 (no return)
Mills, John to Cinthey Williamson 10-14-1847
Minor, Allen to Peggy Southerland 1-3-1849 (no return)
Minor, Jas. Shelton to Bettie Freeman 1-4-1869 (1-8-1869) B
Minson, William to Elvira T. Woollum 5-24-1847 (no return)
Minton, W. L. to I. J. McMillan 8-18-1848 (8-23-1848)
Mitchel, Charley to Catherine Tucker 12-24-1868 (12-26-1868) B
Mitchel, Jerome to Nancy Hester 8-1-1849 (no return)
Mitchel, Jerry to Fanny Wilson 2-1-1867 (2-16-1867) B
Mitchell, Alvay J. to Eliza A. Cox 1-15-1855 (no return)
Mitchell, Ben to Louisa Simpkins 5-13-1870 (5-15-1870) B
Mitchell, Benj. to Sarah? (Mrs.) Griffin 8-20-1839 (9-3?-1839)
Mitchell, Billy to Mollie Jones 12-15-1870 (12-30-1870) B
Mitchell, Charles G. to Elizabeth Blackwell 8-21-1838
Mitchell, Clem to Texanna Heaslett 12-25-1868 (no return) B
Mitchell, H. H. to M. C. Walker 12-12-1860 (12-13-1860)
Mitchell, H. H. to V. C. Walker 12-30-1866 (1-3-1866)
Mitchell, John H. to Lucy A. Harrell 5-13-1862 (5-21-1862)
Mitchell, John H. to Lucy A. Harrell 5-13-1862 (not endorsed)
Mitchell, John H. to Martha A. Ivie 12-13-1854 (no return)
Mitchell, Jonathan P. to Mary E. Notgrass 3-4-1839 (3-13-1839)
Mitchell, Mac McCay to May E. Williamson 10-26-1867
   (10-29-1867) B
Mitchell, Munroe to Amanda Williams 12-27-1870 (12-28-1870) B

Mitchell, Nelson to Nancy Pond 2-3-1840 (2-6-1840)
Mitchell, Peter to Susan Boyd 1-8-1869 (1-9-1869) B
Mitchell, Phillip to Ann H. Patteson 9-17-1867 (9-25-1867) B
Mitchell, W. F. to Mary J. Hollowell 12-19-1853 (no return)
Mitchell, Wm. F. to Bettie A. Cocke 8-22-1860 (8-28-1860)
Moffatt, Frank L. to Mollie M. T. Herndon 1-27-1870
Moncreef, Samuel to Elizabeth Haveway 1-1-1839
Monroe, Henry to Mollie J. Shepard 6-18-1869 (6-20-1869)
Montague, Rhodes to Suck Anderson 2-3-1868 (2-9-1868) B
Montague, Thomas to Fanny Stewart 2-26-1870 (2-27-1870) B
Montague, Young to Martha A. (Mrs.) Batt 5-25-1848
Montcuff, Sanders to Martha Hamblet 8-2-1844 (8-4-1844)
Montgomery, Anda M. C. to Elizabeth Montgomery 9-9-1840
   (9-10-1840)
Montgomery, Hugh to Mary M. Newsom 8-8-1839
Montgomery, J. D. to Susie E. Williams 11-15-1869 (11-18-1869)
Montgomery, Jackson to Martha T. Wright 10-6-1838 (10-8-1838)
Montgomery, Jas. to Susan L. Manley 11-5-1850
Montgomery, S. M. to M. J. Long 3-8-1855 (no return)
Montgomery, W. J. to Anna A. Cassett 2-25-1860 (5-2-1860)
Moody, G. H. to S. J. Johnson 9-20-1849
Moody, Green H. to Eliza D. Johnson 3-1-1848 (3-2-1848)
Moody, John A. to Minerva Branch 6-11-1860 (6-13-1860)
Moody, Joseph E. to Anna M. Laurence 6-14-1849 (6-15-1849)
Moody, Richd. E. to Eliza J. Cocke 1-20-1849 (1-24-1849)
Moore, A. W. to Indiana M. Cabler 8-16-1838
Moore, Benjamin F. to Mary Ann Watson 2-9-1869 (2-11-1869)
Moore, David to Ann Dowdy 11-1-1852 (no return)
Moore, Hugh D. to Mary Ann Thompson 6-20-1844
Moore, J. B. to Mary V. Brown 10-23-1867 (10-24-1867)
Moore, James to Hannah Mitchell 2-18-1869 B
Moore, James to Henrietta Simms 1-29-1866 (2-4-1866)
Moore, John W. to L. V. Farris 11-6-1865 (11-7-1865)
Moore, Johnson to Violet McNeill 5-25-1870 (5-28-1870) B
Moore, Littleton to Susannah Hays 11-12-1869 (11-13-1869) B
Moore, Martin to Jane Jefferson 1-18-1868 (no return) B
Moore, Peyton to Maria Farley 12-30-1865 (12-31-1865) B
Moore, R. M. to Bettie L. McClellan 2-2-1860
Moore, Thad to Adney Chaffin 2-28-1868 (no return) B
Moore, Thos. F. to Martha J. Cogbill 12-19-1870 (12-21-1870)
Moore, William to Georgia Ann Mitchell 10-15-1868 (10-17-1868) B
Moore, Wm. A. to Susan Kerr 7-28-1849 (7-29-1849)
Moore, Wm. L. to Mary C. Abington 12-7-1846 (12-9-1846)
Moore, Wm. to Amy Watkins 10-30-1868 (10-31-1868) B
Moorman, Hiram C. to Frances J. Armstrong 1-27-1870
Moorman, Randal to Louisa Marshall 4-12-1869 B
Mootre, Sam to Mary Ann Murrell 4-29-1870 (5-1-1870) B
Moran, M. Y. to Mary A. Herndon 1-24-1849 (1-26-1849)
Morefield, John to Rebecca E. Rose 7-9-1870 (7-10-1870)
Morgan, Carter to Julia A. Tate 4-5-1867 (no return) B
Morgan, James E. to Nancy Bass 4-16-1844 (4-24-1844)
Morgan, Joe to Ditha Sutherland 9-12-1867
Morgan, John H. to A. Jernigan 3-27-1842 (3-31-1842)
Morgan, Wiley to Martha Bowling 9-16-1870 (9-21-1870) B
Morgan, William N. to Elisabeth A. Bolling 10-24-1848 (11-1-1848)
Morris, D. C. to Elizabeth Reams 4-2-1859 (4-3-1859)
Morris, D. G. to Mary A. Carraway 2-3-1866 (2-8-1866)
Morris, Elisha to Catharine Rodger 6-28-1848 (6-29-1848)
Morris, Freeman to Nancy J. Mayo 12-6-1850 (12-7-1850)
Morris, G. W. to H. M. Granbery 3-26-1855 (no return)
Morris, Henry to Zurie Johnson 12-28-1867 (1-3-1868) B
Morris, J. K. to Cora A. Vanpelt 10-25-1869 (11-26-1869)
Morris, J. W. to Rebeca Boyd 6-15-1855 (no return)
Morris, James B. to Margarett Henley 2-16-1841 (2-18-1841)
Morris, James M. to Dean? Wrightsell 3-24-1842
Morris, James W. to Lucy Granberry 2-5-1845 (2-6-1845)
Morris, Jesse M. to Polly Sullivan 4-6-1850 (4-7-1850)
Morris, John C. to Sallie Brown 2-25-1870 (no return) B
Morris, John to Martha J. Hamilton 3-16-1868 (3-17-1868)
Morris, L. H. to Minerva Hall 12-19-1860
Morris, Lenard W. to Rebecca W. Bell 4-26-1849
Morris, Lovett to Susan J. Rea 4-25-1866 (4-29-1866)
Morris, March to Margaret Williams 1-2-1868 (1-5-1868) B
Morris, Simion to Elvyra Thomason 12-20-1845 (12-23-1845)
Morris, Thomas A. to Amanda Hackney 11-7-1862 (11-9-1862)

Morris, W. J. to Fannie F. Shore 11-30-1859 (12-4-1859)
Morris, Wilie B. to Rebecca E. Rodgers 5-12-1851 (5-14-1851)
Morris, William to Drucilla McDade 3-16-1840 (3-19-1840)
Morris, William to Elizabeth Herington 12-27-1843 (12-28-1843)
Morris, William to Jane Moncreeff 11-5-1838 (11-7-1838)
Morris, Willis to Eliza Knight 12-29-1845 (1-1-1846)
Morris?, W. P. to Judy? Whitehead 11-23-1849
Morrison, Ezra T. to Sophria W. Griffin 1-3-1842 (1-6-1842)
Morrison, R. K. to Elizabeth Bailey 3-13-1866
Morrow, Alfred to Louiza Hart 12-23-1867 (12-24-1867) B
Morrow, George to Millie Ann Morrow 8-20-1868 (8-27-1868) B
Morrow, Ike to Lou Boyd 12-8-1868 (no return) B
Morrow, J. W. to Frances G. Morrow 11-26-1850 (11-27-1850)
Morrow, Joshua to Chaney Shaw 4-28-1871 (5-1-1871)
Morrow, Simon to Donie Holt 9-27-1870 B
Morrow, Thomas to George Anna Wright 4-15-1869 B
Morrow, Tom to Maria Jones 1-7-1867 (1-10-1867) B
Morton, Albert to Mary A. Moody 1-1-1868 (1-27-1868) B
Morton, Horace to Maria Kerr 12-28-1868 (1-3-1869) B
Morton, John M. to Narcissa M. Stewart 2-6-1841
Morton, John Z. to Polly (Mrs.) Harwell 11-12-1862 (not endorsed)
Morton, John Z. to Polly Harwell 11-12-1862 (not endorsed)
Morton, John to Lydia Ann Blackburn 1-13-1870 (1-18-1870) B
Morton, Joseph to Jane C. Alexander 11-10-1847 (11-11-1847)
Mosby, Britton to Lydia Ann Mosby 7-15-1870 (no return) B
Mosby, Dewitt C. to Virginia A. Booker 11-19-1841 (11-20-1841)
Moseley, Burwell S. to Lucy C. J. Stanley 2-16-1846 (2-19-1846)
Mosley, Peterson to Sarah Ann Thornton 9-11-1838
Moss, James R. to Mary E. Blackburn 9-25-1844 (9-26-1844)
Moss, James R. to Mary E. Blackburn no dates (with Feb 1844)
Moss, John H. to Nancy Franklin 6-5-1839
Motley, J. S. to S. J. Luckado 12-17-1866 (12-19-1866)
Motley, John to Sarah Jane Wacker 10-21-1839 (no return)
Mowhorn, Gilbert to Mary Jane Adams 6-5-1869 (6?-1-1869) B
Muncrief, Austin to Caroline Hudspeth 11-3-1845 (11-2?-1845)
Munroe, Albert to Sarah Kinney 12-28-1870 B
Murchison, D. P. to Hilean Ann Herron 10-14-1868 (10-16-1868) B
Murphey, Wm. to Eliza Neal 9-29-1839 (10-3-1839)
Murphy, J. B. to P. A. F. Young 12-31-1859 (1-4-1860)
Murphy, L. E. to Mary J. Hood 10-6-1868 (10-7-1868)
Murray, James H. to Mary G. Wray 1-21-1846
Murray, James M. to Anna Warren 12-22-1870
Murrell, B. F. to Mary Bondurant 6-?-1842 (no return)
Murrell, Charley to Jane Askew 12-31-1869 (no return) B
Murrell, Charley to Mima Minor 4-25-1870 (7-17-1870) B
Murrell, J. Q. to M. A. Williamson 8-30-1859 (8-31-1859)
Murrell, J. T. to A. V. Cartwright 9-27-1852 (no return)
Murrell, J. W. to Judia A. Carroll 1-18-1869 (no return)
Murrell, Joe to Agnis Sawyer 3-30-1867 B
Murrell, Millard to Catharine Williams 3-1-1870 (9-?-1870) B
Murrell, Robert to Josephine Sayers 2-12-1870 (no return) B
Murrell, Robertson to Cynthia Thompson 1-21-1867 (1-22-1867) B
Murry, Pleasant to Mariah Coffman 1-3-1870 (no return) B
Mussy, D. G. to Martha Henly 3-14-1849 (no return)
Mutemas?, Berry to Cornelia A. Carloss 2-3-1871 (2-8-1871) B
Myers, David to Jane C. Hudson 4-24-1852 (no return)
Myers, Frank to Mary S. Taylor 11-13-1868 (11-15-1868)
Myers, William to Martha Hutchins 11-10-1869 (11-11-1869) B
Nance, Nelson to Susana Boyd 8-5-1868 (8-6-1868) B
Nash, Andrew to Sarah Pettit 12-17-1870 (12-18-1870) B
Nash, Isaac to Martha Pane 9-22-1851 (no return)
Nation, Wm. E. to Mary Ann Read 3-22-1843 (no return)
Neal, A. J. to Elizabeth H. Griffin 10-15-1852 (no return)
Neal, Albert to Emily Walker 3-20-1871 (no return) B
Neal, Anderson to Margaret Crawford 1-9-1869 (1-10-1869) B
Neal, James M. to Mary Smith 9-28-1838 (9-30-1838)
Neal, Meredith H. to Harrit Spencer 12-4-1845
Neal, R. B. to M. W. Land 1-27-1868 (1-28-1868)
Neal, Rice to Caroline Reddick 12-23-1865 (12-25-1865) B
Neal, T. S. to Sallie E. Reddick 2-22-1869 (2-24-1869)
Neal, William to M. F. Poore 12-22-1856 (no return)
Neal, Wm. H. to Winiford S. Carraway 7-3-1852 (no return)
Neal, Wm. L. to Kate R. McKinney 6-29-1866 (7-3-1866)
Nealey, W. J. H. to Candis M. Moore 1-2-1849 (no return)
Neel, Drew to Mary Gillespie 10-20-1869 (10-21-1869) B

Neel, James M. to Elizabeth O. Patton 11-22-1841 (11-23-1841)
Neel, John F. to Margaret C. Morrison 10-18-1842
Neel, John to Ella Madore 12-28-1869 (no return) B
Neel, Jurdon to Oma Jackson 1-4-1871 (no return) B
Neel, R. K. to Emma H. Robertson 11-25-1865 (11-29-1865)
Neel, Saml. M. to Mary J. Watkins 11-28-1866
Neeley, Richard to Rachell Biggs 4-14-1849 (4-15-1849)
Neely, C. F. to M. E. Doyle 9-27-1859 (10-6-1859)
Neely, J. A. to Allice C. Kyle 2-6-1871 (2-8-1871)
Neely, J. A. to Belle Irby 12-18-1868 (12-23-1868)
Neely, William T. to Leonora Doyle 1-3-1867 (1-9-1867)
Neesbit, Wm. H. to Catharine Herington 12-27-1843 (12-28-1843)
Nelson, B. F. to Rachel Churchill 1-30-1849
Nelson, M. W. to C. V. Ellington 4-18-1854 (no return)
Nelson, Samul S. to Sophronia L. Linsdey 11-18-1848 (no return)
Nelson, Wm. L. to Mary Bland 3-5-1860 (3-7-1860)
Nelson, Wm. W. to E. A. McClarran 1-28-1842 (2-10-1842)
Nesbit, John A. to Susan Haselett 5-18-1867 (no return) B
Nesbitt, R. N. to Martha R. Thomas 1-3-1855 (no return)
Nevell, Albert G. to M. R. McKinney 8-28-1854 (no return)
Nevil, Jesse to Priscilla Steager 11-15-1869 (11-18-1869) B
Neville, Cain to Laura Strickland 9-7-1867 B
Neville, Wm. B. to C. H. Aston 2-3-1851 (2-11-1851)
Newbern, Wm. W. to Anna L. Mewbern 6-20-1860
Newberry, M. C.? to Gatsy H. Smith 7-20-1842
Newborn, E. W. to Mary Ann Webb 3-23-1869
Newby, J. W. to G. A. Crossett 11-13-1867 (11-14-1867)
Newby, R. W. to Nancy Jane Branch 10-27-1852 (no return)
Newsom, Andrew J. to Elizabeth B. Smith 10-21-1865 (no return)
Newsom, Andrew to Sarah M. C. Johnson 10-13-1851 (no return)
Newsom, George to La Askew 6-8-1867 B
Newsom, Wm. to Tryphenia Newsom 2-25-1868 (2-26-1868)
Nichols, Mathew to Darcas Williams 10-24-1854 (no return)
Nicholson, D. S. to Lucy C. Baxter 12-17-1868
Nicholson, Wyatt to T. C. Wright 12-3-1847 (12-15-1847)
Nickols, Henry to Frances Cocke 1-3-1867 (no return) B
Nickolson, Henry to Rosanna Warran 9-26-1868 (no return) B
Night, W. M. to Emily S. Roberts 11-16-1847 (11-17-1847)
Nobb, D. W. to M. J. Holloway 2-20-1855 (no return)
Noel, John to Rebecca Tolbert 4-26-1845 (4-27-1845)
Nolin, Thos. to Mary McElroy 8-27-1842
Nolly, G. W. to Elizabeth Hilliard 11-3-1862 (not endorsed)
Nolly, Henry to Tilda Rowlett 7-19-1867 (7-20-1867) B
Nolly, Ike to Jenny Rives 1-15-1870 (1-19-1870) B
Nolly, William H. to Mary J. Simmons 10-13-1868 (10-14-1868)
Nonnent, Wm. M. to T. S. Jamson 1-7-1849 (no return)
Norman, H. O. to Emma L. Tatum 4-13-1860 (4-15-1860)
Norman, Wm. P. to Esther Culp 7-14-1849
Norment, Robt. W. to Sallie J. White 11-25-1867 (11-28-1867)
Normont, John S. to Nancy S. Burford 7-27-1847 (7-28-1847)
Norris, David to Elizabeth M. Leath 8-31-1868 (9-2-1868)
Northway, H. K. to Susan E. Parkes 10-14-1852 (no return)
Norton, M. P. to R. F. Davidson 1-27-1869 (1-28-1869)
Notgrass, John W. to Sarah E. Ross 3-22-1852 (no return)
Notgrass, Thos. to Delina Cook 5-10-1845 (5-13-1845)
Nowel, Tom to Amanda Mosby 9-24-1868 (9-27-1868) B
O'Brian, Joseph W. to Amanda M. Walker 3-16-1847 (4-19-1847)
O'Daniel, Wm. to Eliza T. Brooks 12-23-1846 (no return)
O'Kelley, James P. to Rebecca Jane Thorp 9-25-1843 (10-3-1843)
O'Kelly, J. P. to Tempy Wall 8-18-1859 (8-21-1859)
O'Kelly, Lewis J. to Nancy B. Herron 9-5-1866 (9-9-1866)
O'Quinn, A. M. to Annetta Harris 2-3-1866 (2-6-1866)
OKelly, L. J. to Malvina Herron 8-19-1862 (8-23-1862)
O'Kelly, Willis S. to Lucy Cock 12-17-1850 (no return)
Oates, J. A. to Mollie C. Baker 2-18-1871 (no return)
Oates, John H. to Sarah McFadden 9-24-1851 (no return)
Oats, Stephen K. to Celia J. Crittenden 5-11-1867 (5-16-1867)
Oats, Wm. J. to Mary Maxwell 11-21-1844
Okelly, L. J. to Melvina Herren 8-19-1862 (not endorsed)
Old, W. C. to Mary J. Crawford 2-4-1863
Old, William A. to Martha A. Deaner 9-30-1845 (no return)
Oldham, Ned to Phillis Williams 12-26-1866 (12-28-1866) B
Olds, Andrew to Harriet Cooper 12-24-1867 (12-31-1867) B
Olds, Mat to Ella Hayes 6-11-1869 (6-12-1869) B
Olds, Zack to Nancy Brewer 12-28-1870 B

Oliver, Joe to Mandy Beavers 12-3-1868 (12-5-1868) B
Oliver, Richard to Martha Moffett 8-14-1839
Oliver, Wm. B. to Pruda Chappel 9-17-1839 (9-19-1839)
Omesly?, T. H. to Lucy J. Franklin 2-12-1849 (no return)
Organ, Thomas L. to Elizabeth J. Trotter 10-1-1844 (10-9-1844)
Ormann, James L. to Carolin Bryles 1-9-1843 (1-16-1843)
Ormon, Jacob to Elizabeth Jones 3-19-1838
Orr, Allen to Tennessee Cole 12-28-1868 (1-3-1869) B
Orrell, J. C. to Elizabeth Kain 12-10-1862 (12-11-1862)
Orton, Robert W. to Sarah Cochran 8-9-1838
Osborn, Levi P. to Cornelia M. Gregory 7-24-1848 (7-27-1848)
Osborne, Isaac to Augustina Hargiss 9-16-1851 (no return)
Osborne, W. W. to Margaret V. Adams 1-26-1865 (1-31-1865)
Osier, Samuel C. to Maunda Coble 8-19-1851 (no return)
Overton, B. W. to Mattie Reece 12-16-1867 (12-17-1867)
Overton, Henry to Lucy McGowan 11-19-1867 (11-23-1867) B
Overton, Thomas G. to Rozina Gwinn 12-17-1840
Owen, Charles C. to Sarah E. Lancaster 12-6-1855 (no return)
Owen, James to Jane R. Smith 11-5-1838 (no return)
Owen, N. L. to Ann R. Allen 5-7-1855 (no return)
Owens, David O. to Martha E. Lay 8-23-1854 (no return)
Owens, Felix to Permelia H. Plant 1-12-1839 (1-15-1839)
Owens, George to Bitha McFerrin 2-15-1871 (no return) B
Owens, Thomas H. to Jennie Lee Baker 4-16-1866 (4-25-1866)
Owings, R. A. to Rachel E. Holman 9-9-1865 (9-12-1865)
Ozier, C. J. to Luella A. McFadden 3-17-1860
Ozier, George to Sally Wade 1-25-1871 (1-26-1871) B
Ozier, W. C. to Sarah C. Elder 1-2-1863
Ozier, Willie to Winney C. Bostick 12-1-1843
Ozment, Varnum to Emily V. Henderson 5-10-1847 (no return)
Padin, D. M. to Susan E. Settle 7-19-1849
Pagie, Lott to Susan Williamson 3-29-1871 B
Paine, Blueford to Jenny Hunter 12-28-1868 B
Paine, John M. to Margaret A. Porter 11-1-1869 B
Paine, Johnson to Flora Lockhart 1-28-1869 (1-30-1869) B
Palmer, David E. to Ann E. Tucker 1-27-1852 (no return)
Palmer, Henry to Tilda Thompson 1-3-1868 (1-11-1868) B
Palmer, J. T. to Darcas S. Swan 10-31-1839 (11-6-1839)
Palmer, Reubin to Ortry Sanders 12-12-1867 B
Palmore, J. S. to Sarah E. Isbell 6-20-1849 (6-29-1849)
Pankey, John E. to Sarah J. Snellings 8-20-1869 (8-21-1869)
Parchman, Judel? (J. W.?) to Elizabeth Stedham 10-6-1838 (10-8-1838)
Pardew, Thomas J. to Lydia T. Cassell 12-3-1866 (12-4-1866)
Parham, Alfred to Mary Jane Hill 4-11-1867 (5-12-1867) B
Parham, Ben to Jenny Hendly 7-6-1868 (7-10-1868) B
Parham, Jos. D. to Missouri A. J. C. Wilkerson 3-26-1851 (no return)
Parham, R. S. to Annie C. Williamson 2-23-1853 (no return)
Parham, R. S. to Priscilla B. Williamson 11-25-1854 (no return)
Parham, Sikes to Patsy Graves 4-18-1866 (6-16-1866) B
Parham, Williamson H. to Sarah Kendrick 12-23-1847
Parham, Wm. R. to M. E. Lanier 2-20-1860 (2-22-1860)
Parham, jr., Jno. to Anna Harwell 12-18-1860 (12-19-1860)
Parish, A. H. to Catherine (Mrs.) Malone 2-18-1867 (no return)
Parish, Asberry H. to Catharine Malone 2-28-1867 (3-1-1867)
Park, Jacob to Cassanda Moody 1-3-1866 (no return) B
Parke, Wm. to Sarah E. Dowdy 2-13-1851 (no return)
Parker, F. A. to Jullia (Mrs.) Smith 5-13-1869 (5-16-1869)
Parker, Hanks to Nicie Blaydes 2-4-1871 (no return) B
Parker, Hiram to Belle Emma Yancey 12-18-1868 B
Parker, James R. to Mary An Petty (Perry?) 12-18-1848
Parker, John R. to Mary McCartry 10-11-1841 (no return)
Parker, Joseph R. to Rebecca T. Thomas 2-13-1860
Parker, Lemel J. W. to Rebeca H. Dupew 11-21-1840 (11-25-1840)
Parker, Madison to Frances C. Cross 12-27-1847 (12-30-1847)
Parker, O. B. to Martha Williams 10-5-1840 (10-6-1840)
Parker, P. F. to Mollie M. Mason 10-17-1864 (10-18-1864)
Parker, W. E. to Mattie Chapman 5-7-1867
Parkes, William H. to Sarah Wrightsell 11-9-1841 (11-11-1841)
Parks, Chas. to Dilsa Rawlings 9-13-1867 (no return) B
Parks, Moses to Mary A. Culp 12-2-1850 (12-3-1850)
Parks, Oliver to Judy Steger 1-29-1870 (2-22-1870) B
Parks, R. N. to Mattie M. Stewart 2-13-1860 (2-16-1860)
Parks, Robert to Elvira Dowdy 12-29-1868 (12-31-1868) B
Parratt, Geo. W. to Emily F. Boswell 10-6-1848 (10-12-1848)

Parris, Nuggy to Alsey Haselette 12-23-1867 (no return) B
Parrish, Henry to Sarah Ann Marshall 8-2-1847
Parrish, Thomas to Martha L. Manley 8-3-1847 (8-8-1847)
Parrott, Irwin to Lucinda Waller 3-4-1846 (3-5-1846)
Parrott, J. to Margaret E. (Mrs.) Waller 12-11-1854 (no return)
Paschal, R. A. to Nacy (Nancy?) Adkins 11-15-1838
Patillo, J. E. to Martha E. C. Simons 9-11-1850 (9-11-1850)
Patrick, John H. to Elizabeth F. Houston 1-1-1869 (no return)
Patrick, Z. H. to M. S. Curl 6-20-1842 (no return)
Patterson, George W. to Mary Johnson 8-16-1838
Patterson, Robert to Julia Jones 12-6-1866 B
Patterson, Smith to Catharine Humphrey 1-19-1844 (not endorsed)
Patterson, Wm. to Lucy Springfield 11-11-1869 B
Pattillo, John E. to Harriet (Mrs.) Stafford 2-12-1870 (2-13-1870)
Patton, Isaac S. to Mary A. Dickson 9-13-1848
Patton, James M. to Emily N. Kerr 1-19-1848
Patton, Pryus to Lucy Rowder 2-23-1867 (3-11-1867) B
Patton, Wm. E. to Agnes A. Starr 1-27-1840 (1-28-1840)
Patty, R. C. to Ella Campbell 11-8-1869 (11-11-1869)
Paulson, Geor. to Mary B. Adams 4-17-1845
Payne, G. B. to Sarah Ann Webb 12-4-1869 (12-22-1869)
Pearce, Andrew to Anna Warren 12-25-1868 (no return) B
Pearce, J. R. to Maggie Rosser 12-3-1866 (12-5-1866)
Pearce, Jim to Cresia Alexander 3-21-1868 B
Pearce, John A. to Lucy Ann Smith 2-5-1870 (2-10-1870)
Pearce, W. C. to Susan E. Plant 11-30-1866 (12-5-1866)
Pearce, W. S. to Tennessee Branch 11-28-1862 (12-2-1862)
Pearsall, E. J. to J. E. Williams 5-14-1850 (5-16-1850)
Pearson, Alfred to Leathy Turnley 10-19-1867 B
Pearson, Isaac J. to Lannie Lewis 9-24-1870 (10-6-1870) B
Pearson, John D. to Conelia Holland 12-15-1851 (no return)
Pearson, John R. to Margaret L. Lansdon 10-20-1840
Pearson, John R. to Mary W. Cooper 9-14-1854 (no return)
Pearson, Wm. to Carolina E. Stiger 3-13-1841 (no return)
Peebles, Alfred to Emily Hammons 9-28-1870 B
Peebles, E. D. to Nannie Whitaker 4-27-1859 (4-28-1859)
Peeler, Stephen A. to Sarah A. Morris 12-22-1866 (12-25-1866)
Peers, V. C. to Sarah L. Dupuy 10-23-1855 (no return)
Pegees, Jacob to Martha Williamson 4-18-1867 B
Pegram, R. W. to Mary E. Brown 9-10-1847
Pender, Joseph W. to Tralucia L. Durham 4-1-1847
Pendleton, William to Viney Moore 2-18-1869 (2-20-1869) B
Penick, Jno. W. to Susanna C. Miller 8-10-1859
Penick, W. E. to Delia A. Holman 12-12-1870 (12-14-1870)
Penn, James L. to Martha Williamson 6-4-1851
Pennington, B. F. to Rebecca B. Tillman 1-11-1853 (no return)
Pennington, Edwin to Sarah Clift 12-16-1844 (12-19-1844)
Pennington, Marcus J. to Bethany Eason 9-4-1842 (9-20-1842)
Peoples, Nathan M. to Mary L. Williams 2-12-1851 (no return)
Peoples, Nathan M. to Mary S. Williams 11-19-1850 (license lost)
Perkins, David L. to Eliza Watson 12-20-1852 (no return)
Perkins, J. H. to Fannie V. Chitts 10-3-1867
Perkins, Littleton H. to Lou Boyd 3-1-1871
Perkins, R. T. to Belle Baird 8-8-1870
Perry, Abraham to Mary Crook 11-19-1844
Perry, Andrew to Ellen Hilliard 1-19-1871 (1-21-1871) B
Perry, Benjamin to Maria Crowder 1-1-1866 (1-7-1866) B
Perry, Edmund B. to Eliza J. Shaw 1-2-1869 (1-6-1869)
Perry, James to Mary A. Kerr 12-11-1850 (no return)
Perry, John J. to Julia A. Dailey 12-29-1860
Perry, John to E. A. Webb 1-31-1850
Perry, Saml. A. to America Webb 10-5-1846 (no return)
Perry, Solomon to Fanny Gatlin 1-4-1871 (1-5-1871) B
Perry, William to Nancy Holloway 2-25-1851 (2-27-1851)
Perser, Wm. to Caroline Burrow 8-16-1849 (no return)
Person, Willis to Polly Ann Craige 4-30-1864 (5-4-1864)
Peterbock, Jack to Eliza Castles 1-15-1869 (1-16-1869) B
Peters, E. L. to Elizabeth Burton 4-18-1850 (no return)
Peterson, James to Harret M. Martin 1-29-1850 (no return)
Peticats, Arthur E. to _____ 3-15-1852 (no return)
Pettett, James to Eliza V. Grey 1-31-1838
Pettey, Francis M. to Sarah ann Elliott 8-26-1848 (no return)
Pettit, James to Mary Jane Gray 8-3-1852 (no return)
Peyton, Henry S. to Sarah B. Lawrence 12-27-1844 (no return)
Phillips, Bill to Susana Strickland 4-20-1867 B

Phillips, Frank to Caroline Hicks 11-6-1869 (no return) B
Phillips, James Munroe to Sally Makey 12-23-1868 (12-24-1868) B
Phillips, James to Celestia Jones 11-9-1867 B
Phillips, James to Harriett Sherrell 8-6-1853 (no return)
Phillips, John P. to Sarahann Abernathy 10-28-1841 (no return)
Phillips, Joseph W. to Catherine R. Holden 1-21-1868 (1-22-1868)
Phillips, Robert S. to Charley M. Powell 11-20-1855 (no return)
Phillips, S. P. to Mary A. Patterson 1-23-1850
Phillips, Sam to Nancy Warford 1-31-1870 (2-1-1870) B
Phillips, Sam to Roberta Allen 2-28-1866 (3-10-1866) B
Phillips, Samel to Elizabeth Birdsong 12-26-1839 (no return)
Pickens, A. G. to Elizabeth F. Batt 1-17-1842 (1-19-1842)
Pickens, Jas. M. to Jane Singleton 1-24-1853 (no return)
Pickens, Jas. S. to Mary Exum 6-3-1849
Pickens, Robt. T. to Mary W. Pearson 3-14-1870 (3-15-1870)
Pickins, A. L. to Martha Stedham 12-21-1842 (12-22-1842)
Pickins, J. F. to L. J. Zellner 11-15-1852 (no return)
Pickins, J. M. to Harrett J. Churchhill 10-11-1852 (no return)
Pickins, W. H. to Susan E. Stanly 9-29-1849 (9-30-1849)
Pierce, W. W. to M. W. Irwin 11-25-1862 (11-26-1862)
Piller, W. H. to Nancy M. Caraway 12-22-1856 (no return)
Pipkins, J. H. to Margaret A. Pope 7-16-1870 (7-17-1870)
Pippin, Elisah to Emma Clayton 3-16-1869 (3-18-1869)
Pippin, Joseph to Eliza Pullman 11-5-1838 (11-?-1839?)
Pippins, H. S. to Bettie Kindreck 9-6-1869 (9-7-1869)
Pirdle, Ephraim to Charlotte Burford 12-25-1868 (12-28-1868) B
Pitman, Henry M. to Mary J. Kerr 6-30-1849 (no return)
Pitman, R. W. to M. E. Rives 10-29-1866 (10-31-1866)
Pitmon, S. to Sarah A. J. (Mrs.) Bell 5-15-1841 (no return)
Pitt, Anderson to Omy Deener 8-31-1867 B
Plant, Christopher H. to Susan N. Ramsey 11-17-1845 (12-2-1845)
Plant, Mad to Mary A. Cargell 3-14-1853 (no return)
Plant, S. M. to Ellen Elizabeth Stony 7-19-1851 (no return)
Plant, William to Emily W. Sitler 6-20-1843 (no return)
Plattenburg, George to Josephine Howard 9-15-1855 (no return)
Plaxter, Wm. S. to Margarett J. McKinstrey 1-13-1852 (no return)
Pledge, William A. to Elvira J. Yancy 10-27-1849 (11-1-1849)
Plumer, Nathan F. to Eliza D. Stockinger 10-26-1846 (11-5-1846)
Poindexter, Bob to Lutetia Clark 9-16-1867 (9-21-1867) B
Poindexter, C. C. to Virginia Clifton 1-24-1870 (1-25-1870)
Poindexter, Christopher C. to Anna Harris 4-24-1871 (5-5-1871)
Poindexter, Geo. to Mat Tucker 1-1-1868 (1-2-1868) B
Poindexter, Louis H. to Sarah E. Clifton 1-23-1871 (1-25-1871)
Poindexter, Raleigh W. to Winniford L. Hilliard 9-7-1846 (no return)
Poindexter, Rolla to Sarah Wells 12-12-1854 (no return)
Poindexter, T. H. to Hattie V. Farrar 12-6-1866 (12-12-1866)
Poindexter, Thomal C. to Ann E. Cole 9-20-1847
Poindexter, Wm. to Clara Tucker 8-10-1866 (8-12-1866) B
Polk, Britton to Sally Henderson 12-25-1866 (12-26-1866) B
Polk, Osco to Adaline Nelson 1-18-1868 B
Polk, Robert to Laura McNeill 4-11-1867 (4-20-1867) B
Polk, Tho. R. to Lucy N. Cocke 6-11-1846 (6-24-1846)
Polk, Thomas R. to Carolina L. Smith 12-15-1841
Polk, Thos. R. to Bettie Kean 2-27-1862 (3-12-1862)
Polk, Wm. to Mary C. Thomas 7-23-1839 (7-30-1839)
Pollock, George to Mary A. Murphy 6-28-1842
Pool, G. M. to Mary L. Clayton 5-14-1866 (5-16-1866)
Pool, James to Louisa T. Sanders 1-28-1867
Pool, John L. to Deborah M. Sloan 10-11-1839 (10-17-1839)
Poor, Edwin H. to A. S. Boals 3-21-1867
Pope, Andrew R. to Mary A. Murrell 9-2-1865 (9-10-1865)
Pope, John A. to Louisa A. Exum 12-6-1852 (no return)
Pope, John to Lethia Sope 12-15-1842 (no return)
Pope, John to Mary McDowell 11-7-1870 (11-14-1870)
Porter, Andrew A. to Martha A. Taylor 10-17-1846 (10-22-1846)
Porter, Axum to Sarah Dobbin 12-27-1867 B
Porter, Gardner to Jenny Springfield 12-1-1869 (no return) B
Porter, Jeff to Mary Williams 5-3-1870 (no return) B
Porter, Spencer to Nancy Ford 1-17-1866 (1-20-1866) B
Portis, E. D. to Amanda F. Everett 1-27-1853 (no return)
Portis, John C. to Lucy A. Averett 11-23-1855 (no return)
Portis, W. N. to Annie J. Lee 5-12-1860 (5-16-1860)
Portis, Wm. N. to Mattie B. Lee 11-1-1869 (11-3-1869)
Posten, John to Mary Moncrief 7-10-1854 (no return)
Posten?, Noah H. to Louisa J. Eskridge 3-2-1854 (no return)

Poston, J. W. to Sarah E. Compton 10-20-1863 (10-21-1863)
Potts, Charles to Jane S. Bordley 9-1-1840 (9-10-1840)
Potts, Noah to Marietta Goode 8-23-1867 (8-24-1867) B
Potts, Tho. J. to Lucy Lanier 9-18-1865 (9-20-1865)
Pouge?, John to Susan An Williams 12-22-1849 (12-23-1849)
Powell, B. A. to Sallie E. Nelson 2-28-1866 (3-1-1866)
Powell, James to Eliza Ivie 12-11-1866 (12-13-1866)
Powell, John to Annis Rawlings 12-17-1869 (no return) B
Powell, Rufus W. to Margaret R.? Baxter 2-6-1850
Powelson, Simon to Jane Bickers 9-18-1863
Power, Wm. to Mary E. Kelly 11-?-1853 (no return)
Powers, Benj. F. to Martha C. Whitney 10-7-1850 (10-6?-1850)
Powers, L. T. to Elizabeth Knight 1-15-1848 (1-17-1848)
Preston, C. W. to Sarah E. Taylor 12-19-1849 (12-22-1849)
Previtt, N. H. to Mary J. Perkins 3-?-1852 (no return)
Prewitt, Berry to Phoeba A. Jones 12-24-1867 (no return) B
Prewitt, Milton W. to Lucy V. Gates 12-9-1867 (12-10-1867)
Price, A. H. to Mary Ann Chambers 10-9-1848 (10-23-1848)
Price, Anthony to Dicy Mosby 2-15-1867 (2-16-1867) B
Price, Arthur to Emeline Maris 12-29-1866 B
Price, Henry to Caroline Maddox 8-23-1867 (8-24-1867) B
Price, James to Sarah F. Stidam 12-14-1868 (12-16-1868)
Price, Mothen? R. to Frances G. Bounds 12-17-1849 (no return)
Price, N. B. to Mollie E. Millikin 6-9-1868 (6-10-1868)
Price, Peter to Willie Ann Williamson 2-4-1871 (no return) B
Price, Sam to Camelia Hobson 1-5-1867 (1-6-1867) B
Price, William M. to Minerva Teague 7-17-1846 (7-23-1846)
Price, Wm. M. to Frances Humphrey 2-26-1855 (no return)
Prichard, A. A. to Ella E. Chaffin 9-23-1868
Prichard, E. S. to Julia Moore 1-25-1859
Priddy, H. Leigh to C. D. Cole 10-29-1866 (10-31-1866)
Prince, Tom to Laura Williamson 8-3-1867 (no return) B
Proctor, Joseph M. to Joanna L. Scott 10-26-1868
Pugh, John to Mary Carnes 8-29-1867 (9-6-1867) B
Pulliam, A. B. to E. V. Pettit 6-4-1862
Pulliam, Bob to Easter Skipper 12-31-1867 (1-4-1868) B
Pulliam, Campbell to Mina Thornton 12-18-1865 (12-26-1865) B
Pulliam, D. K. to Mary E. Farley 2-5-1867 (no return)
Pulliam, J. J. to Lucy F. Burton 4-24-1850
Pulliam, John to Sophia Gray 12-20-1868 (12-28-1868) B
Pulliam, Zeb to Lucinda Thornton 1-22-1866 (2-28-1866) B
Qualls, Davy to Lucy Douglas 2-20-1869 B
Queen, Geo. W. to Caroline W. Griffin 1-31-1859
Quinn, G. W. to Virginia Griffin 9-21-1853 (no return)
Quinn, Robert to Jane A. Harris 5-14-1852 (no return)
Rachel, Thomas D. to Maryan Davis 1-8-1848
Rafe, J. W. to Martha A. Galleway 3-18-1847 (3-26-1847)
Ragland, Burrel to Eliza Mebane 12-29-1869 (12-9?-1869) B
Ragland, John to Betsy Watkins 12-28-1865 (12-30-1865) B
Ragsdale, Edward to Eliza A. L. Whitmore 8-20-1855 (no return)
Ragsdale, William to Paulina M. Pleasants 10-18-1847 (10-20-1847)
Rainey, Josiah F. to Tempy M. Irwin 9-9-1839 (9-10-1839)
Rainey, Samuel to Edie Dix 8-12-1865
Rains, Wm. H. to Eliza J. Tidwell 8-1-1848 (no return)
Ralph, A. G. to Mary A. Beavers 1-2-1860 (not endorsed)
Ralph, Absolum C. to Martha E. Waller 7-28-1852 (no return)
Ramsey, P. H. to Darthula Koonce 11-24-1852
Ramsey, T. J. to Sallie J. Newall 3-18-1862
Ramsey, Wm. B. to Sarah Moncreif 10-17-1854 (no return)
Randal, Alexander to Bettie Heaslett 3-27-1869 (no return) B
Randle, John B. to Elizabeth Moncrief 12-10-1853 (no return)
Raney, William R. to C. A. Coltharp 9-6-1839 (9-9-1839)
Rankin, Joseph to Lee Holloway 2-15-1870 (2-17-1870)
Rawlings, Reuben to Eliza Harris 4-24-1871 (4-25-1871) B
Rawlings, Wm. A. to Nancy M. May 4-30-1849 (5-2-1849)
Ray, William to Laura M. Alexander 12-14-1846 (12-22-1846)
Rayner, Eli to Maryann C. Jones 8-18-1841 (no return)
Raynor, Hill to Rose Gardner 12-24-1869 (no return) B
Read, Charles L. to Mary S. Taylor 7-20-1852 (no return)
Read, R. N. to S. A. Moore 9-22-1838 (no return)
Ready, Thos. J. to Duann W. Warford 9-18-1855 (no return)
Reames, G. H. to Mollie E. Hood 12-11-1867 (12-12-1867)
Reames, Henry J. to Mary T. Baker 1-29-1842 (2-1-1842)
Reames, J. B. to Sue Johnson 12-11-1867 (12-12-1867)
Reams, R. W. to Sarah A. Carter 7-12-1849

Reams, jr., M. J. to Bettie E. Hood 11-3-1870
Red, Jesse to Rosanna Pool 12-30-1869 (no return) B
Redd, Jesse to Martha A. Sumner 3-8-1859 (3-13-1859)
Reddick, Benj. F. to Laura A. Cleaves 1-27-1840
Reddick, D. to Martha W. Harmon 3-13-1852 (no return)
Reddick, Edward G. to Harriet Ann Mayo 3-13-1846 (3-18-1846)
Reddick, Henry to Mary Donnily 1-15-1869 (no return) B
Reddick, Thomas to Matilda Brown 3-16-1867 (3-18-1867) B
Redding, Forney W. to Martha Ann Ralph 8-2-1851 (no return)
Redding, George W. to Mary Payne 12-16-1869 (12-23-1869)
Redding, Sidney to Elizabeth Galloway 12-6-1853 (no return)
Redmond, M. A. to Mary Boswell 1-12-1848
Reed, David S. to Emma E. Blalock 12-19-1863 (12-24-1863)
Reed, Ephraim to Winney Ann Swift 1-7-1869 (2-4-1869) B
Reed, George to Lucy Battle 12-2-1869 (no return)
Reed, Pinkney to Cyntha Barker 5-9-1855 (no return)
Reeves, Benjamin to Jane Shields 12-27-1869 (12-30-1869) B
Reeves, P. J. to R. J. Martin 1-3-1863 (1-4-1863)
Reeves, Solomon to Lottie A. Miller 5-7-1868 (5-15-1868) B
Reeves, Thomas C. J. to Nancy W. Holmes 4-14-1853 (no return)
Reeves, W. C. to Mary McCarley 12-21-1852 (no return)
Reid, A. to Mary J. Roach 11-20-1838
Reid, Jno. B. to Wallace L. Neal 2-3-1859 (2-8-1859)
Reid, T. J. to Kate M. Neal 1-15-1868 (1-22-1868)
Reid, W. C. to Analine Bentley no date (with Jun 1855)
Renfroe, Jno. S. to H. C. Worrell 12-22-1868 (12-23-1868)
Renfroe, M. S. to Amanda Dougan 1-25-1860 (1-26-1860)
Revis, Hilliard to Fannie Williamson 1-11-1868 (1-12-1868) B
Rhea, James to Rebecca Bracken 3-30-1867 (no return) B
Rhea, John to E. L. Rhea 12-22-1840
Rhea, M. to Addie A. Tucker 12-14-1870
Rhea, Wm. A. to Mollie R. Irvin 2-11-1869
Rhea, jr., Matthew to H. H. (Mrs.) Boyd 9-15-1859
Rhodes, Bob to Jane Williamson 1-15-1868 (1-16-1868) B
Rhodes, Daniel to Malvina Mebane 3-19-1866 (3-22-1866) B
Rhodes, Henry to Rena Ward 11-13-1868 (11-16-1868) B
Rhodes, Henry to Sarah Coffy 1-12-1867 (not executed) B
Rhodes, James to Mary A. P. Morgan 6-26-1838
Rhodes, M. S. to H. J. Patton 12-11-1847 (12-23-1847)
Rhodes, Martin to Ann Cruis 12-21-1867 (12-22-1867) B
Rhodes, R. J. to Mattie T. Nevill 4-9-1866 (4-15-1866)
Rhodes, Robert E. to E. H. Lancaster 4-8-1839 (4-9-1839)
Rhodes, Simon to Sarah Williamson 1-15-1868 (1-16-1868) B
Rhodes, Vernon to Sarah M. Moody 7-22-1845 (7-23-1845)
Rhodgers, L. M. to M. E. Hilliard 4-5-1869 (4-9-1869)
Rice, C. H. to Ella Capers 12-19-1870 (12-20-1870)
Rice, Miles to Luella Jones 12-31-1868 B
Rich, C. W. to Elenor L. Alexander 8-22-1854 (no return)
Rich, Chas. W. to Mary E. Bounds 12-3-1844 (no return)
Rich, Joseph to Eliza Jane Grissom 12-23-1844 (12-25-1844)
Richards, Orrange to Caroline Tanner 10-29-1867 (10-30-1867) B
Richardson, C. W. to Mary Eliza Trotter 2-17-1845 (no return)
Richardson, Henry to Lizzie Wray 3-11-1871 (3-14-1871) B
Richardson, Jno. L. to Martha (Mrs.) Chives? 10-14-1844
   (10-17-1844)
Richardson, Saml. to Cary Rice 5-2-1846 (5-3-1846)
Richardson, Stephen to Laura Little 1-2-1871 (1-12-1871) B
Richardson, Wm. to Adaline Dickinson 5-26-1866 B
Richerson, Caleb W. to Eliza F. Gober 7-12-1839 (7-18-1839)
Richey, A. G. to Louving Gaitley 11-29-1869 (11-26?-1869)
Richey, James R. to Tennessee J. Baker 8-11-1852 (no return)
Richey, James to Gennett Humphrey 4-18-1840 (4-19-1840)
Richey, John M. to Lucy A. Sanders 1-6-1856 (1-9-1859)
Richey, Y. W. to Rutha Jane Baker 7-21-1852 (no return)
Richie, Jas. L. to Martha Humphrey 1-19-1850 (1-20-1850)
Richie, W. T. to Josephine Baker 10-10-1855 (no return)
Richison, Davy to Harriet Lester 1-2-1868 (1-4-1868) B
Richmond, Ben to Silva Coppedge 6-18-1869 (6-20-1869) B
Richmond, Esekel P. to Matilda Moore 7-31-1848 (4?-3-1848)
Richy, John to Louisa Bennett 2-3-1846 (2-5-1846)
Rickett, Thomas to Caroline Harris 1-7-1870 (1-8-1870) B
Rideout, Richard to Mollie Fields 12-28-1867 (no return) B
Ridley, Henry A. to Mary E. Smith 9-15-1853 (no return)
Ridley, R. R. to Mary C. Walker 9-10-1851 (no return)
Ridley, Thomas J. to Sarah L. Smith 6-9-1852 (no return)

Riggs, John W. to E. A. Gibson 12-26-1867
Riggs, Josiah to Rebecca Dunlap 1-23-1843 (1-24-1843)
Riggs, Thos. to Eliza J. Parish 5-29-1867 (5-30-1867)
Riggs, Thos. to Polly Davis 12-13-1853 (no return)
Riley, Wm. to Nelly Ann Harris 10-1-1869 (10-3-1869) B
Rinklin, Andrew to Christine Matmiller 5-9-1859 (5-10-1859)
Ritchie, J. M. to O. E. Shinault 12-1-1866 (12-4-1866)
Rivers, Archile to Rosietta Patterson 9-24-1870 B
Rivers, Dick to Jane Rivers 2-19-1870 B
Rivers, Dick to Martha Ann Patterson 2-12-1870 (2-13-1870) B
Rivers, Sandy to Jane Murphy 12-24-1868 (not executed) B
Rivers, Wallace to Eliza Jane Patterson 1-19-1871 B
Rivers, Wiley to Julia Williamson 1-24-1871 (2-2-1871) B
Rives, Christopher to Mary Ann Shelton 7-12-1838
Rives, E. D. B. to L. A. Williams 12-27-1854 (no return)
Rives, Evans to Rachel Dickinson 2-20-1869 B
Rives, Grandison to Henrietta Brown 12-25-1867 (12-26-1867) B
Rives, Henry A. to Mary Ann Taylor 11-22-1838
Rives, Jack to Lydia Ewell 11-19-1866 (11-20-1866) B
Rives, Richard to Catharine Poindexter 9-25-1869 B
Rives, Robert to Margaret Harvell 12-25-1866 B
Rives, W. M. to Sally A. Rives 9-17-1838
Rives, William A. to L. A. Scale 11-17-1851 (no return)
Rives, William C. to Lucy T. Ferress 12-16-1839 (12-17-1839)
Rives, William to Evelina Dickenson 1-3-1839
Roach, Kit to Adeline Granberry 8-19-1870 (no return) B
Roach, Kit to Harriet Alexander 12-7-1866 (12-8-1866) B
Roane, Lucas to Elmira Caraway 11-6-1869 (11-7-1869) B
Robards, Henry M. to Mary E. Harris 5-28-1867 (5-29-1867)
Roberson, James H. to Nancy T. Salmon 12-1-1847
Roberts, Calvin to Mary White 12-29-1866 (12-31-1866) B
Roberts, Henry D. to Mildred A. Compton 6-3-1853 (no return)
Roberts, James H. to Lucy Ann Gregg 9-3-1838 (no return)
Roberts, Louis? M. to Martha Jane Rawls 4-3-1848 (no return)
Roberts, Nelson to Milla Smith 1-18-1868 B
Roberts, William to Nancy Ewell 1-22-1869 (1-24-1869) B
Robertson, Alfred C. to Mary Bickerstaff 10-12-1838 (10-16-1838)
Robertson, F. M. to A. E. Erwin 1-10-1852 (no return)
Robertson, G. W. to Marry F. Winfield 2-10-1845
Robertson, G. W. to Mary Bull 1-22-1853 (no return)
Robertson, George to Harriet Baw 8-22-1867 (no return) B
Robertson, Green to Elvira Jones 1-27-1869 (1-28-1869) B
Robertson, Henry to Nannie Studivan 3-2-1870 (3-7-1870) B
Robertson, Joseph J. to Fatis C. Howell 4-12-1845 (4-15-1845)
Robertson, M. L. to Mary Jane Hill 2-25-1842 (3-3-1842)
Robertson, Rawlings to Martia McCarley 7-9-1846
Robertson, Sam to Mary Ozier 1-30-1869 (2-6-1869) B
Robertson, Thos. H. to Mary Jane Gurley 1-28-1848 (2-2-1848)
Robins, William to Jane King 12-17-1840
Robinson, Austin to Catherine Hamer 1-2-1868 (1-5-1868) B
Robinson, Ed to Frances Jones 12-24-1870 (no return) B
Robinson, Jno. B. to E. Douglass 3-26-1851 (no return)
Robinson, Oliver to Martha Ragland 2-17-1866 B
Robinson, Saml. B. to Sophrona J. Goodin 12-14-1848 (12-20-1848)
Robinson, Wm. to Eliza E. James 2-17-1860
Robson, Ira S. to Mary M. Snow 11-12-1870 (11-13-1870)
Rochelle, J. S. to Sarah Jane Jolly 3-27-1848 (3-29-1848)
Rodgers, Beverly A. to Lizzie D. Allison 8-9-1868 (no return)
Rodgers, Edmund S. to Mary Allen 4-18-1840
Rodgers, James to Polly Davis 4-14-1842
Rodgers, Jas. to Cornelia Harris 6-30-1849 (7-1-1849)
Rodgers, Wm. J. to Mary M. Pearce 12-4-1865 (12-6-1865)
Rogan, James W. to Alice L. W. Holloway 4-11-1871 (4-12-1871)
Rogers, G. P. to Mary E. Rivers 7-11-1870 (7-14-1870)
Rogers, H. S. to Susan A. Pickins 11-20-1867 (11-26-1867)
Rogers, James M. to Emila Simmons 5-21-1843 (no return)
Rogers, Louis to Emma Brown 12-7-1869 (no return) B
Rogers, Robert E. to Ann E. Harvey 10-6-1869 (10-7-1869)
Rogers, W. H. to M. E. Simerson 10-23-1866 (10-25-1866)
Rogers, W. J. to Elizabeth Wilds 1-15-1866 (1-18-1866)
Rogers, William to Eugenia Williams 1-30-1867
Rolfe, A. V. B. to Martha D. McClaran 12-12-1853 (no return)
Romine, Thomas to Ann Sneed 9-8-1843 (no return)
Rook, Benjamin to Sarah A. Jones 9-3-1866 (9-4-1866)
Rook, John M. to Martha K. Cheairs 1-17-1859 (1-18-1859)

Roper, Joshua to Nancy Stigall 6-19-1844 (6-20-1844)
Roscoe, William S. to William (Miss) Abington 10-19-1846
  (10-21-1846) B
Rose, Alex P. to Mary D. Gloster 1-22-1867 (1-24-1867)
Rose, J. H. to Mary J. Sullivan 10-28-1869 (10-31-1869)
Ross, Albert to Polly Williams 11-4-1869 (no return) B
Ross, Davy to Lou Taylor 12-23-1867 (12-27-1867) B
Ross, F. M. to Harriet Overton 2-24-1862
Ross, Henry to Fannie Williams 5-8-1869 (no return) B
Ross, LeGrand to Mollie Warren 12-18-1866 (12-19-1866) B
Ross, Peter B. to Rozana Overton 12-19-1849 (12-20-1849)
Ross, Thomas to Ophelia Lofton 1-3-1871 (1-15-1871) B
Row, Henry to M. Pool 4-16-1868 (no return) B
Row, Washington L. to Mary C. Stone 12-7-1842 (12-20?-1842)
Royall, J. P. to Sallie Appleberry 9-27-1869 (9-30-1869)
Roycroft, Calvin C. to Nancy E. Taylor 11-30-1846 (12-2-1846)
Rubotton, J. W. to Virginia C. Smotherson? 8-25-1854 (no return)
Ruby, J. G. to Elizabeth Hurley 12-16-1845
Runnals, Martin to Mary Harvy 4-9-1870
Russel, George to Susan Smith 8-20-1869 (8-22-1869) B
Russell, Cornelius to Lou Crawford 8-8-1868 (no return) B
Russell, David C. to Sarah Jones 12-4-1852 (no return)
Russell, R. P. to S. M. Bullock 1-31-1866 (no return)
Russell, Sidney C. to Julia E. Patterson 12-16-1867
Russell, William B. to Nancy Durham 9-22-1840 (9-24-1840)
Ruth, James V. to Rebecca Ballard 6-19-1843
Rutledge, Mat to Lucy Hammons 12-31-1866 (1-8-1867) B
Rutledge, Nathaniel to Elizabeth Speares 8-23-1843 (8-24-1843)
Rutledge, W. R. to Martha B. Hammons 4-6-1842
Saddler, Geo. to Margaret Tharp 1-23-1869 (no return) B
Sadler, John to Louisa C. David 7-1-1844 (7-10-1844)
Saffoon, Geo. to Puss Ellington 12-15-1868 (12-17-1868)
Sain, Henry to G. A. Clacks 12-10-1851 (no return)
Saines, Solomon to Elizabeth Moore 2-2-1870 (2-3-1870) B
Sale, James to Eliza Hill 5-5-1870 (no return)
Sample, Joseph to Sally Appleton 10-7-1850 (no return)
Sample, William to Bitsy Crain 11-26-1842 (12-1-1842)
Samples, Joseph to Margt. E. Cobb 11-9-1850 (11-10-1850)
Sampson, Henry to Susan Holt 10-27-1866 (no return) B
Samuson?, W. R. to Nancy Knott 12-18-1862 (no return)
Sanders, Aaron T. to Mollie F. Wells 1-18-1870 (1-19-1870)
Sanders, David H. to M. L. England 6-28-1859 (6-30-1859)
Sanders, Elijah B. to Emmeline J. Hailey 2-2-1866 (2-6-1866)
Sanders, J. W. to Elizabeth H. Wisson 1-31-1853 (no return)
Sanders, J. W. to Susan F. Hilliard 12-11-1865 (12-12-1865)
Sanders, Kelly to Elizabeth Pearson 3-12-1844 (no return)
Sanders, W. H. to Nancy E. Grizzle 1-11-1868 (1-12-1868)
Sanders, W. L. to Malissa Elder 7-14-1854 (no return)
Sanders, Wm. to Elmira Smith 12-21-1844 (12-22-1844)
Sandford, Richd. to Jane E. Alexander 5-17-1851 (no return)
Sane, Sampson H. to Lucyann E. Winfield 11-28-1838 (no return)
Sann, Rancelier to Emily L. Magit 6-19-1843 (6-21-1843)
Satterfield, Andrew C. to Caroline Robinson 4-2-1838 (no return)
Saunders, Pleasant P. to Hollandberry Atkins 8-26-1846 (8-27-1846)
Saunders, R. G. to Mahala C. Shaw 2-8-1842
Sawyers, Isaac O. to Martha A. Williams 5-9-1848 (5-10-1848)
Scales, J. M. A. to Virginia Whitmore 9-16-1854 (no return)
Scalhurst?, Washington to O. J. Smith 11-19-1852 (no return)
Scallions, Joseph to Martha Blessing 6-8-1847 (6-9-1847)
Schwar, John M. to Anna W. Rives 9-21-1868 (9-30-1868)
Scisco, Wm. to Martha Moncreif 9-18-1847 (9-23-1847)
Scott, Aleck to Evelin Jones 8-11-1866 (8-12-1866) B
Scott, Benj. to Eliza R. Campbell 1-25-1839 (1-31-1839)
Scott, Dock to Abbie Heaslett 2-11-1871 (no return) B
Scott, Geo. R. to Jennie Brooke 1-4-1870 (1-6-1870)
Scott, Henry F. to A. P. Ewell 8-1-1860 (8-2-1860)
Scott, J. V. to L. V. Cocke 12-20-1869 (no return)
Scott, J. T. to Arbelier F. Snellings 8-6-1869 (8-8-1869)
Scott, Jack to Jinney Fleece 8-15-1868 (8-19-1868) B
Scott, M. C. to Sallie F. Tarley 10-31-1867 (no return)
Scott, Richd. G. to Mary B. W. Edwards 11-2-1867 (11-5-1867)
Scott, T. W. to Roxanna Walker 8-11-1853 (no return)
Scott, William to Lila Hall 4-16-1870 (4-17-1870) B
Scott, Winfrey to Polly Baulkum 2-4-1839 (2-6-1839)
Scott, Wm. M. to Sarah O. Taylor 12-21-1844 (12-29-1844)

Scott, Wm. to Sarah A. Bruce 3-20-1843 (3-22-1843)
Scruggs, Edmund R. to Fannie M. Higgason 3-18-1868
Seaton, Geo. to Delina Griffin 5-13-1845 (5-16-1845)
Seaton, George W. to Heneretta Radford 8-26-1844 (8-27-1844)
Seaton, James to Maryann Helton 12-17-1838 (12-20-1838)
Seaton, John L. to Lucy Hart 11-17-1853 (no return)
Secrest, Jno. M. to Martha N. Parcham 1-16-1846
Selby, Edward to Fanny Shaw 10-9-1869 (10-20-1869) B
Sellas, Thomas to Johnita Isalm? 12-30-1847
Sellers, Archie to Eliza Chunn 3-11-1870 (3-12-1870) B
Sensing, Jno. P. to Margaret T. Bucy 9-5-1867 (9-10-1867)
Sensing, John P. to Nancy Moore 4-24-1841 (no return)
Sensing, William to Martha R. Drake 5-24-1847 (no return)
Session, Charles to Adaline Bott 3-23-1867 (3-30-1867) B
Session, Charles to Ann Pulliam 9-4-1868 (9-5-1868) B
Settle, Geo. Washington to Clara Johnson 1-7-1869 (no return) B
Sevier, Enoch to Rebecca M. Sullivan 1-5-1846 (1-6-1846)
Seward, Frank to Adeline Turnage 2-17-1869 (2-21-1869) B
Seward, Phillip M. to Nancyann Myers 1-27-1840 (2-6-1840)
Sewell, Joe to Arabella Boyle 2-7-1868 (2-8-1868) B
Seymore, Elisha S. to Julia A. Bullock 10-20-1847
Seymore, John K. to Ellin Barton 9-27-1842 (9-29-1842)
Seymour, Billy to Eliza Holloway 12-17-1870 B
Seymour, Henry to Candis Trousdale 12-29-1868 B
Seymour, James A. to M. A. Wall 11-7-1854 (no return)
Seymour, Tom to Lou Catron 1-16-1866 B
Shackelford, David to Sarah Heaslet 4-17-1869 (no return) B
Shackelford, Henry to Mary Heaslitt 3-9-1867 (no return) B
Shackleford, Zachariah M. to Sophia T. Mitchell 11-10-1846
  (11-12-1846)
Shaddinger, Nathan to Adaline Reeves 9-5-1867
Shafnor, B. D. to H. E. Thomas 8-22-1849 (no return)
Sharp, Geo. W. to Lucy E. McClaran 3-25-1846 (3-26-1846)
Sharp, Thomas to Elizabeth Millikin 10-8-1847 (10-10-1847)
Sharpe, Joseph A. F. to Martha C. Cloyed 9-24-1838 (10-2-1838)
Shaull, John to Elizabeth Paschal 8-13-1844 (8-14-1844)
Shaw, C. A. S. to Sallie N. Dickinson 4-25-1866 (4-26-1866)
Shaw, Caswell to Charity Walker 3-3-1866 (3-5-1866) B
Shaw, Charles J. to Malissa Webb 1-19-1848 (1-20-1848)
Shaw, F. to P. C. Burford 10-24-1850 (no return)
Shaw, Frank to Martha Loving 12-13-1867 (no return) B
Shaw, Frank to Sylva Galloway 10-1-1870 (10-8-1870) B
Shaw, Henry to Fannie Greggs 12-25-1867 (12-28-1867) B
Shaw, J. Q. to Pheriba Williams 7-13-1841 (7-14-1841)
Shaw, Jim to Lydia A. Williamson 2-8-1870 (2-10-1870) B
Shaw, John W. to Lizzie L. Higgason 3-3-1870
Shaw, Nelson to Fender Jones 12-28-1868 (1-15-1869) B
Shaw, Offy to Harriet Gaither 6-20-1868 (no return) B
Shaw, R. L. to Sophronia Patton 10-7-1865 (10-10-1865)
Shaw, Solomon H. to Caroline Douglass 4-22-1846
Shaw, Thomas to Joanna Macon 10-1-1869 (no return) B
Shaw, Vig to Annie Granberry 3-30-1871 (3-31-1871) B
Shaw, William to Lucinda Neel 12-27-1870 (1-7-1871) B
Shaw, Zachary to Frances E. Trotter 3-20-1855 (no return)
Shaw, Zack to Lizzie Brown 12-25-1866 (12-27-1866) B
Sheffield, Henry M. to Martha H. Ellington 2-25-1851 (2-26-1851)
Sheldon, E. Henry to Mary C. Cooper 10-3-1843 (no return)
Shelley, James to Mollie Newson 3-13-1869 (3-15-1869) B
Shelley, Wm. to Martha Gorman 2-1-1867 (7-6-1867) B
Shells, Raleigh to Mary Geter 4-7-1866 (4-22-1866) B
Shelton, E. O. to Martha Tucker 10-8-1849 (10-17-1849)
Shelton, J. M. to Martha A. Cross 8-7-1849 (8-21-1849)
Shelton, Jonas C. to Frances Ann Sherrod 12-26-1866 (12-28-1866) B
Shelton, L. V. to M. P. Cole 5-10-1859 (5-11-1859)
Shelton, Thomas to Caroline S. Thomas 2-5-1840 (2-7-1840)
Shelton, Tom to Mary Woodfolk 12-27-1867 (no return) B
Shelton, jr., Tho. Jeffreys to Matilda R. Mulliken 2-22-1864
Shepard, T. M. to Malinda M. Champion 9-28-1867
Shepherd, Alexander to Elizabeth Nettles 8-26-1841
Shepherd, Joe to History Allen 5-19-1870 (5-21-1870) B
Shepherd?, Melzer to Marion Radford 1-15-1851 (1-16-1851)
Sheppard, Isaac to Williametta Allen 2-22-1868 (no return) B
Sherrill, Samel to Elenor Eadon 11-18-1840
Sherrod, Alfred to Rosa Capers 12-27-1869 (12-30-1869) B
Sherrod, Ben to Lizzie Williams 8-31-1867 (no return) B

Sherrod, G. F. to C. H. Sayers 7-2-1868 (7-8-1868)
Sherrod, George to Virginia Sawyers 2-28-1866 (3-1-1866)
Sherrod, H. R. to Lilie C. Sayers 4-5-1869 (4-15-1869)
Shillings, W. J. to M. S. Baugh 7-31-1866
Shinault, A. J. to Amanda Campbell 8-29-1850
Shinault, Isaac to Nancy Brumley 2-2-1843
Shinault, Walter to N. C. Frasier 12-1-1866 (12-2-1866)
Ship, W. L. to N. J. Arbuckle 8-4-1859 (8-10-1859)
Shipley, John T. to Fanny L. Ellizer 6-2-1870 (7-25-1870) B
Shipp, J. W. to B. S. Crenshaw 4-30-1855 (no return)
Shivers, Oliver to Isabella Baird 11-16-1866 (11-25-1866) B
Shore, Thos. W. to Sarah Jane Tharp 3-12-1842 (3-15-1842)
Shryack, E. A. to Lou A. Alderson 3-2-1859 (3-8-1859)
Shuffield, John to Anne Diffy 10-10-1842
Shuford, W. S. to Ellen Grider 2-15-1851 (2-19-1851)
Siddle, John to E. Steel 12-29-1840 (12-31-1840)
Sikes, Joseph to Nancy Ross 3-3-1849
Simerson, John to Delilia Haskeah? 7-1-1841
Simison, John H. to Susan Ann Watson 11-9-1847
Simmerson, J. H. S. to Nancy J. Hall 12-21-1853 (no return)
Simmons, Augustus A. to Mary N. Elliott 11-25-1846 (11-26-1846)
Simmons, Garrett W. to Mary A. Johnson 10-27-1848 (10-29-1848)
Simmons, J. P. to Sarah J. Craig 8-24-1854 (no return)
Simmons, Jas. T. to Martha Thompson 10-7-1851 (no return)
Simmons, John to Matilda Fowler 2-28-1843 (3-1-1843)
Simmons, W. B. to Almeter Thompson 1-20-1852 (no return)
Simmons, W. J. to Mary W. Miller 2-25-1854 (no return)
Simmons, Wesley to Manervy Pryer 1-11-1870 (1-12-1870) B
Simpkins, W. D. to C. T. Chapman 2-6-1866 (2-8-1866)
Simpson, Thomas R. F. to Evelina W. Cash 1-6-1842
Sisco, J. C. to Virginia Carter 12-1-1868 (12-2-1868)
Siscoe, G. H. to Mary Didny? 12-23-1848 (no return)
Siscoe, John to Catharine H. McGehee 7-5-1842 (no return)
Skinner, Bernard E. to N. E. Soape 6-13-1845 (no return)
Skinner, Martin to Sarah A. Davis 12-23-1859 (12-25-1859)
Slater, Charles W. to L. E. Parchman 1-11-1843 (1-12-1843)
Slater, John W. to Nancy Sullivant 2-24-1845 (no return)
Slaughter, John J. to Mary J. Cross 3-8-1866 (3-11-1866)
Slaughter, Munrow to Tobitha Ana Mallard 4-21-1841 (4-25-1841)
Slaughter, W. C. to Frances A. Sullivan 11-18-1867 (11-19-1867)
Slaughter, Wiley to Matilda J. Simmons 12-16-1850 (12-23-1850)
Slaughter, Wilson to Algenie? Ozier 12-21-1839 (12-26-1839)
Sledge, Wm. H. to Ann D. McKendree 8-15-1850 (8-20-1850)
Sloane, James to Darthula Casey 7-18-1848 (no return)
Smith, A. G. to Sallie W. Owen 9-27-1870 (9-29-1870)
Smith, A. J. to Nancy Lakey 5-23-1848
Smith, Abe to Bettie Pearson 7-4-1868 (7-10-1868) B
Smith, Aleck to S. Jackson 12-13-1866 (12-16-1866)
Smith, Allen H. to Harriet D. McKee 1-25-1870 (no return)
Smith, Anthony to Dilcey House 11-23-1869 (11-28-1869) B
Smith, Bird to Jane Burnes 11-27-1839 (12-1-1839)
Smith, Carter to Phebe Ann Jefferson 12-31-1866 (no return) B
Smith, Charles to Adaline Dodson 9-14-1866 (9-16-1866) B
Smith, David L. to Mary Ann Sargent 2-22-1848
Smith, David T. to Malissa G. Boon 10-1-1844 (10-3-1844)
Smith, E. H. to Eliza W. Cater 5-5-1863 (5-6-1863)
Smith, E. J. to Jane Bailey 10-2-1867 (no return)
Smith, G. W. to L. F. Beasley 11-14-1853 (no return)
Smith, G. W. to Maryann McCall 1-15-1848 (1-17-1848)
Smith, G. W. to Sallie E. Hall 1-5-1866 (1-10-1866)
Smith, Geor. A. to Elizabeth Grider 12-27-1844 (1-7-1845)
Smith, George M. to Malinda A. Plant 1-11-1843 (1-12-1843)
Smith, George to Mariah Taylor 9-11-1868 (9-26-1868) B
Smith, Hamilton to Mary Bone 8-21-1866 (8-23-1866)
Smith, Henry to Ellen Burrough 12-4-1869 (no return) B
Smith, Isaac to Delia Harris 11-26-1869 (no return) B
Smith, J. N. to Sallie Campbell 9-1-1860 (9-2-1860)
Smith, J. P. to Mollie B. Alexander 3-23-1868 (3-29-1865)
Smith, J. V. to Mary (Mrs.) Patterson 12-18-1852 (no return)
Smith, James W. to Julia Ann Wright 11-30-1844 (no return)
Smith, James W. to R. O. Durham 12-27-1843 (12-28-1843)
Smith, Jas. P. to Sarah F Willis 3-12-1868 (no return) B
Smith, Jesse J. to Martha C. Batts 10-12-1846
Smith, John P. to Sarah Cleaves 3-10-1843 (no return)
Smith, John to Margaret Williams 10-23-1869 (10-24-1869)

Smith, John to Matilda Jane Wilson 1-20-1844
Smith, Jonas? M. to Mary McCauley 11-1-1848
Smith, Joseph H. to Virginia A. Hall 1-2-1869 (1-6-1869)
Smith, Joshua V. to Elizabeth A. Plant 6-14-1841 (6-15-1841)
Smith, L. J. to Katherine Darden 12-18-1868 (12-20-1868)
Smith, L. J. to Martha McCalley 9-19-1855 (no return)
Smith, M. W. to Bettie B. Hewitt 10-24-1869
Smith, Marion to Martha Perkins 12-7-1866 (12-16-1866)
Smith, P. E. to C. D. Boling 4-27-1853 (no return)
Smith, Peyton J. to Emma C. Sherrod 12-7-1870 (12-11-1870)
Smith, R. E. to S. E. Perkins 4-24-1860 (5-1-1860)
Smith, Robert to Charlotte Johnson 9-11-1869 (no return) B
Smith, Sam H. to Virginia C. Sugget 8-20-1855 (no return)
Smith, Sam to Harriet Taylor 9-6-1870 (9-21-1870) B
Smith, Sam to Nancy Jones 12-4-1869 (no return) B
Smith, Thomas J. to R. F. Whitehead 9-6-1853 (no return)
Smith, Washington to Isabella Adams 7-26-1869 (7-27-1869) B
Smith, William A. to Jane A. Smith 8-10-1848
Smith, William C. to Sally A. Cotton 6-3-1847 (6-10-1847)
Smith, William H. to Henrietta Mebane 7-27-1870 (no return) B
Smith, William M. to Mary E. Phillips 9-29-1869 (12-3-1869)
Smith, William to Fanny Turner 2-17-1869 (2-20-1869) B
Smith, William to Prissilla Gilliam 8-12-1841 (no return)
Smith, William to Susan M. Walker 1-5-1852 (no return)
Smith, Wm. M. to E. Julia Taylor 9-22-1853 (no return)
Smith, Wm. to July Ann Wiley 10-1-1849 (10-2-1849)
Smithwick, J. G. to Roanna Williams 5-24-1850 (5-26-1850)
Sneed, J. G. to Victoria Winston 11-26-1862 (11-27-1862)
Sneed, J. G. to Victoria Winston 11-26-1862 (not endorsed)
Sneed, Wm. B. G. to E. G. Anderson no dates (with Sep 1844)
Snelling, Henry to Judy J. Holloway 12-17-1849 (12-20-1849)
Snoden, Wm. H. to Sarah Taylor 6-17-1844 (6-26-1844)
Snow, Henry to Amelia Morris 4-14-1860 (4-22-1860)
Snow, Henry to Mary Shinalt 12-11-1844 (12-12-1844)
Snow, Stephen H. to Margaret Radford 8-19-1850 (8-22-1850)
Snow, Wm. to Anna Spencer 10-22-1849 (10-24-1849)
Snowden, James to Mahala Renfro 4-16-1855 (no return)
Soap, James S. to Jane Raiford 1-25-1840 (no return)
Somers, W. D. to Maria H. Ewell 12-25-1864
Somerville, Peyton to Margaret Hopper 12-26-1865 (no return) B
Soper, Jones L. to Jane Martin 1-2-1841 (no return)
Sorrel, Arris to Malinda Hall 12-7-1848
Sorrell, A. S. to Malissy Ferrell 5-3-1855 (no return)
Soung, John A. to Jane Rorrell 5-8-1847 (5-28-1847)
Southern, B. F. to Cynthia Averett 5-14-1859 (5-15-1859)
Sparks, J. E. to L. J. D. Matthews 9-28-1859
Sparks, James L. to Laura Mays 11-3-1870
Sparks, S. G. to M. C. McClellan 5-16-1866
Sparrow, George to Lucinda Demril? 4-17-1869 (no return) B
Spaulding, Richard to Phoeba Baird 10-8-1870 B
Speer, Dennis to Lucinda Moncreef 11-7-1838 (11-15-1838)
Spence, K. R. to S. P. (Mrs.) Harvey 12-16-1867
Spence, Wm. W. to Mary E. Butterworth 12-6-1847 (12-8-1847)
Sperry, R. A. to Amanda Goodner 10-1-1850 (10-2-1850)
Spiller, Geo. F. A. to Sarah (Mrs.) Hood 11-11-1862 (11-12-1862)
Springfield, Blunt to Elizabeth Degraftenreid 12-4-1843 (no return)
Springfield, Edward to Matilda Green 12-25-1866 (12-26-1866) B
Sprouce, William to Lucinda H. Broadwaters 12-9-1839 (12-10-1839)
Stacy, B. F. to C. M. Hamner 9-25-1852 (no return)
Stacy, James H. to Sopha Ann Cruse 9-4-1852 (no return)
Stacy, R. F. to Z. A. Farrar 7-21-1866 (7-22-1866)
Stafford, B. R. to D. C. Atkins 4-26-1854 (no return)
Stafford, B. R. to Julia A. Snelling 12-19-1856 (no return)
Stafford, Daniel J. to Hesterann Harrison 8-2-1841 (8-12-1841)
Stafford, J. B. to H. A. Stafford 6-22-1867 (6-23-1867)
Stafford, J. P. to Mary F. Stafford 10-6-1862 (10-7-1862)
Stafford, Jessee to Catharine Taylor 10-17-1851 (no return)
Stafford, Noah to Martha Montgomery 6-23-1868 (7-2-1868)
Stafford, Pinkney to Lucinda Robertson 2-14-1867 (2-15-1867)
Stafford, Thos. J. to Mary E. Bomer 2-24-1840 (2-27-1840)
Stafford, Vincent R. to Anna A. Burton 12-19-1838 (12-20-1838)
Stafford, W. B. to Martha C. Bowers 9-14-1847 (no return)
Stafford, W. J. to Sallie J. Talls (Falls?) 1-25-1868 (no return)
Stafford, Willis to America Walton 8-16-1866 (no return) B
Stafford, Willis to Elizabeth Robertson 12-22-1868

Stafford, Wm. H. to Maryann D. Hood 2-17-1845 (2-18-1845)
Stainback, Henry to Jennie Trent 7-13-1866 (not executed) B
Stainback, W. E. to Priscilla A. Williamson 4-25-1865 (4-26-1865)
Stallings, William to Emaline Amouse 1-8-1862 (1-9-1862)
Stallings, Wm. S. to E. J. Rideout 12-25-1860 (not executed)
Stallion, Archy to Nancy Ann Epps 12-13-1869 (12-26-1869) B
Stanback, Henderson to Matilda Powell 1-4-1871 (1-11-1871)
Stanley, H. J. to Georgia A. Mewborn 1-10-1871 (1-12-1871)
Stanley, John B. to Lucinda J. Crawford 8-26-1846 (no return)
Stanley, Solomon H. to Nancy A. Gilerland 12-16-1839 (no return)
Stanly, J. C. to Harriet J. Pratt 4-16-1847
Stanney, Napoleon to Frances Brown 2-1-1871 (2-4-1871) B
Stark, Joseph B. to Margaret A. Little 12-22-1868 (no return)
Stark, Joseph C. to Lamiza Ann Baird 4-22-1847
Stearns, Lamotte to Lizzie L. Klyce 1-22-1866 (1-23-1866)
Stedham, Anderson to Jane C. Johnson 4-12-1839
Stedham, William to Eliza Sowell 12-14-1848 (no return)
Stedham, Wm. to F. L. Henley 7-2-1860 (7-12-1860)
Steel, Jno. B. to P. E. Slow 9-27-1859 (9-28-1859)
Steel, Ninian F. to Phebe A. Wilson 8-27-1846 (no return)
Steele, Doctr. G. T. to E. A. Williams 9-4-1851 (no return)
Steger, Anderson to Cherry Jones 2-14-1870 (2-23-1870) B
Steger, John J. to Evalina A. Raiford 6-9-1848 (6-11-1848)
Stein, Jefferson W. to Sarah A. Dyre 3-13-1843 (no return)
Stephens, W. D. to Jane Hertle 12-23-1868 (12-25-1868)
Stephens, Wm. H. to Candas Stafford 11-20-1867 (11-21-1867)
Stephenson, Elijah to Dovey L. M. Ammons 10-25-1842
Stevens, John to Cordelia Tatum 12-25-1866 (12-26-1866)
Stevens, Lewis to Frances Stevens 1-19-1844 (1-24-1844)
Stevens, Robert to Ann Maddox 9-23-1860 (not endorsed)
Stevens, Samuel L. to Mary Rosan 8-18-1840 (no return)
Stevens, Wm. H. to Mary M. Stafford 11-1-1862 (not endorsed)
Stevenson, J. C. to Martha Stewart 8-12-1863
Stevenson, W. G. to M. C. Clutch 6-25-1863 (6-28-1863)
Steward, James A. to Emma Dodson 4-22-1862 (4-23-1862)
Steward, Wm. M. to Sarah J. Stram 12-14-1850 (12-17-1850)
Stewart, Calvin E. to Catharin Baw 12-28-1851 (no return)
Stewart, E. A. to Margaret Neel 12-5-1860
Stewart, Edward D. to Winny Ann Baw 12-30-1845
Stewart, Geo. M. to Angelina Branch 1-7-1846
Stewart, George to Frances Fletcher 12-20-1869 B
Stewart, Ham to Ann Caldwell 11-27-1865 (no return)
Stewart, Henry to Joanna Joiner 5-11-1867 (no return) B
Stewart, Marcus H. to Mary Ann Leznik 12-19-1848 (12-21-1848)
Stewart, N. R. to Elizabeth Webb 12-29-1855 (no return)
Stewart, Tom to Emily Armour 11-18-1865 B
Stewart, U. T. to Mary Baugh 9-?-1854 (no return)
Still, J. H. to Eliza Compton 12-1-1854 (no return)
Stith, R. S. to A. M. Phillips 2-14-1854 (no return)
Stokes, Micajah to Virginia A. Hedges 7-7-1870
Stone, Jacob to Mary Jane Williams 5-30-1842
Stone, R. C. to B. A. Thomas 12-31-1866 (1-3-1867)
Stone, Robert to Matty A. Fowler 7-8-1846 (7-13-1846)
Stoops, Geo. N. to J. J. Earnheart 7-2-1869 (7-4-1869)
Stott, Henry to Allice Bridgewater 2-18-1871 (3-1-1871) B
Stout, William to Emeline Hunter 12-26-1868 (12-27-1868) B
Stover, R. B. to Phereby Whyte 9-8-1866 (9-10-1866)
Strange, J. to Delila J. Burns 4-11-1842 (4-12-1842)
Straughn, James M. to Mary L. Abbernathy 7-11-1846
Strickland, Robt. to Caledonia Grantham 7-10-1868 (no return)
Stricklin, George W. to Elizabeth White 9-30-1843 (no return)
Strong, Benjamin to Charlott Hanness 3-15-1847 (no return)
Strong, Thos. J. to Martha Williams 11-11-1870 (11-16-1870)
Studvant, Andrew J. to Frances A. Reeves 9-7-1852 (no return)
Stull, Stephen to Phoebe Cannon 7-21-1866 (7-22-1866) B
Suffield, W. to Mary Rogers 12-21-1841 (12-25-1841)
Suggett, Benjamin B. to Parthena B. Holloway 1-27-1846 (1-28-1845?)
Sullivan, Jeff to Mariah McNeill 8-10-1870 (8-11-1870) B
Sullivan, Thomas to Elizabeth Ann Darley 6-11-1855 (no return)
Sullivant, Charles W. to Mary E. Davis 7-23-1850 (no return)
Sullivant, Jesse H. to Mary An Bell 12-12-1848 (12-14-1848)
Sullivant, Rhesa? R. to Elizabeth Edwards 1-4-1842 (1-11-1842)
Summers, J. A. to Callie E. Burnett 1-25-1869 (1-27-1869)
Summers, John W. to Margaret E. Turner 10-1-1870 (10-6-1870)
Sumner, David W. to Catharine E. Redd 6-7-1841 (not endorsed)

Sumner, Marcus D. L. to Sarrah D. Higganson 4-18-1843 (4-25-1843)
Sutton, B. J. to Martha E. Hampton 9-2-1865 (9-4-1865)
Sutton, Elijah to Vina Mebane 12-12-1867 (12-15-1867) B
Sutton, James T. to Mary Ann Pinchback 4-18-1848 (4-19-1848)
Sutton, James to Susan Brinkly 10-18-1844 (10-19-1844)
Swaggart, Littleberry S. to Ruthy Jane Yarbrough 1-17-1842 (no return)
Swann, T. B. to L. A. Freeman 5-15-1860
Sweat, Emery to Emma Pane 3-30-1868 (4-2-1868)
Sweat, L. T. to Thedonia Harris 3-14-1868 (3-16-1868)
Swift, Andrew to Lotta Morris 2-2-1870 (no return) B
Swift, Carns M. to Mary E. Mayo 7-29-1844
Swift, Thos. J. to Sarah L. Mayo 2-1-1850 (2-5-1850)
Swift, V. H. to Caledonia Harrell 11-12-1859 (11-13-1859)
Swift, William to Cresa Reid 4-20-1867 (no return) B
Swiney, C. to Mary Roberts 1-11-1870 (1-12-1870)
Swinney, John to Mary Ann Bradshaw 3-23-1869 (3-24-1869)
Swinny, Lewis to Elizabeth Wright 12-25-1852 (no return)
Sykes, Miles W. to Jane Fitshugh 11-25-1847 (11-27-1847)
Talafairo, John F. to Ann Mariah Leonard 2-24-1851 (2-26-1851)
Taler, Wm. H. to Chartally Scallions 7-29-1841
Tallent, John H. to Rebecca Adkins 5-16-1842
Tappan, Isaac to Emily Williams 1-4-1867 B
Tappan, Mose to Martha Littlejohn 3-1-1869 (3-5-1869) B
Tappan, Thos. to Amy Carpenter 12-22-1870 B
Targart, A. J. to M. C. Durham 12-18-1854 (no return)
Tarver, Thomas D. to Wilmouth O. Edmondson? 8-22-1854 (no return)
Tarwater, George T. to Lucy Ann E. Lane 12-3-1844 (12-5-1844)
Tate, Andrew to Ann Malone 12-24-1869 (no return) B
Tate, Edmund to Lila Heaslett 1-22-1869 (no return) B
Tate, Henry to Margaret Haselett 7-19-1867 (no return) B
Tate, Samuel to Mary Carnes 4-19-1843
Tate, William to Jane Crook 12-24-1869 (no return) B
Tatem, Edward W. to Rebecca H. Copeland 2-10-1849
Tatom, G. W. to Mary E. Morris 10-8-1867 (10-12-1867)
Tatum, A. J. G. to Susan McAdams 12-26-1839
Tatum, A. R. to Allice B. Stewart 12-20-1869 (12-23-1869)
Tatum, Dick to Sophia Rivers 1-1-1870 (1-27-1870) B
Tatum, E. W. to H. A. E. Oats 12-27-1849 (no return)
Tatum, Edward W. to Elizabeth B. Manning 4-7-1851 (4-8-1851)
Tatum, Frank to Lucinda Taylor 3-31-1866 (4-1-1866) B
Tatum, G. W. to Alletha T. Turnbow 9-28-1852 (no return)
Tatum, Geo. W. to Mattie L. Holt 11-13-1860
Tatum, H. A. to Elizabeth N. Ingram 9-19-1851 (no return)
Tatum, J. G. to E. A. Brown 1-11-1866 (1-14-1866)
Tatum, Jackson to Martha Jane Holliday 9-11-1847
Tatum, John G. to Mary P. Clifton 1-18-1841 (1-21-1841)
Tatum, Nathaniel to Matilda Broyles 11-23-1843 (11-25-1843)
Tatum, R. E. to Susan H. Oates 11-15-1852 (no return)
Tatum, Richard to Margaret Eason 11-4-1845 (no return)
Taylor, Alvin E. to Martha A. Taylor 1-2-1860 (1-3-1860)
Taylor, Anderson to Matty Mathews 12-26-1868 (12-28-1868) B
Taylor, Andrew to Mary C. Mitchell 3-31-1846 (4-2-1846)
Taylor, Anthony to Peggy Miller 12-28-1865 (no return)
Taylor, Frank M. to Mollie D. Thompson 11-24-1868 (11-26-1868)
Taylor, Franklin to Flora Thomas 12-21-1868 (12-25-1868) B
Taylor, H. H. to Roann Houston 7-21-1864
Taylor, H. S. to Jane Eliza Mayo 9-18-1846 (no return)
Taylor, Henry S. to Louise E. Hunter 10-16-1838
Taylor, J. D. to M. W. Williams 1-6-1862 (1-8-1862)
Taylor, J. F. to Martha Chambers 12-29-1866 (12-30-1866)
Taylor, James to Kittie Turnley 5-18-1867 B
Taylor, Jim to Fannie Taylor 4-18-1868 (no return) B
Taylor, Jim to Linda McNeil 1-6-1866 (no return) B
Taylor, John M. to Judis A. Lemons 10-9-1848 (10-11-1848)
Taylor, John M. to Tobitha Speer 8-16-1838
Taylor, Jordan to Emeline Hunter 12-28-1866 (12-28-1866) B
Taylor, Joseph to Ellen Groves 6-2-1866 (6-17-1866) B
Taylor, Lewis to Eliza Morrow 3-27-1869 (4-1-1869) B
Taylor, Lihue to Elenida Woldram 7-29-1839 (8-1-1839)
Taylor, Mat to Adeline Hart 2-5-1869 (2-9-1869) B
Taylor, Peter to Bettie Reddick 3-2-1866 (3-3-1866) B
Taylor, Rufus C. to Mollie Shaw 5-7-1869 (no return)
Taylor, Senson to Amy Coffin 8-21-1869 (8-22-1869) B

Taylor, Stephen to Ann McNeil 1-6-1866 (no return) B
Taylor, W. H. to Rutha E. Christman 2-12-1853 (no return)
Taylor, William A. to Martha W. N. Bland 4-17-1839 (4-24-1839)
Taylor, William P. to Manerva A. Brooks 1-6-1851 (1-7-1851)
Taylor, Wm. to Frances Collier 6-6-1868 B
Teagner, Henry to Caroline Ross 12-26-1867 B
Teague, Anderson to Ellen Strickland 8-25-1866 (8-26-1866) B
Teague, C. M. to N. A. Baird 10-27-1860 (10-30-1860)
Teague, James Welborn to Julia Ann Torrance 12-18-1860 (12-19-1860)
Teague, James to Mary A. Duke 10-23-1866 (10-24-1866)
Teague, Spencer to Lavinia Crutcher 9-20-1866 (9-21-1866) B
Teague, W. S. to M. R. Chambers 1-31-1864 (2-2-1864)
Teague, William to Temperance Whitehead 12-6-1845 (12-11-1845)
Teel, James E. to Mary Ann Gailor 10-18-1841
Teel, P. M. to A. Johnson 11-13-1847 (11-18-1847)
Teel, Westley C. to A. F. Holland 3-23-1843 (3-24-1843)
Temple, J. W. to Harriet E. Wells 12-17-1862 (12-28-1862)
Terry, M. T. to Clara A. Olive 12-21-1868 (12-22-1868)
Tharp, Gilliam to Rebecca Jane Nail 12-25-1847 (12-28-1847)
Tharp, Granville to Dora Wells 12-14-1870 B
Tharp, Jessee J. to Sarah Ann Moor 1-29-1851 (1-30-1851)
Tharp, W. H. (Dr.) to Susan P. Whitmore 11-22-1852 (no return)
Tharp, William A. to Candis A. Evans 2-23-1846 (3-3-1846)
Therrell, Wm. to M. M. Burklow 11-6-1868 (no return)
Thomas, Abner D. to Margarett Ann Thomas 2-12-1845 (no return)
Thomas, Benj. to Sally Brodnax 2-2-1867 (no return) B
Thomas, Friday to Dinah Henderson 1-5-1867 B
Thomas, George to Henrietta Morrow 5-10-1867 (5-20-1867) B
Thomas, Guriah to Sarah Moreland 2-28-1871 (4-3-1871) B
Thomas, J. B. to C. B. Maury 12-21-1865
Thomas, J. M. to Amanda Clark 12-6-1865? (12-9-1862)
Thomas, J. W. to Margaret Thompson 2-27-1865
Thomas, John M. to Lucy Q. (Mrs.) Beasly 4-8-1844 (no return)
Thomas, John to Pink Warren 9-7-1867 (no return) B
Thomas, Joseph to Jane McDowell 2-28-1871 (9-22-1873) B
Thomas, Marshall to Sallie Karr 9-4-1868 (9-12-1868) B
Thomas, Saml. H. to Mattie E. Polk 2-8-1871 (no return)
Thomas, William F. to Lucy A. E. Hally 3-3-1841
Thomas, William to Mattie Thomas 10-24-1870 B
Thomas, Wm. T. to Mary J. Fraser 9-12-1861
Thompson, B. L. to Cornelia Grissom 11-15-1851 (no return)
Thompson, Bonaparte to Harriett Reed 1-22-1870 B
Thompson, Cary to Fanny King 5-2-1867 (5-5-1867) B
Thompson, David to Harriet Wilson 5-4-1866 (5-6-1866)
Thompson, Geo. W. to Catharine G. Green 12-10-1845
Thompson, Henry to Rachael Tatom 12-6-1870 (12-21-1871) B
Thompson, Heyborrow? to Betsy Titcomb 5-19-1866 (no return) B
Thompson, James H. to Julia N. P. Koonce 12-11-1850
Thompson, James M. to Louisa Harrison 10-5-1843
Thompson, James W. to Lucy Janie Waller 2-9-1839 (2-12-1839)
Thompson, John T. to Jane McGehee 5-3-1838 (no return)
Thompson, John T. to Martha Ann Bounds 8-10-1846 (8-13-1846)
Thompson, John to Eliza Duke 12-22-1870 (12-25-1870)
Thompson, John to Lavina Farrar 10-10-1866 (10-15-1866) B
Thompson, John to Mary J. Wilkins 11-10-1843 (no return)
Thompson, Joseph to Perlina McFadden 3-2-1870 (3-17-1870) B
Thompson, Joseph to _____ Kellin no date (with Mar 1838)
Thompson, Joshua to _____ Skillen no dates (with May 1838)
Thompson, Monroe to Vic Williamson 12-25-1867 B
Thompson, P. C. to Virginia A. Hodges 12-3-1868 (no return)
Thompson, Sam to Sarah Ann Temple 3-26-1868 (no return) B
Thompson, Washington to Mary Forbs 12-5-1839 (12-18-1839)
Thompson, William H. to Margarett L. Bell 4-4-1855 (no return)
Thomson, John B. to Eliza F. Beaver 12-23-1867 (12-24-1867)
Thornton, A. H. to Sallie F. Thornton 5-2-1866 (5-3-1866)
Thornton, Hamilton to Mary A. Johnson 12-17-1856 (no return)
Thornton, J. V. to M. C. Lay 9-27-1859 (9-28-1859)
Thornton, James B. to Mary E. Cox 4-21-1870
Thornton, Patrick to Lucy Whitmore 7-26-1867 (7-27-1867) B
Thornton, W. H. to Nancy Mass 11-28-1848 (11-6?-1848)
Thurman, Wash to Bettie Thornton 8-26-1869 (8-28-1869) B
Tilghman, A. G. to Catharine M. Boyet 11-24-1855 (no return)
Tiller, George W. to Maryann Robinson 10-19-1839 (5-13-1840?)
Tiller, John W. to Mary E. Rodgers 8-6-1860 (8-16-1860)

Tiller, Thos. H. to Martha J. Williams 11-7-1868 (11-9-1868)
Tillman, James M. to Nancy C. Davis 7-31-1869 (8-3-1869)
Tillmon, A. D. to E. A. Moffett 11-9-1859
Tilson, Henry to Burda Williamson 4-1-1871 (4-2-1871) B
Tines, Henry to Jane Goode 6-17-1867 (6-22-1867) B
Tipton, P. M. to Charity Tumbough 8-3-1843
Tipton, Quincy A. to Mary C. Chrismon 9-1-1841
Todd, J. K. to Harriet J. Barker 1-1-1867
Todd, J. L. to L. J. Todd 3-3-1866 (3-4-1866)
Todd, James A. to Sarah Ann Ward 9-3-1844 (9-4-1846)
Todd, James A. to Sarah Ann Ware 9-3-1846 (no return)
Todd, Wm. W. to Frances C. Suggett 8-26-1865
Tomlinson, H. C. to D. T. Turner 6-14-1865 (6-15-1865)
Tomlinson, John to Lucy H. Moore 9-3-1850 (9-12-1850)
Tomlinson, Junius to G. A. Yates 2-5-1868
Tonage, David E. to Mary J. Askew 11-25-1851 (no return)
Towles, Anthony to Sally Boals 12-28-1868 (12-30-1868) B
Towlkes, T. J. to Julia A. Burton 7-16-1857
Towns, Archy to Adaline Knox 12-4-1868 (12-7-1868) B
Townsend, O. L. to Sallie E. Bass 12-16-1868 (12-17-1868)
Trainer, Barnett M. to Elizabeth Brumley 6-27-1839 (7-4-1839)
Trainer, John H. to Adaline R. Wiles 1-23-1867 (1-24-1867)
Trent, Adam to Judith Alford 9-2-1866
Trent, William H. to Martha G. Jackson 3-14-1846 (3-17-1846)
Triller?, John to Virginia Whitney 4-22-1853 (no return)
Trimble, Frank to Lilly Shelton 1-6-1870
Tripp, Jno. W. to Louiza Brace 5-4-1868 (5-10-1868) B
Tripp, Thomas A. to Adelia (Dibzorah?) Galloway 3-10-1866 (3-11-1866)
Tripp, Thos. A. to Sallie Hicks 5-26-1869 (5-27-1869)
Trotter, B. Y. to Obediance E. Hall 10-10-1848
Trotter, G. W. to Lucy A. Abernathy 7-21-1851 (7-22-1851)
Trotter, George W. to Elizabeth Ball 1-10-1844
Trotter, Henry J. to Melvina Conner 1-26-1848
Trotter, Joseph H. to Ruth W. Harrison 7-6-1846 (7-9-1846)
Trotter, Joseph H. to Sarah Jane Cloyed 9-22-1852 (no return)
Trotter, W. B. to Frances Jordan 1-13-1844 (1-16-1844)
Trout, Leland to Marietta Swift 12-10-1866 (no return)
Trowell, Francis to Sarah Cook 8-12-1846
Truesdale, Jack to Josephine Ragland 12-4-1866 (no return) B
Trulove, Jas. H. to Mary A. Honey 6-17-1846 (6-18-1846)
Trump, H. to Mitta Beasley 11-2-1867 (11-4-1867)
Trusdale, Andrew to Abby E. Braden 11-22-1869 (no return) B
Tucker, George to Harriett Shelton 1-8-1869 (1-9-1869) B
Tucker, J. W. to Sallie A. Mayfield 9-26-1866 (9-27-1866)
Tucker, Jessie to Sallie Ann Tucker 4-10-1869 (4-11-1869) B
Tucker, Joseph C. C. to Mary A. Jackson 7-3-1843 (7-6-1843)
Tucker, Lewis to Nancy Jones 11-9-1868 (11-13-1868) B
Tucker, Monroe to Hannah Hare 12-28-1865 (1-1-1866) B
Tucker, Robert to Mary Williams 12-25-1868 (12-26-1868) B
Tucker, Robt. G. to Sallie E. Lanier 10-5-1868 (10-6-1868)
Tuggle, Tho. R. to Elizabeth Burford 10-1-1846 (no return)
Tunadge, John D. to Susan Montague 1-22-1844 (1-24-1844)
Turnbull, William to Judy Jenkins 4-13-1866 (4-15-1866) B
Turner, Antny to Lucy Walker 1-28-1870 (1-30-1870) B
Turner, Bob to Lila Armstrong 5-2-1868 (no return) B
Turner, C. L. to India D. Graves 10-28-1867 (10-31-1867)
Turner, Charles B. to Susan A. Keeton 1-7-1867 (1-8-1867)
Turner, E. B. to Roena R. Ruffin 9-21-1867 (9-25-1867)
Turner, H. B. to C. C. Smith 12-16-1867 (12-19-1867)
Turner, J. L. to Mary A. Locke 12-26-1853 (no return)
Turner, J. W. to Sarah J. Mitchell 12-9-1846 (no return)
Turner, James N. to E. C. Culbreth 2-19-1868 (no return)
Turner, John B. to Arminda D. Johnson 4-7-1863
Turner, Joseph to Matilda C. Smith 10-11-1841 (10-21-1841)
Turner, M. L. to Marthann Allen 10-13-1847 (10-19-1847)
Turner, Presley to Mary D. Gillmore 1-4-1869 (1-6-1869)
Turner, Simon to Julia M. Leonard 6-28-1853 (no return)
Turner, W. A. to Ann Eliza Jones 5-14-1850
Turner, William W. to Tryphena Pearson 11-1-1845 (no return)
Turnley, George W. to Anna Miller 7-19-1853 (no return)
Tyler, David C. to Celia A. Askew 3-1-1869
Tyler, George to Betsey Willson 1-2-1869 B
Umphlett, John to Rachell W. Croom 6-4-1853 (no return)
Underwood, W. L. to Margarett Myres 11-5-1838 (11-6-1838)

Ursery, Calvin to Elizabeth Hutchins 12-20-1844 (12-19?-1844)
Van Buren, Martin to Isabella Roberts 12-27-1870 (12-29-1870) B
Van Pelt, John W. to Sarah Ann Bounds 9-7-1840 (9-24-1840)
Van, Charley to Harriet Haselett 5-15-1868 (no return) B
Vance, Hezekiah to Mary Newsom 10-23-1869 (10-29-1869) B
Vanderpool, Samson to Arilia D. Rogers 5-26-1842 (5-29-1842)
Vann, James S. to Eliza Gregory 8-30-1846 (no return)
Vanpelt, Israel to Susan Crawford 11-29-1870 (12-20-1870 B
Vanpelt, Wm. T. to Eliza Roffner? 9-27-1844
Vaughan, Nat to Malinda Brown 12-10-1868 (no return) B
Vaughan, Richard to Matilda P. Trotter 1-8-1840 (1-10-1840)
Vaughn, Peter A. to Mary E. Whitmore 12-18-1848 (1-2-1849)
Vaysor?, Mack to Cornelius Dobbins 4-16-1868 (no return) B
Verser, John L. to Mary A. Dickason 11-23-1846 (11-24-1846)
Verser, Wm. A. to Jane Broom 10-1-1841
Vest, William to N. A. Ross 7-29-1870 (8-4-1870)
Vestal, Thos. N. to Demaris Starrett 1-1-1845 (1-2-1845)
Vick, A. R. to Sarah J. West 10-21-1859
Vick, John T. to Lucy M. Belote 11-15-1851 (no return)
Vinson, Hiram C. to Martha Kendall 11-19-1844
Viser, Wm. C. to Jane E. Watkins 6-25-1844 (no return)
Von Negler, Henry to Mary F. Muller 12-24-1866
Waddall, C. W. to M. C. Smith 8-21-1838
Waddell, Alex P. to Isabella S. Miller 6-6-1853 (no return)
Waddell, John C. to Elizabeth D. Bugg 8-15-1846
Waddell, Wm. to Ella Houston 2-8-1868 (no return) B
Wade, Henry E. to Mary E. Terrence 12-19-1854 (no return)
Wade, John F. to Margarett Farmer 12-22-1870 (12-23-1870)
Wade, Richard T. to Sarah J. Terrence 12-19-1853 (no return)
Wagener, J. L. to S. B. Stafford 10-23-1866 (10-30-1866)
Wain, John to Frances Fartherlain 8-12-1838
Wainwright, Charles to Cornelia Taylor 4-23-1866 (4-28-1866) B
Wainwright, Geo. F. to Sarah O. Limon? 1-4-1847 (1-13-1847)
Walden, B. A. to Unity Cammond 10-3-1853 (no return)
Walden, W. H. to M. M. V. Churchhill 11-7-1865 (11-9-1865)
Walis, John to Mary E. McCully 1-3-1853 (no return)
Walker, Bob to Jinney Norman 1-9-1869 (no return) B
Walker, Cato to Lucinda Perry 1-2-1871 (1-5-1871) B
Walker, Epps to Lucinda Williams 10-30-1869 B
Walker, H. B. to Malinda Southerland 2-9-1842 (2-10-1842)
Walker, Hiram S. to Maryann Biggs 11-29-1847
Walker, J. R. to Sarah Ann Young 10-22-1850
Walker, Jim to Mary Pulliam 12-24-1867 (12-25-1867) B
Walker, Jno. to Martha E. Privett 10-14-1868 (10-21-1868)
Walker, Joe to Ann Pirtle 12-31-1866 (1-1-1867) B
Walker, John B. to Sarah C. Sellers 4-5-1844 (no return)
Walker, John to Eliza Hall 11-25-1852 (no return)
Walker, John to Lucinda Broom 1-4-1868 (no return) B
Walker, M. B. to M. J. Benson 3-17-1848 (3-29-1848)
Walker, Matthew to Nancy Davis 1-28-1868 (2-1-1868) B
Walker, Moses to Mary Bridgewater 5-1-1867 (5-4-1867) B
Walker, Pli to Sarah B. Hamblet 12-31-1849 (1-2-1850)
Walker, R. L. to Sallie A. Pulliam 12-4-1866 (12-29-1866)
Walker, Simon H. to Edna B. Frazier 7-3-1849 (7-4-1849)
Walker, Temple C. to Mary C. Buly? 5-6-1848 (5-7-1848)
Walker, William B. to Sarah Ann Page 6-2-1838
Walker, William J. to Adaline Moore 11-4-1846
Walker, William W. to Nancy H. Taylor 6-22-1848 (no return)
Walker, William to Nellie Baker 12-31-1868
Walkup, James to Mollie Cogbill 8-17-1867 (8-18-1867)
Wall, J. B. to E. M. Love 1-23-1866 (1-24-1866)
Wall, J. J. to Fannie Champion 1-10-1867
Wall, J. N. to M. J. Seymour 4-27-1853
Wall, Nelson to Susan Tharp 8-3-1847 (8-11-1847)
Wall, Oney C. to Fanny Caraway 2-14-1867
Wall, Phil to T. Hayslett 2-12-1869 (no return) B
Wall, W. B. to Susan Herron 1-24-1866 (1-25-1866)
Wall, W. T. to N. B. OKelly 11-22-1864 (11-24-1864)
Wallace, Jas. R. to Laura F. Marshall 10-13-1868 (10-17-1868)
Wallace, R. C. to M. T. Crawford 3-5-1850 (no return)
Wallace, Wm. to Mary Montague 10-29-1867 (11-6-1867)
Waller, A. C. to Mariah C. Hatley 8-4-1845 (8-5-1845)
Waller, A. to M. E. Blain 12-20-1852 (no return)
Waller, C. M. to A. E. Pulliam 2-7-1859 (2-8-1859)
Waller, E. M. to Lucy Reed 1-21-1851 (no return)

Waller, Edward G. to Martha F. Waller 2-7-1845 (2-18-1845)
Waller, H. B. to R. E. Wiggins 12-14-1869 (no return)
Waller, Jesse to Jennie Culp 1-29-1870 (3-6-1870) B
Waller, L. G. to Susan A. Waller 4-27-1846 (5-3-1846)
Waller, M. M. to Margarett N. Leonard 9-30-1847 (no return)
Waller, Thomas J. to Clarissa Reed 1-1-1847 (1-7-1847)
Walls, J. B. to A. C. Richey 1-30-1869
Walls, J. M. to Julia A. Dover 9-8-1870
Walthall, John A. to Sarah ann Elder 6-13-1848 (6-18-1848)
Walton, Alfred J. to Ann E. Currin 3-20-1843 (no return)
Walton, David to Mahala Brown 12-28-1870 (12-29-1870) B
Walton, Frank to Malinda Reams 12-24-1868 B
Walton, John to Nancy Rivers 12-26-1870 (1-2-1871) B
Walton, Peter to Rosena Dickinson 12-25-1866 (12-27-1866) B
Walton, Solomon R. B. to Issabella T. Cobb 4-25-1839
Walton, Thomas to Lucy Walton 1-9-1867 (1-17-1867) B
Walton, Willis to Malinda Waller 12-11-1860
Ward, A. M. to Martha A. McClaron 2-16-1859 (2-17-1859)
Ward, Benj. to C. J. McNamee 3-20-1860 (3-21-1860)
Ward, Chas. to Julia A. F. Canada 12-16-1867 (12-20-1867)
Ward, Geo. to Minerva Hass 11-25-1850 (11-26-1850)
Ward, John A. to Jane H. Morton 1-2-1871 (1-5-1871)
Ward, John to Sarah Mills 10-30-1848 (no return)
Ward, Timothy W. to Mary E. Cooper 1-10-1849
Ward, William L. to Sarah Jane Cook 6-14-1847
Ware, A. V. to A. G. Isbell 2-6-1860 (2-8-1860)
Ware, Samel D. to Sarah E. Blaydes 2-22-1851 (2-27-1851)
Warington, John to Eliza Ann Stacy 9-20-1847 (9-23-1847)
Warner, B. W. M. to Jo Ann E. Parrish 10-28-1844 (no return)
Warner, James H. to Martha J. Slone 10-29-1839 (11-7-1839)
Warr, Miles to Martha Williamson 5-5-1871 (5-6-1871) B
Warr, Rufus to Betty Blain 12-25-1868 (12-27-1868) B
Warr, Scott to Mattie Isbell 3-1-1869 (3-3-1869)
Warr, Thomas J. to Annie E. Wiggins 11-21-1865 (no return)
Warren, Anderson to Salak? McCully 4-20-1866 (no return) B
Warren, Ed to Mary Wirt 12-26-1866 B
Warren, Henry to Susan Temple 12-24-1869 (2-26-1870) B
Warren, London to Jane Jones 3-22-1870 (4-9-1870) B
Warren, Perry to Caroline Warren 12-3-1866 (12-8-1866) B
Warren, Pomfrett H. to Fanny A. Levy 11-22-1870
Warren, R. F. to Mary E. Baugh 2-17-1868 (2-20-1868)
Warren, Thomas to Roxanna Neel 2-27-1869 (3-28-1869) B
Warren, Zedrick to Lizzie Baxler 12-23-1867 (12-24-1867) B
Wash, William to Harrett L. Guarrant 3-30-1840
Washington, Geo. W. to Charlotte Exum 12-21-1868 (no return) B
Washington, Geo. to Matilda Keener 9-3-1866 (9-8-1866)
Washington, George to Clary Warr 9-11-1869 (9-26-1869) B
Washington, George to Harriet Jones 9-22-1870 B
Washington, George to Sarah Lewis 3-10-1868 (no return) B
Washington, Henry to Jane Walls 12-28-1868 (1-18-1869) B
Washington, James to Annie Morgan 12-28-1867 B
Washington, W. B. to Louisa M. Dickason 5-1-1850
Washington, Wm. B. to Virginia Dickason 8-7-1860 (8-8-1860)
Watkins, Benj. to Sarah A. Winfrey 1-23-1851 (no return)
Watkins, James to Lucinda Cargill 12-28-1866 (no return) B
Watkins, Major to Dolly Phillips 10-17-1868 (10-31-1868) B
Watkins, R. to L. M. E. Sneed 7-20-1838
Watkins, Stephen K. to Grace Humphreys 12-12-1866
Watkins, Thomas J. to Rutha J. Kelley 10-28-1847
Watkins, Thomas P. to Martha A. Booth 9-18-1838
Watkins, Wyatt B. to Mary E. Wall 8-23-1853 (no return)
Watson, E. J. to Sarah? Bumpass 3-1-1842
Watson, James G. to Mencus E. Goodlow 3-12-1855 (no return)
Watson, K. J. to N. A. Weaver 9-12-1849 (9-13-1849)
Watson, Nathan to Minerva Murray 5-15-1868 (10-25-1868) B
Watson, W. T. to Cora E. Harris 1-14-1861 (1-15-1861)
Watt, Wm. M. to Cordelia Browne 6-2-1845 (no return)
Weatherly, James H. (W.?) to M. J. Crawford 2-7-1871
Weaver, James to Ann Mcguire 5-26-1838
Weaver, John A. to Martha J. Lancer 10-15-1844 (no return)
Weaver, M. W. to Jane Markham 11-13-1847 (11-14-1847)
Webb, A. to Mary D. Knox 2-1-1850 (no return)
Webb, Andrew J. to Elizabeth Richey 2-18-1838
Webb, B. F. to M. A. Dean 10-31-1866 (11-5-1865?)
Webb, J. M. to Ellen H. Taylor 11-17-1865 (11-20-1865)

Webb, J. M. to M. E. Love 12-20-1865
Webb, James M. to Patina C. Perry 1-14-1848 (1-18-1848)
Webb, James R. to Elizabeth Adams 7-27-1846 (7-30-1846)
Webb, Jas. A. to M. L. Winborn 1-20-1868 (1-21-1868)
Webb, Jno. L. to Isadore Ketchum 12-2-1868
Webb, John L. to Louisa J. Ellison 2-19-1850 (2-23-1850)
Webb, John L. to Nancy Adams 8-29-1846 (8-31-1846)
Webb, M. J. to Sallie L. Black 10-4-1860 (10-5-1860)
Webb, R. C. to Elizabeth E. Dortch 4-30-1851 (5-1-1851)
Webber, A. W. to Arretta Bryant 1-11-1853 (no return)
Webber, Albert to M. F. Ivy 10-24-1866 (11-11-1866)
Webber, Phillip to Martha A. Moncreif 12-18-1849 (no return)
Webber, W. R. to Ally C. Swift 11-16-1867 (no return)
Webster, Daniel to Louisa Turner 12-25-1869 (12-31-1869) B
Webster, James to Isabella Bankhead 3-11-1841
Webster, John to Harriet Paine 11-5-1869 B
Welbourn, C. C. to Annie Show 1-5-1860
Wellborn, Henry E. to Jane Talbott 12-5-1853 (no return)
Wells, A. Dolphis to Mary J. Garrison 1-11-1847 (no return)
Wells, Horatio S. to Mary High 10-26-1842
Wells, J. G. to E. C. Vincent 2-9-1842 (2-10-1842)
Wells, Jim to Harriet Moffit 9-5-1868 (9-6-1868) B
Wells, Nelson to Ann Whitthorn 12-27-1869 B
Wells, Nelson to Judy Mason 12-31-1868 (no return)
Wells, Trenton to V. M. Anderson 11-24-1866 (11-28-1866)
Wells, William H. to Martha G. Evans 12-10-1838 (12-11-1838)
Wells, William T. to Melissa Dougan 9-25-1843 (no return)
Wesbrook, R. A. to Marry J. Phillips 12-4-1854 (no return)
Wesson, George W. to Mary Ann Wesson 2-11-1851 (2-14-1851)
Wesson, John A. to Barbery Warden 7-19-1849
Wesson, Wilkins to Sarah Farley 7-10-1839
West, Noel E. to Mary Jane Harington 2-18-1839 (2-20-1839)
Wheeler, George T. to Sarah L. Bennett 1-16-1867
Wheeler, James H. to Mary A. Ramsey 10-24-1842 (10-27-1842)
Wheeler, James to Mary Hill 12-5-1859 (12-11-1859)
Wheeler, King to Amanda Jefferson 5-2-1868 (no return) B
Wheeler, William H. to Almedia Ann McCrean 9-26-1846 (10-4-1846)
Whitaker, Jno. to Lucy J. Strickland 12-15-1868 (12-16-1868)
Whitby, Andrew J. to Mary E. Stafford 12-21-1868 (12-24-1868)
White, Abraham to Elizabeth Brown no date (with Dec 1856)
White, David C. to Mary V. Webster 1-8-1848 (1-13-1848)
White, John to Charlotte Sadler 5-6-1871 (5-7-1871) B
White, Jordan to Nancy Cove 1-29-1867 (2-5-1867) B
White, Robt. P. to Lavinia A. (Louisa?) Firth 10-20-1866 (10-23-1866)
White, William L. to Mary E. Partlow 9-9-1839 (no return)
White, William T. to Eliza E. Parchman 2-20-1841 (2-23-1841)
Whitefield, Johnson J. to Agnis Gregory 11-19-1839 (no return)
Whitehead, Fletcher to Adaline Boyd 7-20-1867 (8-10-1867) B
Whitehead, R. H. to M. A. Conkey 12-19-1859 (12-20-1859)
Whitehead, Reding to Sarah E. Blanchard 2-4-1852 (no return)
Whitehead, S. D. to Isadora Hollis 3-20-1851
Whitehead, W. W. to M. W. Arnold 8-15-1854 (no return)
Whitelaw, Thomas to Mary S. Hatch 2-4-1841 (2-11-1841)
Whitfield, John to Sally Neally 3-16-1841 (3-18-1841)
Whiting, Silas to Sarah Hester 6-21-1848 (6-23-1848)
Whitley, Jos. D. to Annie M. Field 5-11-1866 (5-15-1866)
Whitly, F. G. to M. C. Anderson 3-14-1849 (no return)
Whitney, Elijah to Mary Anderson 2-17-1842 (2-22-1842)
Whitney, James M. to Amanda E. Hardin 11-19-1867 (11-20-1867)
Whitney, James to Sharlott Adams 8-29-1848 (no return)
Whitson, Charles B. to Nancy ann Whitfield 2-13-1855 (no return)
Whitson, Jno. to Jemimah Ann Young 7-9-1846 (no return)
Whitson, S. B. to Huldah A. Soap 10-31-1845 (no return)
Whittaker, B. H. to Lucretia J. Strickland 1-18-1871
Whittaker, Wm. D. to Sally Ann Abbington 5-18-1846 (5-22-1846)
Whitten, A. to Nancyann Malone 4-25-1842
Whittle, George J. to Fannie Poindexter 5-1-1867 (5-11-1867) B
Whitton, Henry to Mary Crawford 11-27-1869 B
Whorton, Samuel to Artelia E. Walker 9-14-1852 (no return)
Whyte, James C. to Martha C. Wray 10-24-1840 (10-25?-1840)
Wiggins, Archibald to Judy Pulliam 2-7-1871 (2-15-1871) B
Wiggins, Finny to Nancy Harris 10-10-1866 (10-13-1866) B
Wiggins, Jas. W. to Sallie P. Smith 1-14-1871 (1-15-1871)
Wiggins, Ned to Fanny Jones 11-22-1870 (no return)
Wiggins, Ned to Liza Shackelford 5-18-1866 (no return) B

Wiggins, Zang to Celena Granberry 12-23-1869 (no return) B
Wilbourn, J. G. to Mary S. Shaw 12-18-1867
Wilburn, John K. to Mary D. Mayfield 5-7-1866 (5-10-1866)
Wilder, W. L. to S. A. Jackson 12-6-1859 (12-8-1859)
Wilder, W. O. to Louisa McKnight 12-10-1869 (12-15-1869)
Wiles, H. J. to E. J. Wilson 3-24-1866
Wiley, Giles to Caledonia Sneed 11-22-1867 (11-24-1867) B
Wiley, John to Catherine Yancey 8-17-1866 (no return) B
Wiley, R. C. to _____ 3-14-1849 (3-15-1849)
Wiley, Richard to Louisa Frierson 12-29-1865 (12-30-1865) B
Wilkerson, Littleberry G. to Elizabeth G. Oliver 1-24-1844 (no
    return)
Wilkerson, Tom to Nancy Armstrong 7-5-1867 (no return) B
Wilkerson, W. D. to Mary J. Harris 10-9-1854 (no return)
Wilkerson, Wiley to Matilda Kemp 3-20-1866 (no return) B
Wilkerson, Wm. to Sarah Rivers 12-22-1869 B
Wilkes, Andrew to Mollie Lindsey 2-8-1871 (2-9-1871) B
Wilkins, Alfred to Mary Brown 6-15-1869 B
Wilkinson, J. M. to Ella Harris 9-19-1870 (9-24-1870)
Wilkinson, Wm. B. to Maggie L. Locke 1-27-1859 (2-2-1859)
Williams, Alfred to Ammarilla Harris 8-6-1839
Williams, Alfred to Matilda Jones 12-29-1869 (12-30-1869) B
Williams, Andrew J. to Caroline C. Stewart 12-17-1846
Williams, Arthur to Susan J. Orr 2-19-1849 (2-20-1849)
Williams, Barney to Victoria Mason 9-9-1867 (9-12-1867) B
Williams, Billy to Elizabeth Kelly 10-27-1869 (no return) B
Williams, Boyed to Rebeca Willis 2-13-1839 (2-14-1839)
Williams, Cato to Candis Goodlett 2-11-1868 (2-16-1868) B
Williams, Claude to Emily Williams 1-23-1866 (no return) B
Williams, Cloyd to Amanda Badaw 12-29-1869 (no return) B
Williams, Coleman to Louisa Mooreland 8-14-1868 (no return)
Williams, Daniel to Jane Sanders 1-19-1870 (no return) B
Williams, Ed to Siloa Bone 6-9-1870 (6-25-1870) B
Williams, Elisha to Mary Rogers 2-15-1844 (no return)
Williams, Evans to Celia High 4-18-1870 (5-1-1870) B
Williams, George to Lidda Lewis 2-18-1839 (2-25-1839)
Williams, H. H. to Elizabeth Perry 12-30-1867 (12-31-1867)
Williams, Howlbert? to Tempe Reddick 9-1-1866 (no return)
Williams, Isaac A. to Mollie R. J. Wells 12-25-1866 (12-28-1866)
Williams, Isaac to Martha Harrison 3-1-1870 (3-3-1870) B
Williams, J. J. to A. M. Sneed 9-14-1851 (no return)
Williams, J. J. to Ann R. Watkins 10-30-1865 (10-31-1865)
Williams, J. J. to Sarah E. Lemmon 12-20-1852 (no return)
Williams, J. N. to M. A. Harrell 10-29-1860 (11-1-1860)
Williams, J. T. to M. J. Moore 10-1-1866 (no return)
Williams, Jackson to Letha Clifton 6-16-1866 (no return) B
Williams, James B. to Mary J. Allen 9-24-1840 (no return)
Williams, James P. to Catharine Bevins 12-25-1841
Williams, Jesse A. to C. Belle Kelly 9-22-1866 (9-25-1866)
Williams, Jno. to Milla Newby 7-11-1868 (7-12-1868) B
Williams, Joe to Sanna? Williams 9-21-1867 (9-22-1867) B
Williams, John R. to Elizabeth A. Anesworth 12-14-1847 (12-15-1847)
Williams, John W. to Margarett Worley 1-6-1851
Williams, John to Frances Buford 11-2-1866 (11-3-1866) B
Williams, John to Malvina Scott 7-7-1866 (no return) B
Williams, Luke L. to Rebecca C. Blair 7-20-1846 (no return)
Williams, Maddison to Susan Norman 5-16-1868 (no return) B
Williams, Mose to Fanny Isbell 1-18-1868 (no return) B
Williams, N. W. to Tomantana Johnson 7-8-1845 (7-9-1846?)
Williams, Normon to Jane Hurley 12-17-1847 (12-22-1847)
Williams, P. M. to Cynthia Houston 2-12-1842
Williams, Peter to Sylvia Jonakin 5-19-1866 (8-11-1866) B
Williams, Providence to Miss Walker 2-5-1838 (no return)
Williams, Richard N. to Eliza H. Sauls 12-24-1844
Williams, Richmond to Silva Fields 12-24-1868 (12-25-1868) B
Williams, Robt. to Martha Morris 4-3-1868 (no return) B
Williams, S. B. to Sarah Godby 2-10-1848 (no return)
Williams, S. to Sarah Ann Beaver 7-23-1845 (8-7-1845)
Williams, Spencer to Paralee Heaslett 2-2-1867 (no return) B
Williams, Sumpter to Dillah Murrell 3-22-1869 (no return) B
Williams, T. F. to Frances M. Hall 11-26-1849 (no return)
Williams, Thomas to Mollie Ozier 1-7-1870 (1-10-1870) B
Williams, Thomas to Nancy Warren 1-21-1870 (2-19-1870) B
Williams, Thos. to Lucinda W. Duke 2-24-1848
Williams, Thos. to Marthaann Yarborough 12-24-1839 (no return)

Williams, W. B. to Tennessee Tatum 7-14-1849 (no return)
Williams, Wm. H. H. to Nancy C. Oates 1-24-1871 (1-26-1871)
Williams, Wm. H. to Esther Gordon 11-20-1844 (no return)
Williams, Wm. to Eleanor Ammons 5-6-1847 (5-9-1847)
Williamson, Alfred to Catie McFarland 2-5-1869 (1?-14-1869) B
Williamson, Archabald to Lutisha R. Hill 4-15-1852 (no return)
Williamson, Bill to Priscilla Deener? 4-22-1871 (no return) B
Williamson, Buck to Frances Williamson 1-13-1866 (1-14-1866) B
Williamson, Cater to Matilda Williamson 3-19-1866 B
Williamson, Clark to Fanny Irvens 5-2-1871 (5-13-1871) B
Williamson, Frank to Dolly Holloway 5-23-1868 (5-25-1868) B
Williamson, George to Amanda Ross 1-7-1869 B
Williamson, George to Eliza Walker 3-30-1867 (4-7-1867) B
Williamson, George to L. Thornton 7-21-1866 (7-22-1866)
Williamson, George to Mary Wright 2-20-1869 (no return) B
Williamson, Horace to Amanda Trip 2-10-1866 (2-17-1866) B
Williamson, J. W. to Mary L. Taylor 3-5-1860 (3-7-1860)
Williamson, Jack to Barthenia Coe 12-23-1865 (12-26-1865) B
Williamson, Jerry to Harriet Gaither 12-31-1866 (no return) B
Williamson, Ned to Martha Orgain 1-12-1867 B
Williamson, Primus to Maggie Harwell 3-25-1870 B
Williamson, Robin to Rachel Fisher 4-18-1866 B
Williamson, Samuel M. to Mary Jane Sneed 9-29-1841 (10-4-1841)
Williamson, T. M. to Cynthia Houston 2-12-1842 (no return)
Williamson, Willis to Eliza Williamson 5-25-1867 B
Williamson, Wm. L. to Sallie P. Taylor 3-5-1860 (3-7-1860)
Williford, Nathan W. to Frances Milegan 2-16-1838
Willingham, H. T. to Nancy Wallace 11-8-1847 (11-9-1847)
Willingham, W. H. to Nancy McGee 9-22-1841 (9-27-1841)
Willis, James T. to Julia Hutchins 4-9-1845
Willis, N. W. to Elender A. (Mrs.) Hollis 12-16-1854 (no return)
Willis, P. H. to Emila T. Jackson 7-6-1847 (7-7-1847)
Willis, Ruffin to Jane Hutchins 1-10-1844
Wills, John B. to Harriet C. Alexander 6-29-1838
Willson, Thomas to Jerusha Vaughn 4-25-1843 (4-27-1843)
Wilson, A. B. to Margaret Adams 3-23-1840 (3-29-1840)
Wilson, Adolphus B. to Sarah A. Trainer 2-22-1869 (2-24-1869)
Wilson, Anderson to Margaret Watterson? 2-1-1870 (no return) B
Wilson, Bennit to Harriet Cogbill 2-15-1869 (2-16-1869) B
Wilson, Charles to Julia Morris 12-24-1866 (12-27-1866) B
Wilson, David R. to Mary Conway 12-27-1849
Wilson, Dennis to Martha Clure 12-15-1870 (no return) B
Wilson, Fed to Kitty Brinkley 9-3-1870 (9-4-1870) B
Wilson, Francis A. to Hadnah? Boyd 1-29-1850
Wilson, George to Charlotte Murrell 1-22-1870 (1-29-1870) B
Wilson, H. P. R. to M. F. Greenway 10-15-1854 (no return)
Wilson, J. A. to M.F. Reeves 10-19-1870 (10-20-1870)
Wilson, James to A. E. Hall 3-23-1852 (no return)
Wilson, James to Harriet Murrell 2-22-1868 (2-26-1868) B
Wilson, John A. to Nancy Rodgers 1-3-1853 (no return)
Wilson, John J. to Sarah Holloway 1-16-1839 (no return)
Wilson, John to Mary Murrell 12-28-1870 (12-31-1870) B
Wilson, John to Sarah Taylor 7-24-1869 (7-25-1869) B
Wilson, Joseph to Elmira Poindexter 12-20-1869 (12-30-1869) B
Wilson, Loyd to Nancy Coker 10-22-1839 (11-9-1839)
Wilson, Moses to Malinda Jordan 6-29-1867 (7-3-1867) B
Wilson, Richard B. to Martha Burriss 10-14-1847
Wilson, Samuel D. to Matilda M. Henderson 12-27-1839 (SB 1838)
Wilson, Samuel H. to Allice L. Hunter 1-23-1869 (1-27-1869)
Wilson, Thaddeus to Sina Matthews 11-26-1860 (11-27-1860)
Wilson, Thadios to Marinett Cartwright 9-8-1849 (10-3-1849)
Wilson, W. P. to Sarah J. Taylor 10-15-1855 (no return)
Wilson, jr., P. to M. E. Carter 7-25-1863 (7-29-1863)
Wily, W. L. to Sallie Shinault 2-1-1860
Winfield, Curtis to Eleander Brown 12-16-1848
Winfield, Henry to Nan Cox 6-26-1869 (6-25?-1869) B
Winfield, W. W. to Mary E. Harwell 6-1-1859 (6-26-1859)
Winfield, William E. to Lucinda M. Malone 11-10-1845 (11-12-1845)
Winfrey, Jessey to Patsy Cocke 2-24-1869 B
Winfrey, William to Ann Dortch 5-3-1869 (no return) B
Wing, W. H. to Eliza Hood 12-17-1866 (12-20-1866)
Winn, Wm. R. to Casandra Shinault 11-24-1841
Winsett, James A. to Isabella J. Roach 11-18-1845 (11-19-1845)
Winsett, James E. to Eliza A. Bell 5-16-1867
Winsett, R. D. to Anna M. Finney 1-22-1868 (12-23-1868)

Winston, Edmond to Sallie A. Fry 5-21-1852 (no return)
Winston, Isaac to Olivia B. Michee 10-11-1852 (no return)
Winston, John A. to Polly Walker Logwood 10-18-1843
Winters, Joseph to Mary Ann Knight 9-9-1850 (9-10-1850)
Wirt, Green to Mary Warren 1-2-1866 (no return) B
Wirt, Harry to Henrietta Patterson 12-27-1867 (12-31-1867) B
Wirt, S. P. to S. E. Crabtree 5-4-1868 (5-5-1868)
Wirwa, C. W. to Henrietta Richardt 9-21-1868 (9-22-1868) B
Wiseman, John P. to Mariah Blain 12-17-1860 (12-20-1860)
Wiseman, Zachariah to Emeline Morriss 5-4-1842 (no return)
Witt, Geo. R. to Isabella R. Yancey 9-1-1846
Witt, George R. to Mary A. Yancy 2-10-1841 (2-11-1841)
Witt, John to Queen Jones 12-30-1869 (1-1-1870) B
Wolsey, Robt. to Mariah Orgain 12-15-1868 (12-19-1868) B
Womack, A. P. to Eliza Jones 1-3-1842 (1-6-1842)
Womble, J. W. to Mary Jane Stephens 1-4-1841 (1-7-1841)
Womble, P. G. to Nancy McDade 10-22-1844 (10-31-1844)
Wood, George to Mary J. (Mrs.) Williamson 6-8-1853 (no return)
Wood, Green to Martha Ann Lowry 11-18-1844 (7-24-1845)
Wood, Jesse to Adaline Williamson 10-19-1867 (10-20-1867) B
Wood, Spiner to Mary M. Alen 3-20-1848 (no return)
Woodard, Jackson to M. J. A. Hooks 10-27-1848 (no return)
Woodfin, John to Minta Thompson 4-4-1868 B
Woodfork, Ed to Peep Shelton 1-5-1870 (no return) B
Woodruff, S. F. to Miss _____ Harrison 9-20-1855 (no return)
Woods, John to Lutitia M. Locke 1-3-1842 (12?-23-1842)
Woods, Taylor to Zoa Ann Deener 12-26-1867 (no return) B
Woods, William to Fanny Dowdy 1-31-1870 (2-10-1870) B
Woodson, Creed to Emeline T. Shaw 12-20-1847
Woodson, John R. to Amanda E. Pitman 10-7-1848
Woodward, Asa to Sarah Bennett 3-22-1846 (3-24-1846)
Wooten, William L. to Mary N. Baugh 12-31-1851 (no return)
Word, J. C. to M. D. Wilbourn 2-4-1864 (2-10-1864)
Word, Jack to Eliza Boyd 3-27-1869 (no return) B
Worrell, Saml. to Malinda Norman 10-18-1867 (10-19-1867) B
Worrell, T. B. to A. M. (Mrs.) Simpson 3-1-1853 (no return)
Wortham, Benj. H. to Mary J. Burrow 9-8-1846 (no return)
Wray, Aleck to Fanny Barby 7-9-1870 B
Wray, J. A. to Sallie A. Neal 9-6-1862 (9-8-1862)
Wray, John to Mary Atkins 10-27-1859 (11-3-1859)
Wright, A. W. to Georgiana Craig 2-22-1870
Wright, D. W. to Christiana A. Duke 5-30-1853 (no return)
Wright, D. W. to Miss _____ Duke 5-23-1853 (no return)
Wright, F. M. to Mary E. Cotton 10-26-1844 (10-29-1844)
Wright, John W. to Annie Whitthorne 12-26-1870 (1-5-1871)
Wright, Tho. to Mahala Shaw 9-4-1845
Wright, Visen? P. to Martha J. Johnson 2-1-1848 (2-8-1848)
Wright, W. B. to M. J. Bryant 3-27-1866 (3-28-1866)
Wright, William to Lucinda Boyed 4-30-1850 (5-1-1850)
Wroten, Elijah to Sarah Brown 2-14-1846 (no return)
Wyley, Harvey to Elizabeth McHenry 9-29-1841 (9-30-1841)
Wylie, Adam R. to Isabelah Paden 8-6-1838
Wylie, J. F. to B. V. Irby 10-22-1864 (10-29-1864)
Yancey, Alfred to Mildred Allen 4-27-1842 (5-28-1842)
Yancey, Henry to Lucy Jane Moore 8-10-1870 (8-22-1870) B
Yancey, James E. to Demaris A. Bradsher 5-25-1863 (5-26-1863)
Yancey, Jas. E. to Mattie A. Harris 12-5-1866
Yancey, Joe to Lissa Yancey 12-18-1869 (1-9-1869) B
Yancey, Leonidas F. to Mary E. Murphy 9-11-1865 (9-12-1865)
Yancey, W. F. to S. E. Bratcher 9-19-1859 (9-21-1859)
Yancy, A. H. to E. J. Moore 5-23-1860 (5-24-1860)
Yancy, Clayton A. to Frances H. Eddins 12-12-1843
Yancy, E. T. to Mary M. Anderson 11-9-1839
Yancy, H. J. to M. A. C. Kaywood 10-19-1859
Yancy, Marshall P. to Ann T. Eddins 11-20-1843 (11-23-1843)
Yancy, Thomas B. to Narsissa J. Warren 4-13-1871
Yarborough, H. W. to Julia D. Cleaves 9-10-1860 (9-13-1860)
Yarbro, Joseph H. to Ellin King 12-24-1845 (no return)
Yarbrough, Henry W. to Tennessee Ann Williams 2-14-1846 (no return)
Yarbrough, James T. to Martha A. Solomon 1-25-1844 (1-31-1844)
Yarbrough, Joseph to Sarah Baucum 1-21-1845 (1-22-1845)
Yarbrough, William to Sarah F. Fausett 12-17-1850 (no return)
Yates, Harry to Jane McElwain 12-27-1869 B
Yearger, Orville to Virginia S. Sale 10-9-1848 (no return)

Young, Amos to Elizabeth McLain 11-9-1868 (no return) B
Young, J. F. to Emily Rodgers 12-28-1866 (1-2-1867)
Young, John B. to Sallie E. Spain 11-6-1866 (11-8-1866)
Young, Norflet T. to Mary Davis 1-11-1869 (1-14-1869)
Young, Peter to Jane Bently 6-30-1866 (no return) B
Young, Phillip to Sally Anna Tucker 12-24-1866 (no return) B
Young, Sye to Mariah Jones 10-31-1868 (11-1-1868) B
Youngs, John W. to Martha G. Burford 12-21-1840 (12-23-1840)
Youree, William P. to America W. Moss 4-2-1838
Zellner, J. W. to Willie E. Patton 11-3-1866 (11-6-1866)

Aaron, Ann E. to E. M. Dunn 2-7-1849 (no return)
Abbernathy, Mary L. to James M. Straughn 7-11-1846
Abbington, Frances E. to Henry H. Dean 5-18-1846 (5-22-1846)
Abbington, Sally Ann to Wm. D. Whittaker 5-18-1846 (5-22-1846)
Abels, Martha to Francis C. Kizer 2-1-1842
Abernathy, Ann to Uriah M. Alexander 1-30-1871 (2-1-1871)
Abernathy, Belsia to J. J. Brown 1-2-1871 (no return)
Abernathy, Lucy A. to G. W. Trotter 7-21-1851 (7-22-1851)
Abernathy, Sarahann to John P. Phillips 10-28-1841 (no return)
Abington, Elinora to Wm. Lowry 3-25-1839 (4-3-1839)
Abington, Mary C. to Wm. L. Moore 12-7-1846 (12-9-1846)
Abington, Rosa B. to Starke Duprey 2-15-1838
Abington, Rose to Solomon Burris 12-22-1868 (12-23-1868) B
Abington, William (Miss) to William S. Roscoe 10-19-1846 (10-21-1846)
Able, Charlotte to Elijah Isham 4-8-1847 (4-9-1847)
Able, Lucy to Wm. Hammons 7-3-1838
Able, M. F. to D. R. Bull 9-2-1867 (9-5-1867)
Adams, Adaline to James L. Kee 9-4-1865 (9-6-1865)
Adams, Elizabeth to James R. Webb 7-27-1846 (7-30-1846)
Adams, Elling to Haywood Cannon 1-1-1854 (no return)
Adams, Emeline to George Bruce 10-3-1840 (10-4-1840)
Adams, Gerusha to John Hurly 11-26-1839 (11-28-1839)
Adams, Isabella D. to John McNama 2-17-1841 (2-18-1841)
Adams, Isabella to Washington Smith 7-26-1869 (7-27-1869) B
Adams, Margaret V. to W. W. Osborne 1-26-1865 (1-31-1865)
Adams, Margaret to A. B. Wilson 3-23-1840 (3-29-1840)
Adams, Martha F. to Richard M. Firth 2-18-1841
Adams, Mary B. to Geor. Paulson 4-17-1845
Adams, Mary Jane to Gilbert Mowhorn 6-5-1869 (6?-1-1869) B
Adams, Mollie E. to S. H. Lockhart 6-30-1862 (not endorsed)
Adams, Nancy to John L. Webb 8-29-1846 (8-31-1846)
Adams, Sharlott to James Whitney 8-29-1848 (no return)
Adams, _____ to _____ Fitzgerald 9-5-1838 (no return)
Adkins, Darcas to Mathew Nichols 10-24-1854 (no return)
Adkins, Lucinda to James W. Bowen 9-13-1843 (9-14-1843)
Adkins, Nacy (Nancy?) to R. A. Paschal 11-15-1838
Adkins, Rebecca to John H. Tallent 5-16-1842
Agee, Frances to Wm. R. McMullin 3-19-1840
Airs, Sarah And. to A. B. Forbess 9-4-1848 (9-27-1848)
Akin, Susan to Benj. F. Dowdy 2-2-1839 (no return)
Alderson, Lou A. to E. A. Shryack 3-2-1859 (3-8-1859)
Alen, Mary M. to Spiner Wood 3-20-1848 (no return)
Alender?, Salina A. to H. B. McKinley 11-26-1850 (12-3-1850)
Alexander, Cresia to Jim Pearce 3-21-1868 B
Alexander, Elenor L. to C. W. Rich 8-22-1854 (no return)
Alexander, Harriet C. to John B. Wills 6-29-1838
Alexander, Harriet to Kit Roach 12-7-1866 (12-8-1866) B
Alexander, Isabella M. to Fredk. Davis 8-26-1842 (8-31-1842)
Alexander, Jane C. to Joseph Morton 11-10-1847 (11-11-1847)
Alexander, Jane E. to Richd. Sandford 5-17-1851 (no return)
Alexander, Laura M. to William Ray 12-14-1846 (12-22-1846)
Alexander, Margarett C. to James W. Anderson 1-17-1842 (1-23-1842)
Alexander, Martha to James Alexander 1-18-1841 (1-21-1841)
Alexander, Mary C. to Rob. S. Alexander? 11-15-1846
Alexander, Mary J. to J. R. Kerr 11-10-1847
Alexander, Mollie B. to J. P. Smith 3-25-1865 (3-29-1865)
Alexander, N. A. to G. W. Burnett 5-29-1860 (not endorsed)
Alexander, Nancy J. to Hugh A. Cullum 11-17-1854 (no return)
Alexander, Nancy to William Irwin 3-30-1841 (4-1-1841)
Alexander, O. J. to W. C. Champion 10-22-1868
Alexander, Sarah D. to Isaac B. Mercer 8-13-1849 (no return)
Alexander, Sidney to Jacob Cummings 5-19-1866 (8-11-1866) B
Alexander, Susan A. to Wm. Johnson 2-15-1847 (2-16-1847)
Alexander, Susan D. to James B. McClurere? 3-24-1848 (4-16-1848)
Alford, Judith to Adam Trent 9-2-1866
Alkire, Lelia to Isaac Bevlin 2-13-1868
Allen, Ann B. to Andrew A. Allen 12-22-1845 (12-23-1845)
Allen, Ann R. to N. L. Owen 5-7-1855 (no return)
Allen, Catharin to Wm. Hughes 8-26-1850 (9-1-1850)
Allen, Elizabeth P. to David H. Johnson 8-?-1842 (not endorsed)
Allen, Emily to James Brown 12-28-1866 (12-30-1866) B
Allen, Fanny to William Johnson 8-17-1869 B
Allen, History to Joe Shepherd 5-19-1870 (5-21-1870) B
Allen, Jane W. to Wm. McQuistin 2-24-1845 (2-25-1845)

Allen, Jane to James C. Davis 1-16-1855 (no return)
Allen, Josephine to Tecumseh Cockran 1-19-1870 B
Allen, M. B. to L. H. C. Branch 12-18-1865 (12-20-1865)
Allen, Margarett G. to John McCaughan 10-21-1854 (no return)
Allen, Margarett J. to Robt. M. Gabbie (Gallbie?) 1-27-1845 (1-28-1845)
Allen, Martha J. to E. H. Bennett 11-29-1870 (11-30-1870)
Allen, Martha to G. W. Freeman 10-15-1854 (no return)
Allen, Marthann to M. L. Turner 10-13-1847 (10-19-1847)
Allen, Mary J. to Isaac Dodds 4-29-1845 (no return)
Allen, Mary J. to James B. Williams 9-24-1840 (no return)
Allen, Mary to Edmund S. Rodgers 4-18-1840
Allen, Mildred to Alfred Yancey 4-27-1842 (5-28-1842)
Allen, Orelia Ann to James Hunter 5-20-1870 (5-21-1870) B
Allen, R. Jane to Henry Franklin 1-22-1870 (1-27-1870) B
Allen, Roberta to Sam Phillips 2-28-1866 (3-10-1866) B
Allen, Sarah A. B. to John H. Mathews 3-21-1839
Allen, Williametta to Isaac Sheppard 2-22-1868 (no return) B
Allen?, Elizabeth P. to R. L. Evans 10-13-1847 (11-12-1847)
Alley, Kittie to Spencer Johnson 4-12-1868 (no return) B
Allison, Lizzie D. to Beverly A. Rodgers 8-9-1868 (no return)
Alston, Edwanna? to Josephus Loving 1-21-1840 (1-22-1840)
Alston, Elizabeth P. to John Brown 5-25-1840 (5-26-1840)
Alston, Nancy C. to James W. Black 5-8-1848
Amis, Berlin to W. H. McCully 11-10-1866 (11-11-1866)
Amis, Clara to Samuel S. Amis 12-10-1866
Ammons, Dovey L. M. to Elijah Stephenson 10-25-1842
Ammons, Eleanor to Wm. Williams 5-6-1847 (5-9-1847)
Ammons, Mary to Green Bennett 8-20-1845 (8-21-1845)
Amouse, Emaline to William Stallings 1-8-1862 (1-9-1862)
Anderson, A. L. to J. W. Amis 8-12-1867 (8-13-1867)
Anderson, Amanda to _____ Mench? 2-12-1849 (no return)
Anderson, E. G. to Wm. B. G. Sneed no dates (with Sep 1844)
Anderson, J. E. to Wm. M. Mayo 12-23-1844 (12-24-1844)
Anderson, Julia A. to W. F. Jones 3-2-1864
Anderson, L. A. to J. H. Dulin 3-14-1866 (3-15-1866)
Anderson, Lucina T. to Wm. J. Hendrick 12-31-1849 (1-1-1850)
Anderson, M. C. to F. G. Whitly 3-14-1849 (no return)
Anderson, Mary M. to E. T. Yancy 11-9-1839
Anderson, Mary to Elijah Whitney 2-17-1842 (2-22-1842)
Anderson, Suck to Rhodes Montague 2-3-1868 (2-9-1868) B
Anderson, V. M. to Trenton Wells 11-24-1866 (11-28-1866)
Andrews, M. to James McCall 7-27-1866 (no return)
Andrews, Martha E. to John W. Hicks 2-26-1868 (2-27-1868)
Andrews, Rosa L. to R. B. Hicks 12-19-1866 (no return)
Andrews, Sallie to C. A. Duncan 12-14-1870
Anesworth, Elizabeth A. to John R. Williams 12-14-1847 (12-15-1847)
Apleton, Martha A. to Nathaniel M. Hutchins 12-16-1847 (12-18-1847)
Appleberry, P. E. to W. C. Isom 7-20-1864 (7-24-1864)
Appleberry, Sallie to J. P. Royall 9-27-1869 (9-30-1869)
Appleton, R. S. to Burrell Branch 12-18-1847 (no return)
Appleton, Sally to Joseph Sample 10-7-1850 (no return)
Arbuckle, C. C. to Lewis Graves 12-6-1849 (no return)
Arbuckle, Lucy F. to Robert L. McNees 11-6-1854 (no return)
Arbuckle, N. J. to W. L. Ship 8-4-1859 (8-10-1859)
Armour, Emily to Tom Stewart 11-18-1865 B
Armour, Isabella to J. S. Haden 1-4-1844 (no return)
Armour, Mary An to Calvin Beacham 8-?-1842 (no return)
Armstrong, Eliza to Gilliam Jones 12-30-1867 (12-31-1867) B
Armstrong, Eveline to John Holliday 3-12-1848 (no return)
Armstrong, Frances I. to Hiram C. Moorman 1-27-1870
Armstrong, Lila to Bob Turner 5-2-1868 (no return) B
Armstrong, Nancy to Tom Wilkerson 7-5-1867 (no return) B
Arnold, Lucy to James Middlehook 3-5-1867
Arnold, M. W. to W. W. Whitehead 8-15-1854 (no return)
Arnold, Martha E. to Joseph J. Chaney 10-16-1866 (10-17-1866)
Ashe, Charity to London DeGraffenried 1-8-1866 (1-13-1866) B
Askew, Celia A. to David C. Tyler 3-1-1869
Askew, Jane to Charley Murrell 12-31-1869 (no return) B
Askew, Jane to Joseph Harris 5-15-1869 (no return) B
Askew, La to George Newsom 6-8-1867 B
Askew, Mary J. to David E. Tonage 11-25-1851 (no return)
Astin, Josie M. to Samuel B. Kyle 12-12-1868 (12-17-1868)
Astin, Sallie E. to George F. Dupree 12-12-1868 (12-17-1868)

Aston, Ann H. to Nathaniel Gordon 4-22-1838
Aston, C. H. to Wm. B. Neville 2-3-1851 (2-11-1851)
Athens, Christianer to Luke Bowers 4-22-1871 (4-23-1871) B
Atkins, D. C. to B. R. Stafford 4-26-1854 (no return)
Atkins, Hollandberry to Pleasant P. Saunders 8-26-1846 (8-27-1846)
Atkins, Margaret to Charles Bobbitt 11-23-1846 (12-1-1846)
Atkins, Mary to John Wray 10-27-1859 (11-3-1859)
Atkinson, Lucinda to George Holden 12-20-1869 (12-23-1869) B
Atkinson, Sarah to Elias Chambers 12-22-1866 (12-23-1866)
Aulsup, Lucinda to Francis M. Forbes 7-2-1870 (7-4-1870)
Austin, Kate E. to J. A. McNeill 1-9-1865 (1-10-1865)
Averett, Cynthia to B. F. Southern 5-14-1859 (5-15-1859)
Averett, Lucy A. to John C. Portis 11-23-1855 (no return)
Averett, Lucy A. to W. H. Largent 11-26-1860 (12-5-1860)
Averett, Mary J. to G. M. Crook 5-2-1854 (no return)
Aynesworth, Caroline M. to John Limbarger 8-25-1841 (8-29-1841)
Ayres, Mary Jane to James M. S. Jemerson 10-4-1838
Badaw, Amanda to Cloyd Williams 12-29-1869 (no return) B
Bagley, Elizabeth to Edward C. Ford 8-30-1845 (9-25-1845)
Bailey, Ann W. to John McSwine 2-19-1852 (no return)
Bailey, Elenora to J. T. Dudney 11-4-1867 (11-6-1867)
Bailey, Elizabeth to R. K. Morrison 3-13-1866
Bailey, Jane to E. J. Smith 10-2-1867 (no return)
Bailey, Martha to John James 12-14-1868 (12-17-1868)
Bailey, Roan to Willis Houston 1-17-1859 (1-19-1859)
Baily, R. E. to Harris Bailey 12-28-1859
Baird, Belle to R. T. Perkins 8-8-1870
Baird, Hannah to Ben Jones 2-22-1867 (2-23-1867) B
Baird, Isabella to Oliver Shivers 11-16-1866 (11-25-1866) B
Baird, Julia to John Bates 2-1-1867 (2-2-1867) B
Baird, Lamiza Ann to Joseph C. Stark 4-22-1847
Baird, Mary to Andy Bowers 7-6-1867 (no return) B
Baird, N. A. to C. M. Teague 10-27-1860 (10-30-1860)
Baird, Phoeba to Richard Spaulding 10-8-1870 B
Baird, Sallie to Jno. Herron 8-5-1868 (8-6-1868) B
Baker, Elizabeth to James L. Lusby 12-16-1841 (12-23-1841)
Baker, Jennie Lee to Thomas H. Owens 4-16-1866 (4-25-1866)
Baker, Josephine to W. T. Richie 10-10-1855 (no return)
Baker, Lucinda to Wm. P. Goode 12-27-1870 B
Baker, Mary T. to Henry J. Reames 1-29-1842 (2-1-1842)
Baker, Mollie C. to J. A. Oates 2-18-1871 (no return)
Baker, Nellie to William Walker 12-31-1868
Baker, Rutha Jane to Y. W. Richey 7-21-1852 (no return)
Baker, Susannah to James V. Garrison 12-14-1846 (no return)
Baker, Tennessee J. to James R. Richey 8-11-1852 (no return)
Balcum, Penny to Thomas Birdsong 9-29-1866 (9-30-1866)
Baldridge, Nancy to Joseph S. Evans 5-15-1847 (no return)
Baldwin, Lucy to Wm. Franklin 1-1-1869 (1-2-1869) B
Ball, Elizabeth to George W. Trotter 1-10-1844
Ball, Sarah J. to A. S. Hancock 1-11-1841 (1-12-1841)
Ballard, Fanny to James A. Furr 11-5-1870 (11-10-1870)
Ballard, H. A. to C. H. Cogbill 7-21-1859
Ballard, Jane to James C. Graham 1-16-1841 (1-20-1841)
Ballard, Martha to James McCullough 7-11-1855 (no return)
Ballard, Rebecca to James V. Ruth 6-19-1843
Ballaw, Jyncy to J. R. Brobbeck 9-20-1851 (no return)
Bankhead, Agnis M. to George S. Howell 4-24-1841 (4-30-1841)
Bankhead, Isabella to James Webster 3-11-1841
Barby, Fanny to Aleck Wray 7-9-1870 B
Barken, Adeline to Isom Miller 12-22-1869 B
Barker, Cyntha to Pinkney Reed 5-9-1855 (no return)
Barker, Harriet J. to J. K. Todd 1-1-1867
Barnes, Amanda L. to James A. Hargiss 6-11-1852 (no return)
Barnes, Frances E. to Robert F. Benton 8-31-1852 (no return)
Barnes, Sarah E. to William A. Kidd 6-19-1851 (no return)
Barren, Mary L. to R. L. Ivey 7-11-1865
Barrett, Mariam to Hansell Cawbourn? 7-9-1839 (no return)
Barrett, Mary to Dean McCarley 8-9-1838
Barron, F. M. to William Fewell 1-17-1848 (1-18-1848)
Barron, Mary to Sanders Barron 9-18-1869 (no return) B
Bartis, Elizabeth A. (Mrs.) to William J. McLean 7-3-1848 (7-4-1848)
Barton, Ellin to John K. Seymore 9-27-1842 (9-29-1842)
Basin, Dora to Gust Bolder 12-17-1870 (12-24-1870) B
Baskerville, Ann to Monroe Goodman 12-29-1866 B
Baskerville, Nancy to Isaac Jones 12-28-1866 (12-29-1866) B

Bass, Fanny B. to Thos. T. Bowman 4-24-1867
Bass, Mary to John Jesse Lappet 4-13-1871 (no return) B
Bass, Nancy to James E. Morgan 4-16-1844 (4-24-1844)
Bass, Sallie E. to O. L. Townsend 12-16-1868 (12-17-1868)
Batt, Elizabeth Ann to Labon Holt 5-25-1842
Batt, Elizabeth F. to A. G. Pickens 1-17-1842 (1-19-1842)
Batt, Martha A. (Mrs.) to Young Montague 5-25-1848
Batt, Millie to Robert McClerrin 12-6-1870 (no return) B
Battle, Keziah to Harris Chaffin 2-1-1871 (no return) B
Battle, Lucy to George Reed 12-2-1869 (no return) B
Batts, Martha C. to Jesse J. Smith 10-12-1846
Baucum, Ellen to J. H. W. Hughes 6-12-1854 (no return)
Baucum, Sarah to Joseph Yarbrough 1-21-1845 (1-22-1845)
Baugh, M. S. to W. J. Shillings 7-31-1866
Baugh, Martha T. to Gustavus Berdon 6-11-1867 (6-18-1867)
Baugh, Mary E. to R. F. Warren 2-17-1868 (2-20-1868)
Baugh, Mary N. to William L. Wooten 12-31-1851 (no return)
Baugh, Mary to U. T. Stewart 9-?-1854 (no return)
Baulkum, Polly to Winfrey Scott 2-4-1839 (2-6-1839)
Baw, Allice to Robt. Johnson 12-3-1867 (no return)
Baw, Catharin to Calvin E. Stewart 12-28-1851 (no return)
Baw, Harriet to George Robertson 8-22-1867 (no return) B
Baw, Julia to William Farley 12-15-1854 (no return)
Baw, L. M. to C. W. McConnell 4-23-1860 (4-26-1860)
Baw, Winny Ann to Edward D. Stewart 12-30-1845
Baxler, Lizzie to Zedrick Warren 12-23-1867 (12-24-1867) B
Baxter, E. E. to W. H. Beal 12-12-1865
Baxter, Emily A. to E. H. Blankenship 12-12-1865
Baxter, Lucy C. to D. S. Nicholson 12-17-1868
Baxter, Malinda to Isaac Lewis 12-21-1867 (12-24-1867) B
Baxter, Margaret R.? to Rufus W. Powell 2-6-1850
Baxter, Nora to Wm. Lazenby 11-20-1869 (11-25-1869)
Baxter, Sallie E. to J. F. Humphreys 12-18-1860
Bayless, Ellenorah E. to Anguss Greenlaw 7-13-1844 (7-14-1844)
Bazzel, Eliza to Henry Barmon 10-3-1849 (no return)
Beard, Margarett to William Baker 1-25-1844
Beasley, Fanny to Henry Buford 2-6-1867 (2-7-1867) B
Beasley, L. F. to G. W. Smith 11-14-1853 (no return)
Beasley, Louisa F. to James M. Gray 4-17-1839 (4-18-1839)
Beasley, Mitta to H. Trump 11-2-1867 (11-4-1867)
Beasley, Virginia A. to James R. Hodge 6-13-1854 (no return)
Beasly, Lucy Q. (Mrs.) to John M. Thomas 4-8-1844 (no return)
Beaver, Eliza F. to John B. Thomson 12-23-1867 (12-24-1867)
Beaver, Isabella to B. F. Houk 4-20-1867 (4-21-1867)
Beaver, Mary to Henry Ballard 2-1-1867 (8-15-1867) B
Beaver, Rebecca Ann to Mathew Barberry 9-15-1842
Beaver, Sarah Ann to S. Williams 7-23-1845 (8-7-1845)
Beavers, C. M. to A. C. Atherton 1-8-1866 (1-10-1866)
Beavers, Lucinda to John W. Ables 2-26-1839
Beavers, Mandy to Joe Oliver 12-3-1868 (12-5-1868) B
Beavers, Mary A. to A. G. Ralph 1-2-1860 (not endorsed)
Beavers, Mary to Phil May 1-6-1868 (no return) B
Beckham, Elizabeth W. to Wm. Jack 6-26-1868 (7-5-1868)
Beer, Roselia to Joseph Hauf 1-24-1854 (no return)
Bell, Eliza A. to James E. Winsett 5-16-1867
Bell, Lucinda to Lewis Hutchins 9-30-1865 (10-1-1865)
Bell, Margarett L. to William H. Thompson 4-4-1855 (no return)
Bell, Martha M. to C. S. Aston 12-6-1847
Bell, Mary An to Jesse H. Sullivant 12-12-1848 (12-14-1848)
Bell, Nannie B. to Jas. W. Brooks 6-22-1865 (6-23-1865)
Bell, R. J. to Wm. R. Love 9-17-1859 (9-18-1859)
Bell, Rebecca W. to Lenard W. Morris 4-26-1849
Bell, Sarah (Mrs.) to Vinson Kenedy 4-21-1841 (no return)
Bell, Sarah A. J. (Mrs.) to S. Pitmon 5-15-1841 (no return)
Belote, Jane to Dorriss Ammons 7-10-1843 (no return)
Belote, Lucy M. to John T. Vick 11-15-1851 (no return)
Benge, Mary A. to John Gates 8-29-1840 (9-3-1840)
Bennett, Louisa to John Richy 2-3-1846 (2-5-1846)
Bennett, Mary to George W. Hood 2-23-1841
Bennett, Sarah L. to George T. Wheeler 1-16-1867
Bennett, Sarah to Asa Woodward 3-22-1846 (3-24-1846)
Benson, Elenor B. to Charles R. Black 9-8-1864 (9-11-1864)
Benson, M. J. to M. B. Walker 3-17-1848 (3-29-1848)
Benson, P. to J. E. Cole 12-6-1859 (12-13-1859)
Benson, Sally to Jos. B. Lacey 10-13-1866 (10-17-1866)

Benson, Zany Ann to Thos. J. Farrer 12-14-1844 (12-19-1844)
Bentley, Allice to Sam Allen 6-14-1867 (no return) B
Bentley, Analine to W. C. Reid no date (with Jun 1855)
Bently, Jane to Peter Young 6-30-1866 (no return) B
Benton, Ann to T. C. Gardner 10-9-1862 (not endorsed)
Benton, Ella to David L. Bain 7-27-1866 (10-15-1866)
Berry, Jane to Sip Hull (Hall?) 12-30-1869 B
Bever?, Marry Ann to C. F. Culbreth 6-26-1840
Bevins, Catharine to James P. Williams 12-25-1841
Bickers, Jane to Simon Powelson 9-18-1863
Bickerstaff, Mary to Alfred C. Robertson 10-12-1838 (10-16-1838)
Biddy, Aley A. to Wm. R. Blake 11-20-1867 (no return)
Biddy, Sarah to Jesse Bryant 11-21-1866 (11-22-1866)
Biggs, Charlotte to Elijah Grant 2-10-1871 (2-15-1871) B
Biggs, Maryann to Hiram S. Walker 11-29-1847
Biggs, Rachell to Richard Neeley 4-14-1849 (4-15-1849)
Birdson, Winney to Benjamin Griffin 2-8-1847
Birdsong, Altha to Joshua Johnson 9-9-1847
Birdsong, Cinthia A. to W. C. Adkins 6-27-1851 (6-30-1851)
Birdsong, Elizabeth to Samel Phillips 12-26-1839 (no return)
Birdwell, Martha to William Fellow 10-16-1841 (10-17-1841)
Bishop, Priscilla to Robert Jones 10-17-1868 (10-18-1868) B
Bivens, Susan to Ben Brockman 4-9-1845 (4-10-1845)
Bivins, Martha O. to Henry C. Boroughs 12-23-1846 (12-24-1846)
Black, Caroline A. to John O. H. Buford 11-2-1846 (11-5-1846)
Black, Caroline V. to Jas. B. Campbell 1-30-1866
Black, Caroline to Leonard Burnett 1-26-1869 (no return) B
Black, Chaney to Frank Jones 2-3-1871 (5-20-1871) B
Black, Mary P. to Wm. J. Bishop 3-8-1849 (3-13-1849)
Black, Mary to Tom Bailey 8-26-1868 (no return) B
Black, Rosah to Dennis McGinnis 4-30-1868 (no return) B
Black, Sallie L. to M. J. Webb 10-4-1860 (10-5-1860)
Black, Sarah to Isam Beasley 3-3-1845 (no return)
Blackburn, Lydia Ann to John Morton 1-13-1870 (1-18-1870) B
Blackburn, Mary E. to James R. Moss 9-25-1844 (9-26-1844)
Blackburn, Mary E. to James R. Moss no dates (with Feb 1844)
Blackwell, Elizabeth to Charles G. Mitchell 8-21-1838
Blackwood, Martha to Granville Lucas 12-24-1870 (12-25-1870) B
Blain, Adeline W. to M. B. Broyles? 11-30-1855 (no return)
Blain, Betty to Rufus Warr 12-25-1868 (12-27-1868) B
Blain, E. L. to W. C. Jenkins 3-3-1868 (3-5-1868)
Blain, M. E. to A. Waller 12-20-1852 (no return)
Blain, M. E. to James L. Jenkins 11-6-1865 (no return)
Blain, Mariah to John P. Wiseman 12-17-1860 (12-20-1860)
Blain, Sarah to Asburry Harrell 12-13-1866 (no return)
Blaine, Easter to Jesse Heaslett 9-27-1871? (SB 1870?) B
Blair, M. A. E. to A. G. B. Harris 9-14-1866 (9-16-1866)
Blair, Margaretta to Hardamon Abington 9-19-1839 (9-26-1839)
Blair, Martha Ann to David B. Hilliard 2-2-1846 (2-5-1846)
Blair, Mary to Noah Dane 11-1-1841 (11-10-1841)
Blair, Rebecca C. to Luke L. Williams 7-20-1846 (no return)
Blalock, Emma E. to David S. Reed 12-19-1863 (12-24-1863)
Blanchard, Sarah E. to Reding Whitehead 2-4-1852 (no return)
Bland, Martha W. N. to William A. Taylor 4-17-1839 (4-24-1839)
Bland, Mary to Wm. L. Nelson 3-5-1860 (3-7-1860)
Blaw, Mozella to Taylor Broom 12-21-1868 (12-25-1868) B
Blaydes, Nicie to Hanks Parker 2-4-1871 (no return) B
Blaydes, Sarah E. to Samel D. Ware 2-22-1851 (2-27-1851)
Bledsoe, Emma to Haden Miller 2-11-1871 (no return) B
Bledsoe, Martha to Cyrus Elcan 10-10-1870 (10-29-1870) B
Blessing, Elizabeth to Alexander Bowland 7-29-1841
Blessing, Louisa to Mark M. Frazer 9-11-1845 (12-6-1845)
Blessing, Martha to Joseph Scallions 6-8-1847 (6-9-1847)
Bluford, Vina to Andy Hunter 1-10-1871 (no return) B
Boales, Margarett A. to Joseph B. Bounds 9-21-1847 (10-10-1847)
Boals, A. S. to Edwin H. Poor 3-21-1867
Boals, Margaret to Gus Griffin 2-24-1869 (2-25-1869) B
Boals, Sally to Anthony Towles 12-28-1868 (12-30-1868) B
Boatman?, Sarah Ann to William Cain 6-4-1852 (no return)
Bobbitt, Catharine to Jerome Davis 9-16-1870 (9-18-1870) B
Bobbitt, Harriet to Washington Goodwin 12-9-1869 (12-16-1869) B
Bobbitt, Isabella S. to James Gwin 1-10-1853 (no return)
Bobbitt, Susan to Cleiborn Culp 9-27-1869 (10-2-1869) B
Boley, Ann E. to Thomas M. Means 10-4?-1853 (no return)
Boling, C. D. to P. E. Smith 4-27-1853 (no return)

Bolling, Elisabeth A. to William N. Morgan 10-24-1848 (11-1-1848)
Bolling, Patience to Henry Jackson 3-17-1866 (3-21-1866) B
Bomer, Mary E. to Thos. J. Stafford 2-24-1840 (2-27-1840)
Bondurant, Mary to B. F. Murrell 6-?-1842 (no return)
Bone, Mary to Hamilton Smith 8-21-1866 (8-23-1866)
Bone, Siloa to Ed Williams 6-9-1870 (6-25-1870) B
Bonner, Elizabeth A. to W. B. Battle 12-8-1846
Booker, Frances to Richard Baskerville 12-22-1870 (12-28-1870) B
Booker, Virginia A. to Dewitt C. Mosby 11-19-1841 (11-20-1841)
Boon, Malissa G. to David T. Smith 10-1-1844 (10-3-1844)
Boon, Nancy to T. C. Beard 6-7-1852 (no return)
Boon?, Margarette W. to And. F. David 5-20-1844 (5-22-1844)
Booth, Eveline to John Gabley 4-17-1852 (no return)
Booth, Martha A. to Thomas P. Watkins 9-18-1838
Bordley, Jane S. to Charles Potts 9-1-1840 (9-10-1840)
Bostick, Winney C. to Willie Ozier 12-1-1843
Boswell, Callie B. to Charles W. Jordan 12-10-1866 (12-12-1866)
Boswell, Elizabeth A. to John A. Alexander 5-1-1865
Boswell, Emily F. to Geo. W. Parratt 10-6-1848 (10-12-1848)
Boswell, Gray to George Hughes 6-18-1867 (no return) B
Boswell, Martha to Alfred Kelly 3-9-1847 (no return)
Boswell, Mary to M. A. Redmond 1-12-1848
Boswell, Salina to John Coates 4-21-1845
Boswell, Sallie Jane to L. C. Crenshaw 8-18-1866 (no return)
Bott, Adaline to Charles Session 3-23-1867 (3-30-1867) B
Botts, Lucy? J. to John W. Finch 9-16-1849
Bounds, Eliza to Thomas May 1-13-1870 (1-31-1870) B
Bounds, Frances G. to Mothen? R. Price 12-17-1849 (no return)
Bounds, L. A. to Franklin Hooper 2-8-1838
Bounds, Louisa to Allen Coulter 9-18-1854 (no return)
Bounds, Martha Ann to John T. Thompson 8-10-1846 (8-13-1846)
Bounds, Mary Ann to James S. Denniston 10-23-1844
Bounds, Mary E. to Chas. W. Rich 12-3-1844 (no return)
Bounds, Sarah Ann to John W. Van Pelt 9-7-1840 (9-24-1840)
Bounds, Stacy to William Grisham 10-31-1845 (no return)
Bourne, Caroline E. to S. D. Bond? 4-24-1854 (no return)
Bowen, Josephine to J. M. Davis 1-1-1866 (1-4-1866)
Bowers, D. Ellen to R. A. Dunkum 2-25-1854 (no return)
Bowers, E. W. G. to J. H. Johnston 10-14-1868 (10-25-1868)
Bowers, Florrence to Robbin Bowers 1-5-1867 B
Bowers, Martha C. to W. B. Stafford 9-14-1847 (no return)
Bowers, Mary C. to Peterson P. Broom 11-5-1838 (11-17-1838)
Bowes, Mary Jane (Mrs.) to Fondell Carpenter 5-28-1853 (no return)
Bowling, Martha to Wiley Morgan 9-16-1870 (9-21-1870) B
Bowls, Mary Jane to Claiborne Gray 9-22-1866 (no return) B
Boyd, Adaline to Fletcher Whitehead 7-20-1867 (8-10-1867) B
Boyd, Eliza to Jack Word 3-27-1869 (no return) B
Boyd, Eliza to Tom Bracken 5-19-1868 (5-22-1868) B
Boyd, H. H. (Mrs.) to Matthew Rhea, jr. 9-15-1859
Boyd, Hadnah? to Francis A. Wilson 1-29-1850
Boyd, Lou to Ike Morrow 12-8-1868 (no return) B
Boyd, Lou to Littleton H. Perkins 3-1-1871
Boyd, M. E. to Stephen G. Bradsher 12-7-1869 (12-16-1869)
Boyd, Mary E. to J. R. McGinnis 12-21-1862 (1-1-1863)
Boyd, Nancy to Lot Harvey 3-23-1866 (4-1-1866) B
Boyd, Rebeca to J. W. Morris 6-15-1855 (no return)
Boyd, Rose to Henry Harris 3-23-1867 (3-30-1867) B
Boyd, Sallie to Wyatt Bailey 1-11-1871
Boyd, Susan to Mack Bowers 3-27-1869 (3-28-1869) B
Boyd, Susan to Peter Mitchell 1-8-1869 (1-9-1869) B
Boyd, Susana to Nelson Nance 8-5-1868 (8-6-1868) B
Boyed, Lucinda to William Wright 4-30-1850 (5-1-1850)
Boyet, Catharine M. to A. G. Tilghman 11-24-1855 (no return)
Boykin, C. A. to Edmond Burnett 7-20-1866 (8-11-1866) B
Boylan, Missouri to Ben Burt 8-31-1867 (no return) B
Boylan, Priscilla P. (Mrs.) to Wm. F. Brown 3-14-1839
Boyle, Arabella to Joe Sewell 2-7-1868 (2-8-1868) B
Boyssian, Henrietta to Isham Fields 11-28-1843 (11-29-1843)
Brace, Louiza to Jno. W. Tripp 5-4-1868 (5-10-1868) B
Bracken, Bettie to James Chaffin 2-13-1869 (2-16-1869) B
Bracken, Rebecca to James Rhea 3-30-1867 (no return) B
Bradberry, Elizabeth J. to Washington B. Hargus 5-16-1844
   (5-17-1844)
Braden, Abby E. to Andrew Trusdale 11-22-1869 (no return) B
Braden, Harriet J. to W. H. Freeman 11-4-1865 (11-5-1865)

Braden, Julia to Henry Harris 3-8-1867 (3-9-1867)
Braden, Susan E. to J. F. Cranford 11-26-1867 (12-1-1867)
Bradley, Mary to Jesse Hughes 7-7-1840 (7-9-1840)
Bradly, M. E. to James B. Adams 1-23-1860 (1-24-1860)
Bradly, Susanah to Samuel Fitzpatrick 11-2-1840 (11-5-1840)
Bradshaw, Martha A. to C. H. Culwell 5-3-1869
Bradshaw, Mary Ann to John Swinney 3-23-1869 (3-24-1869)
Bradsher, Demaris A. to James E. Yancey 5-25-1863 (5-26-1863)
Brady, Mary J. to Samuel M. Durham 1-27-1852 (no return)
Bram, Sarah J. to James B. Baker 6-19-1854 (no return)
Brame, E. S. to John W. Hester 1-7-1841
Brame, Elizabeth I. to John A. R. Brim 6-14-1838 (no return)
Brame, Elizabeth to W. G. Barker 1-8-1848
Branch, A. V. to S. W. Baxter 12-19-1850
Branch, Amy to P. A.? May 12-7-1852 (no return)
Branch, Angelina to Geo. M. Stewart 1-7-1846
Branch, Darcus to James A. Haselet 9-21-1867 (no return) B
Branch, Frances to Tho. J. Brown 1-14-1846 (1-15-1846)
Branch, Martha A. to William P. Butterworth 2-17-1843 (2-23-1843)
Branch, Mary R. to Geo. R. Lipscomb 2-21-1870 (2-22-1870)
Branch, Maryann to Jesse T. Butterworth 9-13-1847 (9-16-1847)
Branch, Minerva to John A. Moody 6-11-1860 (6-13-1860)
Branch, Nancy Jane to R. W. Newby 10-27-1852 (no return)
Branch, Polly to R. D. Grant 6-23-1849
Branch, S. J. to T. J. Firth 8-28-1868 (9-9-1868)
Branch, Sarah R. to Beverly L. Dyer 10-27-1852 (no return)
Branch, Tennessee to W. S. Pearce 11-28-1862 (12-2-1862)
Branscomb, Lou to Silas Ewell 2-24-1868 (2-29-1868) B
Braswell, Julia to Jacob Cross 1-28-1870 (no return) B
Bratcher, S. E. to W. F. Yancey 9-19-1859 (9-21-1859)
Breene?, S. A. to James D. Hesther 6-28-1842 (7-14-1842)
Brewer, Emma to Bernard Hale 12-20-1867 (12-28-1867) B
Brewer, Frances to Robt. Mason 2-7-1868 (2-9-1868)
Brewer, Jantha to Booker Flippin 1-7-1870 (no return) B
Brewer, Nancy to Zack Olds 12-28-1870   B
Brewster, Lavenia to Albert Gwyn 12-23-1866 (12-27-1866) B
Bridgewater, A. to Eli Cavnes 12-9-1869 (12-25-1869) B
Bridgewater, Allice to Henry Stott 2-18-1871 (3-1-1871) B
Bridgewater, Henrietta to James Johnston 11-15-1865 (11-16-1865)
Bridgewater, Martha A. to John H. Hardin 7-26-1849 (7-31-1849)
Bridgewater, Mary to Moses Walker 5-1-1867 (5-4-1867) B
Bridgwater, L. A. to R. A. Crowder 1-11-1859 (not endorsed)
Bridly, Ellen to Granville Fitzpatrick 1-26-1842 (1-27-1842)
Brinkey, Nancy to Willingham Cooper 6-18-1839 (6-20-1839)
Brinkley, Frances to George Doty 7-3-1841 (no return)
Brinkley, Jane R. to L. D. Keywood 3-7-1855 (no return)
Brinkley, Kitty to Fed Wilson 9-3-1870 (9-4-1870) B
Brinkley, Sarah to Jeremiah Brinkley 1-27-1849 (2-1-1849)
Brinkly, Susan to James Sutton 10-18-1844 (10-19-1844)
Brister, Lutisha to J. W. Conner 2-1-1847 (2-2-1847)
Broadnax, Henrietta to Bevly Maclin 2-20-1869 (2-23-1869) B
Broadnax, Martha to Martin Broadnax 10-16-1869 B
Broadnax, Susan to Neverson Hacklin 12-9-1839 (12-10-1839)
Broadwaters, Lucinda H. to William Sprouce 12-9-1839 (12-10-1839)
Brock, Sailie P. to Jas. P. Love 12-19-1868 (1-13-1869)
Brodnax, Florence to J. N. Maclin 5-24-1869 (5-30-1869)
Brodnax, Mary J. to J. W. Maclin 6-17-1861 (6-19-1861)
Brodnax, Sally to Benj. Thomas 2-2-1867 (no return) B
Bromly, Susan J. to Thomas J. W. Dilliard 12-19-1866
Brook, Marcindy to Henry Luster 3-12-1867 (3-15-1867) B
Brooke, Jennie to Geo. R. Scott 1-4-1870 (1-6-1870)
Brooks, Eliza T. to Wm. O'Daniel 12-23-1846 (no return)
Brooks, Elizabeth A. to G. H. Davis 1-4-1854 (no return)
Brooks, Lila to David Dawson 12-3-1870 B
Brooks, Lucy to Stephen Belan 10-5-1870 B
Brooks, Malissa to George McDowell 9-26-1868 (9-27-1868) B
Brooks, Manerva A. to William P. Taylor 1-6-1851 (1-7-1851)
Brooks, Nancy C. to James B. Caperton 10-15-1844 (no return)
Broom, Ann Eliza to Geo. T. Hunter 11-2-1846 (11-5-1846)
Broom, Clara to Beverly Lacy 12-28-1868 B
Broom, Eliza to John T. Herron 3-22-1838
Broom, Frances to J. Lenow 1-7-1845 (1-9-1845)
Broom, Jane to Wm. A. Verser 10-1-1841
Broom, Lucinda to John Walker 1-4-1868 (no return) B
Broom, Martha to James W. Beasley 10-1-1847 (10-2-1847)

Broom, Mary Jane to James W. Hamlet 5-8-1840 (5-14-1840)
Brown, Adeline to Leonard Lewis 7-23-1869 (7-24-1869) B
Brown, Clara to Landon Harrison 12-12-1868
Brown, E. A. to J. G. Tatum 1-11-1866 (1-14-1866)
Brown, Eda A. to Starky S. Hare 2-14-1859 (2-22-1859)
Brown, Eleander to Curtis Winfield 12-16-1848
Brown, Eleanor C. to Geo. W. Martin 12-11-1849
Brown, Eliza J. to Alex. Field 10-15-1842 (no return)
Brown, Eliza to Enoch Beale 2-22-1868 B
Brown, Elizabeth to Abraham White no date (with Dec 1856)
Brown, Ella to William Lewis 8-28-1869 (8-29-1869) B
Brown, Ellen to Jacob Bell 12-28-1867 (12-13?-1868) B
Brown, Emma to Lewis Bowers 12-27-1869 (12-23?-1869) B
Brown, Emma to Louis Rogers 12-7-1869 (no return) B
Brown, Frances to Napoleon Stanney 2-1-1871 (2-4-1871) B
Brown, Henrietta to Grandison Rives 12-25-1867 (12-26-1867) B
Brown, J. L. to John D. Hunter 5-30-1870 (no return)
Brown, Jane to A. J. Langham 2-7-1842 (no return)
Brown, Jane to William Finley 4-23-1870 (no return) B
Brown, Jane to Wm. Hooker 1-3-1849 (no return)
Brown, L. J. to J. H. Granberry 4-9-1866 (4-11-1866)
Brown, Lizzie to Zack Shaw 12-25-1866 (12-27-1866) B
Brown, Mahala to David Walton 12-28-1870 (12-29-1870) B
Brown, Malinda to Nat Vaughan 12-10-1868 (no return) B
Brown, Malinda to Paul Cash 4-26-1870 (4-30-1870) B
Brown, Margaret to Young Fitch 11-25-1865   B
Brown, Margarett M. to James M. Birdwell 4-6-1853 (no return)
Brown, Martha E. to Wm. A. Lea 6-14-1852 (no return)
Brown, Mary A. to J. C. Clements 2-8-1842 (no return)
Brown, Mary E. to R. W. Pegram 9-10-1847
Brown, Mary V. to J. B. Moore 10-23-1867 (10-24-1867)
Brown, Mary to Alfred Wilkins 6-15-1869 B
Brown, Mary to John Jones 3-16-1867 (3-17-1867) B
Brown, Mary to Saml. Boggs 1-5-1867 (1-6-1867)
Brown, Matilda to Thomas Reddick 3-16-1867 (3-18-1867) B
Brown, Mima to Matthew T. Gibson 5-27-1870 (5-28-1870) B
Brown, Nancy C. to John H. Hill 9-23-1853 (no return)
Brown, Nancy to Jesse Humphrey 11-24-1848
Brown, Nancy to John McShaw 12-5-1870 (no return)
Brown, Peggy to Wash Jones 5-2-1867 (5-5-1867) B
Brown, Penelope A. to Wm. W. Cargil 4-6-1849 (5-2-1849)
Brown, Rebecca to Robt. Gray 7-21-1870 (7-22-1870) B
Brown, Sallie to John C. Morris 2-25-1870 (no return) B
Brown, Sally D. to Samuel Hodge 8-12-1843 (no return)
Brown, Sarah to Elijah Wroten 2-14-1846 (no return)
Brown, Susan to Johnson Bunton 10-23-1845
Browne, Cintha to Joseph Johnson 2-3-1845 (2-4-1845)
Browne, Cordelia to Wm. M. Watt 6-2-1845 (no return)
Brownlow, Edna J. to William J. Floyd 8-8-1846 (no return)
Brownlow, Patsey to Marton McConnell 9-30-1841 (10-15-1841)
Broyles, Matilda to Nathaniel Tatum 11-23-1843 (11-25-1843)
Bruce, Mary J. to Robt. T. Jackson 7-28-1845 (7-30-1845)
Bruce, Sarah A. to Wm. Scoth 3-20-1843 (3-22-1843)
Brumley, Elizabeth to Barnett M. Trainer 6-27-1839 (7-4-1839)
Brumley, Mary to J. J. Holloway 10-27-1849 (10-28-1849)
Brumley, Nancy to Isaac Shinault 2-2-1843
Bryan, Sarah W. to John Bivren 1-22-1839
Bryant, Arretta to A. W. Webber 1-11-1853 (no return)
Bryant, Christina to Isaac A. Henley 1-28-1848 (no return)
Bryant, Demarious to John C. Dolton 10-3-1853 (no return)
Bryant, Eliz. to Chas. McNamee 6-21-1845 (no return)
Bryant, M. J. to W. B. Wright 3-27-1866 (3-28-1866)
Bryant, Tempe. S. to Francis Erickson 1-28-1851
Bryles, Carolin to James L. Ormann 1-9-1843 (1-16-1843)
Bryles, Rebeca to John Holloway 1-8-1841
Buck, Mariah to Jan L. Miller 7-15-1851 (no return)
Buckley, Eliza M. to Franklin McKnight 11-7-1843 (11-14-1843)
Buckley, Rebecca to Hall Kersey 12-1-1863 (12-3-1863)
Bucy, Margaret T. to Jno. P. Sensing 9-5-1867 (9-10-1867)
Buford, A. M. to Jesse B. Brown 6-19-1840 (6-24-1840)
Buford, E. A. to F. C. Manley 12-22-1869
Buford, Frances to John Williams 11-2-1866 (11-3-1866) B
Buford, Hannah to Washington Boile 12-27-1869 (12-31-1869) B
Buford, Jane to William McPherson 2-27-1871 (3-4-1871) B
Buford, Lemon to Rasmus Maclin 12-23-1869 (no return) B

Buford, Malinda to Charley Jones 12-27-1869 (12-30-1869) B
Buford, Susan J. to C. P. Lemons 5-5-1840 (5-7-1840)
Bugg, Elizabeth D. to John C. Waddell 8-15-1846
Bull, Luzenia to D. P. Cowan 3-11-1851
Bull, M. H. to H. C. Able 9-2-1867 (9-5-1867)
Bull, Mary to G. W. Robertson 1-22-1853 (no return)
Bull, Nancy C. to Wm. C. Hunter 5-19-1847 (5-20-1847)
Bull, Rebecca to A. F. Cowan 10-22-1845
Bullock, Jane to Manuel Jones 1-27-1866 (no return) B
Bullock, Julia A. to Elisha S. Seymore 10-20-1847
Bullock, S. M. to R. P. Russell 1-31-1866 (no return)
Buly?, Mary C. to Temple C. Walker 5-6-1848 (5-7-1848)
Bumpass, Mary E. to Robt. Caldwell 11-3-1846
Bumpass, Sarah? to E. J. Watson 3-1-1842
Burdaux, Mary E. to Richard F. Cooper 2-9-1839 (2-10-1839)
Burford, Caroline to Thomas W. Harris 8-21-1843 (no return)
Burford, Charlotte to Ephraim Pirdle 12-25-1868 (12-28-1868) B
Burford, Elizabeth to Tho. R. Tuggle 10-1-1846 (no return)
Burford, Lucy to John S. Herron 10-14-1854 (no return)
Burford, Martha G. to John W. Youngs 12-21-1840 (12-23-1840)
Burford, Nancy S. to John S. Normont 7-27-1847 (7-28-1847)
Burford, P. C. to F. Shaw 10-24-1850 (no return)
Burford, Rebeca C. to Marcus D. Harvey 4-8-1839 (4-9-1839)
Burklow, M. M. to Wm. Therrell 11-6-1868 (no return)
Burnes, Jane to Bird Smith 11-27-1839 (12-1-1839)
Burnett, Callie E. to J. A. Summers 1-25-1869 (1-27-1869)
Burnett, Harriett to W. H. Boswell 12-5-1853 (no return)
Burnett, M. T. to J. G. Garvin 9-6-1862 (9-9-1862)
Burns, Delila J. to J. Strange 4-11-1842 (4-12-1842)
Burnset, Charlotte E. to Mark Holman 9-10-1846 (9-17-1846)
Burriss, Martha to Richard B. Wilson 10-14-1847
Burrough, Ellen to Henry Smith 12-4-1869 (no return) B
Burroughs, Eugenia E. to Sterling M. Black 10-23-1869 (10-27-1869)
Burrow, Caroline to Wm. Perser 8-16-1849 (no return)
Burrow, Jane to John M. Meak 10-24-1848 (no return)
Burrow, Lucinda O. to Miles A. Dillard 7-28-1854 (no return)
Burrow, Mary J. to Benj. H. Wortham 9-8-1846 (no return)
Burrows, Catharine to Wm. M. Chambers 1-29-1855 (no return)
Burt, H. W. to A. B. Finny 10-29-1854 (no return)
Burton, Anna A. to Vincent R. Stafford 12-19-1838 (12-20-1838)
Burton, Elizabeth to E. L. Peters 4-18-1850 (no return)
Burton, Julia A. to T. J. Towlkes 7-16-1857
Burton, Lucy F. to J. J. Pulliam 4-24-1850
Burton, Marieller to James P. Mercer 5-12-1855 (no return)
Burtus, Sarah to William L. Cole 12-22-1847 (12-23-1847)
Busey, Sarah M. to Benj. W. Jeter 4-13-1868 (4-16-1868)
Butler, Mary Ann to A. J. Blane 2-15-1864
Butterworth, Ann to Uel H. Farmer 10-10-1839
Butterworth, Mary E. to Wm. W. Spence 12-6-1847 (12-8-1847)
Butterworth, S. E. to Richd. R. Gwyn 11-10-1859 (11-15-1859)
Bynum, Elizabeth to Washington Eddins 5-12-1846 (5-22-1846)
Cabler, Indiana M. to A. W. Moore 8-16-1838
Cage, Susan to Thomas G. Anderson 4-8-1838 (no return)
Caldwell, Ann to Ham Stewart 11-27-1865 (no return)
Caldwell, Rebecca to Jas. A. Cox 12-15-1868 (12-16-1868)
Cammond, Unity to B. A. Walden 10-3-1853 (no return)
Campbell, Amanda to A. J. Shinault 8-29-1850
Campbell, Eliza R. to Benj. Scott 1-25-1839 (1-31-1839)
Campbell, Elizabeth to A. G. Foster 4-27-1853 (no return)
Campbell, Elizabeth to John Lovelady 7-15-1839
Campbell, Ella to R. C. Patty 11-8-1869 (11-11-1869)
Campbell, Harriet to Edmund Jones 5-21-1868 (5-23-1868) B
Campbell, Jennie to Chas. A. George 6-18-1867 (6-20-1867)
Campbell, Olia to Gilbert Clapp 1-4-1871 (2-14-1871) B
Campbell, Sallie to J. N. Smith 9-1-1860 (9-2-1860)
Campbell, Sarah A. to A. J. Brumley 8-20-1846
Canada, Julia A. F. to Chas. Ward 12-16-1867 (12-20-1867)
Cannon, Phoebe to Stephen Stull 7-21-1866 (7-22-1866) B
Capers, Ella to C. H. Rice 12-19-1870 (12-20-1870)
Capers, Fanny to Virginius A. McEllroy 10-14-1869 (10-18-1869)
Capers, Rosa to Alfred Sherrod 12-27-1869 (12-30-1869) B
Caple, Hepsabeth to Richard Iby 2-22-1841 (2-24-1841)
Caples, Ann Eliza to J. G. Field 10-23-1865 (10-26-1865)
Capp, Artis Y. to David Mendeth? 12-28-1840 (no return)
Capps, Emily C. to Nathan Lewis 8-16-1845 (no return)

Capps, Martha to John E. Jeffries 12-9-1840 (no return)
Caraway, Elmira to Lucas Roane 11-6-1869 (11-7-1869) B
Caraway, Fanny to Oney C. Wall 2-14-1867
Caraway, Martha J. to David J. Jernigan 9-30-1844 (no return)
Caraway, Nancy M. to W. H. Piller 12-22-1856 (no return)
Cargell, Mary A. to Mad Plant 3-14-1853 (no return)
Cargil, L. J. to John L. Evans 12-28-1849 (no return)
Cargill, Lucinda to James Watkins 12-28-1866 (no return) B
Cargill, Lucinda to Tom Cargill 8-8-1867 (12-28-1867) B
Cargit, Martha R. to Isaac D. Evans 10-20-1849 (no return)
Carloss, Cornelia A. to Berry Mutemas? 2-3-1871 (2-8-1871) B
Carnes, Mary to John Pugh 8-29-1867 (9-6-1867) B
Carnes, Mary to Samuel Tate 4-19-1843
Carpenter, Amy to Thos. Tappan 12-22-1870 B
Carpenter, Ann J. to Joel C. Howell 9-13-1851 (no return)
Carpenter, Ellen to Harvy Johnson 3-17-1869 (3-19-1869) B
Carpenter, Ellen to William Gilbert 4-16-1867 (not executed) B
Carpenter, Frances E. to Charles C. Howell 12-21-1847 (12-23-1847)
Carpenter, Julia to Frank Maddox 1-13-1869 (1-14-1869)
Carpenter, L. V. to B. J. W. Cocke 9-17-1860
Carpenter, Lucy Jane to William A. Ealey 7-20-1852 (no return)
Carpenter, Rilda to Richard Henry 5-29-1869 (no return) B
Carpenter, Tennessee C. to Thos. W. Kennon 9-26-18686 (9-27-1866)
Carpenter, Violet to Sam Dickinson 5-1-1869 (5-3-1869) B
Carraway, Mary A. to D. G. Morris 2-3-1866 (2-8-1866)
Carraway, N. B. to R. H. Cook 8-16-1851 (no return)
Carraway, Sarah A. to David H. Johnson 11-26-1845 (11-27-1845)
Carraway, Winiford S. to Wm. H. Neal 7-3-1852 (no return)
Carroll, Charity to Paten Hare 11-16-1869 (no return) B
Carroll, Judia A. to J. W. Murrell 1-18-1869 (no return)
Carter, B. to David Harrell 3-2-1838
Carter, Ciney to L. D. Hood 10-6-1840 (10-27-1840)
Carter, Ellin to Henry Benson 9-2-1839 (no return)
Carter, Julia to Green Levy 10-19-1867 (10-20-1867) B
Carter, Love to Henry Allen 1-13-1867 (1-19-1867) B
Carter, Lucy to Sam Carter 1-7-1867 (1-12-1867) B
Carter, M. E. to P. Wilson, jr. 7-25-1863 (7-29-1863)
Carter, Mary to C. L. Bullock 9-25-1854 (no return)
Carter, Sarah A. to R. W. Reams 7-12-1849
Carter, Virginia to J. C. Sisco 12-1-1868 (12-2-1868)
Cartwright, A. V. to J. T. Murrell 9-27-1852 (no return)
Cartwright, Anna J. to J. A. Clay 11-18-1867 (11-20-1867)
Cartwright, Eliza Ann to Haywood Miller 6-3-1869 (no return) B
Cartwright, Eliza to Henry Clay 12-20-1867 (no return) B
Cartwright, Marinett to Thadios Wilson 9-8-1849 (10-3-1849)
Casey, Darthula to James Sloane 7-18-1848 (no return)
Cash, Evelina W. to Thomas R. F. Simpson 1-6-1842
Cassel, Harriet V. to Joseph M. Figgins 2-16-1867 (2-22-1867)
Cassell, Lydia T. to Thomas J. Pardew 12-3-1866 (12-4-1866)
Cassett, Anna A. to W. J. Montgomery 2-25-1860 (5-2-1860)
Cassett?, Mary C. to R. H. Malone 10-2-1849 (10-3-1849)
Castles, Eliza to Jack Peterbock 1-15-1869 (1-16-1869) B
Cater, Eliza W. to E. H. Smith 5-5-1863 (5-6-1863)
Cathey, Narcissa to John T. Jones 11-9-1848 (no return)
Catron, Lou to Tom Seymour 1-16-1866 B
Catron, Rebecca to William Catron 7-23-1870 (no return) B
Chaffin, Adney to Thad Moore 2-28-1868 (no return) B
Chaffin, Charlott to Wm. Lenard 7-20-1867 (7-27-1867) B
Chaffin, Ella E. to A. A. Prichard 9-23-1868
Chaffin, Eveline to James Blaydes 7-3-1867 B
Chaffin, Mollie A. to P. D. Ewell 8-5-1867
Chaffin, Sue to Beverly Isbell 9-26-1867 B
Chaffin, Viola L. to William S. Green 12-20-1870 (no return)
Chambers, Elizabeth D. to W. A.? Hilliard 2-1-1847 (2-4-1847)
Chambers, Emma C. to J. F. Cox 4-19-1870 (4-21-1870)
Chambers, Hannah to Freeman Holt 11-6-1869 (12-4-1869) B
Chambers, M. R. to W. S. Teague 1-31-1864 (2-2-1864)
Chambers, Martha to J. F. Taylor 12-29-1866 (12-30-1866)
Chambers, Mary A. to J. W. T. Hilliard 12-6-1854 (no return)
Chambers, Mary Ann to A. H. Price 10-9-1848 (10-23-1848)
Chambers, Nancy J. to A. Burkhart 1-24-1855 (no return)
Chambers, Palina to Gloster Chambers 11-6-1869 (12-4-1869) B
Champion, Fannie to J. J. Wall 1-10-1867
Champion, Malinda M. to T. M. Shepard 9-28-1867
Chapman, C. T. to W. D. Simpkins 2-6-1866 (2-8-1866)

Chapman, Mattie to W. E. Parker 5-7-1867
Chappel, Pruda to Wm. B. Oliver 9-17-1839 (9-19-1839)
Cheairs, Martha K. to John M. Rook 1-17-1859 (1-18-1859)
Chesolm, Margaret H. to Willie J. Littlejohn 1-18-1843
Childes, Cinetia M. to Mathew M. Cullum 1-26-1848 (no return)
Childress, Anna to G. W. Davis 7-16-1870 (7-17-1870)
Chitts, Fannie V. to J. H. Perkins 10-3-1867
Chives?, Martha (Mrs.) to Jno. L. Richardson 10-14-1844 (10-17-1844)
Chrismon, Mary C. to Quincy A. Tipton 9-1-1841
Christman, Lucinda H. to Isaac Lacy 2-7-1843 (2-9-1843)
Christman, Rutha E. to W. H. Taylor 2-12-1853 (no return)
Chunn, Eliza to Archie Sellers 3-11-1870 (3-12-1870) B
Churchhill, Harrett J. to J. M. Pickins 10-11-1852 (no return)
Churchhill, M. M. V. to W. H. Walden 11-7-1865 (11-9-1865)
Churchill, Rachel to B. F. Nelson 1-30-1849
Cisco, Ada to James T. Carter 12-30-1867 (1-14-1868)
Cisco, Mollie to J. E. Alexander 1-27-1869 (1-28-1869)
Clacks, G. A. to Henry Sain 12-10-1851 (no return)
Clampit, E. J. to James Hood 1-3-1842 (1-13-1842)
Clancey, Lititia to B. Carter 2-7-1865
Clark, Amanda to J. M. Thomas 12-6-1865? (12-9-1862)
Clark, E. A. to Benj. A. Bailey 11-27-1855 (no return)
Clark, Laura N. to Rufus Bass 2-5-1868 (2-6-1868)
Clark, Lutetia to Bob Poindexter 9-16-1867 (9-21-1867) B
Clark, Matilda J. to David Fuller 4-21-1866 (no return)
Clark, Mildred Ann to Eli R. Compton 8-13-1840
Clark, S. E. to A. F. Hudson 12-24-1853 (no return)
Clark, Susan W. to M. A. May 1-20-1847
Clary, Sarah A. to J. P. Bond 1-21-1867 (1-24-1867)
Clay, Iola to James I. Jones 11-15-1869 (11-17-1869)
Clay, M. P. to W. F. Landreth 4-8-1863 (4-30-1863)
Clayton, Emma to Elisah Pippin 3-16-1869 (3-18-1869)
Clayton, Mary L. to G. M. Pool 5-14-1866 (5-16-1866)
Clayton, Parlee to E. R. Collins 4-28-1863 (4-30-1863)
Clayton, S. J. to J. W. Hughes 11-29-1866 (11-30-1865?)
Clear, Lucy to J. S. Luck 11-5-1869 (11-9-1869)
Cleave, Indiana to Frank Hubbard 8-27-1870 (no return) B
Cleaves, Caroline to Ephraim Chaney 2-20-1869 (2-27-1869) B
Cleaves, Julia D. to H. W. Yarborough 9-10-1860 (9-13-1860)
Cleaves, Laura A. to Benj. F. Reddick 1-27-1840
Cleaves, Mary H. to John T. Garrison 5-7-1863
Cleaves, Sarah to John P. Smith 3-10-1843 (no return)
Cleere, Mary E. to Wm. F. Jones 9-2-1845 (9-4-1845)
Clements, Melvinie to Simon W. Green 6-23-1862
Clendenen, Lydia A. to Robert C. Black 8-15-1840 (8-21-1840)
Clift, Sarah to Edwin Pennington 12-16-1844 (12-19-1844)
Clifton, Letha to Jackson Williams 6-16-1866 (no return) B
Clifton, Mary P. to John G. Tatum 1-18-1841 (1-21-1841)
Clifton, Sarah E. to Louis H. Poindexter 1-23-1871 (1-25-1871)
Clifton, Virginia to C. C. Poindexter 1-24-1870 (1-25-1870)
Cloyd, Cynthia to Albert Johnson 7-23-1870 (7-29-1870) B
Cloyd, Rose to Moses Finney 3-14-1870 (no return) B
Cloyed, Eliza A. to D. T. Boyed 12-6-1854 (no return)
Cloyed, Martha C. to Joseph A. F. Sharpe 9-24-1838 (10-2-1838)
Cloyed, Sarah Jane to Joseph H. Trotter 9-22-1852 (no return)
Cloyeds, Pernalia S. to J. N. Caffey 7-6-1841
Clure, Martha to Dennis Wilson 12-15-1870 (no return) B
Clutch, M. C. to W. G. Stevenson 6-25-1843 (6-28-1863)
Cobb, Issabella T. to Solomon R. B. Walton 4-25-1839
Cobb, Margt. E. to Joseph Samples 11-9-1850 (11-10-1850)
Cobbs, Amy to Henry Boyd 2-6-1869 B
Cobbs, Bettie to Ham Gaither 2-1-1870 B
Coble, Maunda to Samuel C. Osier 8-19-1851 (no return)
Coby, Marcy E. F. to William Hamrick 12-14-1859
Cochran, Sarah to Robert W. Orton 8-9-1838
Cock, Lucy to Willis S. O'Kelly 12-17-1850 (no return)
Cocke, Bettie A. to Wm. F. Mitchell 8-22-1860 (8-28-1860)
Cocke, Eliza J. to Richd. E. Moody 1-20-1849 (1-24-1849)
Cocke, Frances to Henry Nickols 1-3-1867 (no return) B
Cocke, L. V. to J. M. Scott 12-20-1869 (no return)
Cocke, Laura to F. A. Mayo 2-23-1869 (2-25-1869)
Cocke, Lucy N. to Tho. R. Polk 6-11-1846 (6-24-1846)
Cocke, Lucy W. to James W. Burton 7-12-1865
Cocke, Mary A. to Daniel Freeman 4-23-1870 (4-28-1870) B

Cocke, Mary P. to James H. Cocke 5-4-1870 (5-5-1870)
Cocke, Mary R. to James B. Adair 1-20-1849
Cocke, Nancy E. to H. S. Haley 12-16-1867 (no return)
Cocke, Patsy to Jessey Winfrey 2-24-1869 B
Cody, Frances to Henry Coleman 3-15-1871 (1-?-1872) B
Cody, Harriet A. to Jos. L. Cody 1-2-1868 (no return)
Coe, Barthenia to Jack Williamson 12-23-1865 (12-26-1865) B
Coe, Eliza to Jesse Merriwether 12-28-1865 (12-29-1865) B
Coe, Isadore to Granison Brown 2-26-1869 (no return) B
Coe, Mary Frances to Harcus Coe 5-31-1869 (6-13-1869) B
Coffee, Elizabeth to James A. Bentley 12-15-1845 (12-18-1845)
Coffey, Isabella to John Griffin 5-2-1840 (5-3-1840)
Coffin, Amy to Senson Taylor 8-21-1869 (8-22-1869) B
Coffman, Allice to Willis Cook 3-19-1870 (no return) B
Coffman, Mariah to Pleasant Murry 1-3-1870 (no return) B
Coffy, Sarah to Henry Rhodes 1-12-1867 (not executed) B
Cogbell, Elvira to Jack Hooper 6-15-1870 (no return) B
Cogbell, Josephine to William E. Loveless 9-20-1848 (9-27-1848)
Cogbill, F. M. to James H. Johnson 12-15-1852 (no return)
Cogbill, Harriet to Bennit Wilson 2-15-1869 (2-16-1869) B
Cogbill, Martha J. to Thos. F. Moore 12-19-1870 (12-21-1870)
Cogbill, Mollie to James Walkup 8-17-1867 (8-18-1867)
Cogbill, Patsy to William Britton 12-22-1870 (12-27-1870) B
Coker, Nancy to Loyd Wilson 10-22-1839 (11-9-1839)
Coker, Sarah to Jackson Loyd 3-26-1846
Cole, Ann E. to Thomal C. Poindexter 9-20-1847
Cole, C. D. to H. Leigh Priddy 10-29-1866 (10-31-1866)
Cole, M. P. to L. V. Shelton 5-10-1859 (5-11-1859)
Cole, Margaret to Ben DeGraffenreid 10-2-1868 B
Cole, Sarah to Booker Hays 5-11-1871 (5-27-1871) B
Cole, Tennessee to Allen Orr 12-28-1868 (1-3-1869) B
Coleman, Paralee to Moses Bell 4-25-1867 (no return) B
Collier, Frances to Wm. Taylor 6-6-1868 B
Collins, Catherine to F. M. C. Hughes 4-9-1867 (4-11-1867)
Coltharp, C. A. to William R. Raney 9-6-1839 (9-9-1839)
Compton, Eliza to J. H. Still 12-1-1854 (no return)
Compton, Malvina to William Hinson 11-10-1838 (11-11-1838)
Compton, Mildred A. to Henry D. Roberts 6-3-1853 (no return)
Compton, Mildred N. to Jno. Henry Hooks 12-12-1867 (no return)
Compton, Narcessus to John G. Hinson 8-15-1838
Compton, Sarah E. to J. W. Poston 10-20-1863 (10-21-1863)
Conkey, M. A. to R. H. Whitehead 12-19-1859 (12-20-1859)
Conner, Hannah to Owen Mangum 2-27-1871 (2-28-1871) B
Conner, Melvina to Henry J. Trotter 1-26-1848
Conway, Mary to David R. Wilson 12-27-1849
Cook, Delina to Thos. Notgrass 5-10-1845 (5-13-1845)
Cook, M. A. F. to W. T. Lamb 11-22-1851 (no return)
Cook, Sarah Jane to William L. Ward 6-14-1847
Cook, Sarah to Francis Trowell 8-12-1846
Cooker, Mary to Peter Ammen 10-17-1843 (no return)
Cooper, Bettie B. to Stephen G. Carnes 3-30-1869
Cooper, Harriet to Andrew Olds 12-24-1867 (12-31-1867) B
Cooper, Mary C. to E. Henry Sheldton 10-3-1843 (no return)
Cooper, Mary E. to Timothy W. Ward 1-10-1849
Cooper, Mary W. to John R. Pearson 9-14-1854 (no return)
Cooper, Philadelphia F. to A. V. Ivey 5-1-1847 (5-2-1847)
Copeland, Rebecca H. to Edward W. Tatem 2-10-1849
Coppedge, Silva to Ben Richmond 6-18-1869 (6-20-1869) B
Cossett, Mary A. to John W. Base? 8-21?-1843 (9-5-1843)
Cothram, Mary to J. S. Mickleberry 11-30-1841 (12-2-1841)
Cothran, Jane to D. T. Holloway 7-16-1866 (7-18-1866)
Cothran, Louisa to Jonathan Fawlk 1-17-1848 (1-20-1848)
Cothran, Rebecca B. to Edmond S. Jackson 11-30-1866 (12-4-1866)
Cothran, S. to Tobert Sidmoreth 2-8-1838
Cothran, Sarah J. to Curtis Harris 5-27-1854 (no return)
Cotner, Mary (Mrs.) to Harris Bailey 5-5-1852 (no return)
Cotner, S. E. to R. M. Koonce 1-12-1871
Cotter, Tobitha J. to Thos. N. Cotter 1-11-1848 (1-12-1848)
Cotton, Mary E. to F. M. Wright 10-26-1844 (10-29-1844)
Cotton, Sally A. to William C. Smith 6-3-1847 (6-10-1847)
Coulter, Mary S. to William Abel 8-9-1853 (no return)
Cove, Nancy to Jordan White 1-29-1867 (2-5-1867) B
Covington, Jennie to Thos. W. Brinkley 10-18-1870 (10-20-1870)
Cowan, Mariah to William H. Henley 9-9-1840
Cowan, Mary F. to J. M. Abel 12-24-1867 (12-26-1867)

Cowan, Mollie A. to G. W. Brannon 12-11-1862 (12-16-1862)
Cox, Eliza A. to Alvay J. Mitchell 1-15-1855 (no return)
Cox, Mary E. to James B. Thornton 4-21-1870
Cox, Nan to Henry Winfield 6-26-1869 (6-25?-1869) B
Crabtree, Mary to James Kindrick 4-13-1838
Crabtree, S. E. to S. P. Wirt 5-4-1868 (5-5-1868)
Craft, Eliza J. to Abnur Blair 10-21-1853 (no return)
Craig, Elizabeth to Michell G. Hilliard 6-7-1838
Craig, Frances C. to R. S. Hill 9-13-1862 (9-14-1862)
Craig, Georgiana to A. W. Wright 2-22-1870
Craig, Sarah J. to J. P. Simmons 8-24-1854 (no return)
Craige, Polly Ann to Willis Person 4-30-1864 (5-4-1864)
Craigg, Elizabeth A. to Wm. H. Brakefield 1-22-1846
Crain, Bitsy to William Sample 11-26-1842 (12-1-1842)
Crank, Lucy M. to Robert L. Foster 5-6-1852 (no return)
Crawford, Abbie to York Bridges 11-11-1870 (11-20-1870) B
Crawford, Ann to Abraham Abernathy 9-3-1869 (11-25-1869) B
Crawford, C. C. to S. M. Edwards 10-23-1865 (10-24-1865)
Crawford, Jenny to Levi Harrell 10-6-1866 (10-8-1866) B
Crawford, Lou to Cornelius Russell 8-8-1868 (no return) B
Crawford, Lucinda J. to John B. Stanley 8-26-1846 (no return)
Crawford, M. J. to James H. (W.?) Weatherly 2-7-1871
Crawford, M. T. to R. C. Wallace 3-5-1850 (no return)
Crawford, Margaret to Anderson Neal 1-9-1869 (1-10-1869) B
Crawford, Mary A. to James T. Land 8-8-1852 (no return)
Crawford, Mary J. to W. C. Old 2-4-1863
Crawford, Mary to Henry Whitton 11-27-1869 B
Crawford, N. E. to G. T. Johnson 11-27-1865 (11-30-1865)
Crawford, Salina to D. T. Levisay 1-11-1842 (no return)
Crawford, Susan to Israel Vanpelt 11-29-1870 (12-20-1870 B
Crawford, Viney to James Gwynn 3-21-1870 (3-31-1870) B
Crawley, Rebecah to Absolem Broom 6-15-1847 (no return)
Crenshaw, B. S. to J. W. Shipp 4-30-1855 (no return)
Crenshaw, Mary Ann to William E. Griffin 9-11-1846 (9-18-1846)
Crewer, Rosanna to Davy Hardy 12-21-1867 B
Crews, Virginia G. to Andrew Anderson 1-27-1869 (2-4-1869)
Crippin, Rachel A. to John Jones 5-12-1860 (5-13-1860)
Crittenden, Celia J. to Stephen K. Oats 5-11-1867 (5-16-1867)
Crockett, Julia to John Cleare 12-28-1870 (no return) B
Crook, Jane to William Tate 12-24-1869 (no return) B
Crook, Mary to Abraham Perry 11-19-1844
Croom, Rachell W. to John Umphlett 6-4-1853 (no return)
Crosby, Mary to Felix Boyd 1-6-1871 (no return)
Cross, Aminta J. to R. W. Black 10-22-1867 (10-23-1867)
Cross, Emma to Henry Miller 1-4-1870 (no return) B
Cross, Frances C. to Madison Parker 12-27-1847 (12-30-1847)
Cross, Lettie to Charlie Houston 12-27-1870 (12-29-1870) B
Cross, Maria to Abraham Cobern 12-21-1868 (no return) B
Cross, Martha A. to J. M. Shelton 8-7-1849 (8-21-1849)
Cross, Martha A. to J. S. Lalusan? 7-7-1849 (not endorsed)
Cross, Martha A. to Robert H. Black 2-19-1867 (2-20-1867)
Cross, Mary J. to John J. Slaughter 3-8-1866 (3-11-1866)
Cross, Rebecca to G. M. Bartlett 4-4-1854 (no return)
Crossett, Elizabeth to Merite Huchins 11-4-1850 (11-7-1850)
Crossett, G. A. to J. W. Newby 11-13-1867 (11-14-1867)
Crowder, Amelia to Elias James 1-14-1869 (1-16-1869) B
Crowder, Harriet to John Crowder 10-31-1868 (11-14-1868) B
Crowder, Maria to Benjamin Perry 1-1-1866 (1-7-1866) B
Crowder, Mary V. to J. R. Johnson 12-1-1869 (12-8-1869)
Crowder, Mollie to W. A. Ellis 9-13-1869 (9-15-1869)
Cruis, Ann to Martin Rhodes 12-21-1867 (12-22-1867) B
Crump, Elizabeth J. to John F. Goodman 8-9-1854 (no return)
Cruse, Sopha Ann to James H. Stacy 9-4-1852 (no return)
Crutcher, Lavinia to Spencer Teague 9-20-1866 (9-21-1866) B
Crutcher, Sallie E. to John Kennedy 12-5-1866 (12-10-1866)
Culbreth, E. C. to James N. Turner 2-19-1868 (no return)
Cullom, J. M. to J. J. Matty 12-17-1859 (12-20-1859)
Culp, Albenia T. to John A. Garvin 12-11-1866 (12-13-1866)
Culp, E. A. to S. L. Barrow 12-20-1864 (12-24-1864)
Culp, Esther to Wm. P. Norman 7-14-1849
Culp, Fanny to Linsey Dowdy 12-15-1870 (12-28-1870) B
Culp, Jennie to Jesse Waller 1-29-1870 (3-6-1870) B
Culp, Mary A. to Moses Parks 12-2-1850 (12-3-1850)
Culp, Mollie E. to W. J. Barron 12-11-1866 (12-13-1866)
Culp, Sarah J. to Francis Hill 12-2-1850 (12-3-1850)

Culpepper, Laura to S. S. Hollowell 2-16-1869 (2-18-1869)
Cumings, Eliza to Overton Harris 2-23-1867 (3-2-1867) B
Cummins, Dora to William Brooks 3-30-1870 (4-2-1870) B
Cunliffe, Susan H. to B. Bowers 10-31-1859 (11-1-1859)
Curl, M. S. to Z. H. Patrick 6-20-1842 (no return)
Currie, Ellen to Charles Greer 7-5-1869 (7-17-1869) B
Currin, Ann E. to Alfred J. Walton 3-20-1843 (no return)
Cursey, Sarah to W. T. Crawford 11-22-1862 (12-4-1862)
Curtis, Mary to John A. Gilliam 1-22-1853 (no return)
Dailey, Julia A. to John J. Perry 12-29-1860
Dairden, Anna E. to John R. Devenport 10-24-1867
Dalton, Mary E. to John J. Boyed 5-25-1848
Daniel, Elisabeth L. to Benjamin F. Furgason 12-6-1848 (no return)
Daniel, Mary O. to Booker Bomar 12-17-1854 (no return)
Darden, Katherine to L. J. Smith 12-18-1868 (12-20-1868)
Darden, Mary to D. B. Massey 12-16-1850 (no return)
Darden, S. A. to H. F. Freeman 12-15-1862 (12-17-1862)
Darley, Elizabeth Ann to Thomas Sullivan 6-11-1855 (no return)
Darlin, Lillie F. to John Goss 12-30-1868 (no return)
Daugherty, Charity A. to John D. Bishop 12-30-1868 (1-6-1869)
Davenport, Margaret to J. J. Langdon 10-19-1866 (10-28-1866)
David, E. J. to Wm. M. Hope 4-19-1854 (no return)
David, Louisa C. to John Sadler 7-1-1844 (7-10-1844)
David, Milly to Joseph Hughes 12-18-1849 (no return)
Davidson, R. F. to M. P. Norton 1-27-1869 (1-28-1869)
Davis, Amelia to Saml. Kindrick 10-17-1846 (no return)
Davis, Ann E. to Richd. M. Manley 8-5-1846
Davis, Caroline to W. H. Emberson 9-6-1847 (9-9-1847)
Davis, Clara J. to Gabriel Cannon 2-24-1853 (no return)
Davis, Eliza Jane to John Davis, jr. 12-18-1856 (no return)
Davis, Emma E. to Joseph F. Ellis 3-16-1852 (no return)
Davis, Lucy A. to Hamilton J. Green 11-19-1850 (11-21-1850)
Davis, Margaret J. to Thomas Branch 12-19-1846 (no return)
Davis, Maria L. to James Brookes 6-21-1842 (6-22-1842)
Davis, Mariah to Rolling H. Johnson 12-15-1851 (no return)
Davis, Martha E. to John Wesley Davis 3-9-1870 (3-10-1870)
Davis, Martha to John Cannon 3-24-1865 (3-28-1865)
Davis, Mary E. to Abner Alexander 2-26-1853 (no return)
Davis, Mary E. to Charles W. Sullivant 7-23-1850 (no return)
Davis, Mary to Norflet T. Young 1-11-1869 (1-14-1869)
Davis, Maryan to Thomas D. Rachel 1-8-1848
Davis, Minta E. to Silas Hughes 7-11-1863 (7-22-1863)
Davis, Nancy C. to James M. Tillman 7-31-1869 (8-3-1869)
Davis, Nancy to Matthew Walker 1-28-1868 (2-1-1868) B
Davis, Polly to James Rodgers 4-14-1842
Davis, Polly to Thos. Riggs 12-13-1853 (no return)
Davis, Sallie to Richard Jones 3-6-1871 B
Davis, Sarah A. to Martin Skinner 12-23-1859 (12-25-1859)
Davis, Sarah to Edward Buck 7-28-1848 (7-30-1848)
Davis, Sarah to Levy Holmes 12-27-1869 (1-1-1870) B
Davis, Susanah to John Baswell 8-2-1848 (no return)
Day, Felicia to Tom Mamier? 5-19-1866 (8-11-1866) B
Dayley, Mary Ann E. to E. A. Burns 12-25-1848 (12-26-1848)
Dayton, R. E. to N. J. Hess 12-10-1870 (12-13-1870)
Ddupree, Bettie E. to J. A. Flippin 4-11-1864 (4-16-1864)
DeGraffenreid, Fillis to Robt. Henderson 10-3-1868 (10-4-1868) B
Dean, M. A. to B. F. Webb 10-31-1866 (11-5-1865?)
Deaner, Martha A. to William A. Old 9-30-1845 (no return)
Dearren, M. J. to R. H. Best 11-6-1865 (11-14-1865)
Deener, Ann to George Green 11-14-1868 (11-15-1868) B
Deener, Anna to Abraham Heaslet 12-3-1869 (no return) B
Deener, Mary to Robert Heaslet 11-29-1869 (no return) B
Deener, Omy to Anderson Pitt 8-31-1867 B
Deener, Zoa Ann to Taylor Woods 12-26-1867 (no return) B
Deener?, Priscilla to Bill Williamson 4-22-1871 (no return) B
Degraffenreid, Evaline H. to E. L. Evans 10-6-1841 (no return)
Degraffenreid, Sarah B. to Solomon Green 10-30-1848 (no return)
Degraftenreid, Elizabeth to Blunt Springfield 12-4-1843 (no return)
Deloach, Rose Ann to G. G. Looney 6-26-1838 (no return)
Demming, Lucinda J. to Wm. C. Harris 1-21-1850 (1-22-1850)
Demril?, Lucinda to George Sparrow 4-17-1869 (no return) B
Derden, Milly to Green McNeill 12-31-1866 (1-6-1867) B
Devenport, R. E. to John H. Dixon 2-5-1870 (2-10-1870)
Devenport, Sarah to Thomas D. Marler 8-12-1838
Dickason, Fannie to Benj. Elder 3-17-1862

Dickason, Josaphine J. to Simon W. Caldwell 1-23-1867 (1-30-1867)
Dickason, Louisa M. to W. B. Washington 5-1-1850
Dickason, Mary A. to John L. Verser 11-23-1846 (11-24-1846)
Dickason, S. A. to J. M. Elder 1-15-1861
Dickason, Virginia to Wm. B. Washington 8-7-1860 (8-8-1860)
Dickenson, Evelina to William Rives 1-3-1839
Dickenson, Sarah to Sam Ealy 12-29-1868 (12-30-1868) B
Dickinson, Adaline to Wm. Richardson 5-26-1866 B
Dickinson, Anna E. to O. T. Edwards 1-30-1867
Dickinson, Berlin to Silo Fraser 1-3-1868 (no return) B
Dickinson, Dinah to Sam Dickinson 12-25-1866 (no return) B
Dickinson, Hannah to Robt. Leavy 10-17-1868 (10-18-1868) B
Dickinson, Laura to Wiley Jones 5-4-1870 (5-7-1870) B
Dickinson, Manerva to Shed Cole 12-9-1870 B
Dickinson, Margaret to Dennis Hall 9-7-1867 (9-8-1867) B
Dickinson, Martha to Louis Justice 8-28-1869 (10-17-1869) B
Dickinson, Rachel to Evans Rives 2-20-1869 B
Dickinson, Rosena to Peter Walton 12-25-1866 (12-27-1866) B
Dickinson, Sallie N. to C. A. S. Shaw 4-25-1866 (4-26-1866)
Dickson, Mary A. to Isaac S. Patton 9-13-1848
Dickson, Rebecca to William Booth 10-23-1839 (10-31-1839)
Didny?, Mary to G. H. Siscoe 12-23-1848 (no return)
Diffy, Anne to John Shuffield 10-10-1842
Dilliard, A.a C. to Geo. Honley 3-15-1866
Dilliard, Sarah A. to Julias Johnson 9-25-1865 (9-26-1865)
Dinkins, Sarah J. to Wm. H. Largent 2-12-1855 (no return)
Dix, Edie to Samuel Rainey 8-12-1865
Dobbin, Sarah to Axum Porter 12-27-1867 B
Dobbins, Cornelius to Mack Vaysor? 4-16-1868 (no return) B
Dobbs, Blanch Ann to Fielding Heaslet 12-2-1869 (no return) B
Dodd, Sarah E. to Benjamin Davis 12-19-1845 (12-23-1845)
Dodddridge, Frances E. to George Millirons 4-23-1838
Dodds, Penniah to Samuel W. Fisk 3-6-1854 (no return)
Dodson, Adaline to Charles Smith 9-14-1866 (9-16-1866) B
Dodson, Emily Jane to William R. House no dates (with Dec 1845)
Dodson, Emma to James A. Steward 4-22-1862 (4-23-1862)
Dodson, Jane to George Carpenter 3-24-1866 B
Dodson, Margaret Ann to Saml. D. Long 2-9-1846 (2-12-1846)
Dodson, Martha E. to Vincent Middleton 7-14-1855 (no return)
Dodson, Mary A. to John A. Jackson 9?-17-1853 (no return)
Dodson, Mary E. to John S. Herndon 1-18-1854 (no return)
Dodson, Sarah Frances to Michael McNelis 3-9-1869 (3-21-1869)
Donaldson, Mary to M. C. M. Abbernathy 9-9-1846 (9-10-1846)
Donelson, Laura to Edmond Lewis 9-2-1868 (no return)
Donnily, Mary to Henry Reddick 1-15-1869 (no return) B
Dors, Margaret to Carter Holt 1-6-1868 (no return) B
Dortch, Ann to William Winfrey 5-3-1869 (no return) B
Dortch, Elizabeth E. to R. C. Webb 4-30-1851 (5-1-1851)
Dortch, Mary E. to Simon Fletcher 1-25-1870 (1-26-1870) B
Dortch, Sarah to Gaines Johnson 1-2-1869 B
Doss, Charlotte to Alexander Franklin 12-30-1866 (1-1-1866?) B
Doudy, Rebecca H. to Jacob Bowers 4-2-1845 (4-9-1845)
Dougan, Amanda to M. S. Renfroe 1-25-1860 (1-26-1860)
Dougan, Melissa to William T. Wells 9-25-1843 (no return)
Douglas, Lucy to Davy Qualls 2-20-1869 B
Douglas, Margaret to George M. McQuirter 10-20-1869
   (no return) B
Douglas, Martha V. to L. B. Lamb 12-16-1865 (12-19-1865)
Douglass, Caroline to Solomon H. Shaw 4-22-1846
Douglass, E. to Jno. B. Robinson 3-26-1851 (no return)
Douglass, Lucy to Jesse Degraffenreid 12-22-1866 (12-27-1866) B
Douglass, Martha A. to Felix McFarland 6-28-1842
Dover, Julia A. to J. M. Walls 9-8-1870
Dow, Margaret to Warren Blackwell 4-15-1871 (4-17-1871) B
Dowdy, Ann to David Moore 11-1-1852 (no return)
Dowdy, Elvira to Robert Parks 12-29-1868 (12-31-1868) B
Dowdy, Fanny to William Woods 1-31-1870 (2-10-1870) B
Dowdy, Jennie to G. W. Allen 11-29-1870 (11-31?-1870)
Dowdy, Louisa to Davy Branch 12-28-1865 (no return) B
Dowdy, Lucinda to Sam Baker 12-27-1865 (no return) B
Dowdy, Mary F. to Geo. H. Ledger 2-26-1851
Dowdy, Sarah E. to Wm. Parke 2-13-1851 (no return)
Dowdy, Sarah F. to G. W. Fletcher 3-4-1841 (no return)
Dowing, Catharine to Stephen Lacy 2-?-1838
Downey, Catharine to Elisha T. Johnson 12-24-1844

Downey, Catharine to R. Manley 12-27-1839 (3-9-1840)
Downy, S. to Wm. R. Langdon 12-29-1869
Doyle, Leonora to William T. Neely 1-3-1867 (1-9-1867)
Doyle, M. D. to R. J. Johnson 1-6-1868 (1-7-1868)
Doyle, M. E. to C. F. Neely 9-27-1859 (10-6-1859)
Drake, Martha R. to William Sensing 5-24-1847 (no return)
Driver, Sarahann to Patrick H. Elder 7-17-1844 (7-18-1844)
Duberry, Frances to Rob. T. Manuel 12-6-1845 (12-7-1845)
Duberry, Mary to Mathew Hood 10-3-1853 (no return)
Duke, Caroline to Robert W. Conn 2-17-1842 (2-24-1842)
Duke, Christiana A. to D. W. Wright 5-30-1853 (no return)
Duke, Eliza to John Thompson 12-22-1870 (12-25-1870)
Duke, Lucinda W. to Thos. Williams 2-24-1848
Duke, Mary A. to James Teague 10-23-1866 (10-24-1866)
Duke, Miss ____ to D. W. Wright 5-23-1853 (no return)
Dun, Arenar to Squire Clay 1-5-1870 (2-1-1870) B
Dunbar, Sarah C. to William C. Allen 6-20-1846 (6-21-1846)
Dunlap, R. E. to B. F. Craig 1-31-1849 (2-1-1849)
Dunlap, Rebecca to Josiah Riggs 1-23-1843 (1-24-1843)
Dunn, Florida to Robert Kee 8-7-1867 B
Dunn, Harriet to Bird Marsh 12-28-1852 (no return)
Dupew, Rebeca H. to Lemel J. W. Parker 11-21-1840 (11-25-1840)
Dupree, Caroline to William Mewborn 1-3-1871 (no return) B
Dupree, Liddie to John Cleere 12-26-1867 (no return) B
Dupuy, Sarah L. to V. C. Peers 10-23-1855 (no return)
Durham, Amelia L. to Elias Carroll 1-29-1840 (1-30-1840)
Durham, Cornelia B. to William A. Edwards 12-28-1868 (12-31-1868)
Durham, Elizabeth M. to E. J. Hubbard 7-15-1844 (no return)
Durham, M. C. to A. J. Targart 12-18-1854 (no return)
Durham, Margaret G. to Richard Manley 9-6-1854 (no return)
Durham, Martha to George Akin 2-8-1844
Durham, Nancy to William B. Russell 9-22-1840 (9-24-1840)
Durham, R. O. to James W. Smith 12-27-1843 (12-28-1843)
Durham, Sarah to A. J. Cullom 5-8-1850 (no return)
Durham, Tralucia L. to Joseph W. Pender 4-1-1847
Dyer, E. V. to R. T. DeAragan 6-21-1854 (no return)
Dyer, Eugene P. to R. Branch 5-11-1853 (no return)
Dyre, Sarah A. to Jefferson W. Stein 3-13-1843 (no return)
Eadon, Elenor to Samel Sherrill 11-18-1840
Eagan, Helen to H. L. Epps 11-1-1869 (11-2-1869)
Ealy, Harriet to George Matthews 4-8-1871 (4-3?-1871) B
Ealy, Harriet to Russel Jones 8-7-1869 (8-9-1869) B
Earl, Margaret to John H. McCully 12-6-1853 (no return)
Earnheart, J. J. to Geo. N. Stoops 7-2-1869 (7-4-1869)
Eason, Bethany to Marcus J. Pennington 9-4-1842 (9-20-1842)
Eason, Margaret to Richard Tatum 11-4-1845 (no return)
Eason, Mary J. to Jesse Benson 10-17-1846 (no return)
East, Marry A. to Sterling Bounds 8-29-1843 (9-5-1843)
Eastham, Amelia A. W. to A. P. Graves 12-4-1852 (no return)
Eastham, M. E. M. to D. W. Anderson 3-7-1853 (no return)
Eathan, Ann L. to Franklin Crawford 3-2-1840 (3-5-1840)
Eddings, Ida Frances to John H. Crenshaw 11-6-1866 (11-7-1866)
Eddins, Angirary? to John C. Davy 4-18-1843
Eddins, Ann T. to Marshall P. Yancy 11-20-1843 (11-23-1843)
Eddins, Elizabeth W. to Thomas Harwell 1-17-1848 (1-20-1848)
Eddins, Frances H. to Clayton A. Yancy 12-12-1843
Eddins, Mary to H. Garvin 7-27-1863 (8-11-1863)
Eddins, Rebecca M. to Burwell S. Hasbey 1-13-1840 (1-14-1840)
Edmondson?, Wilmouth O. to Thomas D. Tarver 8-22-1854 (no
   return)
Edmunston, Adeline to William Anderson 12-27-1843 (no return)
Edwards, Elizabeth to Rhesa? R. Sullivant 1-4-1842 (1-11-1842)
Edwards, F. M. to W. J. Hemson 11-27-1865 (11-28-1865)
Edwards, Juatt? to Benji. Chambers 9-22-1847 (9-16?-1847)
Edwards, Judah to James Lacy 4-26-1848
Edwards, Lucretia J. to Enoch Galloway 2-2-1855 (no return)
Edwards, Mary B. W. to Richd. G. Scott 11-2-1867 (11-5-1867)
Edwards, Mary to William H. Fitts 1-8-1852 (no return)
Edwards, Rosa A. to William H. Martin 1-10-1848 (1-11-1848)
Edwards, S. A. to J. H. Johnston 12-1-1866 (12-5-1866)
Edwards, Sarah ANn to Joseph Graves 11-7-1844 (11-14-1844)
Elder, Malissa to W. L. Sanders 7-14-1854 (no return)
Elder, Martha J. to John W. Conway no date (with Dec 1847)
Elder, Mary J. to Jabize S. Anderson 12-4-1847 (12-7-1847)
Elder, Mary to Benj. F. Burruss 6-3-1851 (no return)

Elder, Nancy to Asa Clements 10-4-1841 (10-6-1841)
Elder, Sarah C. to W. C. Ozier 1-2-1863
Elder, Sarah F. B. to C. A. Goins 3-17-1843 (no return)
Elder, Sarah ann to John A. Walthall 6-13-1848 (6-18-1848)
Eley, Jane to Morgan Jones 7-13-1867 (7-14-1867) B
Ellington, C. V. to M. W. Nelson 4-18-1854 (no return)
Ellington, Jane Thomas to E. Elington 5-8-1848 (5-9-1848)
Ellington, Martha H. to Henry M. Sheffield 2-25-1851 (2-26-1851)
Ellington, Puss to Geo. Saffoon 12-15-1868 (12-17-1868)
Ellington, Sarah A. T. to Wm. J. Harrison 10-4-1849
Elliott, Agnes A. to Joseph Johnson 1-31-1870 (2-4-1870)
Elliott, Mary J. to W. A. Flemming 5-31-1859 (6-8-1859)
Elliott, Mary N. to Augustus A. Simmons 11-25-1846 (11-26-1846)
Elliott, Sarah ann to Francis M. Pettey 8-26-1848 (no return)
Ellison, Emily to B. Malone 9-16-1847 (no return)
Ellison, Louisa J. to John L. Webb 2-19-1850 (2-23-1850)
Ellison, Manda C. to Isaac P. Henley 12-8-1842
Ellizer, Fanny L. to John T. Shipley 6-2-1870 (7-25-1870) B
Elmore, Rebecca to Robert Brown 4-5-1847
Elmore, Sarah to Harvey Brown 7-29-1847
Ely, Lou to Green Jones 12-30-1868 B
Emerson, Caroline to Alexander Daniel 12-29-1855 (no return)
England, M. L. to David H. Sanders 6-28-1859 (6-30-1859)
England, Mary J. to Q. T. Holloway 10-12-1852 (no return)
Epps, Nancy Ann to Archy Stallion 12-13-1869 (12-26-1869) B
Erwin, A. E. to F. M. Robertson 1-10-1852 (no return)
Erwin, Harriet W. to Samuel Johnson 6-12-1839
Eskridge, Louisa J. to Noah H. Posten? 3-2-1854 (no return)
Eskridge, P. D. A. L. to David Cohn 1-17-1853 (no return)
Eubanks, Mary A. to J. W. Campbell 6-21?-1855 (no return)
Evans, Bettie A. to Frank G. Falls 2-24-1871 (3-1-1871)
Evans, Candis A. to William A. Tharp 2-23-1846 (3-3-1846)
Evans, Elizabeth to N. S. Hilliard 12-29-1865 (1-3-1866)
Evans, Ellen to Elkins Cash 5-3-1845 (5-8-1845)
Evans, Emma to J. N. Dazey 12-3-1869 (12-8-1869)
Evans, Martha G. to William H. Wells 12-10-1838 (12-11-1838)
Evans, Mary F. to W. H. Hill 2-1-1868 (no return)
Evans, Mattie O. to Edward H. Anderson 1-2-1871 (1-8-1871)
Everett, Amanda F. to E. D. Portis 1-27-1853 (no return)
Ewell, A. P. to Henry F. Scott 8-1-1860 (8-2-1860)
Ewell, Julia to Harry Ewell 5-12-1870 (5-15-1870) B
Ewell, Lydia to Jack Rives 11-19-1866 (11-20-1866) B
Ewell, Maria H. to W. D. Somers 12-25-1864
Ewell, Mary S. to Benj. W. Britt 8-3-1846 (no return)
Ewell, Nancy to William Roberts 1-22-1869 (1-24-1869) B
Exum, Charlotte to Geo. W. Washington 12-21-1868 (no return) B
Exum, L. A. to Robert D. Guarrant 8-26-1847 (no return)
Exum, Louisa A. to John A. Pope 12-6-1852 (no return)
Exum, Lucy E. to James Cody 2-1-1870 (no return)
Exum, M. J. to Wm. C. Exum 9-17-1859 (9-20-1859)
Exum, Martha H. to Richd. E. Galloway 5-14-1849 (no return)
Exum, Mary to Jas. S. Pickens 6-3-1849
Exum, Mildred to Richd. Miller 8-30-1867 (8-31-1867) B
Faldwell, Martha A. to Henry Bistwick 9-20-1847 (9-26-1847)
Falls, Bella C. to P. D. Ewell 11-12-1863 (11-17-1863)
Farley, Maria to Peyton Moore 12-30-1865 (12-31-1865) B
Farley, Martha E. to A. Baker 2-9-1846 (2-11-1846)
Farley, Mary E. to D. K. Pulliam 2-5-1867 (no return)
Farley, R. C. to James W. Ham 3-9-1850 (no return)
Farley, Sarah to Wilkins Wesson 7-10-1839
Farmer, Margarett to John F. Wade 12-22-1870 (12-23-1870)
Farrar, Hattie V. to T. H. Poindexter 12-6-1866 (12-12-1866)
Farrar, Lavina to John Thompson 10-10-1866 (10-15-1866) B
Farrar, Susan to Adam Jefferson 12-19-1866 (no return) B
Farrar, Z. A. to R. F. Stacy 7-21-1866 (7-22-1866)
Farrer, Martha S. to J. T. Farrer 7-21-1851 (7-24-1851)
Farrill, Fanny P. to Wm. C. Bailey 10-8-1849 (10-11-1849)
Farris, Amanda to Wesley Harris 3-18-1854 (no return)
Farris, Eliza to John H. Broom 4-1-1844 (no return)
Farris, L. V. to John W. Moore 11-6-1865 (11-7-1865)
Fartherlain, Frances to John Wain 8-12-1838
Fausett, Fidelia A. to Jessee M. Hughes 9-10-1852 (no return)
Fausett, Frances E. to Robert Grifford 12-3-1851 (no return)
Fausett, Sarah F. to William Yarbrough 12-17-1850 (no return)
Featherston, Mary to A. H. Herron 2-6-1838

Felts, Dennie to R. T. D. Arragon 6-26-1866 (7-4-1866)
Ferrell, Malissy to A. S. Sorrell 5-3-1855 (no return)
Ferress, Lucy T. to William C. Rives 12-16-1839 (12-17-1839)
Field, Annie M. to Jos. D. Whitley 5-11-1866 (5-15-1866)
Fields, Eliza to Ed Lemons 1-6-1871 (no return) B
Fields, Margarett to Henry McCraw 1-3-1871 (no return) B
Fields, Mollie to Richard Rideout 12-28-1867 (no return) B
Fields, Rose to Jack Fields 12-24-1866 (12-29-1866) B
Fields, Silva to Richmond Williams 12-24-1868 (12-25-1868) B
Fillmore, Jane C. to John H. A. Knight 7-26-1844 (no return)
Finch, Emily to Charles McNamee 1-11-1849 (no return)
Finch, Lucy F. to John Falls 5-13-1862 (5-14-1862)
Finch, Mary to James Dick 1-22-1841 (1-27-1841)
Finney, Anna M. to R. D. Winsett 1-22-1868 (12-23-1868)
Finney, Caroline to Mack Curray 12-17-1870 B
Finney, Ellen to Billy Day 12-31-1866 (1-5-1867) B
Finney, Frances to Isaac Cox 6-23-1866 B
Finney, Margaret to George Ligon 9-3-1869 B
Finney, Martha Ann to Richd. F. Finney 1-5-1839 (1-6-1839)
Finney, Martha J. to W. P. Finney 9-28-1849 (9-10?-1849)
Finney, Martha to Joseph L. Edwards 10-23-1844
Finney, Patience to Sandy Douglas 8-27-1869 B
Firth, Lavinia A. (Louisa?) to Robt. P. White 10-20-1866 (10-23-1866)
Firth, Martha to Richd. Mc. Kirtland 8-24-1863
Fisher, Clara Jane to Thomas S. Damron 3-8-1851 (3-12-1851)
Fisher, Harriet A. to William J. King 9-12-1846 (9-17-1846)
Fisher, Josephine to Henry Fisher 3-10-1868 (no return) B
Fisher, Margaret L. to Isaac C. Dodds 3-1-1848 (3-2-1848)
Fisher, Margarett J. to Alexander J. McClarren 2-4-1840 (2-19-1840)
Fisher, Martha P. to G. W. Ham 1-4-1841 (1-7-1841)
Fisher, Martha to Thomas I. Ham (Haines?) 2-1-1838
Fisher, Mary E. to George Kelly 10-25-1849
Fisher, Rachel to Robin Williamson 4-18-1866 B
Fisher?, Lucinda A. to Hugh J. Cooper 10-5?-1853 (no return)
Fitsgerald, Willie A. to John Cowan 8-17-1867 (8-18-1867)
Fitshugh, Jane to Miles W. Sykes 11-25-1847 (11-27-1847)
Fleece, Jinney to Jack Scott 8-15-1868 (8-19-1868) B
Fleming, Ann E. to Wm. B. Douglass 8-25-1866 (8-29-1866)
Fletcher, Arena to Isam Cross 1-31-1867 (1-8?-1867) B
Fletcher, Frances to George Stewart 12-20-1869 B
Fletcher, Mary Ann to George Hardy 5-18-1868 (no return) B
Flippin, Anna to Henry Bowers 12-17-1868 (no return) B
Flippin, Darcus to Ben Jones 11-3-1866 (11-4-1866) B
Flippin, Frances R. to William Aston 11-18-1845
Flippin, Lizy to Julius Broom 11-26-1869 B
Flippin, Virginia E. to Geo. W. Farrar 11-5-1866 (11-7-1866)
Flowers, Julia to William Bledsoe 12-29-1870 (12-31-1870) B
Flowers, Lucinda to John Johnson 10-29-1870 B
Floyd, Lucy J. to Reddick Arnold 10-14-1839 (10-24-1839)
Floyed, Margarett to Thomas Bounds 12-7-1841 (12-9-1841)
Floyed, Nancy Emily to Wm. R. Brinkley 2-1-1841 (no return)
Flurnoy, Gracey to Saml. Jones 12-28-1870 B
Folwell, Mary to Needham Horton 5-1-1840 (5-6-1840)
Folwell, Mary to Wily Cargil 7-7-1851 (no return)
Forbbs, Carolin M. to Wm. H. Evans 4-28-1846
Forbs, Mary Isabella to Sterling Harris 3-25-1851 (no return)
Forbs, Mary to Washington Thompson 12-5-1839 (12-18-1839)
Ford, Ann Henry to Ambrose E. Green 10-3-1868 (10-8-1868)
Ford, Harriett to Saml. F. Halloway 11-9-1847
Ford, Nancy to Spencer Porter 1-17-1866 (1-20-1866) B
Ford, Sallie to Isaac McNary 5-21-1868 (5-27-1868) B
Forest, Abby to Jerry Crawford 2-2-1867 B
Fort, Eliza to Wm. Carpenter 6-19-1869 (6-20-1869) B
Foster, Matilda to Henry Clay 10-8-1870 B
Foust, Barbary to Isham Higgs 1-9-1840 (no return)
Foust, Elizabeth Jane to William Bogsen? 2-20-1846 (2-22-1846)
Fowler, Mary A. to Robert Stone 7-8-1846 (7-13-1846)
Fowler, Matilda to John Simmons 2-28-1843 (3-1-1843)
Franklin, Emeline to Robert Douglass 4-1-1867 (no return) B
Franklin, Lucy J. to T. H. Omesly? 2-12-1849 (no return)
Franklin, Nancy to John H. Moss 6-5-1839
Fraser, Catherine to Harry Green 3-20-1866 (3-28-1866) B
Fraser, Elizabeth to Washington Green 2-13-1869 (2-17-1869) B
Fraser, Feddie to John Catron 12-9-1868
Fraser, Hattie E. to Wm. L. Fraser 6-8-1865

Fraser, Mary J. to Wm. T. Thomas 9-12-1861
Frasier, N. C. to Walter Shinault 12-1-1866 (12-2-1866)
Frasier, Virginia Bell to Columbus Bryant 10-21-1865 (10-22-1865)
Frasier?, Rhody to J. C. Harriss 1-6-1845 (1-8-1845)
Frazier, Edna B. to Simon H. Walker 7-3-1849 (7-4-1849)
Frazier, Sallie E. to Daniel J. Crisp 12-13-1869 (12-15-1869)
Frazier, Tempy to Nelson Kennon 4-15-1871 (4-17-1871)
Freeman, Bettie to Jas. Shelton Minor 1-4-1869 (1-8-1869) B
Freeman, Fannie M. to W. F. McNamee 11-2-1866 (11-7-1866)
Freeman, L. A. to T. B. Swann 5-15-1860
Freeman, Sarah W. to Joshua J. Jones 10-23-1843
Frierson, Louisa to Richard Wiley 12-29-1865 (12-30-1865) B
Fry, Sallie A. to Edmond Winston 5-21-1852 (no return)
Fuller, Ann J. to H. H. Bailey 2-4-1867 (2-5-1867)
Gablin, Mary A. E. to Barney Mathews 3-5-1841 (3-9-1841)
Gage, Caroline to Pink Davis 11-26-1870 (11-21?-1870)
Gailor, Mary Ann to James E. Teel 10-18-1841
Gaines, Maryann to James Cavenness 2-8-1840 (2-11-1840)
Gaither, Genett to Thos. Lovelace 11-9-1865
Gaither, Harriet to Jerry Williamson 12-31-1866 (no return) B
Gaither, Harriet to Offy Shaw 6-20-1868 (no return) B
Gaitley, Louving to A. G. Richey 11-29-1869 (11-26?-1869)
Galeor, Susanah M. to Thos. W. Deener 11-20-1848 (11-23-1848)
Gallery, Martha J. to August Branan 8-6-1855 (no return)
Galleway, Martha A. to J. W. Rafe 3-18-1847 (3-26-1847)
Galloway, A. P. to J. C. Hancock 3-14-1859 (3-28-1859)
Galloway, Adelia (Dibzorah?) to Thomas A. Tripp 3-10-1866
     (3-11-1866)
Galloway, Elizabeth to Sidney Redding 12-6-1853 (no return)
Galloway, Ellen to R. W. Ing 12-3-1856 (no return)
Galloway, Sylva to Frank Shaw 10-1-1870 (10-8-1870) B
Gambrell, Susan to Jesse Gordon 2-14-1844 (no return)
Gammons, Sally to Peter Anthony 1-9-1869 (1-10-1869) B
Gardner, E. M. to W. C. Malone 7-20-1850 (8-8-1850)
Gardner, Mary E. to Wilson Miller 12-21-1847 (12-30-1847)
Gardner, Rose to Hill Raynor 12-24-1869 (no return) B
Gardner, S. A. to A. C. Finch 11-17-1859 (11-18-1859)
Gardner, S. E. C. to Reuben Harris 5-5-1851 (no return)
Gardner, Susan E. to Wm. C. Armour 9-2-1850 (9-4-1850)
Gardon, Mary B. to James Jones 1-24-1840
Garrett, Maryann to Benson F. Lynn 12-20-1840
Garrett, Patsy to Thos. J. Hollis 11-16-1867 (11-17-1867)
Garrison, Isabella to J. K. Hutchison 8-20-1867
Garrison, Jane to James Ketcham 10-4-1848
Garrison, Martha E. to James H. Irvy? 4-12-1844 (no return)
Garrison, Mary J. to A. Dolphis Wells 1-11-1847 (no return)
Garrison, Rebeccca to J. D. Blaydes 2-26-1866 (3-1-1866)
Garvin, Adelia N. to Joshua E. Bennett 3-18-1864 (3-22-1864)
Garvin, Caroline to Joe Harris 5-9-1866 B
Gate, Caroline C. to William H. Beninger 12-25-1843 (12-28-1843)
Gates, Emily F. to Henry C. Fox 3-17-1862 (3-20-1862)
Gates, Lucy V. to Milton W. Prewitt 12-9-1867 (12-10-1867)
Gatlin, Fanny to Solomon Perry 1-4-1871 (1-5-1871) B
Gay, Emeline to John Davis 4-9-1870 (4-12-1870)
Geter, Mary to Raleigh Shells 4-7-1866 (4-22-1866) B
Gibson, E. A. to John W. Riggs 12-26-1867
Gilbreth, Mary E. to B. S. Ables 7-8-1844 (no return)
Gilerland, Nancy A. to Solomon H. Stanley 12-16-1839 (no return)
Giles, Sarah F. to Alfred W. Campbell 10-13-1851 (no return)
Gill, Amanda to Thompson James 10-16-1840 (no return)
Gill, Laura E. to Henry R. Brooks 12-21-1866 (12-30-1866)
Gillaspie, Martha to G. G. Hudson 12-26-1860 (12-3?-1860)
Gillespie, Mary to Drew Neel 10-20-1869 (10-21-1869) B
Gilliam, Mary P. to T. N. Hughes 2-18-1868 (2-27-1868)
Gilliam, Prissilla to William Smith 8-12-1841 (no return)
Gilmore, Mary D. to Presley Turner 1-4-1869 (1-6-1869)
Gilmore, Jane C. to William M. Claunch 7-22-1844 (7-25-1844)
Gilmore, Sintha to Albert G. Jeter 6-9-1847 (no return)
Glasgow, Elizabeth G. to Gabriel M. Bartlet 12-3-1846
Gloster, Martha to Edmond Dortch 4-9-1866 (4-30-1866) B
Gloster, Mary D. to Alex P. Rose 1-22-1867 (1-24-1867)
Gloster, Roberta to Marion Allen 4-25-1866 (6-17-1866) B
Glover, Mary A. to Thos. S. Carson 4-20-1853 (no return)
Gober, Eliza F. to Caleb W. Richerson 7-12-1839 (7-18-1839)
Gober, S. A. to J. J. Deener 11-12-1851 (no return)

Godbey, Mary F. to John M. Beloate 1-10-1871 (1-11-1871)
Godbey, Susan to Michael B. Martin 9-14-1846 (no return)
Godby, Sarah to S. B. Williams 2-10-1848 (no return)
Gofourth, Alzora to Leroy Culp 2-29-1844
Gohlson, Sarah to Wm. Dunlap 8-9-1867 (8-11-1867) B
Golen, Levena to Jesse Baker 10-18-1840
Goode, Adeline D. to David W. Fort 12-6?-1841 (no return)
Goode, Allice to Dennis Cline 1-5-1869 (1-6-1869) B
Goode, Jane to Henry Tines 6-17-1867 (6-22-1867) B
Goode, Marietta to Noah Potts 8-23-1867 (8-24-1867) B
Goode, Mary to J. W. Harris, jr. 9-12-1865 (9-13-1865)
Gooden, Polly to Peyton Babb 7-13-1870 (7-14-1870) B
Goodin, Sophrona J. to Saml. B. Robinson 12-14-1848 (12-20-1848)
Goodlett, Candis to Cato Williams 2-11-1868 (2-16-1868) B
Goodloe, Martha to Flanders Elliott 3-6-1871 (3-11-1871) B
Goodlow, Mencus J. to James G. Watson 3-12-1855 (no return)
Goodner, Amanda to R. A. Sperry 10-1-1850 (10-2-1850)
Goodwin, Eliza to A. H. Darden 7-30-1869 (8-1-1869)
Goodwin, Elizabeth A. to Joseph J. Crossett 12-26-1846 (1-14-1847)
Goodwin, Matilda to H. B. Dilliard 7-4-1851 (7-6-1851)
Goodwin, Winny to Benj. Dickinson 12-19-1866 (1-16-1867) B
Gordon, Esther to Wm. H. Williams 11-20-1844 (no return)
Gordon, Polly to William Branch 7-13-1866 (no return) B
Gorman, Martha to Wm. Shelley 2-1-1867 (7-6-1867) B
Gowen, Sarah Jane to E. F. Atkin 1-28-1848 (1-30-1848)
Graham, Mollie to R. C. Fraser 9-5-1866 (9-6-1866)
Gramer, Mary A. to James Mayo 12-12-1854 (no return)
Granberry, Adeline to Kit Roach 8-19-1870 (no return) B
Granberry, Annie to Vig Shaw 3-30-1871 (3-31-1871) B
Granberry, Celena to Zang Wiggins 12-23-1869 (no return) B
Granberry, Louisa to Henry Edwards 6-1-1866 (6-3-1866) B
Granberry, Lucy to James W. Morris 2-5-1845 (2-6-1845)
Granberry, Luvenia to Milton Granberry 1-18-1868 (1-26-1868) B
Granberry, Margaret to Everett Granberry 10-23-1869
     (10-24-1869) B
Granberry, Sarah E. to Richard B. Gatling 7-8-1844 (7-9-1844)
Granberry, Winney to George Fortson 4-27-1869 (no return) B
Granbery, H. M. to G. W. Morris 3-26-1855 (no return)
Granbery, Louisa to Richard A. Dunaho 4-3-1848 (4-5-1848)
Granbery, Mary Jane to Wm. A. Jones 3-2-1848
Grantham, Caledonia to Robt. Strickland 7-10-1868 (no return)
Gravault, Eliza to Robert McCall 9-2-1848 (9-3-1848)
Graves, Antoinette A. to James S. Eastham 10-11-1852 (no return)
Graves, Dixie E. to M. D. Hollowell 12-21-1868 (no return)
Graves, India D. to C. L. Turner 10-28-1867 (10-31-1867)
Graves, Isabella to Danl. Baucum 1-7-1841 (1-10-1841)
Graves, Patsy to Sikes Parham 4-18-1866 (6-16-1866) B
Gray, Mary Jane to James Pettit 8-3-1852 (no return)
Gray, Sophia to John Pulliam 12-20-1868 (12-28-1868)
Green, A. J. to J. A. McCharen 11-9-1868 (11-11-1868)
Green, Ann S. to Edward T. Jordan 10-27-1846 (10-28-1846)
Green, Catharine G. to Geo. W. Thompson 12-10-1845
Green, Charlotte to Carter Green 6-16-1866 (no return) B
Green, Eliza to M. M. Boyd 7-19-1865
Green, Jane to Sip Hull 12-29-1865 (1-30-1865) B
Green, Matilda to Edward Springfield 12-25-1866 (12-26-1866) B
Green, Mollid A. to W. T. Anderson 7-6-1869 (7-8-1869)
Green, Nancey to Wmson. Henley 3-10-1845
Green, Rose to John Calway 4-30-1868 (no return) B
Green, Slalie to John Kirksey 12-27-1869 B
Green, Victoria to Madison Matmass 12-14-1870 (12-18-1870) B
Greenwall, Ginnett to Solomon Anker 6-21-1856 (no return)
Greenway, M. F. to H. P. R. Wilson 10-15-1854 (no return)
Gregg, Lucy Ann to James H. Roberts 9-3-1838 (no return)
Greggs, Fannie to Henry Shaw 12-25-1867 (12-28-1867) B
Gregory, Agnes to O. T. Hendron 11-28-1842
Gregory, Agnis to Johnson J. Whitefield 11-19-1839 (no return)
Gregory, Cornelia M. to Levi P. Osborn 7-24-1848 (7-27-1848)
Gregory, Eliza to James S. Vann 8-30-1846 (no return)
Gresham, Mary to Lewis W. Harper 9-2-1850 (9-4-1850)
Grey, Eliza V. to James Pettett 1-31-1838
Grider, Elizabeth to Geor. A. Smith 12-27-1844 (1-7-1845)
Grider, Ellen to W. S. Shuford 2-15-1851 (2-19-1851)
Grider, Mary to Mitchell Heaslett 1-11-1870 (no return) B
Griffin, Ada F. to W. P. Logan 2-13-1860 (2-14-1860)

Griffin, Agness to Thos. J. Beasley 1-21-1867 (1-24-1867)
Griffin, Callie V. to W. J. Harrel 9-14-1869 (no return)
Griffin, Caroline W. to Geo. W. Queen 1-31-1859
Griffin, Delina to Geo. Seaton 5-13-1845 (5-16-1845)
Griffin, Eliza J. to Marshall B. Jones 12-15-1870
Griffin, Eliza Jane to John Glenn 10-25-1845 (10-28-1845)
Griffin, Elizabeth H. to A. J. Neal 10-15-1852 (no return)
Griffin, Mariah S. to Robert S. Allen 1-13-1844 (1-25-1844)
Griffin, Sarah? (Mrs.) to Benj. Mitchell 8-20-1839 (9-3?-1839)
Griffin, Sophria W. to Ezra T. Morrison 1-3-1842 (1-6-1842)
Griffin, Virginia to G. W. Quinn 9-21-1853 (no return)
Griggs, Agnes to R. D. Atkinson 1-30-1869 (2-4-1869)
Grisham, Manerva S. to Ezra Holtzclaw 12-8-1852 (no return)
Grissom, Cornelia to B. L. Thompson 11-15-1851 (no return)
Grissom, Eliza Jane to Joseph Rich 12-23-1844 (12-25-1844)
Grissom, Elizabeth D. F. to Joseph Allen 12-27-1852 (no return)
Grissom, M. V. to R. G. DeBow 12-14-1868 (12-15-1868)
Grissum, Pantha to Elijah Henley, jr. 9-28-1843
Grizzle, Nancy E. to W. H. Sanders 1-11-1868 (1-12-1868)
Groves, Ellen to Joseph Taylor 6-2-1866 (6-17-1866) B
Groves, J. D. to Thomas Birdsong 10-22-1859 (8-12-1860)
Grundy, Dilly to George Hardy 12-28-1867 (no return) B
Guarrant, Elizth. to John A. Jelks 11-25-1844 (no return)
Guarrant, Harrett L. to William Wash 3-30-1840
Gurley, Mary Jane to Thos. H. Robertson 1-28-1848 (2-2-1848)
Guy, Emily T. to E. Gaither 3-14-1864 (3-15-1864)
Guyn, Elizabeth to Thomas Black 10-21-1840 (12-6-1840)
Gwin, Pamelia to John Falkner 11-30-1850
Gwinn, Rozina to Thomas G. Overton 12-17-1840
Gwyn, Julia A. to Oswell F. Jones 10-31-1838 (11-1-1838)
Gwyn, Mary G. to S. J. Hooker 12-8-1866 (no return)
Gwyn, Sarah A. M. to Thomas J. Massey 9-5-1866 (7?-11-1866)
Gwynn, Elizabeth J. to Neill S. Brown 2-14-1871
Gwynn, Judy to William Ewing 12-23-1866 (12-29-1865?) B
Gwynn, S. M. to S. J. Gwynn 1-28-1866 (1-30-1866)
Hackney, Amanda to Thomas A. Morris 11-7-1862 (11-9-1862)
Hackney, Fanny C. to John R. L. Huffman 12-20-1869 (12-23-1869)
Hailey, Emmeline J. to Elijah B. Sanders 2-2-1866 (2-6-1866)
Haily, Candis to John Fuller 12-22-1853 (no return)
Hale, Frances A. E. to William S. Knox 8-24-1847 (no return)
Haley, E. C. to W. H. Hilliard 10-5-1866 (10-7-1866)
Hall, A. E. to James Wilson 3-23-1852 (no return)
Hall, Caroline to Thomas Beck 4-16-1849 (4-18-1849)
Hall, Eliza to John Walker 11-25-1852 (no return)
Hall, Elizabeth F. to James M. Gilliam 6-3-1852 (no return)
Hall, Fannie W. to James A. Mann 1-2-1869 (1-6-1869)
Hall, Frances M. to T. F. Williams 11-26-1849 (no return)
Hall, Lila to William Scott 4-16-1870 (4-17-1870) B
Hall, Malinda to Arris Sorrel 12-7-1848
Hall, Malisa to Daniel S. Farrell 11-17-1851 (no return)
Hall, Minerva to L. H. Morris 12-19-1860
Hall, Nancy J. to J. H. S. Simmerson 12-21-1853 (no return)
Hall, Obediance E. to B. Y. Trotter 10-10-1848
Hall, Sallie E. to G. W. Smith 1-5-1866 (1-10-1866)
Hall, Virginia A. to Joseph H. Smith 1-2-1869 (1-6-1869)
Halloway, Mary to John M. Burton 11-4-1847 (11-5-1847)
Hally, Lucy A. E. to William F. Thomas 3-3-1841
Hamblet, Martha to Sanders Montcuff 8-2-1844 (8-4-1844)
Hamblet, Sarah B. to Pli Walker 12-31-1849 (1-2-1850)
Hamblet, Virginia to Jno. W. Hodges 12-2-1867 (12-11-1867)
Hamer, Catherine to Austin Robinson 1-2-1868 (1-5-1868) B
Hamer, Junetta to Jerry Estridge 4-30-1868 (5-10-1868) B
Hamilton, Martha Jr to John Morris 3-16-1868 (3-17-1868)
Hamilton, Mary to Addison McFerrin 7-23-1869 (no return) B
Hamlett, Mary to Thomas W. Brown 12-15-1838 (12-20-1838)
Hamlett, Rose Ann to Buckner Harwell 7-8-1840 (7-9-1840)
Hammon, Patience to Henderson Grundy 2-20-1869 (2-12?-1869) B
Hammon, Priscilla J. to M. L. Jackson 3-11-1850
Hammons, Emily to Alfred Peebles 9-28-1870 B
Hammons, Emla to Jesse Lassiter 11-11-1840
Hammons, Frances to James Hollice 12-15-1863 (12-17-1863)
Hammons, Lucy to Mat Rutledge 12-31-1866 (1-8-1867) B
Hammons, Martha B. to W. R. Rutledge 4-6-1842
Hammons, Mary to Isaiah Crabb 2-23-1839 (2-26-1839)
Hamner, C. M. to B. F. Stacy 9-25-1852 (no return)

Hampton, C. A. to E. W. Dougan 11-16-1869 (11-18-1869)
Hampton, Eliza B. to Bodley Johnson 11-23-1846 (11-24-1846)
Hampton, Martha E. to B. J. Sutton 9-2-1865 (9-4-1865)
Hampton, Virginia to E. W. Dougan 10-16-1866 (11-10-1866)
Hamrick, Jane to John E. G. Covey 11-13-1865 (no return)
Hamrick, Sally to J. T. Garrett 12-31-1866 (no return)
Haney, Nancy to John A. Hughes 2-9-1869 (2-11-1869) B
Hanley, Marion W. to Edwin K. Austin 7-15-1845 (7-18-1845)
Hanness, Charlott to Benjamin Strong 3-15-1847 (no return)
Hansel?, Susan R. to W. L. Hall 2-14-1852 (no return)
Hansil, Mary S. to John R. Manning 12-23-1851 (no return)
Hardin, Amanda E. to James M. Whitney 11-19-1867 (11-20-1867)
Hardin, Rocky (Rody) to William Bridgewater 2-2-1871 (2-8-1871) B
Hardy, Eliza J. to Francis A. Merweather 3-2-1853 (no return)
Hare, Celia to Emanuel Bartlett 12-13-1869 (12-14-1869) B
Hare, Fannie to Jim Loving 1-15-1868 B
Hare, Hannah to Monroe Tucker 12-28-1865 (1-1-1866) B
Hare, Maria to James Goode 12-24-1866 (no return) B
Hare, Sarah S. to Eaton Bond 7-27-1840 (no return)
Hare, Virginia A. to James F. Green 10-14-1848 (10-18-1848)
Hargas, Sarah Ann to Riley S. Kennedy 9-17-1842 (9-21-1842)
Hargess, J. P. to J. D. Brook 1-16-1852 (no return)
Hargis, Augustine L. to J. W. L. Hargis 12-22-1841 (12-23-1841)
Hargis, Nancy S. to Robert Calewell 1-29-1844 (2-5-1844)
Hargiss, Augustina to Isaac Osborne 9-16-1851 (no return)
Hargrove, Elizabeth to James Barnes 9-22-1845 (9-25-1845)
Hargrove, Mary J. to Thos. D. Baum 11-26-1849
Hargus, Sarah Ann to Allen H. Bobo 6-3-1844 (no return)
Harington, Mary Jane to Noel E. West 2-18-1839 (2-20-1839)
Harmon, Martha W. to D. Reddick 3-13-1852 (no return)
Harp, Araminta Eveline to John Daviss 3-4-1845
Harper, Jennie to Abraham Brown 5-26-1869 (5-29-1869) B
Harper, Mary A. to P. H. W. Grammar 12-24-1853 (no return)
Harper, Permelia to Joseph B. Anderson 1-20-1845 (no return)
Harrell, Adaline to Henry Jones 6-2-1866 (no return) B
Harrell, Caledonia to V. H. Swift 11-12-1859 (11-13-1859)
Harrell, Lucy A. to John H. Mitchell 5-13-1862 (5-21-1862)
Harrell, Lucy A. to John H. Mitchell 5-13-1862 (not endorsed)
Harrell, M. A. to J. N. Williams 10-29-1860 (11-1-1860)
Harris, A. E. to Pinkny Dickson 10-22-1851 (no return)
Harris, Ammarilla to Alfred Williams 8-6-1839
Harris, Anna to Christopher C. Poindexter 4-24-1871 (5-5-1871)
Harris, Annetta to A. M. O'Quinn 2-3-1866 (2-6-1866)
Harris, Annis to Steven Cannon 3-11-1863 (3-17-1863)
Harris, Caroline to Thomas Rickett 1-7-1870 (1-8-1870) B
Harris, Cora E. to W. T. Watson 1-14-1861 (1-15-1861)
Harris, Cornelia to Jas. Rodgers 6-30-1849 (7-1-1849)
Harris, Delia to Isaac Smith 11-26-1869 (no return) B
Harris, Delila to W. H. Lindsy 10-22-1839
Harris, Eliza to Reuben Rawlings 4-24-1871 (4-25-1871) B
Harris, Elizabeth P. to Jonathan McCraw 1-4-1851 (no return)
Harris, Elizabeth to Ridley Clifton 4-11-1846 (no return)
Harris, Ella to J. M. Wilkinson 9-19-1870 (9-24-1870)
Harris, Esther to Wesley Davis 8-21-1869 (8-13?-1869) B
Harris, Fannie F. to J. I. Johnson 2-7-1866 (2-8-1866)
Harris, Jane A. to Robert Quinn 5-14-1852 (no return)
Harris, Malsey to Newit Harris 2-14-1853 (no return)
Harris, Martha to Wm. P. Ingram 6-4-1849 (6-5-1849)
Harris, Marthena to Joseph T. Leverett 11-26-1870 (11-27-1870)
Harris, Mary A. to Alexder. Burkhart 12-4-1856 (no return)
Harris, Mary E. to Henry M. Robards 5-28-1867 (5-29-1867)
Harris, Mary J. to John W. Hester 12-12-1854 (no return)
Harris, Mary J. to W. B. Beavers 2-19-1866 (2-20-1866)
Harris, Mary J. to W. D. Wilkerson 10-9-1854 (no return)
Harris, Mary to D. C. King 2-6-1869 (2-8-1869)
Harris, Mary to John Dickason 10-25-1851 (no return)
Harris, Mary to Thos. S. Jackson 5-26-1845 (no return)
Harris, Mattie A. to Jas. E. Yancey 12-5-1866
Harris, Nancy to Finny Wiggins 10-10-1866 (10-13-1866) B
Harris, Nelly Ann to Wm. Riley 10-1-1869 (10-3-1869) B
Harris, Patience to Ben Hill 8-29-1868 (8-30-1868) B
Harris, R. to J. S. Farrar 1-21-1861 (1-23-1861)
Harris, Ritteran to John Dougan 1-15-1845
Harris, Rose Ann to Wm. Mason 12-26-1867 (12-29-1867) B
Harris, Sarah A. E. to George W. Hardin 6-11-1838 (no return)

Harris, Sarah E. to D. J. Herrington 1-27-1842 (2-2-1842)
Harris, Sarah J. to James Amones 9-12-1865 (9-13-1865)
Harris, Sarah to B. P. Braden 2-3-1849
Harris, Susan H. to N. W. Galloway 5-1-1871 (5-2-1871)
Harris, Thedonia to L. T. Sweat 3-14-1868 (3-16-1868)
Harris, Virginia A. to John A. Covington 2-26-1866 (2-27-1866)
Harrison, Hesterann to Daniel J. Stafford 8-2-1841 (8-12-1841)
Harrison, Louisa to James M. Thompson 10-5-1843
Harrison, Martha to Isaac Williams 3-1-1870 (3-3-1870) B
Harrison, Miss ___ to S. F. Woodruff 9-20-1855 (no return)
Harrison, Ruth W. to Joseph H. Trotter 7-6-1846 (7-9-1846)
Harrison?, Della Ann to Richd. H. Harvey 12-19-1848
Harriss, Eady to Binkley Freeman 4-17-1839 (4-18-1839)
Hart, Adeline to Mat Taylor 2-5-1869 (2-9-1869) B
Hart, Eliza H. to Edward Coates 9-13-1852 (no return)
Hart, J. M. to Wm M. Alexander 3-28-1854 (no return)
Hart, Lizzie S. to H. G. Miller 12-7-1859
Hart, Louiza to Alfred Morrow 12-23-1867 (12-24-1867) B
Hart, Lucy to John L. Seaton 11-17-1853 (no return)
Hart, Mary M. to Robert B. Harper 9-12-1864 (9-13-1864)
Hart, Mary to J. M. McMillon 12-15-1849 (12-18-1849)
Hart, Susan to Ned Gooden 12-30-1869 (12-31-1869) B
Harvell, Ann to James Henderson 12-25-1866 (12-26-1866) B
Harvell, Margaret to Robert Rives 12-25-1866
Harvey, Ann E. to Robert E. Rogers 10-6-1869 (10-7-1869) B
Harvey, Caroline to George Lowrey 8-18-1866 (not endorsed) B
Harvey, Lee to Alfred Jones 2-26-1870 (12-28-1870) B
Harvey, Mary H. to Milton G. Frazer 2-11-1854 (no return)
Harvey, Mary to Larkin Adkins 5-29-1851 (no return)
Harvey, R. C. to Abel Grace 10-20-1849 (10-28-1849)
Harvey, S. P. (Mrs.) to K. R. Spence 12-16-1867
Harvy, Mary to Martin Runnals 4-9-1870
Harvy, Netty to Manuel Butcher 1-14-1870 (1-16-1870) B
Harwell, Anna to Jno. Parham, jr. 12-18-1860 (12-19-1860)
Harwell, Maggie to Primus Williamson 3-25-1870 B
Harwell, Mary A. S. (Mrs.) to Leander Black 5-20-1844 (5-29-1844)
Harwell, Mary E. to W. W. Winfield 6-1-1859 (6-26-1859)
Harwell, Polly (Mrs.) to John Z. Morton 11-12-1862 (not endorsed)
Harwell, Polly to John Z. Morton 11-12-1862 (not endorsed)
Hase?, Amanda C. to Wm. Little 10-6-1840
Haselett, Artemecia to Jake Johnson 1-18-1868 (no return) B
Haselett, Harriet to Charley Van 5-15-1868 (no return) B
Haselett, Margaret to Henry Tate 7-19-1867 (no return) B
Haselett, Susan to John A. Nesbitt 5-18-1867 (no return) B
Haselette, Alsey to Nuggy Parris 12-23-1867 (no return) B
Haselette, Martha to Frank Dunkin 12-23-1867 (12-28-1867) B
Haskeah?, Delilia to John Simerson 7-1-1841
Haskins, Cloe to Dock Hendon 7-30-1870 B
Haskins, Martha to Cash McDonald 1-5-1871 B
Hass, Minerva to Geo. Ward 11-25-1850 (11-26-1850)
Hatch, Mary S. to Thomas Whitelaw 2-4-1841 (2-11-1841)
Hatley, Mariah C. to A. C. Waller 8-4-1845 (8-5-1845)
Hatley, Martha A. to Samuel H. Bayless 7-22-1844
Haveway, Elizabeth to Samuel Moncreef 1-1-1839
Hawkins, M. J. to J. Geyer 7-23-1853 (no return)
Hawley, Laura E. to James M. Allen 9-14-1852 (no return)
Hayes, Ella to Mat Olds 6-11-1869 (6-12-1869) B
Hays, Emelia to Calvin M. Blankenship 9-22-1838 (9-23-1838)
Hays, Susannah to Littleton Moore 11-12-1869 (11-13-1869) B
Hayslett, T. to Phil Wall 2-12-1869 (no return) B
Hazlewood, B. J. to W. T. Hazlewood 12-19-1865 (12-20-1865)
Hazlewood, Letitia F. to David C. House? no date (with Dec 1852)
Hazlewood, Mollie E. to Lewis C. Howse 11-9-1866 (11-14-1866)
Heaslet, Fanny to Daniel Alexander 12-24-1869 (no return) B
Heaslet, Sarah to David Shackelford 4-17-1869 (no return) B
Heaslet, Virtue to Ned Herron 3-5-1870 (3-6-1870)
Heaslett, Abbie to Dock Scott 2-11-1871 (no return) B
Heaslett, Adaline to Henry Cogbill 2-2-1867 (no return) B
Heaslett, Bettie to Alexander Randal 3-27-1869 (no return) B
Heaslett, Lila to Edmund Tate 1-22-1869 (no return) B
Heaslett, Paralee to Spencer Williams 2-2-1867 (no return) B
Heaslett, Texanna to Clem Mitchell 12-25-1868 (no return) B
Heaslitt, Mary to Henry Shackleford 3-9-1867 (no return) B
Heathcock, Amanda J. to William A. Johnson 11-9-1870 (11-10-1870)
Hedges, Virginia A. to Micajah Stokes 7-7-1870

Heit (Hart), Lizzie to James W. D. Henry 2-8-1867 (2-12-1867)
Helton, Maryann to James Seaton 12-17-1838 (12-20-1838)
Henderson, Dinah to Friday Thomas 1-5-1867 B
Henderson, Emily V. to Varnum Ozment 5-10-1847 (no return)
Henderson, Locky Mariah to Whitfield Boyed 2-25-1841
Henderson, Margaret to John H. George 1-24-1845 (no return)
Henderson, Matilda M. to Samuel D. Wilson 12-27-1839 (SB 1838)
Henderson, Sally to Britton Polk 12-25-1866 (12-26-1866) B
Hendley, Juli Ann to Eli Culp 12-27-1842 (no return)
Hendly, Jenny to Ben Parham 7-6-1868 (7-10-1868) B
Hendrix?, Samantha to John Faulk 6-22-1850
Henley, Elizabeth Jane to M. C. Holloway 11-20-1845
Henley, F. L. to Wm. Stedham 7-2-1860 (7-12-1860)
Henley, Margarett to James B. Morris 2-16-1841 (2-18-1841)
Henley, Martha to Green Burrow 5-19-1840
Henley, Sarah E. to Wm. H. Henley 11-9-1868 (11-11-1868)
Henley, Susan to Armsted Dowdy 3-1-1852 (no return)
Henly, Martha to D. G. Mussy 3-14-1849 (no return)
Henry, Laura to Jerry Criddle 12-25-1869 (6-25-1871) B
Henshaw, Margaret A. to David Kirkland 7-6-1846 (7-12-1846)
Herington, Catharine to Wm. H. Neesbit 12-27-1843 (12-28-1843)
Herington, Elizabeth to William Morris 12-27-1843 (12-28-1843)
Herndon, Mary A. to M. Y. Moran 1-24-1849 (1-26-1849)
Herndon, Mollie M. T. to Frank L. Moffatt 1-27-1870
Hernes, Mary F. to George Barnes 12-5-1867
Herren, Melvina to L. J. Okelly 8-19-1862 (not endorsed)
Herrod, Charlotte to Jordan Dickerson 5-26-1866 B
Herron, Fannie A. to Henry M. Cocke 1-16-1861
Herron, Hilean Ann to D. P. Murchison 10-14-1868 (10-16-1868)
Herron, Malvina to L. J. OKelly 8-19-1862 (8-23-1862)
Herron, Nancy B. to Lewis J. O'Kelly 9-5-1866 (9-9-1866)
Herron, Susan to W. B. Wall 1-24-1866 (1-25-1866)
Hertle, Jane to W. D. Stephens 12-23-1868 (12-25-1868)
Hesler, Ann J. to H. M. Farmer 7-13-1849 (7-17-1849)
Hester, Nancy to Jerome Mitchel 8-1-1849 (no return)
Hester, Sarah to Silas Whiting 6-21-1848 (6-23-1848)
Hewitt, Bettie B. to M. W. Smith 10-24-1869
Hickey, Susan to Francis M. Hobbs 8-23-1865
Hicks, Caroline to Frank Phillips 11-6-1869 (no return) B
Hicks, Sallie to Thos. A. Tripp 5-26-1869 (5-27-1869)
Higenbothem, Sarah P. to Bernard G. Hendrick 2-19-1851 (no return)
Higganson, Sarrah D. to Marcus D. L. Sumner 4-18-1843 (4-25-1843)
Higgarson, Mary S. to N. J. Cocke 9-1-1847
Higgason, Alice to Mat Carpenter 4-12-1871 B
Higgason, Ann to Logan Jones 3-19-1866 (no return) B
Higgason, Fannie M. to Edmund R. Scruggs 3-18-1868
Higgason, Lizzie L. to John W. Shaw 3-3-1870
Higgason, Mallissa to Wm. C. Burton 10-23-1860 (10-24-1860)
High, Analiza to C. H. Brumley 5-6-1841
High, Celia to Evans Williams 4-18-1870 (5-1-1870) B
High, Mary to Horatio S. Wells 10-26-1842
High, Nancy Jane to Freman Hubbard 9-11-1850 (9-12-1850)
High, Sarah to Thomas P. Gilliam 12-23-1847
Hill, Betsey J. to Daniel G. Frazier 2-23-1846 (2-25-1846)
Hill, Eliza to James Sale 5-5-1870 (no return)
Hill, Laura to Owen Lewis 1-12-1867 (1-13-1867) B
Hill, Lutisha R. to Archabald Williamson 4-15-1852 (no return)
Hill, Mary Jane to Alfred Parham 4-11-1867 (5-12-1867) B
Hill, Mary Jane to M. L. Robertson 2-25-1842 (3-3-1842)
Hill, Mary to James Wheeler 12-5-1859 (12-11-1859)
Hill, Sarah E. to Richard Campton 5-20-1854 (no return)
Hilliard, Eliza W. to Saml. B. Jordon 1-31-1849
Hilliard, Elizabeth to G. W. Nolly 11-3-1862 (not endorsed)
Hilliard, Ellen to Andrew Perry 1-19-1871 (1-21-1871) B
Hilliard, Harriet to Nelson Boals 9-13-1867 (9-14-1867) B
Hilliard, Julia to Abram Greenlee 7-25-1870 B
Hilliard, L. B. to P. M. Bondurant 4-3-1854 (no return)
Hilliard, M. E. to L. M. Rhodgers 4-5-1869 (4-9-1869)
Hilliard, Mary J. to D. S. Haley 2-15-1853 (no return)
Hilliard, Ruthy to Andy Jefferson 8-17-1869 (8-18-1869) B
Hilliard, Susan F. to J. W. Sanders 12-11-1865 (12-12-1865)
Hilliard, Winniford L. to Raleigh W. Poindexter 9-7-1846 (no return)
Hinson, Eliza T. to John L. Balthrop 12-20-1869 (12-22-1869)
Hobson, Agnes to Charles Ancromb 12-11-1869 (no return) B

Hobson, Camelia to Sam Price 1-5-1867 (1-6-1867) B
Hodges, Elizabeth C. to Theophilus Caldwell 1-19-1846 (no return)
Hodges, Mary E. to Larkin P. Jones 8-9-1838
Hodges, Sarah T. to Joseph B. Edwards 11-6-1865 (11-15-1865)
Hodges, Virginia A. to P. C. Thompson 12-3-1868 (no return)
Hogan, Mary E. to George Ervin 9-28-1848 (9-29-1848)
Holden, Catherine R. to Joseph W. Phillips 1-21-1868 (1-22-1868)
Holland, A. F. to Westley C. Teel 3-23-1843 (3-24-1843)
Holland, Conelia to John D. Pearson 12-15-1851 (no return)
Holland, Lucinda to Rawley Fields 11-10-1869 (not executed) B*
Holland, M. E. to J. B. Armstrong 1-13-1870 (1-18-1870)
Holland, Sarah M. to Daniel Earnhart 10-17-1855 (no return)
Hollemon, Martha to Calvin D. Maddin 6-10-1847
Holliday, Martha Jane to Jackson Tatum 9-11-1847
Hollis, Elender A. (Mrs.) to N. W. Willis 12-16-1854 (no return)
Hollis, Isadora to S. D. Whitehead 3-20-1851
Holloway, Alice L. W. to James W. Rogan 4-11-1871 (4-12-1871)
Holloway, Dolly to Frank Williamson 5-23-1868 (5-25-1868) B
Holloway, Eliza J. to Thos. Barham 1-5-1848
Holloway, Eliza to Billy Seymour 12-17-1870 B
Holloway, Elizabeth to Merrit D. Hix 9-14-1853 (no return)
Holloway, Emma D. to Wm. A. Gilliam 2-17-1869
Holloway, Judy J. to Henry Snelling 12-17-1849 (12-20-1849)
Holloway, Lee to Joseph Rankin 2-15-1870 (2-17-1870)
Holloway, M. J. to D. W. Nobb 2-20-1855 (no return)
Holloway, Marta Jane to Curtis Mills 1-27-1848 (no return)
Holloway, Nancy to William Perry 2-25-1851 (2-27-1851)
Holloway, Nora to Wyott Ivy 2-9-1870 (2-10-1870) B
Holloway, Parthena B. to Benjamin B. Suggett 1-27-1846 (1-28-1845?)
Holloway, Rebecca S. to Wm. F. Blankenship 11-7-1854 (no return)
Holloway, Roanna to Daniel Isbell 7-9-1870 B
Holloway, Sarah to John J. Wilson 1-16-1839 (no return)
Holloway, Sarahjennett to Josiah R. Baugh 11-2-1847
Hollowell, Bamley to G. W. Anthony 11-8-1862 (not endorsed)
Hollowell, Mary J. to W. F. Mitchell 12-19-1853 (no return)
Holman, Delia A. to W. E. Penick 12-12-1870 (12-14-1870)
Holman, Mollie C. to Jas. C. Cogbill 1-2-1866 (1-11-1866)
Holman, Rachel E. to R. A. Owings 9-9-1865 (9-12-1865)
Holmes, Bettie A. to Burrell Jordan 1-11-1871 (1-12-1871)
Holmes, Cary to Sam Jackson 3-18-1869 B
Holmes, Harriet to Jefferson Carter 10-30-1866 (no return) B
Holmes, Nancy W. to Thomas C. J. Reeves 4-14-1853 (no return)
Holt, Donie to Simon Morrow 9-27-1870 B
Holt, Mattie L. to Geo. W. Tatum 11-13-1860
Holt, Sallie to W. L. Hart 10-16-1865 (10-17-1865)
Holt, Susan to Henry Sampson 10-27-1866 (no return) B
Honey, Adah to Thomas A. Driggers 8-30-1843 (8-31-1843)
Honey, Lucinda to Esau Bates 12-11-1843 (12-14-1843)
Honey, Mary A. to Jas. H. Trulove 6-17-1846 (6-18-1846)
Honey, Nancy to Henry Louch 12-23-1843 (12-24-1843)
Honnell, Sarah J. to Tho. B. Henderson 9-1-1846 (9-3-1846)
Hood, Bettie E. to M. J. Reams, jr. 11-3-1870
Hood, Eliza to Jim Durham 12-26-1866 (12-27-1866) B
Hood, Eliza to W. H. Wing 12-17-1866 (12-20-1866)
Hood, Harriett H. to Ben W. Johnston 10-11-1855 (no return)
Hood, Martha J. to W. F. Carter 3-11-1849 (no return)
Hood, Mary J. to L. E. Murphy 10-6-1868 (10-7-1868)
Hood, Maryann D. to Wm. H. Stafford 2-17-1845 (2-18-1845)
Hood, Mollie E. to G. H. Reames 12-11-1867 (12-12-1867)
Hood, Ragile G. to T. W. Bennett 10-5-1848 (no return)
Hood, S. E. to M. H. Kelley 12-26-1867
Hood, Sarah (Mrs.) to Geo. F. A. Spiller 11-11-1862 (11-12-1862)
Hood, Susan A. to R. R. Grizzle 10-3-1868 (10-7-1868)
Hooker, Caroline C. to Jas. A. Eddins 12-10-1850 (12-11-1850)
Hooks, Josephine to Wiley T. Cargil 12-13-1866 (12-24-1866)
Hooks, M. J. A. to Jackson Woodard 10-27-1848 (no return)
Hooper, Lauryan to Benj. F. Hooper 1-18-1843 (no return)
Hope, Eliza to David P. Cloyed 4-21-1841
Hope, Manerva A. to John S. Johnson 10-1-1851 (no return)
Hopper, Margaret to Peyton Somerville 12-26-1865 (no return) B
Hoskins, Elmira J. to Daniel Hodman 1-20-1850 (no return)
House, Ann M. to A. J. Hunter 1-16-1851 (1-22-1851)
House, Dilcey to Anthony Smith 11-23-1869 (11-28-1869) B
House, Jane C. to Silas C. Irbey 12-15-1846 (12-22-1846)
House, Mary to James House 11-5-1869 (11-11-1869) B

Houston, Cynthia to P. M. Williams 2-12-1842
Houston, Cynthia to T. M. Williamson 2-12-1842 (no return)
Houston, Dinah to Thornton Bolling 3-29-1866 (4-1-1866) B
Houston, Elizabeth F. to John H. Patrick 1-1-1869 (no return)
Houston, Ella to Wm. Waddell 2-8-1868 (no return) B
Houston, Roann to H. H. Taylor 7-21-1864
Howard, Elizabeth to Felix W. Lee 2-12-1839
Howard, Josephine to George Plattenburg 9-15-1855 (no return)
Howard, Martha A. to Wm. M. Herndon 12-5-1856 (no return)
Howell, Fatis C. to Joseph J. Robertson 4-12-1845 (4-15-1845)
Howell, Margart A. to Thos. R. McKnight 12-12-1850 (no return)
Howell, Marinda to M. Garrison 6-24-1869 (6-30-1869)
Howell, Nancy to Stephen L. Carter 2-5-1851
Hubbard, Lucinda to Elijah D. Henley 11-11-1846
Huddleston, Catharine J. to Asa Hewin 5-2-1853 (no return)
Hudson, Arena to Ed Bowers 3-28-1870 (3-29-1870) B
Hudson, Caroline to Henry Gaither 12-28-1869 B
Hudson, Eliza A. to James W. Cole 11-28-1866 (11-29-1866)
Hudson, Jane C. to David Myers 4-24-1852 (no return)
Hudson, Martha F. to Wylie Doyerl? 2-11-1840 (2-13-1840)
Hudson, Susan A. to William H. Johnson 7-28-1842
Hudson, Tempy Ann to C. W. Ferrell 2-9-1846
Hudspeth, Caroline to Austin Muncrief 11-3-1845 (11-2?-1845)
Hudspeth, Lucy A. to Tho. J. Bell 12-16-1845 (12-17-1845)
Hughes, Eliza E. to J. M. Elder 1-6-1871 (1-12-1871)
Hughes, Elizabeth to John Culbreth no date (12-28?-1838)
Hughes, Elizabeth to John Ferrel 5-2-1846 (no return)
Humphrey, Catharine to Smith Patterson 1-19-1844 (not endorsed)
Humphrey, Frances to Wm. M. Price 2-26-1855 (no return)
Humphrey, Gennett to James Richey 4-18-1840 (4-19-1840)
Humphrey, Martha to Jas. L. Richie 1-19-1850 (1-20-1850)
Humphrey, Sarah to Nicholas Long 9-10-1844
Humphreys, A. J. to P. D. Benson 8-18-1843 (9-8-1843)
Humphreys, Grace to Stephen K. Watkins 12-12-1866
Humphreys, Mary H. to Timothy K. David 10-14-1840 (10-22-1841?)
Humphreys, Mary to Henry Matthews 3-22-1870 (3-18?-1870) B
Humphreys, Mary to W. A. Milliken 2-3-1870
Humphreys, Rhoda to Thos. Brown 1-4-1851 (1-5-1851)
Hunsucker, Martha E. to W. W. Lyles 1-30-1867
Hunsucker, Sarah Ann to Archey Burleyson 12-21-1866 (12-22-1866)
Hunt, Bettie M. to Wm. H. Long 11-30-1868 (12-8-1868)
Hunter, Allice L. to Samuel H. Wilson 1-23-1869 (1-27-1869)
Hunter, Caroline to George Martin 12-29-1869 (no return) B
Hunter, Emeline to Jordan Taylor 2-27-1866 (12-28-1866) B
Hunter, Emeline to Ned Giles 12-12-1868 (12-19-1868) B
Hunter, Emeline to William Stout 12-26-1868 (12-27-1868) B
Hunter, Evey to Ed Ballard 12-12-1868 (12-21-1868) B
Hunter, Harriet to Mark Lewis 1-1-1869 (1-2-1869) B
Hunter, Jenny to Blueford Paine 12-28-1868 B
Hunter, Julia to Fred Douglass 1-6-1871 (no return) B
Hunter, Louise E. to Henry S. Taylor 10-16-1838
Hunter, Martha to James Merriwether 11-4-1843 (no return)
Hunter, Mary to John L. Dawson 2-2-1866 (2-4-1866)
Hunter, Nancy Ann to Marvin Hunter 4-3-1869 (4-18-1869) B
Hunter, Rebecca J. to A. A. Black 7-30-1853 (no return)
Hurley, C. F. to Wm. F. Farmer 1-30-1871 (2-14-1871)
Hurley, Elizabeth to J. G. Ruby 12-16-1845
Hurley, Jane to Normon Williams 12-17-1847 (12-22-1847)
Hutchins, Elizabeth to Calvin Ursery 12-20-1844 (12-19?-1844)
Hutchins, Jane to Ruffin Willis 1-10-1844
Hutchins, Julia to James T. Willis 4-9-1845
Hutchins, Martha to William Myers 11-10-1869 (11-11-1869) B
Hutchins, Permelia to Silas M. Chiles 2-28-1838
Hutchinson, Eliza J. to Albert C. G. Burton 2-15-1871 (no return) B
Iley, Elizabeth to A. Bevins 12-18-1847 (12-17?-1847)
Ingram, Caroline J. to Philemon T. Burford 5-22-1839 (5-24-1839)
Ingram, Elizabeth N. to H. A. Tatum 9-19-1851 (no return)
Ingram, Elizabeth to Elisha Lay 9-16-1839 (no return)
Ingram, Julia Ann to Phillip Caple 9-6-1839 (no return)
Ingram, Martha to Stephen C. Durham 1-29-1842 (2-3-1842)
Ingram, Mary to Francis Hite 4-26-1853 (no return)
Irby, B. V. to J. F. Wylie 10-22-1864 (10-29-1864)
Irby, Belle to J. A. Neely 12-18-1868 (12-23-1868)
Irby, Jane W. to Edward P. Luckado 6-23-1845
Irby, Julia S. to J. D. Hazlewood 12-8-1866

Irby, Nancy M. to Silas R. Irby 3-12-1847 (no return)
Irvens, Fanny to Clark Williamson 5-2-1871 (5-13-1871) B
Irvin, Ann to George Crawford 9-14-1867 (9-15-1867) B
Irvin, Mollie R. to Wm. A. Rhea 2-11-1869
Irwin, Dollie to Augustus Harding 11-8-1869 (no return) B
Irwin, Harriett J. to T. J. Duvall 3-17-1851 (no return)
Irwin, M. W. to W. W. Pierce 11-25-1862 (11-26-1862)
Irwin, Margaret to James H. Hailey 3-11-1869
Irwin, Mary Elizabeth to George King 4-8-1869
Irwin, Tempy M. to Josiah F. Rainey 9-9-1839 (9-10-1839)
Isalm?, Johnita to Thomas Sellas 12-30-1847
Isbell, A. G. to A. V. Ware 2-6-1860 (2-8-1860)
Isbell, Bell to Taylor McDonald 1-3-1868 (1-7-1868) B
Isbell, Emma to Collin Humphreys 4-18-1867 B
Isbell, Fanny to Mose Williams 1-18-1868 (no return) B
Isbell, Mattie to Scott Warr 3-1-1869 (3-3-1869)
Isbell, Sarah E. to J. S. Palmore 6-20-1849 (6-29-1849)
Ivey, Louisa to J. B. Culpeper 10-8-1849 (10-10-1849)
Ivey, Lucy Ann to James L. Garrison 8-31-1847 (no return)
Ivie, Araminta H. to W. T. Currie 12-18-1860 (12-20-1860)
Ivie, Eliza to James Powell 12-11-1866 (12-13-1866)
Ivie, Frances to Henry Bone 11-12-1866 (12-1-1866) B
Ivie, Martha A. to John H. Mitchell 12-13-1854 (no return)
Ivy, M. F. to Albert Webber 10-24-1866 (11-11-1866)
Ivy, Sallie to Jeff Johnson 2-15-1868 (2-16-1868) B
Jackson, Clara to Austin Buford 1-8-1867 B
Jackson, Didama to Jefferson V.? Mallard 2-10-1841
Jackson, Emila T. to P. H. Willis 7-6-1847 (7-7-1847)
Jackson, H. E. to J. R. Bruce 7-24-1848 (no return)
Jackson, Julia E. to Robert H. Draper 3-3-1855 (no return)
Jackson, Lucy to Washington Carter 12-28-1867 (12-29-1867) B
Jackson, Malissa to Mack Cleere 2-12-1867 (2-14-1867) B
Jackson, Martha G. to William H. Trent 3-14-1846 (3-17-1846)
Jackson, Martha W. to Wilson T. Beaver 7-19-1841 (7-22-1842?)
Jackson, Mary A. to Joseph C. C. Tucker 7-3-1843 (7-6-1843)
Jackson, Mary B. to Jonathan H. McCraw 10-16-1843
Jackson, Mary E. (Mrs.) to T. J. Manly 2-23-1867
Jackson, Mary to Michael Beavers 11-30-1839 (12-5-1839)
Jackson, Oma to Jurdon Neel 1-4-1871 (no return) B
Jackson, Rebecca to Ira N. Green 10-7-1840 (10-13-1840)
Jackson, S. A. to W. L. Wilder 12-6-1859 (12-8-1859)
Jackson, S. to Aleck Smith 12-13-1866 (12-16-1866)
James, Eliza E. to Wm. Robinson 2-17-1860
James, Elizabeth to William J. Guthra 1-24-1842 (5-16-1842)
Jamson, T. S. to Wm. M. Nonnent 1-7-1849 (no return)
Jarrett, Kitty A. to William S. Mayfield 10-13-1843 (no return)
Jefferson, Amanda to King Wheeler 5-2-1868 (no return) B
Jefferson, Jane to Martin Moore 1-18-1868 (no return) B
Jefferson, Martha to John Daniel 1-2-1869 (no return) B
Jefferson, Phebe Ann to Carter Smith 12-31-1866 (no return) B
Jefferson, Phillis to Albert Hilliard 3-20-1869 (3-24-1869) B
Jeffries, Mahala to Henry Kirkland 1-24-1870 (1-25-1870)
Jenkins, Eliza to Reddick Brown 2-18-1867 B
Jenkins, Judy to William Turnbull 4-13-1866 (4-15-1866) B
Jernigan, A. to John H. Morgan 3-27-1842 (3-31-1842)
Jernigan, Amelia J. to David C. Booth 3-9-1839 (no return)
Jernigan, Elizabeth J. to B. D. Finney 5-18-1846 (5-26-1846)
Johnson, A. to P. M. Teel 11-13-1847 (11-18-1847)
Johnson, Amanda to J. H. Bishop 8-12-1869
Johnson, Arminda D. to John B. Turner 4-7-1863
Johnson, Charlotte to Robert Smith 9-11-1869 (no return) B
Johnson, Clara to Geo. Washington Settle 1-7-1869 (no return) B
Johnson, Clara to Henry McDowell 10-10-1868 (no return) B
Johnson, Easter to Tom Grear 8-2-1867 (no return) B
Johnson, Edna M. to Jno. P. Burns 7-23-1868 (7-24-1868)
Johnson, Eliza D. to Green H. Moody 3-1-1848 (3-2-1848)
Johnson, Elizabeth to R. F. Buckelew 8-30-1851 (no return)
Johnson, Emma H. to C. W. McRee 10-11-1869 (10-12-1869)
Johnson, Florence I. to W. G. Anderson 7-27-1869 (7-29-1869)
Johnson, Frances to William Huffman 9-4-1865
Johnson, Harriet to Jas. M. Crowder 9-4-1849 (9-5-1849)
Johnson, Jane C. to Anderson Stedham 4-12-1839
Johnson, Jane to George F. Johnson 7-6-1844 (no return)
Johnson, Jemima to Frank Braden 2-28-1866 (no return) B
Johnson, Margaret to John McCraw 9-21-1866

Johnson, Margaret to John McVay 11-18-1848 (no return)
Johnson, Martha J. to A. B. Lloyd 12-19-1868 (12-22-1868)
Johnson, Martha J. to Visen? P. Wright 2-1-1848 (2-8-1848)
Johnson, Martha to Baltimore Downs 12-4-1867 (12-5-1867) B
Johnson, Mary A. to Garrett W. Simmons 10-27-1848 (10-29-1848)
Johnson, Mary A. to Hamilton Thornton 12-17-1856 (no return)
Johnson, Mary A. to Moses C. Clark 8-13-1846 (8-14-1846)
Johnson, Mary J. to Robt. E. R. Greer 11-5-1867 (11-7-1867)
Johnson, Mary to George W. Patterson 8-16-1838
Johnson, Mollie to T. W. Cox 11-4-1867 (11-5-1867)
Johnson, Myra to Isiah Brown 12-28-1870 B
Johnson, Nancy J. to Lenard Brown 11-8-1849
Johnson, Nola to Daniel Goode 6-11-1869 (no return) B
Johnson, Rebecca to Amos Elms 7-9-1840 (no return)
Johnson, S. A. M. to D. D. Dacus 10-30-1860 (11-2-1860)
Johnson, S. J. to G. H. Moody 9-20-1849
Johnson, Sarah M. C. to Andrew Newsom 10-13-1851 (no return)
Johnson, Sarah to A. Cook? 7-4-1842
Johnson, Sue to J. B. Reames 12-11-1867 (12-12-1867)
Johnson, Susanah R. to Dandridge M. Jordan 9-25-1852 (no return)
Johnson, Tomantana to N. W. Williams 7-8-1845 (7-9-1846?)
Johnson, Zurie to Henry Morris 12-28-1867 (1-3-1868) B
Johnston, Margaret J. to Joseph J. Freeland 11-15-1870 (11-22-1870)
Johnston, Winny to John Flemming 4-11-1849 (4-12-1849)
Joiner, Joanna to Henry Stewart 5-11-1867 (no return) B
Jolly, Sarah Jane to J. S. Rochelle 3-27-1848 (3-29-1848)
Jonakin, Sylvia to Peter Williams 5-19-1866 (8-11-1866) B
Jones, Ann Eliza to W. A. Turner 5-14-1850
Jones, Cassie to L. T. Culp 12-19-1870 (12-22-1870)
Jones, Catherine to Thomas Matthews 1-19-1866 (1-27-1866) B
Jones, Celestia to James Phillips 11-9-1867 B
Jones, Cherry to Anderson Steger 2-14-1870 (2-23-1870) B
Jones, Clarissa to Robert Clear 1-13-1871 (no return) B
Jones, Cynthia to Josiah Cather 12-25-1866 (12-26-1866) B
Jones, Eliza to A. P. Womack 1-3-1842 (1-6-1842)
Jones, Elizabeth to James A. Carnes 10-28-1840 (10-29-1840)
Jones, Elizabeth to Jacob Ormon 3-19-1838
Jones, Elmira to Wm. H. Davis 4-25-1866 (4-28-1866) B
Jones, Elvira to Green Robertson 1-27-1869 (1-28-1869) B
Jones, Emeline to Wilkerson Harris 12-24-1866 (12-27-1866) B
Jones, Emily W. to G. W. Goodloe 12-29-1852 (no return)
Jones, Evelin to Aleck Scott 8-11-1866 (8-12-1866) B
Jones, Fanny to Ned Wiggins 11-22-1870 (no return)
Jones, Fender to Nelson Shaw 12-28-1868 (1-15-1869) B
Jones, Flora to John W. Bell 5-6-1869 B
Jones, Frances to Ed Robinson 12-24-1870 (no return) B
Jones, Georgia Ann to James Gwynn 7-13-1866 (7-28-1866) B
Jones, H. M. to T. B. Harris 12-13-1859 (12-14-1859)
Jones, Harriet to George Washington 9-22-1870 B
Jones, Isabella to J. B. Booker 6-3-1851 (6-4-1851)
Jones, Jane to George Hardy 3-16-1867 (3-19-1867) B
Jones, Jane to London Warren 3-22-1870 (4-9-1870) B
Jones, Julia to Robert Patterson 12-6-1866 B
Jones, Leonah to Willis Eaton 2-4-1869 B
Jones, Luella to Miles Rice 12-31-1868 B
Jones, Maggie to John Jordan 10-18-1870 (no return) B
Jones, Margaret to Marshall Hunter 6-21-1867 (7-13-1867) B
Jones, Margaret to Robert Dawson 1-12-1871 (no return) B
Jones, Maria to Tom Morrow 1-7-1867 (1-10-1867) B
Jones, Mariah to Sye Young 10-31-1868 (11-1-1868) B
Jones, Martha W. to Stuart McMullen 10-4-1869 (10-6-1869)
Jones, Martha to Buck McNeil 1-6-1866 (1-14-1866) B
Jones, Martha to Henry McNeil 12-28-1865 (1-14-1866) B
Jones, Mary E. to Thomas N. Herly 3-12-1848
Jones, Mary Jane to Thomas R. Cocke 3-5-1840
Jones, Mary L. to Wm. L. Griffin 10-14-1868 (10-15-1868)
Jones, Mary to James Martin 9-25-1869 (no return) B
Jones, Mary to John Jones 12-28-1866 (12-29-1866) B
Jones, Mary to L. H. Malone 7-29-1851
Jones, Mary to Patrick J. Lyons 11-26-1868
Jones, Maryann C. to Eli Rayner 8-18-1841 (no return)
Jones, Matilda to Adolphus Anderson 11-2-1866 (11-3-1866) B
Jones, Matilda to Alfred Williams 12-29-1869 (12-30-1869) B
Jones, Minerva to C. H. Harris 12-2-1865 (12-3-1865) B
Jones, Missouri to Wm. Massey 11-11-1868 (11-14-1868) B

Jones, Mollie to Billy Mitchell 12-15-1870 (12-30-1870) B
Jones, Nancy to Lewis Tucker 11-9-1868 (11-13-1868) B
Jones, Nancy to Sam Smith 12-4-1869 (no return) B
Jones, Patience to Hal Cocke 11-16-1869 (11-18-1869) B
Jones, Phoeba A. to Berry Prewitt 12-24-1867 (no return) B
Jones, Priscilla to Nelson Harris 12-29-1870 B
Jones, Queen to John Witt 12-30-1869 (1-1-1870) B
Jones, Sarah A. to Benjamin Rook 9-3-1866 (9-4-1866)
Jones, Sarah to David C. Russell 12-4-1852 (no return)
Jones, Sidney to Ned McFerrin 1-4-1868 (1-7-1868) B
Jones, Sophia Ann to John Alexander 6-16-1866 (no return) B
Jones, Susan M. to James McKnight 5-5-1841 (5-6-1841)
Jordan, Chaney to Freeman Mebane 6-4-1869 (6-5-1869) B
Jordan, Emily S. to William E. Green 11-4-1845 (11-5-1845)
Jordan, Fanny to Robert Field 9-17-1870 (no return) B
Jordan, Frances to W. B. Trotter 1-13-1844 (1-16-1844)
Jordan, Malinda to Moses Wilson 6-29-1867 (7-3-1867) B
Jordan, Malinda to Wm. Collier 9-21-1869 (no return) B
Jordan, Martha to Edward Gant 8-22-1868 (no return) B
Jordan, Mary E. to William E. Green 10-9-1843 (10-11-1843)
Jordan, Mary Jane to George Bowen 3-11-1840 (no return)
Jordan, Sallie to David Armour 3-29-1869 (4-1-1869) B
Joy, Ann to Gilbert Bass 2-15-1869 (3-8-1869) B
Kain, Elizabeth to J. C. Orrell 12-10-1862 (12-11-1862)
Karr, Jane to J. M. Laine 2-16-1846 (2-17-1846)
Karr, Sallie to Marshall Thomas 9-4-1868 (9-12-1868) B
Kaywood, M. A. C. to H. J. Yancy 10-19-1859
Kean, Bettie to Thos. R. Polk 2-27-1862 (3-12-1862)
Kedd, Mary to Charles McNamee 1-27-1840 (no return)
Kee, Lilly to Joseph Jones 12-8-1868 (12-12-1868) B
Keener, Matilda to Geo. Washington 9-3-1866 (9-8-1866)
Keeton, Susan A. to Charles B. Turner 1-7-1867 (1-8-1867)
Kelley, Nancy A. to William Buckley 4-30-1850 (no return)
Kelley, Rutha J. to Thomas J. Watkins 10-28-1847
Kellin, _____ to Joseph Thompson no date (with Mar 1838)
Kelly, C. Belle to Jesse A. Williams 9-22-1866 (9-25-1866)
Kelly, Caroline to Abram Meacham 1-4-1869 (1-10-1869) B
Kelly, Elizabeth to Billy Williams 10-27-1869 (no return) B
Kelly, Harriet M. to Elsey Humphrey 12-12-1844
Kelly, L. A. O. to Henry Beasly 4-29-1865 (5-2-1865)
Kelly, Martha J. to James Haley 10-2-1849 (no return)
Kelly, Mary E. to Wm. Power 11-?-1853 (no return)
Kemp, Matilda to Wiley Wilkerson 3-20-1866 (no return) B
Kendall, Martha to Hiram C. Vinson 11-19-1844
Kendrick, Sarah to Williamson H. Parham 12-23-1847
Kennedy, Adelia P. to Mike Danaher 7-20-1866 (7-25-1866)
Kennon, M. C. to O. B. Cromwell 4-20-1867 (4-21-1867)
Kent, Mary E. to S. R. Deardolph 10-6-1854 (no return)
Kent, Sarah J. to Thomas H. Herndon 5-17-1865
Kerr, Emily N. to James M. Patton 1-19-1848
Kerr, Esther V.? to Charles Lynn 7-18-1841 (6?-22-1841)
Kerr, Isabella D. to N. W. Coapland no dates (with Jun 1838)
Kerr, Maria to Horace Morton 12-28-1868 (1-3-1869) B
Kerr, Mary A. to James Perry 12-11-1850 (no return)
Kerr, Mary J. to Henry M. Pitman 6-30-1849 (no return)
Kerr, Susan to James A. Coppidge 3-12-1866
Kerr, Susan to Wm. A. Moore 7-28-1849 (7-29-1849)
Ketchum, Isadore to Jno. L. Webb 12-2-1868
Ketchum, Mary J. to Dudley Granberry 10-24-1868 (no return) B
Kincaid, Maggie to Mansell Dover 7-6-1870 (7-14-1870)
Kindreck, Bettie to H. S. Pippins 9-6-1869 (9-7-1869)
King, Agnes to Samuel Irvin 1-13-1844 (1-14-1844)
King, Ann to Hiram B. Jones 1-31-1867 (2-1-1867)
King, Ellin to Joseph H. Yarbro 12-24-1845 (no return)
King, Fanny to Cary Thompson 5-2-1867 (5-5-1867) B
King, Jane to William Robins 12-17-1840
King, Susan T. to Tho. M. Broom 1-19-1865 (1-24-1865)
Kinney, Sarah to Albert Munroe 12-28-1870 B
Kinnon, Margaret A. to W. B. Hyde 12-29-1866 (12-30-1866)
Kirkland, Caroline to Horace Blalock 3-22-1870 (3-26-1870) B
Kirkpatrick, Catharine E. to A. L. Meigs 6-11-1855 (no return)
Kirkpatrick, Pink to Governor Bird 4-9-1866 (no return) B
Klyce, Lizzie L. to Lamotte Stearns 1-22-1866 (1-23-1866)
Knight, Eliza to Willis Morris 12-29-1845 (1-1-1846)
Knight, Elizabeth to L. T. Powers 1-15-1848 (1-17-1848)

Knight, Mary Ann to Joseph Winters 9-9-1850 (9-10-1850)
Knott, Margaret J. to Milton S. Allen 11-9-1868 (no return)
Knott, Nancy to W. R. Samuson? 12-18-1862 (no return)
Knox, Adaline to Archy Towns 12-4-1868 (12-7-1868) B
Knox, Lucinda to Clarence Marshall 12-20-1870 (12-22-1870) B
Knox, Mary D. to A. Webb 2-1-1850 (no return)
Knox, Susan to John Ing 9-15-1855 (no return)
Knox, Tempy to Liz Marshall 4-6-1871 (4-7-1871) B
Koonce, Darthula to P. H. Ramsey 11-24-1852
Koonce, Julia N. P. to James H. Thompson 12-11-1850
Krouth, D. E. C. to W. K. Hodges 6-10-1860 (6-14-1860)
Kyle, Allice C. to J. A. Neely 2-6-1871 (2-8-1871)
Kyle, Mary Ann to E. Harper 1-14-1851 (no return)
Kyle, Mattie to Wm. J. Alexander 11-27-1865 (no return)
Lacey, Julia to Edward Bond 3-19-1867 (3-21-1867) B
Lackey, Mary to David Davis 6-14-1838
Lackie, Elizabth. to Thos. Lackie 12-9-1849 (12-11-1849)
Lacy, Martha to Jim Bryant 8-31-1867 (9-7-1867) B
Lacy, Susan E. to N. M. McKinney 2-6-1865
Lakey, Nancy to A. J. Smith 5-23-1848
Lakey, Sarah to James H. Lakey 1-15-1851
Lancaster, E. H. to Robert E. Rhodes 4-8-1839 (4-9-1839)
Lancaster, Sarah E. to Charles C. Owen 12-6-1855 (no return)
Lancer, Martha J. to John A. Weaver 10-15-1844 (no return)
Land, M. W. to R. B. Neal 1-27-1868 (1-28-1868)
Land, Mary to T. R. David 7-14-1870 (7-17-1870)
Lane, Caroline to Elias Gilford 11-25-1870 (no return) B
Lane, Lavicia to E. B. Hugg 4-13-1869 (4-15-1869)
Lane, Lucy Ann E. to George T. Tarwater 12-3-1844 (12-5-1844)
Lane, Mary D. to Virgil H. Mayfield 7-3-1846
Lane, Nancy to Benjamin B. Dye 1-31-1843 (2-2-1843)
Lanier, Lucy to Tho. J. Potts 9-18-1865 (9-20-1865)
Lanier, M. E. to Wm. R. Parham 2-20-1860 (2-22-1860)
Lanier, Mary E. to James Y. Lucas 12-25-1847 (no return)
Lanier, Mary to Abea Atkins 4-10-1848 (4-11-1848)
Lanier, Sallie E. to Robt. G. Tucker 10-5-1868 (10-6-1868)
Lansdon, Margaret L. to John R. Pearson 10-20-1840
Lanthrop, Mary Ann to James French 7-23-1845
Laughn, Martha Ann to Madison H. Chambers 12-8-1843 (no return)
Laughorn, Eliza M. to Rufus E. Buffum 7-15-1846
Laughter, Cladus to Basel McVay 9-25-1847
Laughter, Susan Jane to John H. Beard 4-29-1846 (4-6?-1846)
Laughter, Susan Jane to Lemuel Langham 1-1-1846 (no return)
Laughy, Virginia J. to Wm. B. (Rev.) Hill 10-30-1851 (no return)
Laurence, Anna M. to Joseph E. Moody 6-14-1849 (6-15-1849)
Lavier, Martha B. to Henry W. Hall 5-15-1867 (5-16-1867)
Lawrence, Sarah B. to Henry S. Peyton 12-27-1844 (no return)
Lay, Clotilda to James C. Griffin 6-25-1851 (no return)
Lay, M. C. to J. V. Thornton 9-27-1859 (9-28-1859)
Lay, Martha E. to David O. Owens 8-23-1854 (no return)
Lay, Mary to Thos. S. Canada 4-8-1868 (no return)
Leach, Maggie G. to W. S. Firth 3-1-1870 (3-2-1870)
Leach, Mattie G. to L. H. Lockheart 10-27-1870 (no return)
Leath, Elizabeth M. to David Norris 8-31-1868 (9-2-1868)
Lee, Annie J. to W. N. Portis 5-12-1860 (5-16-1860)
Lee, Catharine to Lewis Amis 11-11-1839
Lee, Malinda to Franklin Bennett 10-31-1843
Lee, Matilda to Wm. H. McKisick 12-24-1867 B
Lee, Mattie B. to Wm. N. Portis 11-1-1869 (11-3-1869)
Lee, Violet to William Brown 1-20-1870 (1-22-1870) B
Leech, E. V. to A. B. Campbell 6-13-1842
Lemmon, Sarah E. to J. J. Williams 12-20-1852 (no return)
Lemons, A. M. to T.J. Claxton 1-8-1866
Lemons, Judis A. to John M. Taylor 10-9-1848 (10-11-1848)
Lemons, Rose to Jack Dodson 5-10-1871 (no return) B
Leonard, Ann Mariah to John F. Talafairo 2-24-1851 (2-26-1851)
Leonard, Julia M. to Simon Turner 6-28-1853 (no return)
Leonard, Margarett N. to M. M. Waller 9-30-1847 (no return)
Leonard, Martha J. to Nuton A. Hamon 9-7-1852 (no return)
Lester, Harriet to Davy Richison 1-2-1868 (1-4-1868) B
Lester, Juliand to Wm. C. Jordan 12-23-1839 (12-24-1839)
Lester, Tranquilla E. to Marion S. Hargiss 5-30-1846 (6-10-1846)
Leverett, Laura W. to S. T. Dougan 3-3-1871 (no return)
Leverett, Sarah A. E. to F. P. Harris 8-7-1867
Levesque, Nancy to William Clampet 1-30-1839 (1-31-1839)

Levy, Fanny A. to Pomfrett H. Warren 11-22-1870
Levy, Hannah to Carroll Douglass 8-23-1867 (9-7-1867) B
Lewis, Caroline to Tom Balam 12-25-1869 (12-20?-1869) B
Lewis, Eliza D. to A. S. Day 11-9-1854 (no return)
Lewis, Lannie to Isaac J. Pearson 9-24-1870 (10-6-1870) B
Lewis, Lidda to George Williams 2-18-1839 (2-25-1839)
Lewis, Mahala to James Hester 12-25-1865 B
Lewis, Maria Mary to William Evans 2-3-1846 (2-5-1846)
Lewis, Martha Ann to Richard Hood 3-17-1851 (no return)
Lewis, Mary V. to W. M. Edwin 10-26-1849 (10-30-1849)
Lewis, Mary to Wistley Duberry 10-15-1847 (10-17-1847)
Lewis, Nancy A. to Calvin Malone 1-8-1839
Lewis, Sarah to George Washington 3-10-1868 (no return) B
Leznik, Mary Ann to Marcus H. Stewart 12-19-1848 (12-21-1848)
Lightie, Martha A. to Wm. Hicks 3-12-1859 (3-18-1859)
Lightle, Ellen to King Culberson 1-7-1868 (2-9-1868) B
Lile, Candace to J. C. Gill 10-13-1847 (no return)
Lile, H. A. C. to B. P. Griffin 10-5-1860 (10-18-1860)
Limon?, Sarah O. to Geo. F. Wainwright 1-4-1847 (1-13-1847)
Lindsey, Delila to Jesse T. Lindsey 8-29-1843 (9-5-1843)
Lindsey, Delilah to Joseph Abels 10-1-1846 (10-4-1846)
Lindsey, Frances to Carter Anderson 1-2-1869 (1-5-1869) B
Lindsey, Mollie to Andrew Wilkes 2-8-1871 (2-9-1871) B
Linebarger, Mary A. to F. S. Blalock 12-7-1868 (12-9-1868)
Link, Watsie? Ann to Robert Cocke 9-15-1869 B
Linsdey, Sophronia L. to Samul S. Nelson 11-18-1848 (no return)
Lipscomb, Margaret to Jessee Cross 6-6-1842 (no return)
Little, Laura to Stephen Richardson 1-2-1871 (1-12-1871) B
Little, Margaret A. to Joseph B. Stark 12-22-1868 (no return)
Littlejohn, Cathrine to Kit Brewer 3-1-1869 (3-5-1869) B
Littlejohn, Martha to Mose Tappan 3-1-1869 (3-5-1869) B
Litton, Carni to R. Y. Kirkpatrick 7-31-1854 (no return)
Lloyd, Georgia to Wm. P. McMullen 4-20-1868 (4-22-1868) B
Lochridge, Matilda P. to James A. Medley 6-2-1851 (6-5-1851)
Lock, Lenora C. to T. L. Giles 3-7-1853 (no return)
Locke, Jane to D. M. B. Hashler 10-11-1854 (no return)
Locke, Lutitia M. to John Woods 1-3-1842 (12?-23-1842)
Locke, Maggie L. to Wm. B. Wilkinson 1-27-1859 (2-2-1859)
Locke, Mary A. to J. L. Turner 12-26-1853 (no return)
Lockhart, Amanda F. to John L. Leach 2-19-1866 (2-21-1866)
Lockhart, Fannie A. to A. G. Leach 1-14-1868 (1-15-1868)
Lockhart, Flora to Aaron Jones 4-25-1866 (no return) B
Lockhart, Flora to Johnson Paine 1-28-1869 (1-30-1869) B
Lofton, Ophelia to Thomas Ross 1-3-1871 (1-15-1871) B
Logan, Sarah Ann to Silas Bailey 11-13-1869 (11-14-1869)
Logwood, Polly Walker to John A. Winston 10-18-1843
Loney, Lucrecia to Henry Lewis 1-20-1840 (12?-27-1840)
Long, M. J. to S. M. Montgomery 3-8-1855 (no return)
Long, Marthaann M. to Samuel M. Hudspeth 4-19-1840 (6-19-1840)
Long, Nancy to Isaac H. McCoard 11-23-1846 (11-5?-1846)
Looney, Eliza to A. F. Brackin 4-15-1838
Lorrence, Rebeca C. to Huy M. Farmer 11-2-1840 (no return)
Love, E. M. to J. B. Wall 1-23-1866 (1-24-1866)
Love, M. E. to J. M. Webb 12-20-1865
Love, Rebecca A. to Wm. A. Bryant 1-1-1866 (1-4-1866)
Loving, Caroline C. to R. W. Hargrove 10-15-1860 (10-16-1860)
Loving, Caty to Robert Griffin 2-4-1867 (no return) B
Loving, Martha to Frank Shaw 12-13-1867 (no return) B
Loving, Mattie to W. C. McKendree 1-8-1866 (1-9-1866)
Loving, Sallie P. to E. B. Davis 2-6-1860 (2-7-1860)
Lowery, P. A. to C. R. Dickinson 12-12-1867 (12-15-1867) B
Lowry, Martha Ann to Green Wood 11-18-1844 (7-24-1845)
Lucado, Willy Ann to James E. McGowan 9-23-1850 (no return)
Lucas, Anna to Ransom Brown 9-28-1870 (no return) B
Lucas, Lizzie W. to Henry M. Dilliard 12-20-1859
Lucas, Mariah to Henry McDowel 2-23-1867 (2-26-1867) B
Lucas, Martha to William Carroll 8-25-1855 (no return)
Luckado, Rebecca J. to Thos. A. Bostick 1-1-1850 (1-2-1850)
Luckado, S. J. to J. S. Motley 12-17-1866 (12-19-1866)
Luckey, Sarah E. to Rufus K. Garrett 1-21-1851 (1-22-1851)
Lumsley, E. to John E. R. Carter 12-13-1844 (12-14-1844)
Lundal, Susan E. G. to J. W. Jarrett 12-10-1838 (12-12-1838)
Lynch, Mary Ann to John Honey 2-15-1847 (2-21-1847)
Maberry?, Elizabeth to Mark Elam 1-10-1855 (no return)
Mabin, Malissa to Wiley Mabin 5-3-1867 (6-3-1867) B

Mabin, Matilda to Mack Hudson 4-18-1867 (no return) B
Macklin, Mary to James Gallagher 4-23-1867 (not executed)
Macklin, Sucky to Andrew Bland 2-4-1869 (no return) B
Maclin, Anna to Thomas Hodge 3-20-1869 (no return) B
Maclin, Bettie to Jerry Maclin 12-23-1866 (no return) B
Maclin, Priscilla to Mingo Buford 4-1-1870 (12-28-1870) B
Macon, Joanna to Thomas Shaw 10-1-1869 (no return) B
Macon, Julia A. to Thomas G. Boyed 9-17-1840 (9-24-1840)
Maddox, Ann to Robert Stevens 9-23-1860 (not endorsed)
Maddox, Caroline to Henry Price 8-23-1867 (8-24-1867) B
Madore, Ella to John Neel 12-28-1869 (no return) B
Magett, Mary E. to William H. Burnes 4-19-1847 (4-29-1847)
Magit, Emily L. to Rancelier Sann 6-19-1843 (6-21-1843)
Magness, Mary E. to Azariah L. Crenshaw 8-31-1846 (9-2-1846)
Mahaffy, Louisa A. to John McGuirk 5-24-1853 (no return)
Makey, Sally to James Munroe Phillips 12-23-1868 (12-24-1868) B
Mallard, Tobitha Ana to Munrow Slaughter 4-21-1841 (4-25-1841)
Mallory, A. E. to Parish A. Gormon 9-6-1848 (9-12-1848)
Malone, Ann Eliza to George Freeth 1-9-1863 (1-10-1863)
Malone, Ann to Andrew Tate 12-24-1869 (no return) B
Malone, Catharine to Asberry H. Parish 2-28-1867 (3-1-1867)
Malone, Catherine (Mrs.) to A. H. Parish 2-18-1867 (no return) B
Malone, Lucinda M. to William E. Winfield 11-10-1845 (11-12-1845)
Malone, Mary to Geor. C. Colter 1-4-1845
Malone, Mary to Geor. C. Colter 12-20-1844 (no return)
Malone, Nancy B. to J. L. Conn 2-24-1849 (2-25-1849)
Malone, Nancyann to A. Whitten 4-25-1842
Malone, Susa C. to Frederick S. Jackson 5-17-1841 (5-20-1841)
Manees, Martha O. to Samel E. Cole 4-3-1850 (no return)
Mangrum, Rebecca to Oliver Francis 2-14-1842 (2-16-1842)
Manier, A. A. to H. L. Burton 2-4-1862 (2-10-1862)
Manley, Harriett O. to P. H. Duggins 1-24-1854 (no return)
Manley, Martha L. to Thomas Parrish 8-3-1847 (8-8-1847)
Manley, Mary F. to H. C. Durham 12-12-1865 (12-13-1865)
Manley, Mary to Theof J. Manley 5-4-1847
Manley, Susan L. to Jas. Montgomery 11-5-1850
Mann, Ann Mariah to Stephen W. Cocke 4-2-1838
Manning, Elizabeth B. to Edward W. Tatum 4-7-1851 (4-8-1851)
March, Victoria J. to J. N. Gibson 6-3-1868
Marcum, Rebecca to James M. Hammond 10-27-1848 (10-29-1848)
Margrove, Martha F. to John D. Baum 6-26-1865 (6-27-1865)
Marial, Frances to James B. Laudaman 11-5-1850 (11-7-1850)
Maris, Emeline to Arthur Price 12-29-1866 B
Markham, Jane to M. W. Weaver 11-13-1847 (11-14-1847)
Marlar, Bettie A. to H. C. Cocke 5-11-1867 (no return)
Marr, Caroline to Archie Brooks 12-28-1867 (no return) B
Marsh, Tappan to William T. Hudson 1-28-1840 (2-12-1840)
Marshall, Amanda to Orange Harris 12-9-1868 (1-3-1869) B
Marshall, Emeline to E. W. Champion 7-9-1868
Marshall, Eva to A. K. Graham 1-15-1866 (no return)
Marshall, Josaphin to Andrew S. Hartis 10-31-1851 (no return)
Marshall, Laura F. to Jas. R. Wallace 10-13-1868 (10-17-1868)
Marshall, Leana to John Jefferson 1-28-1871 (no return) B
Marshall, Louisa to Randal Moorman 4-12-1869 B
Marshall, Louisa to Samuel Knox 3-27-1869 B
Marshall, Mary A. to Josiah Maples 10-1-1853 (no return)
Marshall, Sarah Ann to Henry Parrish 8-2-1847
Marshall, Sophia S. to Bob E. Jackson 3-17-1845 (no return)
Martin, Ada B. to Rob Roy McGregor 6-10-1867 (7-6-1867)
Martin, Ann to William Cain 3-10-1843 (2-1-1843)
Martin, Betty Ann E. to Sylvester Jones 12-19-1850
Martin, Calidona B. to Addison Hinshaw 1-9-1844
Martin, Caroline to John Douglass 12-29-1866 (12-30-1866) B
Martin, Harret M. to James Peterson 1-29-1850 (no return)
Martin, Jane to Jones L. Soper 1-2-1841 (no return)
Martin, Lucy to Solomon Cocke 2-18-1869 (2-20-1869) B
Martin, Lucy to T. P. Harris 5-13-1863 (5-14-1863)
Martin, Margarett A. to Pleasant Hinshaw 11-6-1841 (11-7-1841)
Martin, Martha A. to L. C. Butts 2-15-1844 (2-25-1844)
Martin, Martha C. to M. L. Crenshaw 12-13-1849 (no return)
Martin, Mary E. to Wm. L. Clayton 3-1-1853 (no return)
Martin, Mary to Gus Braden 8-27-1869 B
Martin, R. J. to P. J. Reeves 1-3-1863 (1-4-1863)
Martin, Sarah Jane to Robt. C. Gregory 12-9-1851 (no return)
Marton, Virginia E. to John W. Hunt 1-13-1842 (1-20-1842)

Mask, Charlotte to Russel Alexander 12-30-1868 (12-31-1868) B
Mask, Lina Ann to Grant Johnson 10-30-1868 (no return) B
Mason, Judy to Nelson Wells 12-31-1868 (no return)
Mason, Margaret to Turner Error 8-30-1867 (8-31-1867) B
Mason, Marietta to Thos. Nash Bland 5-10-1867 (5-11-1867) B
Mason, Mary to L. D. Matkins 1-21-1848 (no return)
Mason, Mary to Nathan Hill 12-24-1869 B
Mason, Mollie M. to P. F. Parker 10-17-1864 (10-18-1864)
Mason, Sidney T.D.H.E. to John D. Cleaves 6-11-1852 (no return)
Mason, Victoria to Barney Williams 9-9-1867 (9-12-1867) B
Mass, Nancy to W. H. Thornton 11-28-1848 (11-6?-1848)
Massey, Sarah E. to George W. Coghill 6-25-1847 (6-29-1847)
Massy, Levina to William C. Hogan 1-26-1842 (1-27-1842)
Mathews, Ann S. to Robert Bullock 9-24-1839
Mathews, M. H. to Henry R. Bond 7-12-1847 (7-15-1847)
Mathews, Margaret Ann to Jesse B. Curl 11-20-1843 (11-28-1843)
Mathews, Mariah to Jesse Dildia 12-29-1847 (1-4-1848)
Mathews, Mary A. E. to Thomas Barrom 2-28-1867 (3-5-1867)
Mathews, Mary to Joseph L. Mewborn 11-16-1866 (11-20-1866)
Mathews, Matty to Anderson Taylor 12-26-1868 (12-28-1868) B
Matmiller, Christine to Andrew Rinklin 5-9-1859 (5-10-1859)
Matthews, Bettie A. to J. H. Fisher 5-7-1866 (5-9-1866)
Matthews, Harriett to Wes Jones 1-2-1868 (1-3-1868) B
Matthews, L. J. D. to J. E. Sparks 9-28-1859
Matthews, Sina to Thaddeus Wilson 11-26-1860 (11-27-1860)
Matthews, Tennie B. to Wm. J. Daley 2-28-1868 (no return)
Matthews, Tommie to John H. McFerrin 1-24-1866 (1-31-1866)
Maury, C. B. to J. B. Thomas 12-21-1865
Maury, Lucy J. to W. R. Baker 3-26-1855 (no return)
Maury, M. E. to D. W. Collier 4-27-1865
Maxwell, Gertrude R. to Nat Harper 12-28-1867 (1-8-1868)
Maxwell, Gracy to Wash Matthews 1-2-1868 (1-3-1868) B
Maxwell, Mary J. to H. L. Heflin 1-2-1868 (1-8-1868)
Maxwell, Mary to Wm. J. Oats 11-21-1844
May, Eveline to Frank Mason 12-24-1868 (12-27-1868) B
May, Fannie W. to Wm. H. Hundly 5-23-1859 (5-24-1859)
May, Levina Ann to Jacob Anderson 4-28-1838
May, Mary S. to Gideon J. Beuford 3-29-1852 (no return)
May, Nancy M. to Wm. A. Rawlings 4-30-1849 (5-2-1849)
May?, Lucy E. to William P. Dowdy 12-15-1846 (12-16-1846)
Mayfield, Mary D. to John K. Wilburn 5-7-1866 (5-10-1866)
Mayfield, Sallie A. to J. W. Tucker 9-26-1866 (9-27-1866)
Mayo, Bettie to Andy Jackson 7-3-1868 (7-4-1868) B
Mayo, Harriet Ann to Edward G. Reddick 3-13-1846 (3-18-1846)
Mayo, Jane Eliza to H. S. Taylor 9-18-1846 (no return)
Mayo, Laura to Washington Johnson 12-30-1869 B
Mayo, Mary E. to Carns M. Swift 7-29-1844
Mayo, Nancy J. to Freeman Morris 12-6-1850 (12-7-1850)
Mayo, S. A. to George W. Bumpass 12-22-1868 (12-23-1868) B
Mayo, Sarah L. to Thos. J. Swift 2-1-1850 (2-5-1850)
Mays, Emily V. to Pleasant Henderson 1-30-1841 (2-3-1841)
Mays, Laura to James L. Sparks 11-3-1870
Mays, Sarah W. to Wm. H. Henderson 5-8-1843 (no return)
McAdams, Susan to A. J. G. Tatum 12-26-1839
McAnulty, Dora to Thos. R. Bankhead 10-10-1868 (10-11-1868)
McAvoy, H. to J. W. Hampton 9-30-1847
McCall, Maryann to G. W. Smith 1-15-1848 (1-17-1848)
McCalley, Martha to L. J. Smith 9-19-1855 (no return)
McCarley, Hariett to Washington Faris 12-16-1850 (12-18-1850)
McCarley, Jane to Joseph McKnight 12-7-1839 (12-10-1839)
McCarley, Martia to Rawlings Robertson 7-9-1846
McCarley, Mary to W. C. Reeves 12-21-1852 (no return)
McCartry, Mary to John R. Parker 10-11-1841 (no return)
McCauley, Frances L. to C. H. Cogbill 10-30-1854 (no return)
McCauley, Lucy A. to F. A. Massey 3?-13-1850 (no return)
McCauley, Mary to Jonas? M. Smith 11-1-1848
McClain, Martha to Ned Cocke 1-5-1871 B
McClane, Lettie to Alfred Johnson 6-15-1867 (no return) B
McClaran, Lucy E. to Geo. W. Sharp 3-25-1846 (3-26-1846)
McClaran, Martha D. to A. V. B. Rolfe 12-12-1853 (no return)
McClaren, Harriet F. to John D. Crossett 11-25-1868 (11-26-1868)
McClaren, Mary to S. M. Davis 1-28-1853 (no return)
McClaron, Martha to A. M. Ward 2-16-1859 (2-17-1859)
McClarran, E. A. to Wm. W. Nelson 1-28-1842 (2-10-1842)
McClellan, Bettie L. to R. M. Moore 2-2-1860

McClellan, M. C. to S. G. Sparks 5-16-1866
McClellan, Margaret E. to William L. Mays 2-5-1851
McClinsley, Louisa E. to David R.? Jackson 4-10-1848 (4-13-1848)
McCombs, Mary J. to John S. Cothran 12-19-1853 (no return)
McConnell, Elizabeth to John Krider 10-3-1851 (no return)
McConnell, Susan to Martin H. Adams 1-24-1854 (no return)
McCraw, Catharine to Braxton Melton 12-29-1869 (no return) B
McCrean, Almedia Ann to William H. Wheeler 9-26-1846 (10-4-1846)
McCree, Mitta A. to Baccus Carmack 11-8-1867 (11-10-1867) B
McCulley, Sarah to James Brinkley 3-1-1847 (3-3-1847)
McCully, Charity to Robt. McCally 2-24-1850 (3-5-1850)
McCully, Lucy to George Matthews 9-4-1868 (no return) B
McCully, M. C. to J. M. McCully 4-3-1860 (4-5-1860)
McCully, Mary E. to John Walis 1-3-1853 (no return)
McCully, Salak? to Anderson Warren 4-20-1866 (no return) B
McCully, Sarah E. to E. W. Harrison 9-18-1854 (no return)
McDade, Drucilla to William Morris 3-16-1840 (3-19-1840)
McDade, Nancy to P. G. Womble 10-22-1844 (10-31-1844)
McDowell, Amanda to Sidney Lynn 12-24-1866 (12-25-1866) B
McDowell, Anna to Jos. McDowell 8-13-1866 (8-15-1866) B
McDowell, Catherine to Aaron Matthews 12-26-1870 (no return) B
McDowell, Effie P. to James S. Matthews 11-17-1866 (11-20-1866)
McDowell, Jane to Joseph Thomas 2-28-1871 (9-22-1873) B
McDowell, Juda to Henry Cleaves 1-6-1871 (1-16-1871) B
McDowell, Lizzie H. to James T. Blair 2-26-1867 (2-28-1867)
McDowell, Mary to John Pope 11-7-1870 (11-14-1870)
McElroy, Mary to Thos. Nolin 8-27-1842
McElwain, Jane to Harry Yates 12-27-1869 B
McFadden, Luella A. to C. J. Ozier 3-17-1860
McFadden, M. J. to T. L. Durrum 10-21-1862
McFadden, Perlina to Joseph Thompson 3-2-1870 (3-17-1870) B
McFadden, S. A. to B. K. Boyd 4-11-1864 (4-12-1864)
McFadden, Sarah J. to George Jordan 7-29-1867 (8-7-1867)
McFadden, Sarah to John H. Oates 9-24-1851 (no return)
McFadden, Sarah to Joseph Carroll 8-30-1842 (no return)
McFaddin, J. B. to H. W. Brown 12-31-1849 (1-1-1850)
McFarland, Catie to Alfred Williamson 2-5-1869 (1?-14-1869) B
McFerrin, Bitha to George Owens 2-15-1871 (no return) B
McFerrin, Mary L. to James C. Mewborn 11-2-1867 (11-7-1867)
McFerrin, Mattie Lou to Joshua W. Mewborn 11-2-1867 (11-7-1867)
McFerrin, Sallie W. to Timothy M. Cartwright 11-7-1870 (11-10-1870)
McGee, Jane to John E. Gardner 9-27-1838
McGee, Mary Jane to R. G. McGee 12-12-1839 (no return)
McGee, Nancy to W. H. Willingham 9-22-1841 (9-27-1841)
McGehee, Catharine H. to John Siscoe 7-5-1842 (no return)
McGehee, Jane to John T. Thompson 5-3-1838 (no return)
McGinnis, Sarah to Mebane Black 2-2-1871 (2-11-1871) B
McGowan, Lucy to Henry Overton 11-19-1867 (11-23-1867) B
McHenry, Elizabeth to Harvey Wyley 9-29-1841 (9-30-1841)
McInteref, Shemima to William Graves 1-30-1849
McIntosh, Laura J. to Robt. B. Hooks 12-12-1867 (12-15-1867)
McKeasy, Sarah Adaline to Silas W. McMullin 12-31-1845
McKee, Harriet D. to Allen H. Smith 1-25-1870 (no return)
McKendree, Ann D. to Wm. H. Sledge 8-15-1850 (8-20-1850)
McKinley, Minda to Jerry Jones 10-29-1870 B
McKinney, Kate R. to Wm. L. Neal 6-29-1866 (7-3-1866)
McKinney, M. R. to Albert G. Nevell 8-28-1854 (no return)
McKinstrey, Margarett J. to Wm. S. Plaxter 1-13-1852 (no return)
McKnight, Louisa to W. O. Wilder 12-10-1869 (12-15-1869)
McKnight, Margarette P. to J. J. Crawford 9-19-1844 (no return)
McLain, Elizabeth to Amos Young 11-9-1868 (no return) B
McLeod, Mary C. to James Blare 2-22-1851 (no return)
McLeod?, Loomy to William Burford 7-6-1844 (7-7-1844)
McLoad, Martha to George F. Hamilton 11-17-1853 (no return)
McMillan, I. J. to W. L. Minton 8-18-1848 (8-23-1848)
McMullen, Iva to James S. Boyd 5-7-1860 (5-10-1860)
McMullin, Anna E. to T. B. Lloyd 12-25-1865 (1-1-1866)
McMurry, Pataline to Vincent Johnson 2-20-1867 (no return)
McNamee, C. J. to Benj. Ward 3-20-1860 (3-21-1860)
McNamee, N. E. (Mrs.) to W. P. Lipscomb 2-15-1870 (3-2-1870)
McNeal, Dicey to Captain Iverson 7-14-1866 (7-15-1866) B
McNeel, Rosanna to Andrew Johnson 7-3-1868 (7-4-1868) B
McNees, Mary A. to J. M. Crenshaw 2-9-1850 (2-10-1850)
McNeil, Ann to Stephen Taylor 1-6-1866 (no return) B
McNeil, Caroline to Horace McNeil 3-17-1866 (8-26-1866) B

McNeil, Linda to Jim Taylor 1-6-1866 (no return) B
McNeill, Anikee to Lindsey Cocke 2-7-1868 (no return) B
McNeill, Laura to Robert Polk 4-11-1867 (4-20-1867) B
McNeill, Mariah to Jeff Sullivan 8-10-1870 (8-11-1870) B
McNeill, Martha to John Chersey 11-9-1867 (no return) B
McNeill, Mary to Perry McKinney 8-5-1867 (8-10-1867) B
McNeill, Octavia to Grandison Irwin 11-10-1868 (11-11-1868) B
McNeill, Violet to Johnson Moore 5-25-1870 (5-28-1870) B
McPherson, Ann Eliza to Jackson R. Henderson 4-30-1846 (no return)
McSpadden, Martha E. to Wm. F. Harris 7-16-1844
Mcguire, Ann to James Weaver 5-26-1838
Mcguire, Susan to Braddock Brooks 1-1-1867 (1-3-1867) B
Mebane, Amanda to Frank Hare 10-1-1870 (10-4-1870) B
Mebane, Clara to King Freeman 12-24-1868 (12-25-1868) B
Mebane, Cornelia to Allen Kirk 9-6-1866 (no return) B
Mebane, Eliza to Burrel Ragland 12-29-1869 (12-9?-1869) B
Mebane, Emeline to Ellet Hines 12-27-1870 (12-30-1870) B
Mebane, Gracey to Henry Culpepper 12-28-1870 (12-29-1870) B
Mebane, Henrietta to William H. Smith 7-27-1870 (no return) B
Mebane, Laura to James Foster 10-28-1868 (no return) B
Mebane, Malvina to Daniel Rhodes 3-19-1866 (3-22-1866) B
Mebane, Mattie to Frank Levett 2-4-1870 (no return) B
Mebane, Tela to Levon H. Cox 6-30-1866 (7-15-1866) B
Mebane, Vina to Elijah Sutton 12-12-1867 (12-15-1867) B
Melton, Elizabeth to Joseph P. Braden 11-1-1843 (11-3-1843)
Menees, Sarah E. to William M. Allen 10-21-1847 (10-23-1847)
Menice?, Frances D. to Gilberth Fall 11-26-1839
Meredith, Ardis to Saml. B. Martin 2-17-1846 (no return)
Meriweather, Amy to John Jones 3-2-1867? (3-3-1867) B
Messenger, Martha to John Douglass 4-9-1867 (4-13-1867) B
Messenger, Mary to James Johnson 4-13-1871 (4-16-1871) B
Mewbern, Anna L. to Wm. W. Newbern 6-20-1860
Mewborn, Georgia A. to H. J. Stanley 1-10-1871 (1-12-1871)
Michee, Olivia B. to Isaac Winston 10-11-1852 (no return)
Middlebrooks, Maria to Louis Malone 12-27-1867 (12-28-1867) B
Milegan, Frances to Nathan W. Williford 2-16-1838
Miligan, Rebecca to Joseph East 2-6-1838
Miller, Amy to James Anderson 8-13-1870 (8-14-1870) B
Miller, Anna to George W. Turnley 7-19-1853 (no return)
Miller, Dicy to Elijah Cross 5-31-1838
Miller, Easter to Stephen Mason 2-21-1871 (2-26-1871) B
Miller, Isabella S. to Alex P. Waddell 6-6-1853 (no return)
Miller, Julia to Joe Bowers 9-7-1867 B
Miller, Lottie A. to Solomon Reeves 5-7-1868 (5-15-1868) B
Miller, Lou to Charley Alexander 11-12-1870 (11-17-1870) B
Miller, Margarett R. to Jesse R. Irwin 9-14-1844 (no return)
Miller, Mary W. to W. J. Simmons 2-25-1854 (no return)
Miller, Peggy to Anthony Taylor 12-28-1865 (no return)
Miller, Rutelia to R. H. Daniel 1-22-1867
Miller, Sally W. to Jas. W. (Rev.) Knott 5-27-1849
Miller, Serena to Moses Lightfoot 10-25-1870 (no return) B
Miller, Susanna C. to Jno. W. Penick 8-10-1859
Miller, Virginia A. to Hankins E. Harendon 9-3-1839
Millikin, Elizabeth to Thomas Sharp 10-8-1847 (10-10-1847)
Millikin, Mollie E. to N. B. Price 6-9-1868 (6-10-1868)
Mills, Sarah to John Ward 10-30-1848 (no return)
Minor, Mima to Charley Murrell 4-25-1870 (7-17-1870) B
Mitchel, Ary Ann to Turner Harris 6-11-1847 (6-17-1847)
Mitchel, R. H. (Mrs.) to C. B. Brame 8-20-1855 (no return)
Mitchell, Ama to Samuel Dunlap 3-27-1867 (no return) B
Mitchell, Arabella E. to Henry B. Chiles 1-4-1851 (1-6-1851)
Mitchell, Elizabeth to Washington Ivie 12-7-1846 (no return)
Mitchell, Eveline to Henry Jones 12-28-1870 B
Mitchell, Fanney to J. C. Harrell 3-16-1859
Mitchell, Georgia Ann to William Moore 10-15-1868 (10-17-1868) B
Mitchell, Hannah to James Moore 2-18-1869 B
Mitchell, Jane to Spencer Bell 8-5-1869 (8-7-1869) B
Mitchell, Jollie? to Alfred Armstrong 8-29-1870 (no return) B
Mitchell, Mary C. to Andrew Taylor 3-31-1846 (4-2-1846)
Mitchell, Mary L. to William Barton 4-30-1847
Mitchell, Mary P. to R. C. Lea 12-6-1847 (12-23-1847)
Mitchell, Mary c. to John F. Greenbery 1-4-1851 (1-6-1851)
Mitchell, Mary to John Elgin 10-18-1844
Mitchell, Puss to Sam Evans 12-25-1868 (12-26-1868) B

Mitchell, Rhodie to John Bullock 1-11-1868 (1-21-1868) B
Mitchell, Sallie A. to John C. Hewlet 2-2-1866 (2-8-1866)
Mitchell, Sarah J. to J. W. Turner 12-9-1846 (no return)
Mitchell, Sophia T. to Zachariah M. Shackleford 11-10-1846 (11-12-1846)
Mitchell, Victoria to Andy Anderson 9-4-1865 (9-6-1865)
Moanings, Elizabeth to William Brown 1-5-1870 (no return)
Moffett, E. A. to A. D. Tillmon 11-9-1859
Moffett, Martha to Richard Oliver 8-14-1839
Moffit, Harriet to Jim Wells 9-5-1868 (9-6-1868) B
Moncreef, Druciller to Joseph Darby 11-7-1838 (11-15-1838)
Moncreef, Lucinda to Dennis Speer 11-7-1838 (11-15-1838)
Moncreeff, Jane to William Morris 11-5-1838 (11-7-1838)
Moncreif, Martha A. to Phillip Webber 12-18-1849 (no return)
Moncreif, Martha to Wm. Scisco 9-18-1847 (9-23-1847)
Moncreif, Sarah to Wm. B. Ramsey 10-17-1854 (no return)
Moncreiff, Ann to Joseph Darby 9-21-1844 (9-22-1844)
Moncreiff, Permelia to Jno. W. Choat 9-19-1844 (9-20-1844)
Moncrief, Elizabeth to John B. Randle 12-10-1853 (no return)
Moncrief, Mary to John Posten 7-10-1854 (no return)
Monroe, Jenney to Ike Hadley 12-4-1865 (12-9-1865) B
Monroe, Martha J. to Geo. R. Green 5-27-1846 (no return)
Montague, Emaly Y. to John C. Brooks 8-8-1848
Montague, Frances to Moses J. Bradshaw 3-12-1844 (3-28-1844)
Montague, Hester to Silas Babbs 9-25-1869 (6-15-1870) B
Montague, Mary to Wm. Wallace 10-29-1867 (11-6-1867)
Montague, Susan to John D. Tunadge 1-22-1844 (1-24-1844)
Montcreath, Elizabeth to William Cassell 10-18-1852 (no return)
Montcrief, Emily to David Lynch 10-30-1853 (no return)
Montgomery, Augusta to Lafayette McCrillis 12-27-1865 (12-28-1865)
Montgomery, Caroline to Wm. McNary 2-3-1870 (2-5-1870) B
Montgomery, Elizabeth to Anda M. C. Montgomery 9-9-1840 (9-10-1840)
Montgomery, Isabella A. M. to Harmon Havercamp 2-5-1867
Montgomery, Martha to Noah Stafford 6-23-1868 (7-2-1868)
Montgomery, Mary M. to Henry Melton 7-17-1850 (7-18-1850)
Montgomery, Mary to Marcus Byles 8-26-1841
Mooberry, Mary A. J. to T. J. Charles 12-24-1855 (no return)
Moodey, Mary L. C. to Thomas D. Franklin 5-3-1845 (5-7-1845)
Moody, Cassanda to Jacob Park 1-3-1866 (no return) B
Moody, Livinia to L. H. Milliken 7-5-1841
Moody, Mary A. to Albert Morton 1-1-1868 (1-27-1868) B
Moody, Millie to Jessee Hill 12-5-1870 (12-8-1870) B
Moody, Nancy to George Anderson 12-22-1866 (no return) B
Moody, Sarah M. to Vernon Rhodes 7-22-1845 (7-23-1845)
Moon, Isabella to Thomas McClerry 12-4-1869 B
Moor, Sarah Ann to Jessee J. Tharp 1-29-1851 (1-30-1851)
Moore, Adaline to William J. Walker 11-4-1846
Moore, Candis M. to W. J. H. Nealey 1-2-1849 (no return)
Moore, Cathrine to Stephen Castleberry 1-8-1867 (1-16-1867) B
Moore, E. J. to A. H. Yancy 5-23-1860 (5-24-1860)
Moore, Elizabeth to Solomon Saines 2-2-1870 (2-3-1870) B
Moore, Frances to Kirk Dickinson 7-16-1870 B
Moore, H. C. to Jas. C. Edenton 11-21-1868 (11-24-1868)
Moore, Hannah to George Gordan 10-16-1867 (10-19-1867) B
Moore, Julia to E. S. Prichard 1-25-1859
Moore, Katherine to Calib Baker 12-31-1868 (1-1-1869) B
Moore, Laura to Handy Cleveland 6-21-1867 (6-22-1867) B
Moore, Lavina to James Davis 11-18-1840 (11-19-1840)
Moore, Lucy H. to John Tomlinson 9-3-1850 (9-12-1850)
Moore, Lucy Jane to Henry Yancey 8-10-1870 (8-22-1870) B
Moore, M. J. to J. T. Williams 10-1-1866 (no return)
Moore, Margaret to Stephen Crawford 12-29-1868 B
Moore, Mariah to George Crooms 1-24-1867 (1-25-1867) B
Moore, Martha A. to Wm. A. Booth 4-2-1845
Moore, Martha L. to F. D. Cossett 6-7-1855 (no return)
Moore, Martha to Isaac Glasgow 1-11-1867 (1-19-1867) B
Moore, Martha to John Harrison 7-6-1867 B
Moore, Martha to Warren Adams 1-11-1849 (no return)
Moore, Matilda to Esekel P. Richmond 7-31-1848 (4?-3-1848)
Moore, Nancy to John P. Sensing 4-24-1841 (no return)
Moore, R. M. to J. A. Humphrey 9-4-1860 (9-5-1860)
Moore, S. A. to R. N. Read 9-22-1838 (no return)
Moore, S. L. to T. H. Lovelady 9-28-1854 (no return)
Moore, Sarah M. to Huel D. Culbreath 1-3-1868 (no return)

Moore, Sarah to Thos. McGee 8-?-1842 (no return)
Moore, Viney to William Pendleton 2-18-1869 (2-20-1869) B
Mooreland, Louisa to Coleman Williams 8-14-1868 (no return)
Moorman, Charity to Willis Asbury 1-28-1870 (2-5-1870) B
Moorman, Eliza to John Golden 1-28-1869 (1-30-1869) B
Moreland, Sarah to Guriah Thomas 2-28-1871 (4-3-1871) B
Morgan, Annie to James Washington 12-28-1867 B
Morgan, Emma to Newt Marshall 3-13-1871 (4-5-1871) B
Morgan, Martha to William Johnson 4-28-1871 (no return) B
Morgan, Mary A. P. to James Rhodes 6-26-1838
Morgan, Mary E. to D. L. Blakeley? 5-14-1851 (5-15-1851)
Morgan, Mary E. to Tobias Anderson 11-6-1869 (11-9-1869) B
Morgan, Nancy to William Burton 2-13-1851 (no return)
Morison, Amelia J. to John W. Griffin 12-30-1848 (12-31-1848)
Morphis, Ann R. to A. F. Calhoun 4-10-1865 (4-13-1865)
Morris, Amelia to Henry Snow 4-14-1860 (4-22-1860)
Morris, Harriet to Daniel Lane 6-8-1867 (no return) B
Morris, Julia to Charles Wilson 12-24-1866 (12-27-1866) B
Morris, Lotta to Andrew Swift 2-2-1870 (no return) B
Morris, Lucy Ann to Gus Gooden 11-5-1869 (11-6-1869) B
Morris, M. H. to James M. Gore 10-30-1866 (11-2-1865?)
Morris, Martha Ann to Davis Gillespie 6-17-1848 (no return)
Morris, Martha to Robt. Williams 4-3-1868 (no return) B
Morris, Mary C. to Isaac J. Carter 5-25-1844
Morris, Mary E. to G. W. Tatom 10-8-1867 (10-12-1867)
Morris, Mary Jane to Hiram M. Jones 2-3-1845 (no return)
Morris, Mary to Robt. Lee 1-5-1866 (1-6-1866) B
Morris, Sarah A. to Stephen A. Peeler 12-22-1866 (12-25-1866)
Morris, Sarah to M. A. Jones 1-8-1850
Morrison, Margaret C. to John F. Neel 10-18-1842
Morrison, Martha E. to A. J. Biggers 2-11-1850 (2-12-1850)
Morrison, Mary M. to John M. McFadden 11-27-1844 (no return)
Morrison, S. C. to James J. Covey 11-21-1865 (11-26-1865)
Morrison? Charlotte M. to H. P. Maxwell 3-19-1841
Morriss, Emeline to Zachariah Wiseman 5-4-1842 (no return)
Morriss, Perlina C. to Daniel W. Frazier 12-1-1843 (11?-16-1843)
Morrow, Ann to David Griffith 11-9-1868 (11-13-1868) B
Morrow, Eliza to Lewis Taylor 3-27-1869 (4-1-1869) B
Morrow, Emily to Jessee Boyd 1-19-1867 B
Morrow, Frances G. to J. W. Morrow 11-26-1850 (11-27-1850)
Morrow, Henrietta to George Thomas 5-10-1867 (5-20-1867) B
Morrow, Jane to Aleck Boyd 3-28-1866 (3-31-1866) B
Morrow, Mary to Joseph Jackson 1-13-1845
Morrow, Millie Ann to George Morrow 8-20-1868 (8-27-1868) B
Morrow, Rachel A. to Robert Allen 8-26-1870 (8-28-1870) B
Morton, Eliza E. to J. F. Baxter 1-7-1870 (1-13-1870)
Morton, Jane H. to John A. Ward 1-2-1871 (1-5-1871)
Morton, M. M. to A. J. McCoy 1-4-1869 (1-5-1869)
Morton, Margaret C. to Candour McKinny 11-20-1844 (no return)
Morton, Rhoda C. to Wm. C. McNeely 1-1-1869 (no return)
Morton, Victoria to Solomon McDowell 1-6-1871 (no return) B
Mosby, Amanda to Tom Nowel 9-24-1868 (9-27-1868) B
Mosby, Dicy to Anthony Price 2-15-1867 (2-16-1867) B
Mosby, Lydia Ann to Britton Mosby 7-15-1870 (no return) B
Mosby, Paralee to John McClellan 11-16-1867 (1-4-1868) B
Moseley, Molly to Cyrus Mackey 12-26-1868 (12-29-1868) B
Mosley, Jennie to Henry Dilliard 12-27-1866 (1-2-1867) B
Mosley, Judy to William T. Bonner 7-25-1843
Mosley, Sallie to Bernard Cox 12-27-1866 (1-12-1867) B
Moss, America W. to William P. Youree 4-2-1838
Moss, Nancy to J. W. D. Haring 3-26-1850 (3-28-1850)
Motley, Mary A. to Rufus Archie 1-29-1861 (1-30-1861)
Muller, Mary F. to Henry Von Negler 12-24-1866
Mulliken, Matilda R. to Tho. Jeffreys Shelton, jr. 2-22-1864
Munn, Mary to John Eddins 12-13-1846
Muray, Nancy J. to Jno. M. Daniel 11-21-1860
Murphey, Elizabeth F. to J. A. V. Goode 11-30-1853 (no return)
Murphey, O. E. to Jno. E. Harrison 8-13-1838 (no return)
Murphy, Catharine to Spencer Hull 5-19-1866 (8-11-1866) B
Murphy, Jane to Sandy Rivers 12-24-1868 (not executed) B
Murphy, Mary A. to George Pollock 6-28-1842
Murphy, Mary E. to Leonidas F. Yancey 9-11-1865 (9-12-1865)
Murray, Minerva to Nathan Watson 5-15-1868 (10-25-1868) B
Murrell, Ann to Dallis Kyle 12-26-1870 (no return) B
Murrell, Betty to John Jones 1-11-1870 (2-9-1870) B

Murrell, Charlotte to George Wilson 1-22-1870 (1-29-1870) B
Murrell, Dillah to Sumpter Williams 3-22-1869 (no return) B
Murrell, Harriet to James Wilson 2-22-1868 (2-26-1868) B
Murrell, Lou to Sam Allen 2-22-1868 (2-26-1868) B
Murrell, Mary A. to Andrew R. Pope 9-2-1865 (9-10-1865)
Murrell, Mary Ann to Sam Mootre 4-29-1870 (5-1-1870) B
Murrell, Mary to John Wilson 12-28-1870 (12-31-1870) B
Murrell, Permelia to Reuben Burrow 3-7-1842 (4-5-1842)
Murry, Eliza A. (Mrs.) to John Cloyd 11-26-1855 (no return)
Myers, Nancyann to Phillip M. Seward 1-27-1840 (2-6-1840)
Myres, Margarett to W. L. Underwood 11-5-1838 (11-6-1838)
Nail, Rebecca Jane to Gilliam Tharp 12-25-1847 (12-28-1847)
Neal, Cornelia A. to Edwin D. Dickinson 4-21-1841
Neal, Eliza to Wm. Murphey 9-29-1839 (10-3-1839)
Neal, Josephine M. to Robert E. Mason 5-16-1854 (no return)
Neal, Kate M. to T. J. Reid 1-15-1868 (1-22-1868)
Neal, Margarett E. to Jacob Hare 10-31-1853 (no return)
Neal, Marthaann to Thomas S. Evans 1-30-1841 (2-18-1841)
Neal, Sallie A. to J. A. Wray 9-6-1862 (9-8-1862)
Neal, Wallace L. to Jno. B. Reid 2-3-1859 (2-8-1859)
Neally, Sally to John Whitfield 3-16-1841 (3-18-1841)
Neblett, Sue T. to T. K. Archibald 7-6-1870 (no return)
Neel, Gracy to Lewis Kendrick 10-19-1867 (11-6-1867) B
Neel, L. A. to John D. Castles 10-19-1866 (10-23-1866)
Neel, Lucinda to William Shaw 12-27-1870 (1-7-1871) B
Neel, Margaret to E. A. Stewart 12-5-1860
Neel, Marietta C. to E. C. Douglass 12-1-1868 (12-3-1868)
Neel, Mary to John J. Crouch 10-1-1847
Neel, Roxanna to Thomas Warren 2-27-1869 (3-28-1869) B
Neely, Margery E. to John W. Jordan 10-7-1842 (12-12-1842)
Neesbit, Mary E. to A. B. Jones 11-23-1839 (11-27-1839)
Neil, Mariah to Phil Ellington 2-16-1867 B
Neiley, Mary C. to John C. Brown 1-8-1849 (1-10-1849)
Nellums, Penny Ann to Wm. Johnson 3-14-1839
Nelson, Adaline to Osco Polk 1-18-1868 X
Nelson, Callie to Wm. Cobbs 2-16-1867 B
Nelson, Elsworth to James A. Claxton 10-4-1865 (10-5-1865)
Nelson, Malinda to David Evans 12-14-1839 (12-24-1839)
Nelson, Mary A. to J. N. Hicks 2-7-1866 (2-8-1866)
Nelson, Sallie E. to B. A. Powell 2-28-1866 (3-1-1866)
Nelson, Sarah A. to N. G. Curtis 12-5-1855 (no return)
Nesbit, Martha R. to John W. Boals 5-22-1869 (5-23-1869)
Nettles, Elizabeth to Alexander Shepherd 8-26-1841
Nevill, Mattie T. to R. J. Rhodes 4-9-1866 (4-15-1866)
Neville, Cassanda H. to Henry Biggs 4-3-1854 (no return)
Nevills, Claricy to Edmund Boykin 10-30-1869 B
Newall, Sallie J. to T. J. Ramsey 3-18-1862
Newby, M. A. to P. D. Crawford 10-10-1866 (10-11-1866)
Newby, Milla to Jno. Williams 7-11-1868 (7-12-1868) B
Newby, Susan to B. B. Horner 2-16-1850 (2-20-1850)
Newby, Verda to Burrell Cogbell 2-11-1871 (no return) B
Newsom, Charlotte to Zack Lewis 12-10-1868 (12-11-1868) B
Newsom, Jane to David P. Jarrett 4-10-1839 (no return)
Newsom, Mary M. to Hugh Montgomery 8-8-1839
Newsom, Mary to Alfred Carter 8-26-1868 B
Newsom, Mary to Hezekiah Vance 10-23-1869 (10-29-1869) B
Newsom, Penelope to J. S. Baird 9-24-1866 (9-25-1866)
Newsom, Sallie M. to Newitt Harris 10-24-1867
Newsom, Tryphenia to Wm. Newsom 2-25-1868 (2-26-1868)
Newson, Mollie to James Shelley 3-13-1869 (3-15-1869) B
Newton, M. A. D. to W. W. Baswell 3-17-1860 (3-22-1860)
Newton, Mary L. to Richd. Appleberry 9-21-1846 (no return)
Nicholson, V. J. to A. J. Johnson 12-23-1865 (12-26-1865)
Nobles, Ida A. to George Bounds 2-28-1870 (3-2-1870)
Nokes, Nancy E. to Daniel M. Craig 12-23-1848 (12-24-1848)
Nolly, Eleanor A. to John R. Johnston 11-15-1865 (11-22-1865)
Norman, Elizabeth L. to Judson A. Culp 12-13-1850 (12-15-1850)
Norman, Jinney to Bob Walker 1-9-1869 (no return) B
Norman, Louisa to Nathan Boles 3-31-1845 (4-1-1845)
Norman, Malinda to Saml. Worrell 10-18-1867 (10-19-1867) B
Norman, Margaret to Nelson Boals 5-12-1866 (no return) B
Norman, Mary E. to Jacob E. Carl 12-26-1853 (no return)
Norman, Susan to Maddison Williams 5-16-1868 (no return) B
Norris, Laura to C. C. McCarson 8-14-1867 (8-15-1867)
Notby, Mary to Joseph S. Mercer 8-13-1849 (no return)

Notgrass, Ann to Robt. Kendrick 5-7-1846 (no return)
Notgrass, Ann to Thomas T. Borun 11-11-1847 (no return)
Notgrass, Mary E. to Jonathan P. Mitchell 3-4-1839 (3-13-1839)
Notgrass, Susanah to Booker Boner 8-7-1851 (no return)
Nowlin, Louisa W. to James C. Kelly 11-15-1846 (11-19-1846)
Nutson, Margaret to Lacey Fisher 1-22-1870 (no return) B
Nutt, Sarah to Leonard Coker 7-11-1846 (7-12-1846)
O'Kelly, Cornelia to Jack Bland 8-10-1866 (8-11-1866) B
O'Kelly, Susan to John W. Bobins 5-3-1847 (5-13-1847)
OKelly, N. B. to W. T. Wall 11-22-1864 (11-24-1864)
Oates, Nancy C. to Wm. H. H. Williams 1-24-1871 (1-26-1871)
Oates, Susan H. to R. E. Tatum 11-15-1852 (no return)
Oats, H. A. E. to E. W. Tatum 12-27-1849 (no return)
Oberley, Paulina to J. T. Hampton 2-5-1842 (no return)
Okelly, Matilda to Isaac Adkins 8-17-1867 B
Okelly, Rebecca J. to Jackson Ashford 12-6-1870 (12-7-1870)
Old, Martha A. to B. G. Hendrick 5-30-1842 (no return)
Old, Mary E. to Shadrack Dickinson 1-24-1843 (1-25-1843)
Old, Sallie Anna to Henry E. Hilliard 7-18-1860
Oliphant, Nancy to Robert Bankhead 3-4-1846 (3-5-1846)
Olive, Clara A. to M. T. Terry 12-21-1868 (12-22-1868)
Oliver, Elizabeth G. to Littleberry G. Wilkerson 1-24-1844 (no return)
Oliver, Elizabeth to Wm. Arter 11-18-1838
Oliver, Mary B. to William H. Jones 6-6-1855 (no return)
Orgain, Mariah to Robt. Wolsey 12-15-1868 (12-19-1868) B
Orgain, Martha to Ned Williamson 1-12-1867 B
Orr, Henry to Charles Lynn 1-4-1869 (1-5-1869)
Orr, Susan J. to Arthur Williams 2-19-1849 (2-20-1849)
Outlaw, Elizabeth to Joseph Lavender 4-28-1852 (no return)
Outlaw, Mary to John W. Grissom 11-15-1869 (11-16-1869)
Overton, Harriet to F. M. Ross 2-24-1862
Overton, Rozana to Peter B. Ross 12-19-1849 (12-20-1849)
Owen, Lucy A. to Thos. C. Cogbill 10-18-1867 (10-30-1867)
Owen, Mary F. to R. Moses Green 11-25-1854 (no return)
Owen, Sallie W. to A. G. Smith 9-27-1870 (9-29-1870
Owen, Sallie to L. P. Jones 1-17-1861
Owens, Isabella to James Heaggins 2-11-1871 (no return) B
Ozier, Algenie? to Wilson Slaughter 12-21-1839 (12-26-1839)
Ozier, Mary M. to Wm. C. McCaskill 10-5-1854 (no return)
Ozier, Mary to Sam Robertson 1-30-1869 (2-6-1869) B
Ozier, Mary to W. M. Eitle 1-13-1869
Ozier, Mollie to Thomas Williams 1-7-1870 (1-10-1870) B
Ozier, Piny E. to Tho. Malone 12-16-1846 (12-17-1846)
Paden, Isabelah to Adam R. Wylie 8-6-1838
Page, Sarah Ann to William B. Walker 6-2-1838
Paine, Eliza W. to Robt. Drysdale 7-30-1849 (8-2-1849)
Paine, Harriet to John Webster 11-5-1869 B
Paine, Laura to James P. Braden 11-10-1869 (11-11-1869)
Palmer, Ann to Simon Carter 10-22-1870 (10-23-1870) B
Palmer, Mary Belle to W. D. F. Hafford 3-8-1859
Palmer, Susan Jane to William J. Brown 2-3-1847 (2-4-1847)
Palmor, Lucy Ann to Moses P. Martin 11-22-1848
Palmore, Mary J. to Royal F. Brown 1-15-1847 (1-17-1847)
Pane, Emma to Emery Sweat 3-30-1868 (4-2-1868)
Pane, Martha to Isaac Nash 9-22-1851 (no return)
Parcham, Martha N. to Jno. M. Secrest 1-16-1846
Parchman, Eliza E. to William T. White 2-20-1841 (2-23-1841)
Parchman, L. E. to Charles W. Slater 1-11-1843 (1-12-1843)
Parham, Aregon to Henry Jones 8-22-1867 (no return) B
Parham, Harriet to Geor. C. Gray 1-22-1845
Parish, Catharine to Wm. J. Gant 3-16-1870
Parish, Eliza J. to Thos. Riggs 5-29-1867 (5-30-1867)
Parish, Lizzie to Jones Baker 4-24-1867 (4-28-1867) B
Parker, Eliza to John Bedford 9-12-1862 (9-18-1862)
Parker, Jane to Richard Fields 8-28-1869 (no return) B
Parker, Mary to Washington Ingram 12-13-1869 (12-26-18689) B
Parkes, Susan E. to H. K. Northway 10-14-1852 (no return)
Parks, Ann to Isaac Hunt 12-24-1867 (12-26-1867) B
Parks, Biney to Robert Gately 2-1-1859
Parks, Ella to Frank McKindry 12-20-1870 (no return) B
Parks, Mahala to W. S. Knox 3-17-1866 (3-18-1866)
Parr, Emma R. to John J. Bailey 1-6-1851
Parrish, Jo Ann E. to B. W. M. Warner 10-28-1844 (no return)
Parrish, Martha to Alfred Hill 9-7-1870 (9-18-1870) B

Parrott, P. E. to J. W. McKinstry 11-16-1869 (11-17-1869)
Partlow, Mary E. to William L. White 9-9-1839 (no return)
Paschal, Elizabeth to John Shaull 8-13-1844 (8-14-1844)
Paschal, Sarah to Geo. W. David 12-9-1845 (12-10-1845)
Patrick, Sallie to Robert Miller 12-22-1869 B
Patterson, Alsey to Jim Delap 8-11-1866 (8-12-1866) B
Patterson, Eliza Jane to Wallace Rivers 1-19-1871 B
Patterson, Henrietta to Harry Wirt 12-27-1867 (12-31-1867) B
Patterson, Julia E. to Sidney C. Russell 12-16-1867
Patterson, Martha Ann to Dick Rivers 2-12-1870 (2-13-1870) B
Patterson, Mary (Mrs.) to J. V. Smith 12-18-1852 (no return)
Patterson, Mary A. to S. P. Phillips 1-23-1850
Patterson, Minerva to George Dortch 8-16-1867 (8-18-1867) B
Patterson, Nancy J. to Henry McClanahan 2-2-1869 (2-7-1869) B
Patterson, Rosietta to Archile Rivers 9-24-1870 B
Patteson, Ann H. to Phillip Mitchell 9-17-1867 (9-25-1867) B
Pattillo, Jennie to Henry Fraser 1-2-1867 B
Pattilo, Amanda to Wm. F. Crook 6-25-1849 (no return)
Patton, Armelia to William L. Hall 12-11-1847 (12-23-1847)
Patton, Elizabeth O. to James M. Neel 11-22-1841 (11-23-1841)
Patton, Frances to W. G. Day 12-7-1853 (no return)
Patton, H. J. to M. S. Rhodes 12-11-1847 (12-23-1847)
Patton, Margaret C. to E. G. Coleman 10-12-1847
Patton, Martha Ann to Thomas Dodson 10-21-1844 (10-23-1844)
Patton, Sophronia to R. L. Shaw 10-7-1865 (10-10-1865)
Patton, Tommie to Calvin L. Barringer 12-24-1862 (no return)
Patton, Willie E. to J. W. Zellner 11-3-1866 (11-6-1866)
Paulson, Laura J. to R. M. Haden 6-23-1869 (6-24-1869)
Payne, Mary to George W. Redding 12-16-1869 (12-23-1869)
Payne, Nancy C. to William H. Fowler 12-26-1846 (12-27-1847?)
Payton, Sarah B. to Elisha W. Harris 11-19-1846 (11-24-1846)
Peak, F. H. to R. H. Herndon 12-24-1854 (no return)
Pearce, Mary M. to Wm. J. Rodgers 12-4-1865 (12-6-1865)
Pearson, Bettie to Abe Smith 7-4-1868 (7-10-1868) B
Pearson, Elizabeth to J. F. Brown 7-24-1854 (no return)
Pearson, Elizabeth to Kelly Sanders 3-12-1844 (no return)
Pearson, Mary W. to Robt. T. Pickens 3-14-1870 (3-15-1870)
Pearson, Tryphena to William W. Turner 11-1-1845 (no return)
Peebles, Catharine to Arter Bailey 11-4-1869 (11-9-1869) B
Peebles, Chany to Bently Cal 4-22-1867 B
Penn, M. A. to M. A. Gober 11-24-1865 (11-29-1865)
Perkins, Elizabeth to Solm. O. Graves 9-9-1853 (no return)
Perkins, Kitty L. to T. M. Milam 12-20-1865 (12-27-1865)
Perkins, Martha to Marion Smith 12-7-1866 (12-16-1866)
Perkins, Mary B. to Hugh J. Douglass 9-7-1843 (9-8-1843)
Perkins, Mary E. to P. T. Hudson 5-9-1866
Perkins, Mary J. to N. H. Previtt 3-?-1852 (no return)
Perkins, S. E. to R. E. Smith 4-24-1860 (5-1-1860)
Perry, Elizabeth to H. H. Williams 12-30-1867 (12-31-1867)
Perry, Lucinda to Cato Walker 1-2-1871 (1-5-1871) B
Perry, M. P. to J. R. McNeill 12-16-1862 (12-24-1862)
Perry, Mary E. to Simon McNeill 12-9-1867 (12-16-1867)
Perry, Patina C. to James M. Webb 1-14-1848 (1-18-1848)
Perry, Rebecca to J. W. Glover 7-8-1868 (7-9-1868)
Pettis, Tillah to Haywood Chaffin 1-2-1869 B
Pettit, E. V. to A. B. Pulliam 6-4-1862
Pettit, Sarah to Andrew Nash 12-17-1870 (12-18-1870) B
Pettus, Becky to Lewis Bowers 12-27-1869 (12-23?-1869) B
Petty (Perry?), Mary An to James R. Parker 12-18-1848
Petty, Carolin to William T. Hunt 7-1-1844 (no return)
Petty, Sarah C. to John J. Eliott 9-1-1840 (9-2-1840)
Pety, Sarah R. to Hiram Fain 4-5-1842
Peviard?, A. H. to E. H. Amis 6-26-1869 (6-27-1869)
Pewett, Julia Ann to Fed Davis 5-2-1867 (no return) B
Philips, S. E. to Robert B. Bailey 3-15-1843 (3-18-1843)
Phillips, A. M. to R. S. Stith 2-14-1854 (no return)
Phillips, Adeline to Willis Dowdy 3-13-1869 (3-27-1869) B
Phillips, Ann to Frank Johnson 2-22-1867 (2-24-1867) B
Phillips, Dolly to Major Watkins 10-17-1868 (10-31-1868) B
Phillips, Elizabeth C. to D. H. Bently 12-27-1852 (no return)
Phillips, Julia A. to W. W. Graves 12-25-1850
Phillips, Leah to Felix D. Lane 8-11-1847
Phillips, M. N. to G. S. Flemmings 12-7-1864 (not endorsed)
Phillips, Marry J. to R. A. Wesbrook 12-4-1854 (no return)
Phillips, Martha to Robert Culp 1-12-1866 (1-15-1866) B

Phillips, Mary E. to W. D. Buckley 3-20-1869 (3-23-1869)
Phillips, Mary E. to William M. Smith 9-29-1869 (12-3-1869)
Phillips, Sallie A. to W. C. Armstrong 10-21-1868 (10-22-1868)
Philpott, Mary A. (Mrs.) to John Blackwell 1-18-1843 (no return)
Pickens, M. C. to W. C. Baldwin 1-31-1842 (2-6-1842)
Pickens, Mary A. to T. H. Foote 11-23-1869 (11-25-1869)
Pickens, S. A. to B. Finch no date (1864 or 65?)
Picket, Ellen to Henry Burris 8-2-1851 (no return)
Pickett, Mary to Ed D. Jenkins 9-23-1844 (9-26-1844)
Pickins, Eliza J. to James L. Crawford 2-6-1867 (2-7-1867)
Pickins, Margaret E. to Francis M. Griffin 12-24-1847 (12-28-1847)
Pickins, Nancy O. to Benjamin F. Meliam 10-13-1851 (no return)
Pickins, Susan A. to H. S. Rogers 11-20-1867 (11-26-1867)
Pierce, Nancy M. to Calvin Carelton 1-9-1861 (1-10-1861)
Pinchback, Mary Ann to James T. Sutton 4-18-1848 (4-19-1848)
Pinket, Margarett to Samuel Maurach? 11-2-1840
Pippin, Margaret to Louis Jones 3-15-1871 (3-20-1871)
Pippin, Susan to James Lindley 7-30-1866 (7-31-1866)
Pirtle, Ann to Joe Walker 12-31-1866 (1-1-1867) B
Pitman, Amanda E. to John R. Woodson 10-7-1848
Pittman, Nannie to Dave Mebane 2-20-1871 (2-21-1871)
Plant, Elizabeth A. to Joshua V. Smith 6-14-1841 (6-15-1841)
Plant, Malinda A. to George M. Smith 1-11-1843 (1-12-1843)
Plant, Mary J. to W. T. Abbington 12-3-1866 (12-4-1866)
Plant, Permelia H. to Felix Owens 1-12-1839 (1-15-1839)
Plant, Sarah to Green W. Bobbitt 12-15-1845 (12-16-1845)
Plant, Susan E. to W. C. Pearce 11-30-1866 (12-5-1866)
Pleasant, M. A. to T. L. Anthony 10-29-1849 (11-4-1849)
Pleasants, Lucy W. to N. J. Cocke 10-14-1845 (10-15-1845)
Pleasants, Paulina M. to William Ragsdale 10-18-1847 (10-20-1847)
Pleasants, Sarah J. to Nathanl. Blain 4-9-1842 (4-14-1842)
Plummer, Annie E. to W. R. Johnson 1-21-1869
Poindexter, Angeline to Henry McFarland 5-11-1868 (5-16-1868) B
Poindexter, Betsy to Tom Jordan 1-4-1869 B
Poindexter, Catharine to Richard Rives 9-25-1869 B
Poindexter, Elmira to Joseph Wilson 12-20-1869 (12-30-1869) B
Poindexter, Elvira to John Boyd 12-26-1867 (12-27-1867) B
Poindexter, Emily J. to William Johnson 3-20-1869 B
Poindexter, Fannie to George J. Whittle 5-1-1867 (5-11-1867) B
Poke, Margaret to Hal Anderson 12-28-1869 (1-1-1870) B
Polk, Dilly to C. P. James 9-17-1849 (no return)
Polk, Emma O. to R. M. Bouchette 12-31-1842 (1-3?-1843)
Polk, Henrieta E. to A. H. Avery 4-10-1848 (4-12-1848)
Polk, Martha H. to Robert D. Durrett 11-8-1841
Polk, Mary A. to Geo. Davis 11-19-1842 (11-17?-1842)
Polk, Mary E. to Douglass R. Hunt 4-3-1846 (4-8-1846)
Polk, Mattie E. to Saml. H. Thomas 2-8-1871 (no return)
Polk, V. G. to P. H. Bowen 3-9-1864 (3-15-1864)
Pollerd, Blanch to Charney Hilliard 2-4-1871 (2-12-1871) B
Pollock, Martha A. to Geo. W. Bryant 7-24-1865 (7-25-1865)
Pollock, R. P. to D. W. Eaton 11-5-1869
Pollock, Samanthy to Charles Edmonds 12-13-1869 (12-16-1869)
Pond, Nancy to Nelson Mitchell 2-3-1840 (2-6-1840)
Pool, Levina to Moses Cowan 6-13-1844
Pool, M. E. C. to Jesse Boon 12-12-1865 (12-15-1865)
Pool, M. to Henry Row 4-16-1868 (no return) B
Pool, Rosanna to Jesse Red 12-30-1869 (no return) B
Poor, America J. to H. L. Gwyn 2-4-1865 (2-6-1865)
Poor, Cornelia to Joe Holleman 12-26-1866 (12-27-1866) B
Poore, M. F. to William Neal 12-22-1856 (no return)
Pope, Cornelia W. to A. T. Gossett 1-14-1871 (1-17-1871)
Pope, Margaret A. to J. H. Pipkins 7-16-1870 (7-17-1870)
Porter, Camilla to Charles G. Jones 10-9-1865 (10-11-1865)
Porter, Frances E. to T. D. G. McClellan 8-29-1848
Porter, Harriet to Dempsie Mabin 4-28-1868 (no return) B
Porter, Julia Ann to Dennis Jackson 7-2-1869 (no return) B
Porter, Margaret A. to John M. Paine 11-1-1869 B
Porter, Mary A. to William R. Cullum 7-20-1848 (no return)
Porter, Nancy to James Christian 7-16-1870 (5?-11?-1870) B
Porter, Susan Ann to John Jackson 4-6-1867 (4-14-1867) B
Porter, Virginia W. to R. H. Deener 2-27-1869 (2-28-1869)
Portis, Martha A. to B. H. Cullum 11-?-1853 (no return)
Posey, Mary to Harvey W. Brown 1-28-1854 (no return)
Powell, Binga H. to J. W. Keeble 9-10-1855 (no return)
Powell, Charley M. to Robert S. Phillips 11-20-1855 (no return)

Powell, Matilda to Henderson Stanback 1-4-1871 (1-11-1871)
Pratt, Harriet J. to J. C. Stanly 4-16-1847
Preston, Dionitia A. to Lawson T. Barnett 1-5-1847 (no return)
Preston, Sarah J. to J. W. Darden 1-7-1855 (no return)
Prewitt, Lucy to Jordan Douglass 12-27-1867 (1-5-1868) B
Price, Adaline to Johnun? Carroll 12-30-1839 (no return)
Price, Fannie to Anthony Bordeaux 8-4-1869 (no return) B
Price, Jane to John C. Allen 3-21-1844 (3-23-1844)
Price, Luncinda to Abraham Jenkins 11-9-1840 (11-12-1840)
Price, Mary Ann to Harry (Henry) M. Farmer 4-27-1871
Price, Mollie Jane to Nathan Daughety 8-3-1867 (no return)
Price, Susan E. to B. F. Magee 9-1-1852 (no return)
Privett, E. A. to J. D. Appleberry 12-23-1863 (12-29-1863)
Privett, Martha E. to Jno. Walker 10-14-1868 (10-21-1868)
Privette, Matilda J. to R. G. Appleberry 1-13-1865 (1-18-1865)
Provine, Maryann to E. R. Alexander 12-15-1841 (no return)
Pryer, Manervy to Wesley Simmons 1-11-1870 (1-12-1870) B
Pucket, Mary C. to Thomas J. Irwin 4-23-1841
Pullen, Mary to W. P. Lipscomb 2-4-1868 (2-26-1868)
Pulliam, A. E. to C. M. Waller 2-7-1859 (2-8-1859)
Pulliam, Almira to John Michie 4-9-1866 (no return) B
Pulliam, Ann to Charles Session 9-4-1868 (9-5-1868) B
Pulliam, Ann to Peter McCarley 6-11-1868 (6-13-1868) B
Pulliam, Judy to Archibald Wiggins 2-7-1871 (2-15-1871) B
Pulliam, Louisa to Jack Jones 4-14-1866 (4-22-1866) B
Pulliam, Mary to Jim Walker 12-24-1867 (12-25-1867) B
Pulliam, Rachel C. to Joseph A. Hill 6-6-1859 (6-7-1859)
Pulliam, Sallie A. to R. L. Walker 12-4-1866 (12-29-1866)
Pullman, Eliza to Joseph Pippin 11-5-1838 (11-?-1839?)
Pyron, Martha M. to Thos. D. Baggett 2-21-1853 (no return)
Rachel, Sarah Ann to Wm. Davis 10-7-1850 (no return)
Rachels, Mary to Benjn. Davis 8-27-1850 (8-29-1850)
Radford, Heneretta to George W. Seaton 8-26-1844 (8-27-1844)
Radford, Margaret to Stephen H. Snow 8-19-1850 (8-22-1850)
Radford, Marion to Melzer Shepherd? 1-15-1851 (1-16-1851)
Ragan, Margaret M. to Benjamin F. Koen 10-7-1839
Ragland, Josephine to Jack Truesdale 12-4-1866 (no return) B
Ragland, Martha to Oliver Robinson 2-17-1866 B
Ragland, Sara to George McFarland 11-27-1865 (12-30-1865) B
Ragland, Sarah to Lewis Edwards 3-9-1868 (3-21-1868) B
Raiford, Evalina A. to John J. Steger 6-9-1848 (6-11-1848)
Raiford, Jane to James S. Soap 1-25-1840 (no return)
Rainer, Frances to Jasper Jones 8-29-1867 (9-23-1867) B
Rainer, Rosella to Frank Ketchum 10-28-1868 (no return) B
Rains, Fanny to Aleck Mackey 11-30-1870 (12-1-1870)
Ralph, Martha Ann to Forney W. Redding 8-2-1851 (no return)
Ramsey, Mary A. to James H. Wheeler 10-24-1842 (10-27-1842)
Ramsey, Nancy to S. E. Hogan 9-21-1843
Ramsey, Susan N. to Christopher H. Plant 11-17-1845 (12-2-1845)
Randal, Martha to Wm. Jones 1-8-1869 (1-16-1869) B
Raper, Nancy C. to Stephen C. Ball 11-28-1859 (11-29-1859)
Rawlings, Annis to John Powell 12-17-1869 (no return) B
Rawlings, Caroline R. to James Floyd 12-21-1865 (12-24-1865)
Rawlings, Dilsa to Chas. Parks 9-13-1867 (no return) B
Rawlings, Lizzie to Archy Dowdy 2-14-1868 (2-21-1868) B
Rawlings, Lucinda to Wash Fitchugh 1-8-1867 (1-12-1867) B
Rawls, Martha Jane to Louis? M. Roberts 4-3-1848 (no return)
Ray, Angeline to Jno. A. Hood 3-10-1860 (3-13-1860)
Ray, Areadna to Andrew H. Farrington 7-15-1845
Ray, C. A. to W. R. Coody 11-14-1853 (no return)
Ray, Maggie to Kitchen Boggs 12-7-1869 (12-8-1869)
Rayn, Susan T. to Francis Loving 11-28-1839 (no return)
Rea, Susan J. to Lovett Morris 4-25-1866 (4-29-1866)
Read, Jane to Pleasant Guardner 8-31-1838 (no return)
Read, Mary Ann to Wm. E. Nation 3-22-1843 (no return)
Read, Sarah Jane to Thomas H. Cargal 11-8-1851 (no return)
Reames, S. J. to J. S. Amis 11-14-1865 (11-16-1865)
Reams, Elizabeth to D. C. Morris 4-2-1859 (4-3-1859)
Reams, M. J. to A. M. Hood 2-3-1864 (not endorsed)
Reams, Malinda to Frank Walton 12-24-1868 B
Redd, Catharine E. to David W. Sumner 6-7-1841 (not endorsed)
Reddick, Bettie to Peter Taylor 3-2-1866 (3-3-1866) B
Reddick, Caroline to Rice Neal 12-23-1865 (12-25-1865) B
Reddick, Casandra to Charles Jones 10-13-1866 (no return) B
Reddick, Edy to Sandy Askew 1-15-1869 (no return) B

Reddick, Mahala to Monroe Eddins 9-8-1866 (no return) B
Reddick, Sallie E. to T. S. Neal 2-22-1869 (2-24-1869)
Reddick, Tempe to Howlbert? Williams 9-1-1866 (no return)
Redus, D. F. to J. L. Ayers 4-16-1850
Reece, Mattie to B. W. Overton 12-16-1867 (12-17-1867)
Reed, Clarissa to Thomas J. Waller 1-1-1847 (1-7-1847)
Reed, Harriett to Bonaparte Thompson 1-22-1870 B
Reed, Lucy to E. M. Waller 1-21-1851 (no return)
Reed, Martha to Silas Douglas 1-6-1870
Reed, Melvina to Frederick Burton 12-28-1868 (12-29-1868) B
Reed, Milla to James Brown 9-25-1868 B
Reed, Priscilla to H. C. Cunliff 11-28-1860 (11-29-1860)
Reeder, Sarah to Alonzo Herrick 12-23-1868 (12-24-1868)
Reese, Eliza to Charles E. Copeland 11-23-1841 (no return)
Reese, Evelina to James M. Miller 12-24-1844 (no return)
Reeves, Adaline to Nathan Shaddinger 9-5-1867
Reeves, Frances A. to Andrew J. Studvant 9-7-1852 (no return)
Reeves, Frances to Plummer Evans 1-21-1869 B
Reeves, H. T. to James H. Clayton 10-24-1855 (no return)
Reeves, Lyddia to Nat Howard 12-25-1869 (12-31-1869) B
Reeves, M.F. to J. A. Wilson 10-19-1870 (10-20-1870)
Reeves, Mary F. to T. W. Crowder 12-16-1865
Reeves, Musadora to L. L. Boyd 1-27-1866 (1-30-1866)
Reeves, Nancy Witt to Joshua Darden 11-23-1865 (11-28-1865)
Reeves, Rebecca to Wesley Harris 3-11-1869
Reeves, Rose to Jordan McNeill 11-9-1867 (no return) B
Reid, Cresa to William Swift 4-20-1867 (no return) B
Reid, Peggie to Andrew Fulks 3-8-1869 (no return)
Renfro, Trilucia to James Snowden 4-16-1855 (no return)
Rhea, E. L. to John Rhea 12-22-1840
Rhea, Ella to H. Cary 5-1-1866
Rhea, Isabell to King Levy 12-29-1868 (1-16-1869) B
Rhea, Lucinda to S. A. Miller 8-28-1849
Rhea, Margarett J. to Nicholas Long 7-12-1848
Rhine, Mary to William House 11-5-1869 (11-11-1869) B
Rhodes, A. K. to James H. M. Hall 4-22-1838
Rhodes, Fannie to Alfred Martin 9-5-1868 (9-6-1868) B
Rhodes, J. C. to W. B. Harvey 3-31-1869 (no return)
Rhodes, Mary A. E. to Wm. W. Greenway 9-5-1850
Rhodes, Sarah A. to R. C. Garrett 5-1-1848 (5-3-1848)
Rice, Cary to Saml. Richardson 5-2-1846 (5-3-1846)
Rice, Celia Ann to Spencer P. Daniel 12-31-1845 (1-8-1846)
Rice, Kerron R. to John N. Lewis 3-16-1846 (no return)
Rich, Frances to J. A. Harper 9-3-1850 (no return)
Rich, Julia L. to Henry C. Gwynn 6-25-1866 (6-28-1866)
Rich, Lucy H. to W. A. Harper 11-11-1853 (no return)
Richardson, Nancy to Wash Bailey 1-25-1871 (1-26-1871) B
Richardt, Henrietta to C. W. Wirwa 9-21-1868 (9-22-1868)
Richey, A. C. to J. B. Walls 1-30-1869
Richey, Elizabeth to Andrew J. Webb 2-18-1838
Richey, Susan J. to A. J. Davis 1-6-1869 (1-7-1869)
Richie, Sarah to Thomas Lowery 12-14-1853 (no return)
Ricketts, A. E. to J. D. Cocke 12-27-1864 (12-29-1864)
Riddle, Charlotte to Haden Johnston 4-24-1850 (no return)
Rideout, E. J. to Wm. S. Stallings 12-25-1860 (not executed)
Rideout, Eliza J. to James H. Hammond 1-17-1861 (1-20-1861)
Rieves, Lou to Henry Harris 8-15-1867 (8-17-1867) B
Riggs, Eliza to John W. Downey 2-20-1860
Riggs, Mary C. to William Malone 12-8-1862
Rightsdale, Mandy to James Johnson 12-16-1867 B
Ritchey, Lucy K. to James B. Gilliam 1-18-1870 (1-20-1870)
Ritchie, Tabitha to John Evans 6-26-1847
Rivers, Jane to Dick Rivers 2-19-1870 B
Rivers, Mariah to Dick Johnson 2-9-1867 (2-10-1867) B
Rivers, Mary E. to G. P. Rogers 7-11-1870 (7-14-1870)
Rivers, Mary Lucette to Edwin Dickinson, sr. 12-27-1870 B
Rivers, Mat to Anderson Boyle 1-12-1869 (1-17-1869) B
Rivers, Nancy to John Walton 12-26-1870 (1-2-1871) B
Rivers, Perlina to Andrew Anderson 11-18-1869 (11-21-1869) B
Rivers, Sallie to Thos. J. Johnson 6-12-1867
Rivers, Sarah to Wm. Wilkerson 12-22-1869 B
Rivers, Sophia to Dick Tatum 1-1-1870 (1-27-1870) B
Rives, A. R. to A. D. Bright 10-18-1867 (10-24-1867)
Rives, Anna W. to John M. Schwar 9-21-1868 (9-30-1868)
Rives, Jenny to Ike Nolly 1-15-1870 (1-19-1870) B

Rives, M. E. to R. W. Pitman 10-29-1866 (10-31-1866)
Rives, Maranda to Ned McElwain 2-19-1870 (2-20-1870) B
Rives, Mary to Wilson Allen 2-3-1841 (2-4-1841)
Rives, Sallie J. to Leonidas C. Chaffin 12-20-1869 (12-21-1869)
Rives, Sally A. to W. M. Rives 9-17-1838
Roach, Isabella J. to James A. Winsett 11-18-1845 (11-19-1845)
Roach, Mary J. to A. Reid 11-20-1838
Roach, Sarah L. to Samuel L. Irwin 4-29-1847
Roberson, Hariett to H. Gray 1-30-1851
Roberson, Missouri to Dennis Barrington 12-28-1867 (1-1-1868) B
Roberts, Clancy D. to William R. Darby 1-12-1841
Roberts, Elizabeth C. to Edward D. Hammons 10-7-1870 (10-9-1870)
Roberts, Emily J. to John Bateman 11-15-1848
Roberts, Emily S. to W. M. Knight 11-16-1847 (11-17-1847)
Roberts, Emily S. to W. M. Night 11-16-1847 (11-17-1847)
Roberts, Isabella to Martin Van Buren 12-27-1870 (12-29-1870) B
Roberts, Janie F. to James D. Darbey 1-28-1839 (1-29-1839)
Roberts, Martha A. to Saml. E. Gaither 3-31-1871 (4-4-1871)
Roberts, Mary to C. Swiney 1-11-1870 (1-12-1870)
Roberts, Susan to Henry C. Gwynn 12-18-1865 (12-20-1865)
Robertson, Edna F. to Jeremiah Bull 7-12-1851 (no return)
Robertson, Elizabeth to Willis Stafford 12-22-1868
Robertson, Emma H. to R. K. Neel 11-25-1865 (11-29-1865)
Robertson, F. J. to W. H. Frank 5-30-1859
Robertson, J. J. to J. D. Green 12-23-1862 (12-30-1862)
Robertson, Lucinda to Pinkney Stafford 2-14-1867 (2-15-1867)
Robertson, Martha An to James A. King 3-6-1848 (3-16-1848)
Robertson, Mary F. to George H. Hiflin 11-28-1854 (no return)
Robertson, Trilucia to John M. Durham 1-23-1845
Robinson, Caroline to Andrew C. Satterfield 4-2-1838 (no return)
Robinson, Maryann to George W. Tiller 10-19-1839 (5-13-1840?)
Rodger, Catharine to Elisha Morris 6-28-1848 (6-29-1848)
Rodgers, Ann P. to G. W. Ammons 8-22-1851 (no return)
Rodgers, Emily to J. F. Young 12-28-1866 (1-2-1867)
Rodgers, Mary E. to Caleb T. Harris 2-3-1869 (2-24-1869)
Rodgers, Mary E. to John W. Tiller 8-6-1860 (8-16-1860)
Rodgers, Nancy A. to Lawrence Kerniham 7-29-1868 (no return) B
Rodgers, Nancy to Jesse Harvey 11-10-1866 (11-20-1866)
Rodgers, Nancy to John A. Wilson 1-3-1853 (no return)
Rodgers, Rebecca E. to Wilie B. Morris 5-12-1851 (5-14-1851)
Roe, Maryann to James C. Foster 1-25-1843 (2-2-1843)
Roffner?, Eliza to Wm. T. Vanpelt 9-27-1844
Rogers, Arilia D. to Samson Vanderpool 5-26-1842 (5-29-1842)
Rogers, Carrie F. to Bernard P. Dickinson 1-28-1869 (no return)
Rogers, Eliza M. to William Denney 7-12-1847 (7-18-1847)
Rogers, Kitty to Wyatt Henderson 11-1-1867 (11-2-1867) B
Rogers, Lydia M. to Smith C. Belote 7-15-1844
Rogers, Martha L. J. to H. P. Guy 1-4-1865
Rogers, Martha to T. M. Holiday 1-24-1871 (1-25-1871)
Rogers, Mary J. to R. H. (Dr.) Harvey 6-16-1869
Rogers, Mary to Berry Lee 10-7-1845 (10-9-1845)
Rogers, Mary to Elisha Williams 2-15-1844 (no return)
Rogers, Mary to W. Suffield 12-21-1841 (12-25-1841)
Rogers, Parisade to John Campbell 12-24-1869 (no return) B
Rogers, Susan E. to George W. Hacket 11-8-1845 (11-18-1845)
Rolyere? (Rogers?), Margier B. to Thos. G. Clark 10-8-1838
     (10-9-1838)
Rorrell, Jane to John A. Soung 5-8-1847 (5-28-1847)
Rosan, Mary to Samuel L. Stevens 8-18-1840 (no return)
Rose, Rebecca E. to John Morefield 7-9-1870 (7-10-1870)
Ross, Amanda to George Williamson 1-7-1869 B
Ross, Ann to Mansfield Manifee 9-1-1869 (no return) B
Ross, Arabella to Wm. Black 4-19-1851
Ross, Caroline to Henry Teagner 12-26-1867 B
Ross, Celia to William Blaydes 1-19-1871 B
Ross, Louisa to A. Hunsucker 3-11-1869 (3-23-1869)
Ross, Lydia A. to Clem S. Cole 12-17-1867 (12-19-1867) B
Ross, Mary J. to Buckner Harwell 10-2-1867 (10-3-1867)
Ross, N. A. to William Vest 7-29-1870 (8-4-1870)
Ross, Nancy to Joseph Sikes 3-3-1849
Ross, Sallie to Alfred Cobb 3-2-1867 (not endorsed) B
Ross, Sarah E. to John W. Notgrass 3-22-1852 (no return)
Rosser, Maggie to J. R. Pearce 12-3-1866 (12-5-1866)
Rosser, Maria to Durell Griffin 11-3-1870 (11-8-1870)
Rowder, Lucy to Pryus Patton 2-23-1867 (3-11-1867) B

Rowlett, Tilda to Henry Nolly 7-19-1867 (7-20-1867) B
Ruffin, Agnes C. to David S. Bass 8-9-1866 (8-12-1866)
Ruffin, Roena R. to E. B. Turner 9-21-1867 (9-25-1867)
Rushen, Matilda to Silas Hughes 11-17-1852 (no return)
Rutledge, Mary F. to Jno. H. Garnett 12-15-1868
Sadler, Charlotte to John White 5-6-1871 (5-7-1871) B
Sale, Mary Lucinda to Alford W. Harris 2-24-1846 (no return)
Sale, Virginia S. to Orville Yearger 10-9-1848 (no return)
Salmon, Elizabeth J. to James A. Douglass 10-26-1841 (10-27-1841)
Salmon, Nancy T. to James H. Roberson 12-1-1847
Sample, Fanny H. to James Lewis 5-10-1842 (5-12-1842)
Sanderman? Bucy, Julia to James D. Cleaves 5-11-1852 (no return)
Sanders, Anna to Allen McDowell 10-6-1869 B
Sanders, Elizabeth to Charles Bradberry 2-9-1843
Sanders, Elizabeth to L. S. Hailey 12-22-1847 (no return)
Sanders, Emily to Charles Hill 12-17-1869 (no return) B
Sanders, Isabella to William Gibson 7-21-1841 (7-22-1841)
Sanders, Jane to Daniel Williams 1-19-1870 (no return) B
Sanders, Louisa T. to James Pool 1-28-1867
Sanders, Lucy A. to John M. Richey 1-6-1856 (1-9-1859)
Sanders, Lucy A. to Samuel McKinney 8-15-1854 (no return)
Sanders, M. J. to J. C. Adams 4-15-1859 (4-20-1859)
Sanders, Martha to Asberry Fletcher 4-6-1866 (4-10-1866) B
Sanders, Ortry to Reubin Palmer 12-12-1867 B
Sanders, Polly to Littleton Caple 1-8-1840 (1-9-1840)
Sanford, Mary A. to N. W. Lambeth 7-10-1865 (7-12-1865)
Sargent, Mary Ann to David L. Smith 2-22-1848
Sasser, Sarah J. to Jas. M. Martin 2-16-1853 (no return)
Sauls, Eliza H. to Richard N. Williams 12-24-1844
Saunders, F. C. to B. A. England 12-2-1859 (12-6-1859)
Sawyer, Agnis to Joe Murrell 3-30-1867 B
Sawyers, A. E. to Richard Brinkley 2-16-1842 (2-17-1842)
Sawyers, Virginia to George Sherrod 2-28-1866 (3-1-1866)
Sayers, C. H. to G. F. Sherrod 7-2-1868 (7-8-1868)
Sayers, Josephine to Robert Murrell 2-12-1870 (no return) B
Sayers, Lilie C. to H. R. Sherrod 4-5-1869 (4-15-1869)
Scale, L. A. to William A. Rives 11-17-1851 (no return)
Scalion, Elizabeth to Tho. Cunningham 1-8-1846
Scallions, Chartally to Wm. H. Taler 7-29-1841
Scarbrough, A. J. to C. L. Barnard 9-28-1852 (no return)
Scott, Ann to Milton Gourdlock 9-4-1869 B
Scott, Harriet H. to Richard W. Green 5-8-1839 (5-15-1839)
Scott, Joanna L. to Joseph M. Proctor 10-26-1868
Scott, Julia Ann to Sterling Carlton 1-3-1867 (1-6-1867) B
Scott, Maggie A. to J. G. King 10-22-1866 (10-4?-1866)
Scott, Malvina to John Williams 7-7-1866 (no return) B
Scott, Mary E. to G. W. Earnhart 11-13-1867 (11-14-1867)
Scott, Vernelia to A. J. Langum 12-21-1844 (no return)
Scott, Virginia M. to T. M. Downing 9-10-1850 (9-11-1850)
Scott, Virginia to D. P. Carney 11-4-1867 (11-5-1867)
Sellers, Sarah C. to John B. Walker 4-5-1844 (no return)
Settle, Mary to Wm. W. Anderson 3-16-1866 (no return)
Settle, Susan E. to D. M. Padin 7-19-1849
Sevier, Sarah E. to Richd. Aiken 12-13-1851 (no return)
Seward, Julian to J. A. House 11-15-1838
Seymour, Ella to Wm. Braswell 7-19-1866 (7-21-1866) B
Seymour, Isabella to B. P. Garrison 4-4-1864
Seymour, M. J. to J. N. Wall 4-27-1853
Shackelford, Liza to Ned Wiggins 5-18-1866 (no return) B
Shackelford, Lucinda to Henry Clay Cole 5-14-1866 (no return) B
Shackleford, Celia to John Mathews 3-23-1867 (no return) B
Shackleford, Emily to Adam Heaslett 11-15-1867 (no return) B
Shafter, Sarah C. to Levi Couch 12-1-1849 (no return)
Shaine, Mary to James Coker 3-22-1844 (3-23-1844)
Sharp, Armedia A. to Charles J. Maxwell 9-21-1852 (no return)
Sharp, Fannie to J. M. McFadden 11-4-1863 (11-5-1863)
Shaw, Annie L. to Thomas H. Brightwell 1-14-1869
Shaw, Becky to Cornelius Franklin 12-25-1867 B
Shaw, Bettie L. to Ed Dickinson, jr. 12-17-1868
Shaw, Chaney to Joshua Morrow 4-28-1871 (5-1-1871)
Shaw, Clarecy A. to Joseph T. Baldwin 11-14-1851 (no return)
Shaw, Eliza J. to Edmund B. Perry 1-2-1869 (1-6-1869)
Shaw, Eliza J. to William Blake 1-8-1852 (no return)
Shaw, Eliza N. to C. C. Glover 4-29-1854 (no return)
Shaw, Eliza to Joseph Fowler 2-25-1869 (2-26-1869) B

Shaw, Emeline T. to Creed Woodson 12-20-1847
Shaw, Fanny to Edward Selby 10-9-1869 (10-20-1869) B
Shaw, Frances M. to John S. Biles 6-23-1845 (6-24-1845)
Shaw, Mahala C. to R. G. Saunders 2-8-1842
Shaw, Mahala to Tho. Wright 9-4-1845
Shaw, Malina to R. S. McComack 11-29-1841 (12-9-1841)
Shaw, Mariah to Sam Cross 8-9-1866 (no return) B
Shaw, Martha Jane to Edward B. Baw 1-15-1844 (1-18-1844)
Shaw, Mary S. to J. G. Wilbourn 12-18-1867
Shaw, Mollie to Rufus C. Taylor 5-7-1869 (no return)
Shaw, Nellie to Austin Harris 10-25-1870 (10-30-1870) B
Shaw, Valeria to Robt. N. Christian 7-28-1866 (8-?-1866)
Shelton, Harriett to George Tucker 1-8-1869 (1-9-1869) B
Shelton, Lilly to Frank Trimble 1-6-1870
Shelton, Mary Ann to Christopher Rives 7-12-1838
Shelton, Mary to Dave Archbell 12-26-1868 (12-28-1868) B
Shelton, Mattie to Charles Bailey 12-23-1869 (no return) B
Shelton, Peep to Ed Woodfork 1-5-1870 (no return) B
Shepard, Mollie J. to Henry Monroe 6-18-1869 (6-20-1869)
Shephard, Amy to Andrew Jackson 3-13-1869 (3-15-1869)
Shephard, Noah to Emanuel Alexander 7-21-1869 (7-29-1869) B
Shepherd, Nancy E. to William Ballard 10-26-1846 (10-27-1846)
Sherfield, Mallissa C. to Wm. A. Browne 11-29-1844 (11-30-1844)
Sherrell, Harriett to James Phillips 8-6-1853 (no return)
Sherrod, Eliza to Calvin Bond 12-24-1866 (no return) B
Sherrod, Emma C. to Peyton J. Smith 12-7-1870 (12-11-1870)
Sherrod, Frances Ann to Jonas C. Shelton 12-26-1866 (12-28-1866) B
Shields, Jane to Benjamin Reeves 12-27-1869 (12-30-1869) B
Shinalt, Mary to Henry Snow 12-11-1844 (12-12-1844)
Shinault, Casandra to Wm. R. Winn 11-24-1841
Shinault, Mary A to W. E. Ballard 2-22-1866
Shinault, O. E. to J. M. Ritchie 12-1-1866 (12-4-1866)
Shinault, Sallie to W. L. Wily 2-1-1860
Shinel, Hetty to Francis C. Keyor? 9-21-1841 (no return)
Shinn, Rebecca to F. M. Mays 9-24-1851 (no return)
Shirley, Anna to J. A. Lipscomb 12-29-1868 (12-31-1868)
Shoemaker, Margaret F. to W. S. Hawley 2-9-1871 (2-24-1871)
Shoemaker, Martha J. to S. Ellis 1-25-1871 (1-26-1871)
Shore, Elizabeth to Joe Cross 12-20-1867 (12-22-1867) B
Shore, Fannie F. to W. J. Morris 11-30-1859 (12-4-1859)
Shore, Sallie A. V. to Harrison Herron 10-7-1867 (10-17-1867)
Shore, Sarah A. O. to James D. Carter 5-28-1846 (6-10-1846)
Show, Annie to C. C. Welbourn 1-5-1860
Simerson, M. E. to W. H. Rogers 10-23-1866 (10-25-1866)
Simmons, Alice to Lou Jones 12-26-1870 B
Simmons, Caroline to L. B. Hammons 3-2-1854 (no return)
Simmons, E. J. to W. A. Bryan 4-26-1853 (no return)
Simmons, Emely M. to Peter A. Crook 9-17-1853 (no return)
Simmons, Emila to James M. Rogers 5-21-1843 (no return)
Simmons, Mary Ann to Anderson Miller 12-28-1868 B
Simmons, Mary J. to William H. Nolly 10-13-1868 (10-14-1868)
Simmons, Mary to James Lee 2-8-1842
Simmons, Matilda J. to Wiley Slaughter 12-16-1850 (12-23-1850)
Simmons, Polly to John Conish 7-2-1870 B
Simmons, Priscilla S. to George A. Lipscomb 12-25-1854 (no return)
Simmons, Sarah Eliz. to Jno. W. High 9-11-1850
Simmons, Sarah to G. A. Isham 1-8-1870 (1-13-1870)
Simmons, Sophia W. to Joshua? C. Lundy 8-4-1845 (8-5-1845)
Simmons, Tempe to Dock Forrest 2-22-1866 (no return) B
Simms, Allice E. to Saml. E. Champion 3-4-1868 (3-5-1868)
Simms, G. A. to Jas. M. Culbreath 3-25-1868 (3-26-1868)
Simms, Henrietta to James Moore 1-29-1866 (2-4-1866)
Simms, Mattie O. to B. H. Lucas 10-2-1865 (10-3-1865)
Simons, Martha E. C. to J. E. Patillo 9-11-1850 (9-11-1850)
Simpkins, Louisa to Ben Mitchell 5-13-1870 (5-15-1870) B
Simpson, A. M. (Mrs.) to T. B. Worrell 3-1-1853 (no return)
Sims, Fannie R. to Benj. J. Allen 11-6-1855 (no return)
Singleton, Jane to Jas. M. Pickens 1-24-1853 (no return)
Sisco, Elizabeth F. to Calvin S. Floyd 10-16-1850 (10-17-1850)
Sisco, Mary to George N. Allen 11-24-1845 (no return)
Sitler, Emily W. to William Plant 6-20-1843 (no return)
Skeggs, Rosina B. to J. W. Brewer 11-21-1866 (11-22-1866)
Skillen, _____ to Joshua Thompson no dates (with May 1838)
Skipper, Easter to Bob Pulliam 12-31-1867 (1-4-1868) B
Skipper, Lizzie to King Bird 12-24-1869 (12-29-1869) B

Slaughter, Aillvice? to Wm. S. Jones 12-31-1839
Slaughter, Laura L. to W. W. McClarty 4-7-1868 (4-12-1868)
Slaughter, M. A. to G.? J. Green 10-22-1866 (10-25-1866)
Slaughter, M. A. to J. R. McCarty 1-29-18686 (2-1-1866)
Slaughter, M. F. to R. E. McCheven 12-3-1866 (12-5-1866)
Slaughter, Mary F. to Wm. Booth 2-12-1868
Slaughter, O. J. to J. M. Black 1-29-1866 (2-1-1866)
Slauson, Grissey to Wilson Luckado 6-20-1853 (no return)
Sloan, Anna to J. H. Alford 12-14-1870 (12-15-1870)
Sloan, Deborah M. to John L. Pool 10-11-1839 (10-17-1839)
Slone, Martha J. to James H. Warner 10-29-1839 (11-7-1839)
Slow, P. E. to Jno. B. Steel 9-27-1859 (9-28-1859)
Smalman, Mary A. D. to Jehu Graham 6-26-1851
Smith, Adaline to William McVey 6-12-1867 (6-25-1867)
Smith, C. C. to H. B. Turner 12-16-1867 (12-19-1867)
Smith, Carolina L. to Thomas R. Polk 12-15-1841
Smith, Catharine A. to Daniel K. Cockrahane 5-17-1843 (5-18-1843)
Smith, Cordelia to M. Logan Anderson 3-25-1870 (3-30-1870)
Smith, Cornelia A. to Wm. B. Langly 3-12?-1842 (no return)
Smith, Cynthia to Jesse Marlar 8-15-1846 (no return)
Smith, D. E. to M. B. Dyer 4-26-1859 (4-28-1859)
Smith, E. A. to W. H. Farris 2-3-1868 (2-5-1868)
Smith, Eliza to Felix Fletcher 11-19-1869 (no return) B
Smith, Elizabeth A. to R. R. Gwyn 12-19-1842
Smith, Elizabeth B. to Andrew J. Newsom 10-21-1865 (no return)
Smith, Elizabeth to Jesse Bowden 2-19-1847 (no return)
Smith, Elizah to J. W. S. Long 8-29-1838 (8-30-1838)
Smith, Ellen to Daniel T. Hooey 7-9-1869 (7-11-1869)
Smith, Elmira to Wm. Sanders 12-21-1844 (12-22-1844)
Smith, F. A. to G. W. F. Crunch 4-27-1852 (no return)
Smith, F. E. to James A. McCaskill 12-19-1856 (no return)
Smith, Frances A. to Philemon T. Burford 3-4-1842 (no return)
Smith, Gatsy H. to M. C.? Newberry 7-20-1842
Smith, Jane A. to William A. Smith 8-10-1848
Smith, Jane R. to James Owen 11-5-1838 (no return)
Smith, Jullia (Mrs.) to F. A. Parker 5-13-1869 (5-16-1869)
Smith, Lucy Ann to John A. Pearce 2-5-1870 (2-10-1870)
Smith, M. C. to C. W. Waddall 8-21-1838
Smith, Martha E. to Wm. T. Firth 11-15-1859 (12-13-1859)
Smith, Martha J. to Jno. B. Caroway 1-14-1868 (1-16-1868)
Smith, Martha J. to Victor Clampet 10-17-1854 (no return)
Smith, Martha W. to James W. Manning no date (with Oct 1852)
Smith, Mary E. to B. W. McAdams 4-6-1869
Smith, Mary E. to Henry A. Ridley 9-15-1853 (no return)
Smith, Mary to James M. Neal 9-28-1838 (9-30-1838)
Smith, Mary to William Jackson 2-6-1867 B
Smith, Matilda Ann to Aden Johnson 10-1-1842 (10-6-1842)
Smith, Matilda C. to Joseph Turner 10-11-1841 (10-21-1841)
Smith, Mattie to Charles Carter 4-11-1871 (4-15-1871) B
Smith, Milla to Nelson Roberts 1-18-1868 B
Smith, O. J. to Washington Scalhurst? 11-19-1852 (no return)
Smith, Penelolpe to Thos. Eskridge 4-7-1849
Smith, Rebecca M. to Edmond Allen 12-30-1838
Smith, Sallie P. to Jas. W. Wiggins 1-14-1871 (1-15-1871)
Smith, Sarah L. to Thomas J. Ridley 6-9-1852 (no return)
Smith, Susan to F. H. Lockett 6-2-1847 (no return)
Smith, Susan to George Russel 8-20-1869 (8-22-1869) B
Smith, Susan to S. A. Hart 7-31-1855 (no return)
Smithson, E. S. to W. G. Brooks 12-31-1866 (no return)
Smotherson?, Virginia C. to J. W. Rubotton 8-25-1854 (no return)
Sneed, A. M. to J. J. Williams 9-14-1851 (no return)
Sneed, Ann M. (Mrs.) to Joseph B. Littlejohn 1-9-1843 (1-10-1843)
Sneed, Ann to Thomas Romine 9-8-1843 (no return)
Sneed, Caledonia to Giles Wiley 11-22-1867 (11-24-1867) B
Sneed, L. M. E. to R. Watkins 7-20-1851
Sneed, Lottie to Wilson Allen 2-1-1871 (no return) B
Sneed, Mary Jane to Samuel M. Williamson 9-29-1841 (10-4-1841)
Snelling, Julia A. to B. R. Stafford 12-19-1856 (no return)
Snellings, Arbelier F. to J. T. Scott 8-6-1869 (8-8-1869)
Snellings, Sarah J. to John E. Pankey 8-20-1869 (8-21-1869)
Snow, Lucinda to A. S. Pasco Elliott 12-19-1844
Snow, Mary M. to Ira S. Robson 11-12-1870 (11-13-1870)
Snow, Permilia to W. T. Davis 9-27-1865 (9-28-1865)
Soap, Huldah A. to S. B. Whitson 10-31-1845 (no return)
Soap, Sarah T. to Johnson G. Ford 12-19-1842 (no return)

Soape, N. E. to Bernard E. Skinner 6-13-1845 (no return)
Solomon, Martha A. to James T. Yarbrough 1-25-1844 (1-31-1844)
Sope, Lethia to John Pope 12-15-1842 (no return)
Southall, Lee G. to Wilie A. Glover 12-5-1863 (12-13-1863)
Southerland, Malinda to H. B. Walker 2-9-1842 (2-10-1842)
Southerland, Peggy to Allen Minor 1-3-1849 (no return)
Southern, Martha J. to James B. Crook 7-?-1844
Sowell, Eliza to William Stedham 12-14-1848 (no return)
Spain, Sallie E. to John B. Young 11-6-1866 (11-8-1866)
Sparkes, Sally P. to Thomas Jones 7-7-1853 (no return)
Speares, Elizabeth to Nathaniel Rutledge 8-23-1843 (8-24-1843)
Speer, Tobitha to John M. Taylor 8-16-1838
Spencer, Anna to Wm. Snow 10-22-1849 (10-24-1849)
Spencer, Harrit to Meredith H. Neal 12-4-1845
Spencer, Mary W. (Mrs.) to Creed P. Halley 7-18-1839
Spike, Lucy to Sam Drake 8-19-1868 (no return) B
Spiller, Sallie to James Doolin 12-23-1869 (12-29-1869) B
Spivey, Emaline E. to John M. McCall 8-30-1843 (8-31-1843)
Springfield, Jenny to Gardner Porter 12-1-1869 (no return) B
Springfield, Judy to Nathan Degraffenreid 12-25-1866 (12-27-1866) B
Springfield, Lucy to Wm. Patterson 11-11-1869 B
Springfield, Nellie to Tennessee Hunt 12-31-1868 (1-2-1869) B
Springfield, Susan to Wm. Jones 1-23-1869 (no return) B
Spurlock, Eliza J. to G. W. Griffin 12-21-1852 (no return)
Stackerd, Sarah J. to W. J. Kirkpatrick 5-10-1854 (no return)
Stacy, Eliza Ann to John Warington 9-20-1847 (9-23-1847)
Stacy, Susan to Earby Benson 9-25-1852 (no return)
Stafford, Ann E. to G. W. Boling 1-14-1854 (no return)
Stafford, Candas to Wm. H. Stephens 11-20-1867 (11-21-1867)
Stafford, Cornelia A. to J. M. Adams 2-7-1866
Stafford, Emley to Stephen Hern 8-5-1844 (8-8-1844)
Stafford, H. A. to J. B. Stafford 6-22-1867 (6-23-1867)
Stafford, Harriet (Mrs.) to John E. Pattillo 2-12-1870 (2-13-1870)
Stafford, Margaret to William Johnson 8-1-1870 (8-2-1870)
Stafford, Martha B. to John K. Earl 10-7-1863 (10-8-1863)
Stafford, Mary E. to Andrew J. Whitby 12-21-1868 (12-24-1868)
Stafford, Mary F. to J. P. Stafford 10-6-1862 (10-7-1862)
Stafford, Mary M. to Wm. H. Stevens 11-1-1862 (not endorsed)
Stafford, Nancy to Stephen Cannon 3-16-1866 (3-21-1866)
Stafford, S. B. to J. L. Wagener 10-23-1866 (10-30-1866)
Stainback, Allice M. to Wm. M. Ingram 10-21-1867 (10-24-1867)
Stainback, Lucy E. to Levin H. Coe 12-20-1866
Stainback, Maria to David Green 11-27-1866 (12-2-1866) B
Stallings, Lucinda to Joseph Denton 4-2-1849
Stamper, Mary A. to Burgess Bolling 5-5-1851 (no return)
Standley, Martha A. D. to John M. Eddins 12-22-1841 (12-23-1841)
Standley, Mary Elizabeth to Isaac Bason 12-26-1840 (12-29-1840)
Stanley, Lucy C. J. to Burwell S. Moseley 2-16-1846 (2-19-1846)
Stanly, Susan to W. H. Pickins 9-29-1849 (9-30-1849)
Stansberry, Ellen to J. S. Evans 9-18-1855 (no return)
Starling, Elizabeth to Nathanl. Harris 7-23-1850 (no return)
Starling, Elizabeth to Nathl. Harris? 7-25-1850 (no return)
Starr, Agnes A. to Wm. E. Patton 1-27-1840 (1-28-1840)
Starrett, Demaris to Thos. N. Vestal 1-1-1845 (1-2-1845)
Stations, Lusinda to William A. Bennett 7-22-1848 (no return)
Steadham, Jane C. to John C. Lightle 12-20-1864 (12-22-1864)
Steadham, Ripsey to Wm. H. C. Johnson 12-17-1838 (12-20-1838)
Steager, Priscilla to Jesse Nevil 11-15-1869 (11-18-1869) B
Stedham, Elizabeth to Judel? (J. W.?) Parchman 10-6-1838 (10-8-1838)
Stedham, Jane to Aretny Mathews 4-2-1849 (5-3-1849)
Stedham, Martha to A. L. Pickins 12-21-1842 (12-22-1842)
Steel, E. to John Siddle 12-29-1840 (12-31-1840)
Steel, Jane E. to Francis E. Davis 5-10-1842 (no return)
Stegall, Eliza J. to Jas. H. Harbson 7-1-1850 (7-9-1850)
Stegar, Frances I. to Joseph E. Douglass 2-15-1838
Steger, Fannie C. to R. L. Knox 1-29-1866 (1-31-1866)
Steger, Judy to Oliver Parks 1-29-1870 (2-22-1870) B
Stephens, Mary Jane to J. W. Womble 1-4-1841 (1-7-1841)
Stephens, Permella to Charley Allen 2-7-1871 (2-9-1871) B
Stephens, Sarah E. to D. L. Chaffin 1-30-1851 (1-31-1851)
Sterling, Susan to Anderson Lucas 4-17-1850 (4-18-1850)
Stevens, F. E. to J. D. Davis 1-15-1866 (1-16-1866)
Stevens, Frances to Lewis Stevens 1-19-1844 (1-24-1844)
Stewart, Allice B. to A. R. Tatum 12-20-1869 (12-23-1869)

Stewart, C. V. to T. M. Melugin 12-11-1862
Stewart, Caroline C. to Andrew J. Williams 12-17-1846
Stewart, Caroline to Turner Earl 9-9-1870 (no return) B
Stewart, Catharine to John P. Hampton 8-23-1869 (8-26-1869)
Stewart, Elisabeth to John D. Braden 11-23-1848 (11-30?-1848)
Stewart, Fanny to Thomas Montague 2-26-1870 (2-27-1870) B
Stewart, Katie to Balam Boylan 2-18-1871 (no return) B
Stewart, L. A. to D. T. Jones 8-11-1869 (8-13-1869)
Stewart, Martha to J. C. Stevenson 8-12-1863
Stewart, Mattie M. to R. N. Parks 2-13-1860 (2-16-1860)
Stewart, Narcissa M. to John M. Morton 2-6-1841
Stewart, Rose to Harrison Brown 6-9-1868 (6-10-1868) B
Stewart, Susan A. to Saml. Jones 9-9-1867 (not endorsed)
Stidam, Sarah F. to James Price 12-14-1868 (12-16-1868)
Stidham, Mary J. to W. A. King 1-13-1868 (1-14-1868)
Stidham, Mary to G. W. S. Johnson 1-8-1845 (1-9-1845)
Stidham, Milla to Moses Gardner 9-13-1867 (no return) B
Stigall, Nancy to Joshua Roper 6-19-1844 (6-20-1844)
Stiger, Carolina E. to Wm. Pearson 3-13-1841 (no return)
Stockinger, Eliza D. to Nathan F. Plumer 10-26-1846 (11-5-1846)
Stockinger, M. A. to D. G. Hineman 2-9-1859
Stockinger, Margaret to David Fausett 4-27-1862 (4-30-1862)
Stokes, Sarah H. to Meredith Holmes 5-25-1838
Stone, Julina to William A. Baw 1-13-1852 (no return)
Stone, Lucinda F. to Sterling Farley 7-7-1847
Stone, Manerva Ann to William Farley 10-4-1848 (no return)
Stone, Martha D. to John R. Cherry 4-10-1849
Stone, Mary C. to Washington L. Row 12-7-1842 (12-20?-1842)
Stony, Ellen Elizabeth to S. M. Plant 7-19-1851 (no return)
Stovall, Mary to Thomas Harris 12-6-1842 (12-7-1842)
Stram, Sarah J. to Wm. M. Steward 12-14-1850 (12-17-1850)
Strickland, Candis to Dick Baker 4-4-1868 B
Strickland, Ellen to Anderson Teague 8-25-1866 (8-26-1866) B
Strickland, Laura to Cain Neville 9-7-1867 B
Strickland, Lucretia J. to B. H. Whittaker 1-18-1871
Strickland, Lucy J. to Jno. W. Whitaker 12-15-1868 (12-16-1868)
Strickland, Susan to James C. Martin 2-27-1869 (2-28-1869) B
Strickland, Susana to Bill Phillips 4-20-1867 B
Studivan, Nannie to Henry Robertson 3-2-1870 (3-7-1870) B
Suckett, Elizabeth to John Egan 1-6-1855 (no return)
Sugget, Virginia C. to Sam H. Smith 8-20-1855 (no return)
Suggett, Frances C. to Wm. W. Todd 8-26-1865
Sulivant, Rutha An to L. A. Buchanon 2-3-1848 (2-7-1848)
Sullivan, Frances A. to W. C. Slaughter 11-18-1867 (11-19-1867)
Sullivan, Katty to Richard McDonald 10-17-1868 B
Sullivan, L. F. to E. Ammons 12-9-1854 (no return)
Sullivan, Lydia to Isaac Kee 3-30-1844
Sullivan, Mary J. to J. H. Rose 10-28-1869 (10-31-1869)
Sullivan, Nancy E. to David McDonald 12-24-1866 (12-26-1866)
Sullivan, Polly to Jesse M. Morris 4-6-1850 (4-7-1850)
Sullivan, Rebecca M. to Enoch Sevier 1-5-1846 (1-6-1846)
Sullivan, Sarah E. to Blunt Harvey 3-4-1868 (3-10-1868)
Sullivan, Temperance J. to W. H. Hobson 4-27-1840 (5-2-1850)
Sullivan, Tennessee to James Gallagher 1-4-1870 (1-6-1869?)
Sullivant, Nancy to John W. Slater 2-24-1845 (no return)
Sumner, Alice to Tom Johnson 1-12-1871 (no return) B
Sumner, Martha A. to Jesse Redd 3-8-1859 (3-13-1859)
Sumner, Penelope to Wm. C. Jenkins 12-21-1840
Sumner, Sarah to John Bryant 3-5-1849 (3-11-1849)
Surpit, M. L. to Wm. J. Devenport 2-13-1849 (2-14-1849)
Sutherland, Ditha to Joe Morgan 9-12-1867
Sutherland, Selena C. (Mrs.) to Moses Lynch 12-31-1839
Sutherland, Susan J. to W. J. Devenport 3-28-1870 (3-29-1870)
Suttle, Martha D. to Robt. C. Buford 11-27-1848 (no return)
Swan, Darcas S. to J. T. Palmer 10-31-1839 (11-6-1839)
Swift, Ally C. to W. R. Webber 11-16-1867 (no return)
Swift, Eliza C. to Arther B. Jones 12-14-1852 (no return)
Swift, Frances to John Fraser 2-21-1867 (no return)
Swift, India M. to Henry D. Green 12-21-1859 (12-22-1859)
Swift, Marietta to Leland Trout 12-10-1866 (no return)
Swift, Martha A. to John A. Cole 3-13-1843 (3-22-1843)
Swift, Winney Ann to Ephraim Reed 1-7-1869 (2-4-1869) B
Talbott, Jane to Henry E. Wellborn 12-5-1853 (no return)
Talls (Falls?), Sallie J. to W. J. Stafford 1-25-1868 (no return)
Tanner, Caroline to Orrange Richards 10-29-1867 (10-30-1867) B

Tanner, Mary T. to Jas. H. Cobbs 4-11-1850
Tappan, Mariah to Matthew Brewer 3-1-1871 (3-2-1871) B
Tarley, Sallie F. to M. C. Scott 10-31-1867 (no return)
Tarry?, P. A. to Newton Johnson 9-8-1849 (no return)
Tate, Betsy to Henry Alexander 7-19-1867 (no return) B
Tate, Julia A. to Carter Morgan 4-5-1867 (no return) B
Tate, Margarett V. to William Johnson 5-25-1848 (5-31-1848)
Tatom, Rachael to Henry Thompson 12-6-1870 (12-21-1871) B
Tatom, Ruth to Giles Dennis 6-1-1868 (no return) B
Tatum, Cordelia to John Stevens 12-25-1866 (12-26-1866)
Tatum, Elizabeth J. to Samuel C. Brooks 3-23-1843 (3-24-1843)
Tatum, Emma L. to H. O. Norman 4-13-1860 (4-15-1860)
Tatum, Martha to Thomas Farley 10-6-1843 (10-10-1843)
Tatum, Mary E. to Wm. C. Linebarger 11-21-1865 (11-22-1865)
Tatum, Mary to John W. Baker 1-31-1842 (2-2-1842)
Tatum, Mary to Willis Dickinson 12-26-1868 B
Tatum, Rachel to Hamp Billeps 12-14-1869 (no return) B
Tatum, Rebeca to Joseph J. Farley 11-20-1840 (11-26-1840)
Tatum, Rebecca to George Golin 8-27-1869 (no return) B
Tatum, Tennessee to W. B. Williams 7-14-1849 (no return)
Taylor, Ann Jane to Robert Douglass 12-22-1866 (12-26-1866) B
Taylor, Bettie to Sam Adkins 4-6-1867 (4-7-1867) B
Taylor, Catharine to Jessee Stafford 10-17-1851 (no return)
Taylor, Cornelia to Charles Wainwright 4-23-1866 (4-28-1866) B
Taylor, Cressy to David Archer 12-26-1866 (12-28-1866) B
Taylor, E. Julia to Wm. M. Smith 9-22-1853 (no return)
Taylor, Ellen H. to J. M. Webb 11-17-1865 (11-20-1865)
Taylor, Ellen to Jack Dewitt 12-26-1870 (12-27-1870) B
Taylor, Emma to Michael Burrell 12-30-1868 (12-31-1868) B
Taylor, Fannie to Jim Taylor 4-18-1868 (no return) B
Taylor, Frankey to Wm. Jones 9-20-1867 (9-21-1867) B
Taylor, H. R. E. to John G. Martin 5-23-1859 (5-25-1859)
Taylor, Hardenia A. to H. G. Ballard 5-3-1847 (5-4-1847)
Taylor, Harriet to Sam Smith 9-6-1870 (9-21-1870) B
Taylor, Jenny to Ransom Lewis 4-4-1868 (4-5-1868) B
Taylor, Laura to Richmond Matthews 12-24-1868 (12-28-1868) B
Taylor, Lou to Davy Ross 12-23-1867 (12-27-1867) B
Taylor, Lucinda to Frank Tatum 3-31-1866 (4-1-1866) B
Taylor, Lucretia to David Madding 12-20-1869 (12-28-1869) B
Taylor, Lucy A. to Jackson Granberry 1-18-1868 (1-26-1868) B
Taylor, Lucy to Bill Anderson 4-5-1871 (4-6-1871) B
Taylor, Mariah to George Smith 9-11-1868 (9-26-1868) B
Taylor, Martha A. to Alvin E. Taylor 1-2-1860 (1-3-1860)
Taylor, Martha A. to Andrew A. Porter 10-17-1846 (10-22-1846)
Taylor, Martha A. to Lewis D. Fortner 12-16-1854 (no return)
Taylor, Mary Ann to Henry A. Rives 11-22-1838
Taylor, Mary F. to J. G. Chambers 8-3-1859
Taylor, Mary Jane to Granville H. Hogan 7-23-1845 (7-24-1845)
Taylor, Mary L. to J. W. Williamson 3-5-1860 (3-7-1860)
Taylor, Mary M. to Robert F. Allison 1-3-1871 (1-5-1871)
Taylor, Mary S. to Charles L. Read 7-20-1852 (no return)
Taylor, Mary S. to Frank Myers 11-13-1868 (11-15-1868)
Taylor, Mary to Thomas Humphrey 12-25-1869 (12-26-1869) B
Taylor, Nancy E. to Calvin C. Roycroft 11-30-1846 (12-2-1846)
Taylor, Nancy H. to William W. Walker 6-22-1848 (no return)
Taylor, Nancy to Archibald Bennett 7-25-1839
Taylor, Polly to William Hill 5-18-1866 (5-19-1866) B
Taylor, Puss to John Keer 3-4-1868 (3-7-1868) B
Taylor, Sallie P. to Wm. L. Williamson 3-5-1860 (3-7-1860)
Taylor, Sarah E. to C. W. Preston 12-19-1849 (12-22-1849)
Taylor, Sarah J. to W. P. Wilson 3-10-1855 (no return)
Taylor, Sarah M. to R. B. Alexander 3-29-1838
Taylor, Sarah O. to Wm. M. Scott 12-21-1844 (12-29-1844)
Taylor, Sarah to John Wilson 7-24-1869 (7-25-1869) B
Taylor, Sarah to Wm. H. Snoden 6-17-1844 (6-26-1844)
Taylor, Susan to William Miller 2-25-1871 (no return) B
Taylor, Veniann to Isaac Bowers 5-19-1868 B
Teage?, Catharine to Robertson Hood 10-10-1848
Teague, Emily to Milton H. Knox 12-30-1843 (no return)
Teague, Eveline to Daniel Jones 1-1-1867 B
Teague, Minerva to William M. Price 7-17-1846 (7-23-1846)
Teague, Sarahann to Jerome B. Gressom 7-16-1844 (no return)
Teams, L. A. to James Davis 12-9-1865 (12-10-1865)
Teller, Margarett E. to John A. Bryan 9-12-1854 (no return)
Temple, Sarah Ann to Sam Thompson 3-26-1868 (no return) B

Temple, Susan to Henry Warren 12-24-1869 (2-26-1870) B
Terrence, Mary E. to Henry E. Wade 12-19-1854 (no return)
Terrence, Sarah J. to Richard T. Wade 12-19-1853 (no return)
Terrill, Mary E. to L. S. Mayo 12-27-1850 (12-28-1850)
Thacker, Barthema to Samuel Crabtree 7-6-1844 (no return)
Tharp, Margaret to Geo. Saddler 1-23-1869 (no return) B
Tharp, Margaret to Thomas Cofield 3-9-1870 (no return) B
Tharp, Sarah Jane to Thos. W. Shore 3-12-1842 (3-15-1842)
Tharp, Susan to Nelson Wall 8-3-1847 (8-11-1847)
Thomas, B. A. to R. C. Stone 12-31-1866 (1-3-1867)
Thomas, Caroline S. to Thomas Shelton 2-5-1840 (2-7-1840)
Thomas, Elizabeth to Augustus Hatcher 1-11-1868 (1-12-1868) B
Thomas, F. A. to Thos. Hemly 12-23-1851 (no return)
Thomas, Flora to Franklin Taylor 12-21-1868 (12-25-1868) B
Thomas, H. E. to B. D. Shafnor 8-22-1849 (no return)
Thomas, Liza Jane to James Comer 8-5-1867 (8-9-1867) B
Thomas, Lucy Ann to John L. Davis 12-2-1844 (12-20-1844)
Thomas, M. to M. McCray 10-26-1869 (10-28-1869)
Thomas, Margarett Ann to Abner D. Thomas 2-12-1845 (no return)
Thomas, Martha R. to R. N. Nesbitt 1-3-1855 (no return)
Thomas, Mary C. to Wm. Polk 7-23-1839 (7-30-1839)
Thomas, Mattie to William Thomas 10-24-1870 B
Thomas, Rebecca T. to Joseph R. Parker 2-13-1860
Thomas, Z. A. to James H. Griffin 1-6-1851 (no return)
Thomason, Elvyra to Simion Morris 12-20-1845 (12-23-1845)
Thompson, Almeter to W. B. Simmons 1-20-1852 (no return)
Thompson, Ann E. to D. M. Barwell 10-8-1860 (10-24-1860)
Thompson, Cyntha to Fountain McGehee 1-13-1839 (1-24-1839)
Thompson, Cynthia to Fountain McGehee 1-13-1839 (no return)
Thompson, Cynthia to Robertson Murrell 1-21-1867 (1-22-1867) B
Thompson, E. A. C. to John S. R. Cowan 2-8-1869 (2-10-1869)
Thompson, Edie to William Littleton 12-29-1870 (no return) B
Thompson, Jane to William Clark 6-30-1866 (no return) B
Thompson, Julia A. to John A. Anderson 12-13-1870 (12-17-1870) B
Thompson, Margaret to J. W. Thomas 2-27-1865
Thompson, Margarett to Benjamin Frierson 12-24-1870
  (no return) B
Thompson, Martha G. to W. C. Johnson 6-1-1867 (6-2-1867)
Thompson, Martha to Jas. T. Simmons 10-7-1851 (no return)
Thompson, Mary Ann to Hugh D. Moore 6-20-1844
Thompson, Mary to Lawrence A. Campbell 4-26-1869 (4-27-1869)
Thompson, Mary to Taylor Malone 2-28-1870 (3-2-1870)
Thompson, Mary to Thomas Allen 1-7-1869 B
Thompson, Minta to John Woodfin 4-4-1868 B
Thompson, Mollie D. to Frank M. Taylor 11-24-1868 (11-26-1868)
Thompson, Nancy to James C. Merrick 4-17-1839 (4-21-1839)
Thompson, Nannie J. to A. J. Ivy 1-21-1867 (1-24-1867)
Thompson, Patsey to James Madison 2-1-1867 (2-16-1867) B
Thompson, Tilda to Henry Palmer 1-3-1868 (1-11-1868) B
Thornton, Bettie to Wash Thurman 8-26-1869 (8-28-1869) B
Thornton, L. to George Williamson 7-21-1866 (7-22-1866)
Thornton, Lucinda to Zeb Pulliam 1-22-1866 (2-28-1866) B
Thornton, Mina to Campbell Pulliam 12-18-1865 (12-26-1865) B
Thornton, Sallie F. to A. H. Thornton 5-2-1866 (5-3-1866)
Thornton, Sarah Ann to Peterson Mosley 9-11-1838
Thornton?, Martha E. to Abraham W. Berry 5-20-1849
Thorp, Rebecca Jane to James P. O'Kelley 9-25-1843 (10-3-1843)
Thorpe, Virginia to J. M. Farley 12-29-1870 (no return)
Thrift, Eliza S.? to John C. Marler 1-1-1841 (1-5-1841)
Tidwell, Eliza J. to Wm. H. Rains 8-1-1848 (no return)
Tiller, Lavinia F. to James D. Bryant 1-27-1852 (no return)
Tiller, R. J. to John F. Able 10-19-1867 (10-23-1867)
Tillman, Rebecca B. to B. F. Pennington 1-11-1853 (no return)
Tilman, Sarah C. to Alen R. Luck 11-26-1849 (12-5-1849)
Tipton, Lucretia to B. Brewer 10-30-1849 (11-2-1849)
Titcomb, Betsy to Heyborrow? Thompson 5-19-1866 (no return) B
Todd, L. J. to J. L. Todd 3-3-1866 (3-4-1866)
Tolbert, Rebecca to John Noel 4-26-1845 (4-27-1845)
Tomblinson, Ellen J. to W. L. Burnett 12-20-1852 (no return)
Tomlin, L. C. to L. C. Crenshaw 5-16-1867
Tomlinson, C. A. to H. P. Guy 8-9-1854 (no return)
Tomlinson, Catharine E. to T. G. Benchbark 7-8-1852 (no return)
Tomlinson, E. J. to John Guy 7-3-1849 (7-11-1849)
Torrance, Julia Ann to James Welborn Teague 12-18-1860
  (12-19-1860)

Torrence, Malinda to G. Graves 9-22-1849 (11-27-1849)
Torrence, Nancy to Robert Flemming 2-21-1859 (2-23-1859)
Towls, Lucey A. to E.H. Freear 4-29-1853 (no return)
Trainer, Sarah A. to Adolphus B. Wilson 2-22-1869 (2-24-1869)
Traylor, Caraline to Charles A. Combes 1-26-1848 (1-27-1848)
Trent, Emily to Wesley Baxter 7-6-1867 (7-7-1867) B
Trent, Jennie to Henry Stainback 7-13-1866 (not executed) B
Trent, Louisa C. to James A. Anderson 5-24-1852 (no return)
Trent, Maggie to W. C. (Rev.) Gray 5-11-1863 (5-20-1863)
Trent, Tabby to Dandrage Farris 12-1-1868 (12-27-1868) B
Trezvant, Lucyann to James T. Fuller 7-25-1848 (no return)
Trip, Amanda to Horace Williamson 2-10-1866 (2-17-1866) B
Trip, Mary Jane to Lewis Miller 12-25-1867 (12-28-1867) B
Tripp, Amelia to James Beasley 2-23-1867 (3-4-1867) B
Tripp, C. S. to J. P. Hilliard 3-24-1866 (3-29-1866)
Trotter, Caroline to John H. Boult 12-9-1839 (12-19-1839)
Trotter, Cornelia F. to James S. Evans 1-28-1851 (1-29-1851)
Trotter, Elizabeth J. to Thomas L. Organ 10-1-1844 (10-9-1844)
Trotter, Frances E. to Zachary Shaw 3-20-1855 (no return)
Trotter, Manervy Ann to Presley D. Boyed 10-28-1852 (no return)
Trotter, Martha A. to C. B. Mayo 4-1-1850 (4-9-1850)
Trotter, Mary Eliza to C. W. Richardson 2-17-1845 (no return)
Trotter, Mary V. to J. T. Z. Hilliard 9-24-1860 (9-25-1860)
Trotter, Matilda P. to Richard Vaughan 1-8-1840 (1-10-1840)
Trousdale, Candis to Henry Seymour 12-29-1868 B
Trousdale, Emily to Caswell Edwards 1-7-1867 B
Tucker, Addie A. to M. Rhea 12-14-1870
Tucker, Ann E. to David E. Palmer 1-27-1852 (no return)
Tucker, Catherine to Charley Mitchel 12-24-1868 (12-26-1868) B
Tucker, Clara to Wm. Poindexter 8-10-1866 (8-12-1866) B
Tucker, Lina to Isiah Boylan 4-8-1871 (no return) B
Tucker, Martha to E. O. Shelton 10-8-1849 (10-17-1849)
Tucker, Mary E. to Wiley Durden 11-14-1870 (11-15-1870)
Tucker, Mat to Geo. Poindexter 1-1-1868 (1-2-1868) B
Tucker, Nerva to Adam Brown 7-13-1867 (8-3-1867) B
Tucker, Polly A. to Joshua Macklin 12-24-1870 (no return) B
Tucker, Rose to John Cabness 3-17-1869 (no return) B
Tucker, Sallie Ann to Jessie Tucker 4-10-1869 (4-11-1869) B
Tucker, Sally Anna to Phillip Young 12-24-1866 (no return) B
Tucker, Sally to Henry Ashley 2-18-1869 (2-21-1869) B
Tuckniss, Jennie R. to A. T. Hilliard 12-1-1866 (12-2-1866)
Tumbough, Charity to P. M. Tipton 8-3-1843
Turbeville, Oliver B. to Thomas P. Hare 1-10-1848 (1-13-1848)
Turnage, Adeline to Frank Seward 2-17-1869 (2-21-1869) B
Turnbow, Alletha T. to G. W. Tatum 9-28-1852 (no return)
Turner, D. T. to H. C. Tomlinson 6-14-1865 (6-15-1865)
Turner, Estell to Thos. A. Ewell 2-9-1870 (2-10-1870) B
Turner, Fanny to William Smith 2-17-1869 (2-20-1869) B
Turner, Louisa to Daniel Webster 12-25-1869 (12-31-1869) B
Turner, Margaret E. to John W. Summers 10-1-1870 (10-6-1870) B
Turner, Mary Jane to William J. Miller 3-9-1852 (no return)
Turner, Missouri S. to Rodwier? J. Boyers 5-19-1843 (5-21-1843)
Turnley, Emeline to Ned Jones 1-11-1868 B
Turnley, Kittie to James Taylor 5-18-1867 B
Turnley, Leathy to Alfred Pearson 10-19-1867 B
Upshaw, Ann E. to A. H. Adams 12-3-1847
Van Campen, Ellen to Joseph Frothschild 9-18-1866 (9-20-1866)
Vanpelt, Cora A. to J. K. Morris 10-25-1869 (11-26-1869)
Vanpelt, Lydia to David Haney 10-1-1869 (10-2-1869) B
Vaughan, Clara A. to Geo. W. Jackson 1-7-1847 (1-14-1847)
Vaughn, Jerusha to Thomas Willson 4-25-1843 (4-27-1843)
Vaughn, Mary Jane to J. B. Chaffin 11-30-1838 (no return)
Vaughn, Matilda P. to M. High 1-11-1851 (1-16-1851)
Vincent, E. C. to J. G. Wells 2-9-1842 (2-10-1842)
Wacker, Sarah Jane to John Motley 10-21-1839 (no return)
Wade, Beckey to Adrian Hood 7-10-1868 (no return) B
Wade, E. F. to M. L. Chambers 10-24-1859 (10-26-1859)
Wade, Liza to York Londa 7-13-1867 B
Wade, Lucinda to John Deener 1-7-1869 (no return) B
Wade, Mandy to Jesse B. Curl 2-20-1847 (3-10-1847)
Wade, Mary to Henry C. Bert? 10-26-1844 (10-31-1844)
Wade, Sallie Ann to R. E. Hughes 12-18-1868 (12-20-1868)
Wade, Sally to George Ozier 1-25-1871 (1-26-1871) B
Wainwright, Cornelia to Matthews Crawford 12-29-1868 B
Wainwright, Sarah (Mrs.) to Wm. Mavis 7-17-1855 (no return)

Walker, Ada to Simon Crawford 7-16-1870 (no return) B
Walker, Amanda M. to Joseph W. O'Brian 3-16-1847 (4-19-1847)
Walker, Amanda to Lee Green 2-12-1870 (2-25-1870) B
Walker, Angeline to A. Cartwright 1-19-1869 (2-5-1869) B
Walker, Artelia E. to Samuel Whorton 9-14-1852 (no return)
Walker, Charity to Caswell Shaw 3-3-1866 (3-5-1866) B
Walker, Daffne to Dee Caruthers 1-17-1868 B
Walker, Eliza to George Williamson 3-30-1867 (4-7-1867) B
Walker, Elizabeth A. to James L. Harvy 11-14-1842 (11-15-1842)
Walker, Emily to Albert Neal 3-20-1871 (no return) B
Walker, Fanny to James Maberry 2-9-1867 (2-16-1867) B
Walker, Georgeann to Levi Kitchem 1-19-1844
Walker, Helen to Champ Hubbard 10-4-1869 (no return) B
Walker, Hester to John Baker 10-19-1868 (10-30-1868) B
Walker, Louisa to L. Black 8-14-1854 (no return)
Walker, Lucy to Antny Turner 1-28-1870 (1-30-1870) B
Walker, Lucy to George Carnes 4-28-1866 (5-13-1866)
Walker, M. C. to H. H. Mitchell 12-12-1860 (12-13-1860)
Walker, Mariah to Charles Beasley 12-12-1868 (12-13-1868) B
Walker, Mary Ann to A. W. Caldwell 11-2-1868 (no return)
Walker, Mary C. to R. R. Ridley 9-10-1851 (no return)
Walker, Mary Catharine to R. W. Floyed 4-13-1852 (no return)
Walker, Miss to Providence Williams 2-5-1838 (no return)
Walker, Nancy M. to William M. McFerren 11-20-1852 (no return)
Walker, Pricilla S. to David Adams 9-19-1855 (no return)
Walker, Roxanna to T. W. Scott 8-11-1853 (no return)
Walker, Susan M. to William Smith 1-5-1852 (no return)
Walker, V. C. to H. H. Mitchell 12-30-1866 (1-3-1866)
Wall, Elizabeth A. to John S. Herndon 11-5-1862 (11-6-1862)
Wall, Louiza E. to Jeremiah Frazure 11-13-1851 (no return)
Wall, M. A. to James A. Seymour 11-7-1854 (no return)
Wall, Margaret M. to William C. Allen 12-23-1847
Wall, Margaret R. to Wm. T. Humphreys 11-2-1850 (no return)
Wall, Margarett A. to James M. Gilliam 1-16-1843 (1-17-1843)
Wall, Martha J. to A. G. Holt 10-28-1847 (no return)
Wall, Mary E. to Wyatt B. Watkins 8-23-1853 (no return)
Wall, Sarah A. to J. B. Crawford 4-21-1859 (4-20?-1859)
Wall, Sinia E. to William H. Hester 4-3-1841 (4-5-1841)
Wall, Tempy to J. P. O'Kelly 8-18-1859 (8-21-1859)
Wallace, Margarett to George W. Carroll 12-21-1870 (12-22-1870)
Wallace, Nancy to H. T. Willingham 11-8-1847 (11-9-1847)
Wallace, Sarah to Geo. W. Bill 7-10-1850 (no return)
Waller, Billy to Jas. Abington 12-12-1851 (no return)
Waller, Lucinda to Irwin Parrott 3-4-1846 (3-5-1846)
Waller, Lucy Janie to James W. Thompson 2-9-1839 (2-12-1839)
Waller, M. N. to N. P. Ferrell 10-2-1854 (no return)
Waller, Malinda to Willis Walton 12-11-1860
Waller, Margaret E. (Mrs.) to J. Parrott 12-11-1854 (no return)
Waller, Martha E. to Absolum C. Ralph 7-28-1852 (no return)
Waller, Martha F. to Edward G. Waller 2-7-1845 (2-18-1845)
Waller, Susan A. to L. G. Waller 4-27-1846 (5-3-1846)
Walls, Jane to Henry Washington 12-28-1868 (1-18-1869) B
Walton, America to Willis Stafford 8-16-1866 (no return) B
Walton, Lucy to Thomas Walton 1-9-1867 (1-17-1867) B
Walton, Sarah to M. L. Davis 1-19-1854 (no return)
Ward, Barbary A. to Thos. F. Babbett 5-16-1860
Ward, Martha R. to Daniel B. Jack 1-21-1871 (1-24-1871)
Ward, Mary Ann to James Lashley 8-17-1840
Ward, Mary to John Cunningham 12-27-1869 (12-28-1869) B
Ward, Rena to Henry Rhodes 11-13-1868 (11-16-1868) B
Ward, S. D. to T. F. Bobbitt 1-6-1871 (1-10-1871)
Ward, Sarah Ann to James A. Todd 9-3-1844 (9-4-1846)
Warden, Barbery to John A. Wesson 7-19-1849
Ware, Ann T. J. to Starkey S. Hare 8-15-1846 (8-18-1846)
Ware, Sarah Ann to James A. Todd 9-3-1846 (no return)
Warford, Duann W. to Thos. J. Ready 9-18-1855 (no return)
Warford, Nancy to Sam Phillips 1-31-1870 (2-1-1870) B
Warr, Clary to George Washington 9-11-1869 (9-26-1869) B
Warr, Lizzie Ann to Calvin Culpepper 7-2-1870 (no return)
Warran, Rosanna to Henry Nickolson 9-26-1868 (no return) B
Warren, Amanda to Joseph Brown 12-24-1870 (12-25-1870) B
Warren, Anna to Andrew Pearce 12-25-1868 (no return) B
Warren, Anna to James M. Murray 12-22-1870
Warren, Bettie to Henry Johnson 12-24-1869 (no return) B
Warren, Caroline to Perry Warren 12-3-1866 (12-8-1866) B

Warren, M. F. to A. J. Connell 10-5-1868 (no return)
Warren, Mary to Green Wirt 1-2-1866 (no return) B
Warren, Mira to Ed Gant 3-1-1871 (3-3-1871) B
Warren, Mollie to LeGrand Ross 12-18-1866 (12-19-1866) B
Warren, Nancy to Thomas Williams 1-21-1870 (2-19-1870) B
Warren, Narsissa J. to Thomas B. Yancy 4-13-1871
Warren, Pink to John Thomas 9-7-1867 (no return) B
Warren, Rosa to Joe Harrison 12-27-1865 (12-30-1865) B
Warren, Sarah to James Farrell 8-4-1866 (no return)
Wash, Elizabeth G. to H. B. Baty 12-18-1838 (12-20-1838)
Washington, Frances to Harrison Graham 1-2-1871 (1-4-1871)
Washington, Rebeca M. to Peter M. Dupree 11-21-1840 (11-25-1840)
Watkins, Amy to Wm. Moore 10-30-1868 (10-31-1868) B
Watkins, Ann R. to J. J. Williams 10-30-1865 (10-31-1865)
Watkins, Betsy to John Ragland 12-28-1865 (12-30-1865) B
Watkins, Catharine T. to E. M. Leake 3-20-1844 (no return)
Watkins, Elnory E. to Jonathan T. Bryan 3-23-1844 (3-28-1844)
Watkins, Frances J. to J. G. Crossett 1-18-1854 (no return)
Watkins, Jane E. to Wm. C. Viser 6-25-1844 (no return)
Watkins, Margarett to Robert M. Bondurant 7-2-1847 (no return)
Watkins, Mary J. to Saml. M. Neel 11-28-1866
Watkins, Milly to Henry Allen 9-25-1869 (no return) B
Watkins, N. J. to T. J. Cook 11-5-1867 (no return)
Watkins, Sarah A. to Daniel Johnson 2-11-1871 (2-16-1871) B
Watkins, Sarah T. to Samuel A. Grable 3-28-1862 (4-4-1862)
Watson, Agnes to Daniel Baker 12-17-1868 (12-25-1868) B
Watson, Eliza to David L. Perkins 12-20-1852 (no return)
Watson, Ida to Finis Bowers 12-26-1870 (no return) B
Watson, Mary Ann to Benjamin F. Moore 2-9-1869 (2-11-1869)
Watson, Ruth to Thomas McFadden 11-10-1838
Watson, Sarah C. to William Burton 8-23-1848
Watson, Sarah E. to Jno. M. McFadden 1-8-1846
Watson, Susan Ann to John H. Simison 11-9-1847
Watters, Eliza H. to James A. Gober 8-6-1845 (8-7-1845)
Watterson?, Margaret to Anderson Wilson 2-1-1870 (no return) B
Watts, Mary W. to William M. Allen 12-2-1847 (12-14-1848?)
Weaver, N. A. to K. J. Watson 9-12-1849 (9-13-1849)
Webb, America to Saml. A. Perry 10-5-1846 (no return)
Webb, Callie to W. G. Herron 1-15-1868 (1-16-1868)
Webb, E. A. to John Perry 1-31-1850
Webb, Elizabeth to N. R. Stewart 12-29-1855 (no return)
Webb, Ellen to C. C. Daniels 1-23-1867 (1-24-1867)
Webb, Emily to Robt. Allen 12-20-1848
Webb, Fannie G. to Henry T. Forbes 9-12-1855 (no return)
Webb, Lucinda to A. T. Booker 1-21-1845 (no return)
Webb, Malissa to Charles J. Shaw 1-19-1848 (1-20-1848)
Webb, Mary Ann to E. W. Newborn 3-23-1869
Webb, Mary to Clark Bryant 6-15-1867 (6-20-1867) B
Webb, Mary to R. W. Lynch 6-3-1854 (no return)
Webb, Sarah Ann to G. B. Payne 12-4-1869 (12-22-1869)
Webb, Sarah to Frank Carroll 7-17-1866 (7-26-1866)
Webber, M. L. to F. B. Crenshaw 7-11-1859 (7-13-1859)
Webster, Martha J. to James M. Gardner 5-13-1869 (5-17-1869)
Webster, Martha to James Bankhead 2-5-1845 (2-6-1845)
Webster, Mary V. to David C. White 1-8-1848 (1-13-1848)
Wellar, Virginia to John W. Dyer 1-29-1849 (1-30-1849)
Weller, Mary Ann to Richd. Brinkley 12-26-1848 (no return)
Wells, Dora to Granville Tharp 12-14-1870 B
Wells, Harriet E. to J. W. Temple 12-17-1862 (12-28-1862)
Wells, Martha P. to John Burton 6-28-1839 (6-29-1839)
Wells, Mollie F. to Aaron T. Sanders 1-18-1870 (1-19-1870)
Wells, Mollie R. J. to Isaac A. Williams 12-25-1866 (12-28-1866)
Wells, Rosina to W. F. Harwell 11-15-1865 (11-21-1865)
Wells, Sarah to Rolla Poindexter 12-12-1854 (no return)
Wells, Sophia Ann to Mike Lucas 4-5-1869 (4-6-1869)
Wesson, Lucy M. to F. A. Lock 3-12-1853 (no return)
Wesson, Mary Ann to George W. Wesson 2-11-1851 (2-14-1851)
West, Rosa to Jas. K. Johnson 1-8-1867 (no return)
West, Sarah J. to A. R. Vick 10-21-1859
Westbrook, Levinia to John Davis 12-29-1846 (12-31-1846)
Westmoreland, Lucy to Ephraim Evans 2-1-1871 (2-6-1871) B
Weston, F. D. to C. A. Foster 12-4-1838 (1-22-1839)
Wheeler, Tonser to Wm. P. Hutchins 11-3-1866 (11-4-1866)
Whitaker, Mary M. to Phillip Catnar 11-14-1848 (11-16-1848)
Whitaker, Nannie to E. D. Peebles 4-27-1859 (4-28-1859)

White, Ann C. (Mrs.) to Benj. H.? Legon 5-11-1855 (no return)
White, Ann to William Ligon 3-15-1867 (3-17-1867) B
White, Arbella to W. P. Dickson 10-13-1870 B
White, Elizabeth to George W. Stricklin 9-30-1843 (no return)
White, L. A. to E. H. Chaffin 2-9-1854 (no return)
White, Lanith to G. B. Frazier 11-13-1855 (no return)
White, Leathy to Reuben Beasley 12-3-1870 (12-29-1870) B
White, Mary to Calvin Roberts 12-29-1866 (12-31-1866) B
White, Sallie J. to Robt. W. Norment 11-25-1867 (11-28-1867)
Whitehead, Elizabeth Jane to William Clark 1-29-1839
Whitehead, J. A. R. to J. C. Davison 9-25-1848 (9-28-1848)
Whitehead, Judy? to W. P. Morris? 11-23-1849
Whitehead, M. to John Jordan 12-11-1847 (12-16-1847)
Whitehead, R. F. to Thomas J. Smith 9-6-1853 (no return)
Whitehead, Temperance to William Teague 12-6-1845 (12-11-1845)
Whitfield, Nancy ann to Charles B. Whitson 2-13-1855 (no return)
Whitmore, Eliza A. L. to Edward Ragsdale 8-20-1855 (no return)
Whitmore, Lizzie A. to Jerry Bracken 1-1-1868 (2-3-1868) B
Whitmore, Lucy to Patrick Thornton 7-26-1867 (7-27-1867) B
Whitmore, Mary E. to Peter A. Vaughn 12-18-1848 (1-2-1849)
Whitmore, Sally P. to Newel W. Harris 10-4-1852 (no return)
Whitmore, Susan P. to W. H. (Dr.) Tharp 11-22-1852 (no return)
Whitmore, Virginia to J. M. A. Scales 9-16-1854 (no return)
Whitney, Jane to Matthew Bronte 8-2-1842
Whitney, Martha C. to Benj. F. Powers 10-7-1850 (10-6?-1850)
Whitney, Virginia to John Triller? 4-22-1853 (no return)
Whitt, Ellen to Owen Ligon 12-27-1866 B
Whittaker, Sarah E. to F. J. Izard 5-2-1854 (no return)
Whitten, Mary Jane to Edward A. Anderson 11-9-1846 (11-12-1846)
Whitthorn, Ann to Nelson Wells 12-27-1869 B
Whitthorne, Annie to John W. Wright 12-26-1870 (1-5-1871)
Whitton, Rebecca Ann to Sam Dishourgh 8-10-1844 (8-13-1844)
Whyte, M. D. C. to Benjamin W. Evans 3-19-1839 (3-21-1839)
Whyte, Phereby to R. B. Stover 9-8-1866 (9-10-1866)
Wiggins, Annie E. to Thomas J. Warr 11-21-1865 (no return)
Wiggins, R. E. to H. B. Waller 12-14-1869 (no return)
Wigglesworth, Edmonia to Baker Mebane 12-29-1870 (no return) B
Wilborn, Nannie to John Calhoon Davis 1-5-1854 (no return)
Wilborne, J. P. to Meshack Franklin 4-26-1866 (5-2-1866)
Wilbourn, M. D. to J. C. Word 2-4-1864 (2-10-1864)
Wilburn, Sarah E. to Sampson Lane 9-7-1854 (no return)
Wilds, Elizabeth to W. J. Rogers 1-15-1866 (1-18-1866)
Wiles, Adaline R. to John H. Trainer 1-23-1867 (1-24-1867)
Wiley, Elizabeth J. to J. P. Love 3-22-1855 (no return)
Wiley, July Ann to Wm. Smith 10-1-1849 (10-2-1849)
Wilkerson, Mary to Elijah Gwyn 12-28-1868 (12-5?-1868) B
Wilkerson, Missouri A. J. C. to Jos. D. Parham 3-26-1851 (no return)
Wilkerson, Susan to N. Gwynn 8-10-1866 (8-12-1866) B
Wilkerson?, Nancy to Joseph Cheairs 11-7-1842 (no return)
Wilkes, Emily to Pleasant Batts 1-26-1871 (1-28-1871) B
Wilkins, Ann Eliza to John Holden 12-11-1841
Wilkins, Henrietta O. to Benjamin Houston 10-27-1845 (10-29-1845)
Wilkins, Mary J. to John Thompson 11-10-1843 (no return)
Wilkinson, Willie to Wm. E. Franklin 2-7-1871 (2-8-1871)
Wilks, Manerva to Baker Dandridge 8-26-1865
Williams, Amanda to Munroe Mitchell 12-27-1870 (12-28-1870) B
Williams, Ann E. to William H. Devereux 11-18-1852 (no return)
Williams, Annie to George Braden 8-9-1867 (8-10-1867) B
Williams, Catharine to Millard Murrell 3-1-1870 (9-?-1870) B
Williams, E. A. to Doctr. G. T. Steele 9-4-1851 (no return)
Williams, Edney J. to James J. Brownlow 7-13-1840 (no return)
Williams, Ela Ann to Edmond Kelley 7-5-1838
Williams, Elizabeth to W. H. Hill 12-27-1845 (12-28-1845)
Williams, Emily to Claude Williams 1-23-1866 (no return) B
Williams, Emily to Isaac Tappan 1-4-1867 B
Williams, Emma J. to Wm. C. Elliot 12-17-1870 (12-22-1870)
Williams, Eugenia to William Rogers 1-30-1867
Williams, Fannie to Henry Ross 5-8-1869 (no return) B
Williams, J. E. to E. J. Pearsall 5-14-1850 (5-16-1850)
Williams, Jennie to Belton Brown 9-17-1868 (9?-19-1868)
Williams, Julia A. to George W. Holliday 8-6-1847 (8-15-1847)
Williams, Kitty to Andy McKinley 1-17-1871 B
Williams, L. A. to E. D. B. Rives 12-27-1854 (no return)
Williams, Lizzie to Ben Sherrod 8-31-1867 (no return) B
Williams, Louisa to Henry Clayton 1-14-1869 (1-16-1869) B

Williams, Lucinda to Epps Walker 10-30-1869 B
Williams, Lucy to Mack Jordan 4-24-1869 (4-29-1869) B
Williams, Lydia to John Granberry 12-25-1866 (12-27-1866) B
Williams, M. W. to J. D. Taylor 1-6-1862 (1-8-1862)
Williams, Maggie E. to Levin Lake 10-28-1864 (10-29-1864)
Williams, Margaret to John Smith 10-23-1869 (10-24-1869)
Williams, Margaret to March Morris 1-2-1868 (1-5-1868) B
Williams, Marth M. to Henry Lee 10-11-1854 (no return)
Williams, Martha A. to Isaac O. Sawyers 5-9-1848 (5-10-1848)
Williams, Martha J. to Thos. H. Tiller 11-7-1868 (11-9-1868)
Williams, Martha Jane to H. Harris 7-30-1851 (no return)
Williams, Martha P. to Augustus Kelly 7-20-1846 (7-23-1846)
Williams, Martha to Nickolas Mason 12-24-1868 (12-26-1868) B
Williams, Martha to O. B. Parker 10-5-1840 (10-6-1840)
Williams, Martha to Thos. J. Strong 11-11-1870 (11-16-1870)
Williams, Mary F. to Samuel O. Ballard 3-25-1841
Williams, Mary Jane to Jacob Stone 5-30-1842
Williams, Mary L. to Nathan M. Peoples 2-12-1851 (no return)
Williams, Mary S. to Nathan M. Peoples 11-19-1850 (license lost)
Williams, Mary V. to James Marsden 5-23-1842 (5-24-1842)
Williams, Mary to Henry Guy 7-5-1870 (7-17-1870)
Williams, Mary to Jeff Porter 5-3-1870 (no return) B
Williams, Mary to Robert Tucker 12-25-1868 (12-26-1868) B
Williams, Mary to V. Dozier 3-1-1854 (no return)
Williams, Maryann to Smith C. Belote 7-10-1848 (no return)
Williams, Nancy J. to Nelson Hunter 2-13-1868 (no return) B
Williams, Nancy to P. L. Dowdy 4-7-1842 (4-13-1842)
Williams, Pheriba to J. Q. Shaw 7-13-1841 (7-14-1841)
Williams, Phillis to Ned Oldham 12-26-1866 (12-28-1866) B
Williams, Polly to Albert Ross 11-4-1869 (no return) B
Williams, Rebecca O. to Samel M. Kerr 12-21-1850 (12-25-1850)
Williams, Roanna to J. G. Smithwick 5-24-1850 (5-26-1850)
Williams, Sanna? to Joe Williams 9-21-1867 (9-22-1867) B
Williams, Sarah Jane to A. Manning 2-14-1852 (no return)
Williams, Susan An to John Pouge? 12-22-1849 (12-23-1849)
Williams, Susan to Abraham Eaton 1-18-1847 (no return)
Williams, Susan to Isaac Hudson 12-30-1868 (12-31-1868) B
Williams, Susanah E. to James M. Godby 9-14-1852 (no return)
Williams, Susie E. to J. D. Montgomery 11-15-1869 (11-18-1869)
Williams, Tempy R. to James M. Duke 1-28-1854 (no return)
Williams, Tennessee Ann to Brown Belote 8-28-1846 (no return)
Williams, Tennessee Ann to Henry W. Yarbrough 2-14-1846 (no return)
Williams, Virginia to Wm. Dickinson 12-27-1865 (12-28-1865) B
Williamson, Adaline to Jesse Wood 10-19-1867 (10-20-1867) B
Williamson, Anna M. to C. W. Cherry 7-17-1849 (7-18-1849)
Williamson, Annette to John Hall 6-23-1866 B
Williamson, Annie C. to R. S. Parham 2-23-1853 (no return)
Williamson, Burda to Henry Tilson 4-1-1871 (4-2-1871) B
Williamson, Caroline to Fielding C. Gardner 5-21-1839 (5-25-1839)
Williamson, Cinthey to John Mills 10-14-1847
Williamson, Cordelia to Thos. W. Jones 5-29-1866
Williamson, Cornelia to Henry Cocke 1-23-1869 B
Williamson, Eliza to Willis Williamson 5-25-1867 B
Williamson, Fannie to Hilliard Revis 1-11-1868 (1-12-1868) B
Williamson, Frances to Buck Williamson 1-13-1866 (1-14-1866) B
Williamson, H. L. to D. J. Meriwether 4-2-1860 (4-4-1860)
Williamson, Jane to Bob Rhodes 1-15-1868 (1-16-1868) B
Williamson, Julia to George Henderson 12-27-1869 B
Williamson, Julia to Wiley Rivers 1-24-1871 (2-2-1871) B
Williamson, Laura to Tom Prince 8-3-1867 (no return) B
Williamson, Louisa to Isaac Allen 1-16-1871 (1-19-1871) B
Williamson, Louisa to Joe Matthews 9-5-1868 (9-6-1868) B
Williamson, Lucy L. to John B. Fields 1-3-1868 (1-9-1868)
Williamson, Lydia A. to Jim Shaw 2-8-1870 (2-10-1870) B
Williamson, M. A. to J. Q. Murrell 8-30-1859 (8-31-1859)
Williamson, Mag to Lewis Jones 4-24-1867 (no return) B
Williamson, Margaret J. to J. M. Johnson 1-10-1849 (1-11-1849)
Williamson, Martha to Jacob Pegees 4-18-1867 B
Williamson, Martha to James L. Penn 6-4-1851
Williamson, Martha to Miles Warr 5-5-1871 (5-6-1871) B
Williamson, Mary J. (Mrs.) to George Wood 6-8-1853 (no return)
Williamson, Matilda to Cater Williamson 3-19-1866 B
Williamson, May E. to Mac McCay Mitchell 10-26-1867 (10-29-1867) B

Williamson, Minerva to Fil Chester 5-11-1868 (no return) B
Williamson, Nancy P. to A. J. Anderson 7-4-1853 (no return)
Williamson, Nancy to Wesley Dickinson 3-16-1867 B
Williamson, Priscilla A. to W. E. Stainback 4-25-1865 (4-26-1865)
Williamson, Priscilla B. to R. S. Parham 11-25-1854 (no return)
Williamson, Sallie T. to J. L. Granberry 10-9-1865 (10-12-1865)
Williamson, Sarah to Simon Rhodes 1-15-1868 (1-16-1868) B
Williamson, Susan to Lott Pagie 3-29-1871 B
Williamson, Tempy to Fayette Jones 12-25-1866 (12-29-1866) B
Williamson, Vic to Monroe Thompson 12-25-1867 B
Williamson, Willie Ann to Peter Price 2-4-1871 (no return) B
Willingham, Nancy T. to Francis C. Folkner 11-10-1855 (no return)
Willis, Nancy A. to J. W. T. Hilliard 9-16-1854 (no return)
Willis, Rebeca to Boyed Williams 2-13-1839 (2-14-1839)
Willis, Sarah F to Jas. P. Smith 3-12-1868 (no return) B
Willis, Susan to Gabriel Jackson 11-20-1841 (11-23-1841)
Wills, Artelia J. to Thomas J. Graves 1-28-1840 (1-30-1840)
Wills, Frances to Briggs Gantling 1-12-1839 (1-15-1839)
Wills, Lizzie to Tom Ewing 12-23-1866 (12-29-1865?) B
Willson, Betsey to George Tyler 1-2-1869 B
Willson, Sarah A. to James H. Melton 3-16-1853 (no return)
Wilson, Annis to John W. Lawrence 12-14-1841 (12-21-1841)
Wilson, E. J. to H. J. Wiles 3-24-1866
Wilson, Fanny to Jerry Mitchel 2-1-1867 (2-16-1867) B
Wilson, Harriet to David Thompson 5-4-1866 (5-6-1866)
Wilson, Ibby to John Carter 4-10-1840 (4-12-1840)
Wilson, Isabella to Jonathan Medford 4-20-1871
Wilson, Laura Ann to Stephen Baker 7-5-1866 (7-6-1866) B
Wilson, Mareno to Mack Johnson 2-12-1868 (2-15-1868) B
Wilson, Mary A. to F. M. Cody 1-14-1860 (1-17-1860)
Wilson, Mary A. to William S. Brown 8-27-1846 (no return)
Wilson, Mary Ann to Thomas Holland 11-23-1852 (no return)
Wilson, Mary J. to Isaac Kendall ?-24-1844 (2-29-1844)
Wilson, Matilda Jane to John Smith 1-20-1844
Wilson, Mattie to Martin Bell 8-19-1867 (8-24-1867) B
Wilson, Phebe A. to Ninian F. Steel 8-27-1846 (no return)
Wilson, Sallie M. to Hukbald? D. Hunt 12-21-1848
Winborn, M. L. to Jas. A. Webb 1-20-1868 (1-21-1868)
Winbourne, Mary F. to J. R. Harris 12-15-1869
Winder, Harriet to John S. Hollin 5-11-1866 (5-12-1866) B
Winfield, Lucy to H. Walter Lewis 8-9-1870 (8-10-1870)
Winfield, Lucyann E. to Sampson H. Sane 11-28-1838 (no return)
Winfield, Marry F. to G. W. Robertson 2-10-1845
Winfield, Nisha A. to J. J. Bounds 7-18-1865
Winfrey, Lelia to William Matthews 10-27-1865 (10-28-1865) B
Winfrey, Priscilla to William Langley 12-30-1868 (12-31-1868) B
Winfrey, Sarah A. to Benj. Watkins 1-23-1851 (no return)
Winn, Agnis to Seaton Hudspeth 10-17-1848 (10-19-1848)
Winn, Agnis to Seten Hudspeth 10-17-1848
Winn, Elizabeth to John W. Conway 11-4-1841
Winsett, Joe to Wm. A. Bell 10-19-1865 (10-22-1865)
Winston, Emily A. to John W. Mayo 2-2-1842
Winston, Mary E. to Whitson A. Harris 1-24-1848 (1-28-1848)
Winston, Victoria to J. G. Sneed 11-26-1862 (11-27-1862)
Winston, Victoria to J. G. Sneed 11-26-1862 (not endorsed)
Wirt, Catharine to Willis M. Green 3-15-1838
Wirt, Catharine to Wm. J. Cannon 11-9-1854 (no return)
Wirt, Frances to Peter Jordan 2-20-1869 (3-21-1869) B
Wirt, Mary to Ed Warren 12-26-1866 B
Wisson, Elizabeth H. to J. W. Sanders 1-31-1853 (no return)
Witt, Drucilla B. to Saml. E. Champion 1-12-1871
Witt, Kitty to Tom Lewis 2-1-1868 (2-2-1868) B
Woldram, Elenida to Lihue Taylor 7-29-1839 (8-1-1839)
Wollerford, Frances to Wm. Bragg 9-30-1850 (no return)
Womac, Eliza E. to Andrew B. Hurley 6-6-1848 (6-8-1848)
Womble, Josephine to John McDade 10-22-1844
Wood, Jane L. to Jonathan Buckner 1-21-1846 (1-28-1846)
Woodard, Martha to Benjamin Bickers 8-15-1840 (8-17-1840)
Woodfin, Elizabeth F. to John M. Batt 9-19-1840 (9-24-1840)
Woodfolk, Lucy to Gabe McCully 12-24-1870 (no return) B
Woodfolk, Mary to Tom Shelton 12-27-1867 (no return) B
Woods, Ann J. to Stephen J. Lester 2-7-1838
Woods, Ella to Adam Higbee 12-25-1868 (12-26-1868) B
Woodson, Sallie P. to W. W. Bondurant 11-8-1869 (11-9-1869)
Woolley, Mary Jane to Jno. W. Hollis 8-15-1868 (8-16-1868)

Woollum, Elvira T. to William Minson 5-24-1847 (no return)
Woolly, Harriet to Allen Dorman 12-5-1846
Wootten, Marthaan to Saml. B. Burge 10-20-1839 (10-24-1839)
Word, Betty N. to T. J. Flippin 2-24-1864 (2-25-1864)
Word, Emma V. to J. V. Jones 12-11-1867 (no return)
Word, Louisa to Tom McCulley 12-25-1866 (no return) B
Word, Minerva to J. L. Cleere 10-3-1854 (no return)
Word, Sarah to John S. Burtus 7-27-1853 (no return)
Worley, Margarett to John W. Williams 1-6-1851
Worrell, Eliza J. to J. M. Martin 12-26-1863 (1-17-1864)
Worrell, H. C. to Jno. S. Renfroe 12-22-1868 (12-23-1868)
Worrell, M. B. to R. T. Cobb 11-9-1870 (11-10-1870)
Worrell, Mary B. to Tobias Grider 1-5?-1839
Worrell, Rebecca C. to B. H. Grider 1-28-1845
Worrell, Sallie A. to G. B. Hawkins 1-17-1866
Worsham, Lavenia to Andrew Johnson 12-28-1869 (12-9?-1869) B
Wortham, Harriet to M. G. Fraser 2-20-1867
Wortham, Mary to Joseph Y. Gray 8-19-1840 (9-22-1840)
Worthan, Estelia to John G. Henry 2-18-1840 (2-20-1840)
Worthen, Maryan to George Dougan 11-27-1843
Wray, Frances to Andrew Jones 7-9-1870 B
Wray, Lizzie C. to J. W. Karr 1-3-1853 (no return)
Wray, Lizzie to Henry Richardson 3-11-1871 (3-14-1871) B
Wray, Martha C. to James C. Whyte 10-24-1840 (10-25?-1840)
Wray, Martha to Matt Hood 12-27-1867 (12-31-1867) B
Wray, Mary G. to James H. Murray 1-21-1846
Wray, Virginia A. to J. Y. Boyd 1-1-1851
Wright, Bettie to Saml. Low 1-1-1868 (no return) B
Wright, Celia to Harry Edwards 8-4-1870 (8-11-1870) B
Wright, Elizabeth to Lewis Swinny 12-25-1852 (no return)
Wright, George Anna to Thomas Morrow 4-15-1869 B
Wright, Hester to John Greenberry 10-7-1867 (no return) B
Wright, Julia Ann to James W. Smith 11-30-1844 (no return)
Wright, Julia ann to Andrew J. Gillespie 2-12-1844 (2-13-1844)
Wright, Juliana to Saml. Hamerick 3-13-1847 (3-16-1847)
Wright, Martha T. to Jackson Montgomery 10-6-1838 (10-8-1838)
Wright, Mary to George Williamson 2-20-1869 (no return) B
Wright, Puss to John Allen 3-19-1870 (4-16-1870) B
Wright, Sarah A. to Samuel Howard 12-29-1868 (12-30-1868) B
Wright, T. C. to Wyatt Nicholson 12-3-1847 (12-15-1847)
Wrightsell, Dean? to James M. Morris 3-24-1842
Wrightsell, Sarah to William H. Parkes 11-9-1841 (11-11-1841)
Wylie, Martha to Wm. A. Clark 9-28-1868
Yancey, Belle Emma to Hiram Parker 12-18-1868 B
Yancey, Catharine G. to George A. Lipscomb 9-4-1847 (no return)
Yancey, Catherine to John Wiley 8-17-1866 (no return) B
Yancey, Charlotte to Harris Chaffin 12-28-1868 B
Yancey, Isabella R. to Geo. R. Witt 9-1-1846
Yancey, Lissa to Joe Yancey 12-18-1868 (1-9-1869) B
Yancey, Lizzie J. to Wm. H. Allen 5-14-1866 (5-15-1866) B
Yancey, P. T. to W. F. Chambliss 11-27-1866
Yancy, Analiza to Thomas S. Black 3-6-1852 (no return)
Yancy, Bettie to Z. W. Heath 1-26-1869 (1-27-1869)
Yancy, Elvira J. to William A. Pledge 10-27-1849 (11-1-1849)
Yancy, Louisa E. V. to Thomas M. Broom 3-20-1860 (3-22-1860)
Yancy, Mary A. to George R. Witt 2-10-1841 (2-11-1841)
Yancy, Mattie V. to Jno. H. Gates 12-2-1867 (12-6-1867)
Yarborough, Marthaann to Thos. Williams 12-24-1839 (no return)
Yarbrough, Ellen to William Clayton 2-3-1871 B
Yarbrough, Ruthy Jane to Littleberry S. Swaggart 1-17-1842 (no return)
Yates, G. A. to Junius Tomlinson 2-5-1868
Yeates, Caroline to Simpson L. Marler 3-4-1841
York, Nancy J. to J. P. Irby 1-16-1871 (no return)
Young, Amanda to Wash Conner 12-26-1866 (12-27-1866) B
Young, E. C. to John W. Harris 4-3-1871 (5-2-1871)
Young, Elisabeth M. to William W. Greenway 5-2-1848
Young, Elizabeth to Mumphred H. Cole 4-24-1840 (5-5-1840)
Young, Ellen to Alfred Currin 10-31-1866 B
Young, Emma to Chas. G. Mason 1-22-1866 (1-24-1866) B
Young, Jane to John Exum 4-15-1840 (4-16-1840)
Young, Jemimah Ann to Jno. G. Whitson 7-9-1846 (no return)
Young, Lucy H. to Edwin H. Cobbs 12-15-1845 (no return)
Young, Mary to Calvin Haskins 12-22-1866 (12-24-1866) B
Young, Matilda to B. F. Burrows 3-2-1866 (no return)

Young, P. A. F. to J. B. Murphy 12-31-1859 (1-4-1860)
Young, Sarah Ann to J. R. Walker 10-22-1850
Young, Sarah to Tom Brown 8-31-1867 (9-7-1867) B
Zellner, Helen M. to Pliney B. Londrith 6-21-1859 (6-23-1859)
Zellner, L. J. to J. F. Pickins 11-15-1852 (no return)
_____, Martha A. to James A. Coulter 9-19-1855 (no return)
_____, Martilla to P. Holcomb 8-28-1851 (no return)
_____, _____ to Arthur E. Peticats 3-15-1852 (no return)
_____, _____ to Wilson J. Godby 7-19-1849 (no return)
_____, _____ to R. C. Wiley 3-14-1849 (3-15-1849)

www.ingramcontent.com/pod-product-compliance
Lightning Source LLC
Chambersburg PA
CBHW050356100426
42739CB00015BB/3421